Item Generation
for
Test Development

Item Generation
for
Test Development

Edited by

Sidney H. Irvine
University of Plymouth

Patrick C. Kyllonen
Air Force Research Laboratory and
Educational Testing Service

LAWRENCE ERLBAUM ASSOCIATES, PUBLISHERS

2002   Mahwah, New Jersey   London

The final camera copy for this work was prepared by the editors
and therefore the publisher takes no responsibility for consistency
or correctness of typographical style. However, this arrangement
helps to make publication of this kind of scholarship possible.

Lawrence Erlbaum Associates, Inc., Publishers
10 Industrial Avenue
Mahwah, New Jersey 07430

Cover design by Kathryn Houghtaling Lacey

Library of Congress Cataloging-in-Publication Data

ISBN: 0-8058-3441-9

Books published by Lawrence Erlbaum Associates are printed on acid-free paper,
and their bindings are chosen for strength and durability.

Printed in the United States of America
10   9   8   7   6   5   4   3   2   1

This book is dedicated to the memory of

Samuel J. Messick

A great scientist, an extraordinary colleague,
and a good friend

Contributors

Russell G. Almond
Educational Testing Service

Dave Bartram
SHL Group

Isaac I. Bejar
Educational Testing Service

Randy E. Bennett
Educational Testing Service

Peter Bradon
University of Plymouth, UK

Ian Dennis
University of Plymouth, UK

Susan E. Embretson
University of Kansas

Mary K. Enright
Educational Testing Service

Jonathan Evans
University of Plymouth, UK

Klaus-Martin Goeters
DLR German Aerospace Center

Simon Handley
University of Plymouth, UK

Lutz F. Hornke
Aachen University of Technology

Sidney H. Irvine
University of Plymouth, UK

Patrick C. Kyllonen
*Air Force Research Laboratory and
Educational Testing Service*

Charles Lewis
Educational Testing Service

Bernd Lorenz
DLR German Aerospace Center

Robert J. Mislevy
Educational Testing Service

Rick Morgan
Educational Testing Service

Stephen Newstead
University of Plymouth, UK

Kathleen M. Sheehan
Educational Testing Service

Mark K. Singley
IBM T.J. Watson Research Center

Linda S. Steinberg
Educational Testing Service

Len Swanson
Educational Testing Service

Howard Wainer
National Board of Medical Examiners

David Wright
Univerisity of Plymouth, UK

Contents

Contributors   vii

Foreword   xiii
    Henry Braun

Item Generation for Test Development: An Introduction   xv
    Sidney H. Irvine

Acknowledgments   xxvii

Prologue and Epilogue: Remembering Samuel J. Messick   xxix

PART I: PSYCHOMETRIC AND COGNITIVE THEORY OF ITEM GENERATION

Chapter One
The Foundations of Item Generation for Mass Testing   3
Sidney H. Irvine

Chapter Two
Using the Psychology of Reasoning to Predict the Difficulty   35
of Analytical Reasoning Problems
Stephen Newstead, Peter Bradon, Simon Handley, Jonathan Evans,
and Ian Dennis

Chapter Three
Approaches to Modeling Item-Generative Tests   53
Ian Dennis, Simon Handley, Peter Bradon,
Jonathan Evans, and Stephen Newstead

Discussant Remarks   73
Len Swanson

Discussion   77

PART II: CONSTRUCT-ORIENTED APPROACHES TO ITEM GENERATION

Chapter Four
On the Roles of Task Model Variables in Assessment Design   97
Robert J. Mislevy, Linda S. Steinberg, and
Russell G. Almond

Chapter Five
Modeling the Difficulty of Quantitative Reasoning Items: 129
Implications for Item Generation
Mary K. Enright and Kathleen M. Sheehan

Chapter Six
Item-Generation Models for Higher Order Cognitive Functions   159
Lutz F. Hornke

Discussant Remarks   179
Charles Lewis

Discussion   187

PART III: FROM THEORY TO IMPLEMENTATION

Chapter Seven
Generative Testing: From Conception to Implementation   199
Isaac I. Bejar

Chapter Eight
Generating Abstract Reasoning Items With Cognitive Theory   219
Susan E. Embretson

Chapter Nine
Item Generation for Repeated Testing of Human Performance   251
Patrick C. Kyllonen

Chapter Ten
Scoring Tests When Items Have Been Generated   277
David Wright

Chapter Eleven
On the Automatic Generation of Test Items: Some Whens,   287
Whys, and Hows
Howard Wainer

PART IV: APPLICATIONS OF ITEM-GENERATIVE PRINCIPLES

Chapter Twelve
The MICROPAT Pilot Selection Battery: Applications   317
of Generative Techniques for Item-Based and Task-
Based Tests
Dave Bartram

Chapter Thirteen
On the Implementation of Item-Generation Principles   339
for the Design of Aptitude Testing in Aviation
Klaus-Martin Goeters and Bernd Lorenz

Chapter Fourteen
Item Generation and Beyond: Applications of Schema Theory   361
to Mathematics Assessment
Mark K. Singley and Randy E. Bennett

Discussant Remarks   385
Rick Morgan

Discussion   391

Author Index   399

Subject Index   405

About the Editors   411

Chapter Eleven

Foreword

It is my pleasure to introduce this landmark volume on item generation. It presents much of the best thinking and current research of many of the leaders in the field. The conference on which this volume is based was jointly sponsored by the Air Force human research laboratory, through the good offices of Patrick Kyllonen (now at ETS) and by ETS Research. The measurement community owes both organizations a vote of thanks.

This conference was conceived and organized by Sidney Irvine, and the late Sam Messick. Sam's untimely death just a month before the conference left us all bereft. We lost a great scientist, an extraordinary colleague, and a wonderful friend. Sam had a longstanding interest in item generation, and the talk that he intended to present would certainly have proved illuminating. Unfortunately his illness, starting in the September before the conference, prevented him from realizing his plans, and we had to make our way without his guidance. It is also most appropriate to recognize three very important women in Sam's life: Betty Messick, his wife: Ann Jungblut, his longtime research partner who died just a few months before Sam; and Kathy Howell, his administrative assistant. Sam would be the first to acknowledge his debt to all of them and we should do no less. I want especially to thank Kathy Howell, who labored mightily under trying circumstances to help bring the conference together and was instrumental in assisting the editors in seeing this volume to publication.

At first blush, the topic of this conference appears to be so technical, so esoteric, that it could not be of general interest or concern. Actually, I think nothing could be further from the truth. It's certainly the case that the topic is technical, but I think it has important implications for anyone who is concerned with testing, or touched by testing, and that is just about everyone. But some of the reasons for this interest may not be entirely obvious. I believe we have to consider item generation in the context of the general trajectory of test design and test construction. In the future, test developers are going to have to become more responsive to the complex, and often competing, demands that society places on us—and this, I predict, will force the design process to become both more disciplined and more innovative. What is true for test design, must also be true of the elements that give a test substance, namely items. Certainly at ETS the advent of continuous testing through technology, CBT we call it, has placed increased demands on item capacity, primarily because of concerns with security. We also have learned that while good items are a necessity, expensive items are a luxury we can ill-afford. Economic reality has forced us to examine, or re-examine, a central activity that we have long thought of as an honorable craft. And so this conference comes, for us at least, at a very timely moment.

We shall see that research efforts in this area have a long history and, in the first chapter, we will be ably conducted on a tour of that history, by one of its founders. We will learn that a far-seeing few recognized the value in item generation, quite apart from its potential economic returns: That in combination with technology delivery, it makes possible testing paradigms that were heretofore impossible. But I want to draw your attention to another aspect of this enterprise. Principled item generation must depend on deep understanding of what is being done. As we are challenged with new content domains and new formats, we will have to extend our ability to describe and delineate the targets of the generation engine, as well as to establish sources of difficulty and their relative magnitude. Simply put, once this is done there will be a much more substantial and defensible foundation for asserting the construct validity of our tests than ever before. It will also enable us to convey much more useful information about a candidate's performance, particularly if this work has been embedded in a test that is designed for such a purpose.

Further progress will depend on the dynamic interplay between theoretical developments and careful empirical work. The classic version of the scientific method will stand us in good stead here. Failures in prediction will be welcomed, at least to some extent, because they will be of great value in signaling gaps in our understanding, and lead eventually to greatly strengthened theory. Pushing up against the boundaries will be an essential strategy and expecting serendipity, quite sensible. The conference, and this volume, will be seen to have both marked an important milestone in the field and provided the impetus for further rapid development. It is a privilege for me to have been a small part of this enterprise.

Henry Braun
Educational Testing Service

Item Generation for Test Development: An Introduction

Sidney H. Irvine
University of Plymouth

The avowed aim of any introduction to a book of contributed chapters is a conceptual voyage fueled and provisioned by individual contributions. It may often and perhaps should in this particular instance provide, through the spyglass of hindsight, an alternative to following the order in which the late Samuel Messick drew up the program of events that marked the invitational seminar held in the Henry Chauncey Conference Center of Educational Testing Service in October, 1998. Here, then, is one such option, offered as a definition of the field, in the limited sense of a key to its understanding.

To define item-generation theory is somewhat easier than attempting to define all-embracing constructs such as intelligence or personality because it has a much less ambitious role. A concept that grew out of early attempts to harness computer technology to the production, as distinct from the administration and scoring of tests, *item generation* had no portentous mention until about fifteen years ago. It therefore has neither long-established nor indeed any immediate rivals. To bring the concept to life, this volume contains accounts of work by people who pioneered attempts to generate items for tests. In such circumstances contributors offer definitions that produce a key to understanding; and their empirical materials reveal ostensive and operational definitions in practice.

UNDERSTANDING ITEM GENERATION: ORIGINS AND SYNTACTICS

Cronbach's (1957) conception of the two fundamentally different scientific disciplines of psychological enquiry is an essential embarkation point. He characterized these disciplines as the discovery of main effects through controlled experimentation with cognitive tasks; and the exploration of individual differences apparent in psychometric test scores. One branch of the discipline relies on small numbers of subjects and determines the presence or absence of main effects and interactions on tasks through analysis of variance. The other requires large subject pools to produce reliable and robust latent structures and regression equations that can stand up to validity replications in all kinds of different contexts, cultural or dispositional. Cronbach's goal of a unified main line approach is attainable in the development of item-generative tests.

How work in item generation has fostered a unified discipline of psychology is a major feature of this volume. Readers will find overwhelming evidence of confluence in the pioneering item-generation models of authors Bartram, Bejar, Goeters, Hornke, and Irvine, and in second-generation developments characterized in the chapters by Dennis, Embretson, Kyllonen, and Newstead; but not confined to their work as one observes later in this introduction.

Perhaps the obvious and main departure from traditional test construction, which may be described as a technology with an unending sequence of empirical questions, is the emergence of a basis for item-construction requiring *mental models*. Mental models are founded in theory: and test items have become increasingly dependent on the verification of cognitive models in whole or part. These have been sought, applied, and clarified using different approaches to item generation owing very little to each other but contributing essential parts of a new theory of test development.

Good illustrations of how the earliest adventures in item generation could influence later test development are immediately evident in the chapters written by Bejar and Hornke. Both were concerned to generate *figural*[1] items. Bejar's work in the 1980s (Bejar, 1986a, 1986b, 1986c) was based on two unique and seminal approaches. First, he stipulated that to construct items a logical syntax, or *grammar* was essential. This made explicit the need for a verifiable internal logic used by the computer to produce items. Second, he applied an objective method (the Hough [1962] transform) to produce an external, computer-driven referent for item difficulty based on figural complexity. With these two original moves, Bejar provided an *early definition of the process of item generation* that was an indispensable key to its understanding. He also based test development of spatial orientation items derived from three-dimensional representations on Roger Shepard's chronometric models (Shepard & Metzler, 1971), using that paradigm as a foundation for making items progressively more difficult to solve. He thus used two different methods for item construction and subsequent verification—one a machine-driven algorithm and the other a specific mental model based in time to complete an item (see also Bejar &

---

[1] I offer a parenthesis for clarity and in a forlorn hope that psychologists will abandon the term non-verbal when describing figural items, because the term has been and still is systematically misleading. These were figural representations, but such items are *not* non-verbal when they are processed. Film of people solving figural items shows subvocalisation at every stage of item solution.

Yocom, 1991). In doing this he was some years ahead of practice and combined in one series the two basic approaches to item generation described in the chapter by Dennis.

Hornke and Habon's (1986) equally portentous contribution to the generation of complex figural tests of inference was published at the same time as Bejar's early reports, although the field work was independently completed in Germany much earlier. The scale of the research is astonishingly broad. Taking Matrix type item features as the universe, Hornke devised a population of some 600 items. The item features were constructed from a-priori rules based on research findings about cognitive process and inferences about their relation to item difficulty. After testing more than 7,000 subjects, a set of 450 items was retained. Cognitive operations conceived as main effects on item difficulty explained item-response parameters well. Hornke summarizes this approach as having two outcomes, unifying cognitive and psychometric models and freeing "item construction from item writer idiosyncrasies" (loc.cit. p. 369). This quotation foreshadowed the need to provide tools for item-writers, exemplified by the work of Singley and Bennett in this volume, and which we have defined as "the third way."

Today, the complex cognitive demands of Matrix items are now becoming fully understood because of his approach; and these demands are further demonstrated in Susan Embretson's (1995, 1996) more recent experiments involving exemplary protocols with these item types. Even so, her work and Hornke's uncovers no complete delineation of all of the mental operations employed in the solution of matrix items. Nevertheless, their successful efforts to generate the items from a common grounding in cognitive functions have left a permanent contribution to psychological theory. They demonstrate the complete inadequacy of psychometric g as a construct for a-priori item construction of items that have had their claim to recognition, or perhaps notoriety, as stipulated *nonverbal g* markers. As a consequence of their work, one understands more about the theoretical *limits* of broad constructs like g. Such primitive[2] explanatory constructs now require detailed redefinition in cognitive terms before they can be understood to the point of providing the basis for consistent operational definition through item construction. Embretson and Hornke prove that this harmony occurs in *g-loaded* figural tests only when items are generated to specify individual differences in their constituent cognitive markers.

One of the explicit efforts to predefine both cognitive and psychometric syntactics for item-generation in the mid-1980s can be seen in Irvine's

---

[2] Primitive is used here in the sense of explanatory but incapable of further explanation. As a type of unitary semantic entity it presents barriers to further decomposition and explanation.

review chapter of the published efforts of his colleagues at the University of Plymouth (Irvine, Dann, & Anderson, 1990; Irvine, Dann, & Evans, 1987). They started in 1986 with the aim of combining the work of Carroll (1976, 1980, 1983) on psychometric tests as cognitive tasks with known current models of cognitive functioning. They deduced and had confirmation from co-operation with Kyllonen and the late Raymond Christal (Christal, 1987; Kyllonen & Christal, 1988; Kyllonen & Christal, 1989) that Baddeley's (Baddeley, 1968; Baddeley & Hitch, 1974) work on the role of working memory in cognitive tasks was central to their aims. They knew, because of Jonathan Evans's direct involvement, that the results of cognitive modeling of deductive reasoning tasks (Evans, 1982) was almost immediately transferable to the construction of psychometric tests. From this and their own experimental work, the inference that the discovery of consistent main effects would effectively point the way to *prediction* of item difficulty was a short stride. In fact, they began their test construction as a series of experiments to verify in item types certain main effects found in generic cognitive tasks widely known in the literature (see pp. 14–15)). Irvine called these main effects as they were introduced to the grammar of item construction *radicals*. These were the essential constituents that Bejar predicated as a requirement of the system. The grammar was built to produce computer-delivered and paper-and-pencil analogues of the test items. By 1992, the system was operational throughout the United Kingdom with each army recruit undertaking a unique version of each of the tests, known as the British Army Recruit Battery (BARB).

In the course of their work, they realized that to sample extensively and reliably the processes involved in item completion, items had to seem different even if they remained the same beneath their surface characteristics. Changes in these necessary surface characteristics were defined as *incidentals*. They were indeed supposed to be only incidental to the delivery of items whose cognitive demands could be *changed* by *radicals* derived from models of cognitive competence.[3] It is a fundamental part of the grammar of test generation required by Bejar. The discovery of these radicals and their subsequent use is witnessed in large-scale construction attempts by Bartram and Goeters. This emphasis is central to the first of three main approaches to generating items.

---

[3] This same and fundamental distinction between aspects of items that affect and hence serve to predict their difficulty and those that do not, is characterized by Dennis as the difference between *controlling* and *non-controlling* aspects of items. Irvine and Dennis arrive at two different terms for precisely the same distinction.

RUNNING IT UP THE FLAGPOLE
TO SEE IF IT WOULD FLY

If the *radical-incidental* distinctions were not immediately explicit in other large-scale operational efforts to generate items, such as those described in the chapters by Bartram and Goeters, they were certainly implicit. Both of these authors directed nationally funded efforts at constructing a battery of tests for pilot and aviator selection. They required parallel forms of tests, some of which in Bartram's battery, were adaptive from the outset. This is Bartram's signal contribution to early computer-delivered tests. Bartram was able to be adaptive because he went straight to machine delivery, using a relatively portable system with outfiles recording accuracy and latency. Bartram's training in cognitive psychology is evident in most of the machine-delivered tasks, particularly those demonstrating coordination of hand and eye that were created, and whose difficulty was governed by, a control mechanism. In others, conventional pilot-selection wisdom is the basis for test construction.

In these characteristics the Micropat system described by Bartram (1987) has much in common with the comprehensive testing regimen practised in Hamburg in Goeters' laboratory. Goeters, however, kept machine-based testing for secondary stage selection, relying on inexpensive paper-and-pencil versions for first-phase exclusion. The parallelism of the paper-and-pencil test forms is amply demonstrated in Goeters and Rathje (1992). The PARAT system, as it was called, had goals in common with other large-scale first stage screening batteries, such as BARB, the British Army Recruit Battery. These included the distribution of pretest information to ensure knowledge of expectations, computer generation of an infinite number of parallel tests, and the pursuit of equity for applicants to limit the effects of language and educational differences.

This account by Goeters and his team shows that for the first time open testing was considered a real possibility because the disclosure of one form of a test did not imply the construction of a new one at great expense and inconvenience. The new forms were already available and needed no restandardization. In short. technical advance became permanently linked with the desiderata of cost-benefits, administrative convenience, and political defensibility. However, in case one may believe that all such problems have been solved by the availability of multiple parallel forms, Dennis's chapter asserts that without the adoption of very sophisticated models of test generation, the codes for item generation can be derived from the release of items and, should these items be seen to be open to strategic solutions, there would be continued work for the test-coaching industry.

Dennis's chapter has to be read alongside that of Newstead, and both, preferably, after digesting the accounts of earlier attempts by Bejar, Hornke, Irvine, Bartram, and Goeters to provide a universe of discourse. Their work also begins from an applied problem, the creation of many reasoning items; but the flagpole has shifted ground. Both Newstead and Dennis are experimental cognitive psychologists for whom item generation is essentially a strategic application. Dennis in particular offers a syntactic alternative to any generative approach that first finds radical main effects and proceeds to generate items from these and a number of incidentals. He characterizes this alternative, second approach, as a *model semantic* system. Simply put, if an item has a number of semantic elements, the possible number of variants is n! To become a candidate for generation in Dennis's universe, the item has first to pass an internal test of logical consistency as defined by a computer-based algorithm. The emergence of radicals is *secondary* to the item passing this "grammatical" test. In the other approach, the identification of radicals is primary.

One now begins to see how important Bejar's insistence on the derivation of an item grammar has become in the understanding of the second approach. It is foreshadowed by the early work of Bejar himself with the Hough transform, and the instrumental contributions to item generation in the BARB system by Evans (Irvine, Dann, & Evans, 1987) using POPLOG to ensure the internal logical consistency of two and three term transitive inference items. Both of these early attempts point to the eventual emergence of the second, important and complementary approach to item generation encouraged by Dennis and Newstead.

New opportunities for item generation are suggested by Kyllonen and Chaiken in their approach to repeated-measures testing of cognitive performance. First, they offer a somewhat unique perspective on item generation based upon a theory of measurement that is already established (the CAM Model). Examples of radical and incidental variation are given from this coherent structure. In the second part of the chapter they shift ground from difficulty written into the items by radical elements to constructing relatively easy items made difficult by external stressors such as time constraints. They also examine the effect of dispositional variables including experimentally induced fatigue and disruption of cognitive function through sleep deprivation or abrupt change in sleep patterns, such as those induced by jet lag. They assert that special types of items have to be generated for use in such testing models. Empirical evidence for the use of item-generative multiple parallel forms in repeated measures testing is provided in Irvine's case study of a single patient's peformance after general anaesthesia, and 19 weeks later. Finally, of particular interest to Kyllonen and Chaiken are models of item scoring to combat speed-accuracy trade-off. They point out that Dennis and Evans (1996) provide a very full account of various scoring options in item-generative contexts. Similarly, the chapter in this volume by Wright provides possible item response theory expansions using item latencies. If item generation is to be used in online learning contexts, the chapter by Kyllonen and Chaiken is prescribed reading.

THE THIRD WAY: TOOLS FOR ITEM WRITERS

Accounts of several attempts to assist people whose job it is to write items have appeared in the reports of Educational Testing Service. These have not been conceived outside the standard ETS technical framework of item response theory nor of the essential political need to satisfy customers in the educational enterprise. Little in the way of freewheeling in item construction has followed Bejar's lead of the mid-1980s. This is not to imply lack of progress, just to emphasize that progress has been made along other directions and within the unenviable constraints of improving and adapting established test programs to changing times and politically correct fashions in educational assessment. This third approach to generating items from knowledge of their characteristics is witnessed in the provision of *tools of construction and verification* for item production by experts.

Thus far, there has been an emphasis on the internal logic used by item constructors. These are, simply, rules of various kinds. The third way has also a set of rules, but of a different sort. In fact, the chapter by Mislevy and his colleagues prescribes an overarching metaphysic, a credo for ensuring the validity of the form of the item. This validation is part of a painstaking judgmental processs about the content, relevance, and construct validity of the items proposed. It may be exercised by machines, but it first has to be assented to by answers to questions of context. In that sense it begins to trace an operational definition of the criterion of political defensibility that is required of all high-stakes tests.

The third way, of tools to aid conventional methods of item-construction is specifically and *ostensively defined* in the system designed by Singley and Bennett to bring semantic distance theory directly to bear on the modeling of elementary mathematics items; and in the tracing of key elements in predicting the difficulty of mathematical items using *hierarchical* item-response models by Enright and Sheehan. Singley and Bennett, however, can be seen to intersect with the *logical necessity model* for item construction fostered by Dennis. Their item-writer's assistant demands and obtains total consistency from the author of the item within the algorithms for item-construction. There too, item difficulty is secondary to the production of items that are consonant with the algorithms defining their authenticity. In their *weltanschauung*, the derivation of item difficulties is, however, a judgmental as well as a system design function.

Enright and Sheehan are inheritors of *item response theory models of item verification*, and this work is directly descended from the paper by Mislevy and Sheehan (1988) on using item information as additional item response theory parameters. Its value-added element lies in the apparently successful quest for more precise understanding of coherent item-families in mathematics. In the use of item-response technology, readers will see strict rules for the approach to item-generation that seeks to produce generic item types of which there are multiple examples relying on radicals and incidentals for their difficulty parameters.

In the category of tools that are advances on conventional item response theory is the important synthesis made by Wright's chapter on scoring item-generated tests. Wright had collaborated at Plymouth with Dennis (Dennis & Evans, 1989, 1996), and Evans (Evans & Wright, 1992, 1993) and was aware of the progress made by Mislevy at Educational Testing Service (Mislevy, Wingersky, Irvine, & Dann, 1992) on using time to solution as a means of discriminating between identical items and the means to solve them. His own lines of enquiry (Wright, 1990, 1992) have resulted in a major conceptual advance on how to score item-generative tests. This approach uses time envelopes to change the difficulty parameters in systematic fashion. Only with the availability of item response theory and the construction of items that vary only in surface characteristics *(incidentals)* were the conditions for his work satisfied. The result is a convincing demonstration of the advances that can be made once the two disciplines of scientific psychology are consciously brought to bear on an operational definition of item-generation theory.

THE FOURTH HORSEMAN: POLITICAL DEFENSIBILITY

Thus far, the introduction has concerned itself with three of the horsemen of the computer-based testing apocalypse that may yet sweep away paper-and-pencil forms. They ride under the banners of cognitive models, psychometric robustness, and administrative convenience. The fourth horseman carries the flag of political defensibility. Howard Wainer's generous agreement to write his comments on presentations as a separate chapter provides a sharp focus for political issues. When and how should item generation be used and what are its advantages over traditional methods? Suffice it to say that Wainer argues cogently for a particular outcome of the internal debates of major test-producers on how to deliver and construct tests profitably while technology is forcing changes upon constructors and users alike. It is challenging reading; but answers to many of the questions raised by him are either implicit or explicit in the chapters described briefly in this introduction. Whether they are in Wainer's view adequately answered is not of course, a theoretical question. From his perspective item-generation proponents must be asked cost and benefit questions as part of the social justification for the introduction of their methods. That is as it should be. But cost-benefit issues are not always nor are they necessarily scientific censors, even if they are valid considerations in the programmatic funding of item generation as a unified psychometric and cognitive discipline.

THE DISCUSSIONS

Pat Kyllonen spent many unseen hours editing transcripts of the discussions. The fruits of his painstaking labour are now on the table. In September 2001, just before this manuscript went to the printer, I received a proof copy. The discussions were then in their rightful context.

Three years on from the conference itself, the issues and questions raised by discussants are at the limits of our knowledge: and they challenge our creativity, ingenuity and political will in the pursuit of answers. In that quest, protocols for both experimentation and correlational analysis are suggested, debated, pondered, qualified. As the discussions proceed, alternative solutions become standards to follow and if possible, to emulate. The unique focus that discussion leaders and participants have brought to this work has enhanced it greatly. I want to thank them for their signal contribution. Our chief debt is, of course, to Pat Kyllonen for making it available.

REFERENCES

Baddeley, A. D. (1968). A three-minute reasoning test based on grammatical transformation. *Psychonomic Science, 10,* 341–342.

Baddeley, A. D., & Hitch, G.(1974). Working memory. In G. H. Bower (Ed.), *The psychology of learning and motivation* (Vol. 8, pp.47–90).

Bartram, D. (1987). The development of an automated testing system for pilot selection: The Micropat project. *Applied Psychology: International Review, 36,* 279–298.

Bejar, I. I. (1986a). *The psychometrics of mental rotation (RR-86-19).* Princeton, NJ: Educational Testing Service.

Bejar, I. I. (1986b). Analysis and generation of Hidden Figure items: A cognitive approach to Psychometric Modelling (RR-86-20). Princeton, NJ: Educational Testing Service.

Bejar, I. I. (1986c). *Final report: Adaptive testing of spatial abilities (ONR 150 531).* Princeton, NJ: Educational Testing Service.

Bejar, I. I., & Yocom, P. (1991). A generative approach to the modelling of isomorphic hidden-figure items. *Applied Psychological Measurement, 15*(2), 129–137.

Carroll, J. B. (1976). Psychometric tests as cognitive tasks: a new "Structure of Intellect." In L. B. Resnick (Ed.), *The nature of intelligence.* Hillsdale, NJ: Lawrence Erbaum Associates.

Carroll, J. B. (1980). *Individual difference relations in psychometric and experimental cognitive tasks* (Report No. 163). Thurstone Psychometric Laboratory, University of North Carolina, Chapel Hill, NC.

Carroll, J. B. (1983). The difficulty of a test and its factor composition revisited. In H. Wainer & S. Messick (Eds.), *Principals of modern psychological measurement*. Hillsdale, NJ: Lawrence Erbaum Associates.

Christal, R. E. (1987). *A factor-analytic study of tests of working memory*. Unpublished Report, Human Resources Division, USAF Armstrong Laboratory, Brooks AFB, San Antonio, Texas.

Cronbach, L. J. (1957). The two disciplines of scientific psychology. *American Psychologist, 12,* 671–684.

Dennis, I., & Evans J. St. B. T. (1989). *System architecture for computerised assessment*. HAL Report for the Army Personnel Research Establishment (Contract 2021/12). Human Assessment Laboratory, University of Plymouth.

Dennis, I., & Evans, J. St. B. T. (1996). The speed-error trade off problem in psychometric testing. *British Journal of Psychology, 87,* 105–129.

Embretson, S. E. (1995). Working memory capacity versus general control processes in abstract reasoning. *Intelligence, 20,* 169–189.

Embretson, S. E. (1996). Multidimensional latent trait models in measuring fundamental aspects of intelligence. In I. Dennis & P. G. C. Tapsfield (Eds.), *Human abilities, their nature and measurement*. Hillsdale, NJ: Lawrence Erbaum Associates.

Evans, J. St. B. T. (1982). *The psychology of deductive reasoning*. London: Routledge.

Evans, J. St. B. T., & Wright, D. E. (1992) *The Transitive Inference Task*. HAL Technical Report 2-1992, for the Army Personnel Research Establishment, Human Assessment Laboratory, University of Plymouth.

Evans, J. St. B. T., & Wright, D. E. (1993). *The Properties of Fixed-Time Tests: A Simulation Study*. HAL Technical Report for the Army Personnel Research Establishment, Human Assessment Laboratory, University of Plymouth..

Goeters, K-M., & Rathje, H. (1992). *Computer-generiete parallel-tests fur die fahigeitsmessung in der eignungsauswahl von operationellem luftfahrtpersonal.* DLR Institut fur Flugmedizin Abteilung Luft-und Raumfahrtpsychologie, Hamburg.

Hornke, L. F., & Habon, M. W. (1986). Rule-based item bank construction and evaluation within the linear logistic framework. *Applied Psychological Measurement,* 10, 369–380.

Hough, P. V. C. (1962). *Method and means for recognising complex patterns*. U.S. Patent 3,069,654.

Irvine, S. H., Dann, P. L., & Anderson, J. D. (1990). Towards a theory of algorithm-determined cognitive test construction. *British Journal of Psychology, 81,* 173–195.

Irvine, S. H., Dann, P. L., & Evans, J. St. B. T. (1987). *Item generative approaches for computer-based testing: A prospectus for research*. Report for the Army Personnel Research Establishment, Human Assessment Laboratory, University of Plymouth.

Kyllonen, P. C. (1996). Is working memory capacity Spearmans's *g*? In I. Dennis & P. G. C. Tapsfield (Eds.), *Human abilities, their nature and measurement*. Hillsdale, NJ: Lawrence Erbaum Associates.

Kyllonen, P. C., & Christal, R. E. (1988). *Cognitive modelling of learning abilities: A status report of LAMP. (AFHRL-TP-87-66).* Brooks AFB, Texas: Manpower and Personnel Division, Air Force Human Resources Laboratory.

Kyllonen, P. C., & Christal, C. E. (1989). Cognitive modelling of learning abilities. In R. Dillon & J. W. Pellegrino (Eds.), *Testing: Theoretical and applied issues*, San Francisco, Freeman.

Mislevy, R. J., Wingersky, M. S., Irvine, S. H., & Dann, P. L. (1992). Resolving mixtures of strategies in spatial visualization tasks. *British Journal of Mathematical and Statistical Psychology,* 44, 265–288.

Mislevy, R. J., & Sheehan, K. M. (1988). *The role of collateral information about examinees in item parameter estimation.* ETS Research Report (RR-88-55-ONR). Princeton, NJ: Educational Testing Service.

Shepard, R. N., & Metzler, J. (1971). Mental rotation of three-dimensional objects. *Science, 171*, 701–703.

Wright, D. E. (1990). *Item response and theory for item generation: Comment and developments* HAL Technical Report: 3-1990 for Army Personnel Research Establishment, Human Assessment Laboratory, University of Plymouth

Wright, D. E. (1992). *IRT modelling using latent variable generalized linear models.* HAL Technical Report: 3-1992 for Army Personnel Research Establishment, Human Assessment Laboratory, University of Plymouth.

Acknowledgments

This book is based on a conference "Generating Items for Cognitive Tests: Theory and Practice," held at the Chauncey Conference Center on the Educational Testing Service campus in Princeton, New Jersey, November 5-6, 1998. Funding for the conference and preparation of the book was provided by Educational Testing Service's Research Division (Dr. Henry Braun), by the U.S. Air Force Office of Scientific Research (Dr. John Tangney), and by the Air Force Research Laboratory's Human Effectiveness Directorate (Drs. William Strickland, William Alley, and Bruce Gould). The support of these organizations and individuals has brought the project to fruition: and we extend to them the thanks of all who participated.

Educational Testing Service's interest in the sharing and dissemination of knowledge was and continues to be due to the need for larger item pools as a result of the demands of computer adaptive testing, as is documented in several chapters and at various points in the discussions. In addition, the Air Force Research Laboratory had an interest in repeated-testing applications. Large item pool and repeated measure issues are the focus of much of the content of this volume. For the Air Force Office of Scientific Research, the current effort was part of a two conference-book project. The companion project—supplementary to the current project's focus on methodology was devoted primarily to the content of assessments (Ackerman, Kyllonen, & Roberts [Eds.] [1999], *Learning and Individual Differences: Process, Trait, and Content Determinants*. Washington, DC: American Psychological Association).

The two-day conference was organized into four sessions, one each morning and afternoon, with three or four papers presented during each session, and a discussion of the papers at the end of each session. Many people made the discussions and debates lively and informative. Henry Braun's role was pivotal in introducing the conference and speakers, and leading the discussions. Howard Wainer was center stage for Session 3, adding his characteristic wit to the proceedings. Their skills were invaluable.

Apart from these major debts, we wish to thank all those who participated in the stimulating and lively discussions, including, in addition to the chapter authors and discussants, Chris Elshaw, a psychologist in the Centre for Human Sciences, at the United Kingdom's Ministry of Defence Evaluation and Research Agency (DERA); Stephen Luebke, a Senior Test Specialist at the Law School Admission Council in Newtown, Pennsylvania; and the following individuals from ETS: Mary Morley, a Research Scientist with a specialty in assessment design; Douglas Fiero, Group Leader, Arts and Literature, Assessment Division; and Ned Walthall, a content assessment specialist from the Assessment Division.

We also wish to thank Dianne Rein for her assistance on the manuscripts, Sumeet Dandeker, who transcribed the discussions in record time, and Catherine Hombo, who provided excellent technical reviews of some of the manuscripts. Above all, we wish to thank Kathleen Howell for her assistance in all phases of the conference and book planning and execution, including travel arrangements, manuscript collection and editing, subject and author indexes, and arrangements with the conference center. Like her late colleague, Ann Jungblut, she embodies that pursuit of excellence so closely associated with ETS conference organization and book production.

Finally, we note that Sam Messick, to whom this book is dedicated, played a critical role in the initiation of the conference, in developing its theme, and in selecting its speakers. Sam believed the time was right for the conference intellectually, and with characteristic magnanimity and charm he engineered its conception administratively. Without his vision and participation, the conference could not have taken place; and this book would not have been written. All of us were cognizant of his role and conscious of his influence as we prepared and assembled our talks and our chapters. His guiding hand is apparent throughout.

Prologue and Epilogue:
Remembering Samuel J. Messick

The problem of remembering the dead is not that of bringing them to memory, but of dealing with the pain that memory brings. It is especially difficult when one loses people for whom one harbors lasting affection derived from a meeting of minds. And Samuel James Messick was one of those people. To deal with my own sense of loss, and perhaps to comfort others whose loss is immeasurably the greater, I offer this short personal memoir of the happy times we celebrated together.

I met Sam's mind long before first meeting him in person in May of 1967 in Berlin, at the landmark Ingenkamp Conference on Test Construction, for I had read most if not all of his early publications. Because of their content, grasp of issues, intelligence and maturity, my imagination made him much older. When I met him, and as we looked over The Wall together, he appeared to be a veritable youngster. And indeed he was, because he was exactly my age and all people of one's own age are, by definition, youngsters. He was quick, agile, lively, witty, a snappy dresser who loved food, conversation, ideas, and jazz. This list is neither exclusive nor multiple choice unless it includes all of the above, and not necessarily in that order.

While we were in Berlin, Sam offered me a fellowship at ETS and in September I was there. In those days, under Henry Chauncey's benign eye, it was the place to be for anyone dedicated to the study of tests and testing. It became and remained a standard to follow. Our friendship lasted for 30 years, although I left ETS in 1968.

I often wonder what would have become of us had I accepted a generous ETS offer to stay, but we never lost touch. The prospects of collaborative work increased markedly when I found a second spiritual home at Plymouth in 1979. My regular pilgrimages in pursuit of the Holy Grail of item-generation theory always included meetings and cheerful dinner evenings with Sam and Betty. Our closest colleagues became involved and no more so than when Sam first came to Plymouth to address the inaugural Spearman Seminar in 1994 and to represent all of the international delegates at the reception given by the Lord Mayor of Plymouth. He came again in 1996 to give a seminar. In July, 1997, his role was as a co-organizer of the Second Spearman seminar, the title and emphasis of which he created. In December of that year he arrived once more to receive his honorary DSc degree from The University of Plymouth.

His influence has persisted, because Janet Collis, a member of the Human Assessment Laboratory, has edited with Sam and the late, much mourned Ann Jungblut the proceedings of the 1997 Spearman Seminar. Sam also ensured that a surplus hard copy of all ETS research reports from 1947 was gifted to the University and this priceless collection proudly bears his name.

I am honored to represent the University on this occasion and to convey the deep regret of all concerned. While we in Plymouth have lost a distinguished DSc, we know full well that psychology has lost a great mind and that ETS has lost a living embodiment of its worthiest and most cherished ideals.

One does not envy any organization that might seek to replace Sam, or anyone even closely resembling him. They would need to hire at least four people: the world authority on cognitive style, the doyen of editors-in-chief, a legal expert on test use, and a hard-nosed test scientist for whom fads in testing were mere flies in the ointment of validity. As if that were not enough, ETS would have to find a raconteur par excellence of after-dinner stories whose wit increased directly in proportion to their tolerable degree of salaciousness.

In spite of handicap and in his later years a long struggle with failing health, it was as if Sam had rewritten the famous line of the Rupert Brooke poem—Grow old along with me. His own inimitable cognitive style seemed to say, "Grow young along with me, the best is yet to be." He would rejoice and grow younger this evening for seeing you all assembled here in Princeton, his own field of dreams, playing by the rules he did so much to make.

So when we retire for canapés and cocktails and then sit down to a dinner whose menu he personally oversaw, marvel not that a very dry martini made with Bombay gin and a twist of lemon unaccountably disappears from the bar; nor that a story is whispered in your ear after the fine white and red wines have been sampled and the port comes along with the cheese. Sam would want us to embrace this particular evening as much as he surely would have done. Let us enjoy both the dinner he planned and pursue the kind of lively, happy conversation he stimulated as fitting tributes to his memory.

Finally, I invite all of you to remember him gladly and with thankfulness for the enduring example of the human spirit that the gift of his life means to those he left behind. Such a gift comes along only once in a generation. I for one will not look upon his like again.

Sid Irvine

Sam's scholarly accomplishments were well known to everyone in educational measurement and certainly well beyond that field. What is less well known are some of the roles he played here at ETS. And one of the roles that I think was most important was the "keeper of Research values." He instilled those values in others and maintained them over the course of several decades that he spent here at ETS. Those values included a very strong sense of ethics, a sense of objectivity, of academic freedom and a certain independence that he felt the Research division must maintain. Those values helped ETS meet its chartered mission, which included providing unbiased information to the education community, the measurement community and the policy community, even when that information was not necessarily flattering to ETS itself and to ETS's own tests. Sam was very successful in protecting those values, in good part because he was such a formidable presence and because he was so well respected inside ETS, by ETS senior management in particular. I think one of the best ways we can honor his memory is to continue to fight for those values and see that they are preserved. Those values, I feel, represent one of Sam's most important legacies to ETS and to the education community.

Randy Bennett

I've been having trouble dealing with my grief. Once in the past month I found myself halfway between my office and Sam's going over to see him. I caught myself, turned around, and returned to my office my question unanswered. Last week, as I sat in my seat at Richardson auditorium I looked down at the seats that are usually occupied by Sam and Betty. They weren't there, but I kept looking. Each time their absence struck me.

I have a very selfish motive in speaking to you today. I'm hoping that by speaking about Sam in public, my own grief can be assuaged. So far it hasn't helped.

I'd like to tell you about a project I did with Sam and what he taught me. A year or so after I arrived at ETS Sam and I collaborated on a book. It was a festschrift in honor of Fred Lord. Once we started working at it a pattern for the distribution of labor emerged. I did the grunt work and Sam was the brains in the outfit. What I learned was the enormous respect that he had for other people. As the work on the festshrift went on Sam was continually elated when various people would agree to come and participate. The wonderful phrase he used was, "This book will really be something if we could join the labor of our minds to the beauty of theirs." In fact that book was the product of the labor of my mind and the beauty of his. I continue to mourn the loss of his beauty.

Howard Wainer

Sam's untimely death last month, left us all bereft. We lost a great scientist, an extraordinary colleague, and a wonderful friend. As you all know, Sam had a longstanding interest in this area, and the talk that he intended to present for this meeting would certainly have proved illuminating. Unfortunately his illness, starting in September, prevented him from realizing his plans, and we shall have to make our way without his guidance.

One thought that keeps coming back to me as I talk to people about the various projects that Sam unfortunately left undone or incomplete and the refrain is always the same, "Who else is going to do this?" And that is both a tribute and part of the pain.

Henry Braun

I
PSYCHOMETRIC AND COGNITIVE
THEORY OF ITEM GENERATION

1

The Foundations of Item Generation for Mass Testing

Sidney H. Irvine
University of Plymouth

THE SCIENTIFIC BASIS OF ITEM GENERATION

When Cronbach (1957) called for the unification of experimental and correlational universes of discourse in psychology, it was not a consummation that, even if devout and desirable, could occur immediately for tests and measurements. And even now, if a degree of confluence has been achieved in the concepts and operational definitions of item-generation theory, applications to test construction are widespread neither in the domains of test content, nor in the use that is made of theory by large-scale test constructors. But if used, item-generation theory at one and the same time brings about a remarkably robust test-construction medium. To enable a perspective on the state of the art, historical and theoretical influences on the derivation of tests for initial screening of job applicants are outlined and then reviewed.

Origins

The origins of item-generation theory are, as in all new branches of science, more a matter of ostensive than precise definition. One could paraphrase Spearman on intelligence and declare that we do not yet know what item-generation theory is, only where it may be found. Ostensive definitions in published materials are available as historical landmarks; and one may readily fix the location of these in the following: Bartram (1987), Bejar (1986a, 1986b, 1986c), Carroll (1976, 1980, 1983, 1986, 1987), Christal (1984), Collis, Dann, Irvine, Tapsfield, and Wright (1995), Dann and Irvine (1986), Dennis (1993), Dennis, Collis, and Dann (1996), Embretson (1996), Goeters and Rathje (1992), Hornke and Habon (1986), Irvine, Dann, and Anderson (1990), Kyllonen and Christal, (1989, 1990) Mislevy, Wingersky,

3

Irvine, and Dann (1991). Much of the research activity on item generation predates eventual publication by some years, but a new field of algorithm-based test construction was being charted in a number of geographically distant centres from about 1985. History will also relate that these early attempts at item generation (and also at predicting item-difficulty from item elements) were the result of much original and creative work that took place in relative scientific isolation.

Theoretical Substrates

Within these sources are embedded not one grand design of overarching theory, but a number of theoretical substrates, representing the erstwhile two disciplines of psychology—one seeking main effects in controlled cognitive experiments, and the other looking for underlying domains and dimensions of abilities in correlation matrices of varying in extent and robustness (Carroll, 1993). As far as mass testing movements are concerned, the major influences on the development of the operational British Army Recruit Battery have already been published in Irvine et al. (1990), and on The USAF CAM Experimental Battery (Kyllonen & Christal, 1989, 1990). Nevertheless, the benefit of hindsight enables a sharper focus to modify and make more evident details brought to mind by selective attention.

There are at least three measurement paradigms that qualify how item generation has developed in the past and may yet grow in future. These have been described in detail elsewhere (Irvine, Dann, & Evans, 1987; Irvine, Dann, Evans, Dennis, Collis, Thacker, & Anderson, 1989) as R (Accuracy), L (Latency), and D (Dynamic or Change) Models. In the interests of brevity and clarity, their influence on test construction methods is summarized

R-Models. Those who favor accuracy or R-Models mark items as right and wrong and may use classical test theory in which true score variance and error variance are the two determinants of reliability—a notion that began with Spearman. Alternatively, item response theory is employed, a technology dating from 1960 and largely associated with Educational Testing Service (ETS) and Fred Lord (1980). Although many primary sources could be cited to do justice to all those who have contributed to the refinement of R-Models through the use of classical or modern test theory, a balanced contemporary overview can be seen in Crocker and Algina (1987) and in Wainer and Messick (1983). The elaboration of R-Models through item response theory has developed as a method of shortening tests, of replacing or replenishing item-banks annually produced by experts, and of equating one test form with another. They are part of the large item-bank generation and process that is used in the SAT test models developed at ETS, in the Graduate Record Examination, and in the Armed Services Vocational Aptitude Battery (ASVAB) used in the assessment of applicants to all arms of the United States military. The assumptions and practices of item response theory applied to right and wrong answers are at the heart of early and not all together successful attempts to introduce computerised adaptive testing.

L-Models. L-Models use time, or latency, to distinguish fast from slow performance. Moreover, they have relied on differences from baseline times, slopes of times when task difficulty has increased, intercepts when latency has been made to increase over homogeneous items by their external manipulation. Much has been written of reaction-time paradigms, and attempts have been made to determine stage processes by decomposing gross times into estimates of stage times within individuals. The experimental literature dealing with main effects in cognitive tasks directly related to ability formation testifies to their universality. For example, Chase, 1969; Clark and Chase, 1972; Evans, 1982; Miller and McKean, 1964, provide specific latency performance models for deductive reasoning tasks. The use of these methods to generate test scores for individuals suffers, nevertheless, from the inadequacy of procedures for estimating individual differences in abilities from them (cf. Lohman, 1994). Such individual scores as may be generated become even more problematic when structural relations among stage processing measures are sought by correlational methods. Latency measures within a fixed time interval are invariably experimentally dependent upon each other (Sternberg, 1977), making traditional validation by intercorrelation and latent-trait methods at best risky and at worst tendentious. It is hardly surprising that Lohman (1994) describes attempts to produce a unified theory of measurement derived from latency studies of process stages as a qualified failure. Nevertheless, attempts to grapple with a model for individual differences in latencies have a long history (Dennis & Evans, 1996; Furneaux, 1952; Restle & Davis, 1962; White, 1982; Wright, 1997).

D-Models. Dynamic, learning, or D-Models involve the repeated measurement of individuals while they are learning either the task they are performing, or some other task whose outcome the task being measured is expected to predict. While they may be constructed either from scores for accuracy (R) or latency (L), D-Models operate most effectively when they require some asymptotic level of performance in the predictor, or the criterion, or both. Even if elegant mathematical models have been in place for some time (see, e.g., Neimark & Estes [1967] on stimulus sampling theory) that precisely allocate main effects they have had little or no lasting influence on the measurement of individual differences. Change scores are difficult to use in regression equations unless they are highly reliable. The need to preserve serial independence of items that are generated is nevertheless paramount in the exercise of test theory (Royer, 1971). What the subject may be predicted to learn, or operationally just as salient, be prevented from learning during the test greatly influences the choice of item generation algorithms.

The Fourth Estate

On the whole, the work that went into creating a large-scale operational model from tests that were wholly item generative, and thereby guaranteed a *new* test for every applicant, deliberately collected data that would reveal aspects of these three models. In the outfiles that were generated for each subject. the item order, item characteristics, latencies for each stage of item delivery and response, correct and actual response, were all collected. Nevertheless, test scores were invariably constructed around R-Models adjusted for guessing, without totally resolving the question of speed–accuracy trade off (Dennis & Evans, 1996). To enable the outfiles to be created, the nature of changes in testing that were brought with the microcomputer had to be understood and invoked as principles.

Traditionally, large-scale testing was and still is carried out in groups, using paper-and-pencil tests as the medium. This technology restricted the range of operational variables that could be constructed; and has defined ability theory in a very constrained fashion. Indeed, item response theory was a function of that delivery system because of the need to equate paper-and-pencil annual aptitude test forms that were never quite parallel in the hands of item-construction teams. Much of the early literature on computer-based testing is preoccupied with transferring old paper-and-pencil tests to computers to see if they will produce the same results. This apart, other research teams concerned with the promise of computer-adaptive testing used the computer to administer individually tailored tests.

For progress to be made, the microcomputer could not become an expensive form of continuing paper-and-pencil test conventions into the millennium. Moreover, the implications of the capacity of microcomputers to shape the future of measurement were realised much earlier than the capacity of scientists to deliver the necessary changes. At least two independent major reports outlined where decision-making functions could be left to algorithms in the machine (Bunderson, Inouye, & Olsen, 1988; Dennis & Evans, 1989). Today, computer-based testing can be said to have increased the boundaries of theory to such an extent that the limits to mental measurement require a new form of boundary specification. Here, confined to the obvious, tests in computers have been defined, in the sense of providing a key to understanding their new operational dimensions; *by hardware, by software and by knowledge-based systems created for score production according to preconceived paradigms.*

The most important context for item generation is the microcomputer itself, not its operating system, but in how the ergonomics of test delivery and subject response may serve to shape the tests themselves. The microcomputer can be a variable, or more exactly can be made to define a number of quasi-independent variables (which are called *radicals*) that will constrain and alter the nature of the mental process to be measured. *These variables include display mode, information sequence, and response mode.* Table 1.1 summarises these.

Display Modes. Visual displays can be made to vary from a completely static representation of an item (as if it were transferred without change from paper to screen) to a wholly dynamic item where parts actually move (as in an arcade game environment where movement is a precondition). Old-fashioned apparatus tests (using puzzles, cards, beads, jig-saw pieces) administered to individuals also introduce movement and manipulation of the apparatus as sources of variation, for example in the so-called Non-Verbal, but more accurately Performance, scales of omnibus intelligence tests administered individually. Interactive modes allow changes in displays depending on responses. This can be seen in adaptive paper-and-pencil questionnaires that require people to go on to answer *different* questions, depending on whether the answer is yes or no to any one question. Note that the information categories in particular may vary within each one. *Quality* refers to the amount of degradation on the screen. *Order, pace, and*

TABLE 1.1
Microcomputer Display and Response Variables Affecting Test Scores

Display	*Information*	*Response*
Static	Modality	Keyboard
Moving	Amount	Console
Sequential	Order	Touch Screen
Interactive	Pace	Mouse
	Quality	Voice

amount of information are not necessarily correlated attributes, although in practice they are likely to be. Finally, another modal category *(Medium)* to distinguish prose from representations from geometrical figures in visual displays may need to be specified. Voice-over, and/or voice-only, delivery is not a forgotten condition: but it has not been used in the empirical work here described.

Information Modes. Whatever the medium of test delivery, *information modes can vary in the modality, quality, amount, order, pace, and medium of presentation.* For example, much of information delivery in traditional paper-and-pencil testing is quasi-linear and is processed serially, fixed by what may be printed on a page of given size. It is most controlled in the medium of verbal items using sentences, and least controlled in a figural or pictorial item medium where subjects are free to extract what they will in whatever order they wish, because a figure or a picture does not prescribe a directional mode of attack on comprehension. In using the screen of the computer to determine amount, order, pace and medium of information delivery, the test constructor may control the range of all of them. By knowing that range for each variable, the test constructor can choose to limit or extend it.

Response Modes. Whereas the meanings of most categories are transparent, *response input* is perhaps one of the least obvious but most important variables in computer-based testing. How the subject makes the response is no longer a form of multiple-choice on the printed test or on a separate answer sheet, but can vary from standard computer keyboards to modified keyboards, to custom-made consoles (including joysticks), to different forms of mouse, or · to analogues of paper and pencil involving touchscreens.

These are qualitative differences that do *not* represent a single continuous variable. Hence, for any specific type of test, mode of response must follow function wherever possible (Collis et al., 1995). For example, recording an accurate answer in a non-speeded test is a relatively trivial task whatever the mechanics of it. The true-score variance in subjects is not related to the speed with which they record the answer, or if it is, time to complete all the test items is of no consequence. In a speeded test, the variance introduced by the form of response is as critical in paper and pencil as in computer-based tests. Just as separate answer sheets are inappropriate for paper-and-pencil tests requiring a fast processing rate, so *any* response mode that requires a long answer-search period or a prolonged learning period to master how to record an answer will introduce unreliability in tests whose items take only seconds to complete. In either form, hunting around for the correct location for the answer will invalidate the test by introducing variance that is irrelevant. In general, in comparison to the relatively few ways in which responses are made in paper-and pencil tests, nearly all computer-based tests may be made to vary in what they measure by the idiosyncrasies of the response mode.

Table 1.2 sets out a scheme to outline how computer presentation of items in a simple error-detection (perceptual speed) task (see Irvine & Reuning, 1981, and Irvine, Schoeman, & Prinsloo, 1988 for the rationale for and antecedents to this type of task) can be made to change their difficulty, and very probably, their factorial composition. The task is to compare two versions of series of symbols and to count the errors in the copy. In computer delivery there are variables (or if not variables, categories that produce individual variations in performance) related to display, information, and response functions. In constructing a system, these display functions can be manipulated to produce six versions of the task. Table 1.2 lists a number of factors that could be varied to alter the difficulty of the generic task. Although they may not all be implemented, it is important to set out the ways in which the test format could be altered with consequences for item difficulty at the outset of task design.

The test described in Table 1.2 can be made available by item-generation methods in traditional paper-and-pencil form as well as in computer-delivered form. This means that certain items are only analogues (and occasionally are no more than approximate analogues) of what appears on

TABLE 1.2
Error Detection Task Framework Screening Variations

Correct	Copy	Answer	Screen Mode	Pace Controls
	Original	Item	Format	
TX 3142	TZ 3246	0 1 2 **3** 4		
1 Screen 1	Screen 1	Screen 2	Static	No time
	Potential	Item	Variants	
2 Screen 1	Screen 1	Screen 2	Static	Time
3 Screen 1	Screen 1	Screen 2	Sequential	No time
4 Screen 1	Screen 1	Screen 2	Sequential.	Time Screen 2
5 Screen 1	Screen 1	Screen 2	Sequential	Time Screens 1, 2
6 Screen 1	Screen 1	Screen 2	Time-Square Tickertape Screen 1	Time Screen1 Time Screens 1, 2

screen; but that other potentially useful item types are not available because they depend on the computer's delivery properties for their existence. Nevertheless, the principles behind test construction in computers apply equally to analogues constrained by a different medium of delivery.

The computer itself is a means to explore the possibilities of factors that will alter the difficulty of items. Bejar (1986) demonstrated the use of various methods of estimating item difficulty by having the computer both construct and solve items. He used the Hough transform (Hough, 1962) in the generation and solution of embedded figures test items. Irvine, Dann, and Evans (1987) were able to design algorithms to produce and solve Baddeley's (1968) deductive reasoning tasks. They were able to estimate difficulty from the number of grammatical transformations required by the computer to reduce any one variant of the task to its simplest form. They also used Markov chain approaches to a spatial search task involving learning; so that *learning scores* could be estimated from subject gains over a random walk to solution.[1] In recent extensions (Irvine, 1998) the computer produced a file for each computer-delivered version, an analogue camera-ready paper-and-pencil form in a standard word-processor, a key, and a specification file showing how each parallel form had been constructed.

CONTRIBUTIONS TO PSYCHOLOGY BY TESTS USING ITEM-GENERATIVE TECHNIQUES

A substantial literature now exists to demonstrate the effectiveness of test construction using item-generation theory. To enable a systematic evaluation, the results of research have been organized along the lines of the previous section, dealing in turn with R-Models, L-Models, and D-Models; and ending with some illustrations of computer use beyond the realm of item presentation and response.

Item-Generation Theory in Right–Wrong Models

As far as mass-testing was concerned, the original aims of the work carried out by The Human Assessment Laboratory of the University of Plymouth in the period 1986–1990 were: to provide multiple parallel forms of tests created in real time that did not require equating by IRT methods; to deliver them on a client basis to applicants whose literacy and numeracy skills were basic; to constrain testing time to less than one hour; and to predict degree

---

[1] Jonathan Evans did this work using *Poplog*. Its significance has not yet, perhaps, been fully realised.

of success in primary and secondary training contexts using conventional right-wrong scoring procedures and classical test theory (Irvine et al., 1990). Operational requirements apart, there were fundamental questions to be answered about the success or failure of item-generation theory in determining the parallelism of the tests, their reliability, and not least, their construct and predictive validity.

Parallelism and Reliability. If item-generation theory is to be a bulwark against test compromise through overexposure, the notion of a new test for every person constructed from generic item types has to be conceived not just as a real possibility, but an attainable goal. In Table 1.3 are summarized results of creating parallel forms of the British Army Recruit Battery in three different versions, and of recently developed (Irvine, 1998a, 1998b) Tests for Selection Interviews (T_SI). These results are from paper-and pencil versions generated for group administration. The sources for the summary data include Collis and Irvine (1991a, 1991b, 1991c, 1991d, 1991e), Harris and Tapsfield (1995), Irvine (1998a, 1998b), Tapsfield and Wright, (1993), Wright, Irvine, and Tapsfield (1992).

In Table 1.3, means are shown for parallel forms and reliabilities (internal consistency and parallel form) for, respectively, *Reasoning, Orientation, and Working Memory* tests in three different difficulty formats of BARB, the British Army Recruit Battery (Recruits, Army Regular Commissions Board [ARCOM], and Navy); and for one completely new set of tests (T_SI) bearing no physical resemblance to BARB. Although these versions differ in difficulty, in item types and in the populations sampled, the results are coherent. A separate cadre of research about computer-delivered tests and their reliabilities confirms the consistency of these illustrations across delivery modes (Harris & Tapsfield, 1995; Tapsfield, 1993a, 1993b; Tapsfield & Wright, 1993). Multiple parallel forms of high reliability, the longest of which takes only 10 minutes to administer, can be generated in paper and pencil and in computer-delivered forms.

What Makes Items Difficult?

Parallelism is not all that complicated a matter if item difficulty variations in graduated item-banks are counterbalanced in blocks of relatively small size through the application of algorithms (Armstrong, Jones, & Wang, 1994). These variations are then incidental to the production of forms with identical group means. However, if one wishes to vary difficulty in a predictable and construct-congruent way where there are no item-banks, then the elements of items that change their difficulty have a root-causal or *radical* function. These elements are the basis of parallel forms that are both

Table 1.3
Parallelism and Reliability in
Item-Generation Theory Tests for Mass Testing

Test Batteries

| | Army Recruits | | | ARCOM (Difficult) | | | Navy | | | | T_SI | |
	TI	OR	WM	TI	OR	WM	TI	OR	WM	RC	OR	WM
Form												
A	54	57	37	36	30	18	51	33	46	19	23	42
B	53	58	36	36	29	19	51	34	45	19	23	43
N	279			240			294			3000		
rtt	76	92	90	.86	.88	.84	88	89	90	.82	.86	.87
rpf/rt	75	82	80	-	-	-	78	73	84	.77	.74	.73

Note: RC Reasoning Categories; OR Rotated Symbol/Locations; TI Transitive Inference; WM Working
Memory Tasks.

reliable and valid. From the outset, work in the Human Assessment Laboratory, University of Plymouth, tried to distinguish between *incidental* elements of items and *radical* elements. *Radicals* are defined as those theoretically consonant structural elements of items, which, as quasi-independent variables, will cause statistically significant changes in item difficulties measured by error rate and/or time to completion. These can be distinguished from *incidentals*, those surface characteristics of items that preserve serial independence but, when allowed to vary randomly within item strata, exert no significant influence on item difficulty.

Predicting Item Difficulty. Carroll and Johnson (1991) showed how classical item-difficulty (p values) for a variety of items could be predicted from *radicals*. Block Counting, and two of Thurstone's (1938) orientation tests (Flags, Hands), Shepard and Metzler's (1971) Rotation Task, the Seashore Pitch Test and a Vocabulary test were all used. The p values for items were predicted from observed item *radicals* with a multiple R ranging from .72 at least, and .99 at best. As far as the work in mass testing was concerned, it is possible to offer results in the domains of Working Memory (Woltz, 1987)) and Orientation (Irvine et al., 1990; Mislevy et al., 1991); and to record further advances made by Dennis (1993, 1995; Dennis, Collis, & Dann, 1995). Woltz (1987) was able to determine p values for an alphabet reconstruction task that had been adopted for BARB, and which is described in more detail in the section on latency models. The p values varied with the number of letters in the stimulus and in the number of steps required to reconstruct the alphabet from memory. When this data was reanalyzed, we observed that the p values were additive functions of set size and step size, with no interactions. In the Mislevy et al., study, it was possible to predict the mean RT per item to a rotation task involving the rotation of two right triangles. The stimuli varied line length, angle of rotation, and identity vs. mirror image. Latency was almost perfectly predicted knowing line lengths, angle of rotation and identity vs. mirror image ($R = .92$). Another study in the Human Assessment Laboratory, involved the Wegfiguren[2] test (Goeters, 1979; Kirsch, 1971). This task requires the subject to follow a drawn path visually on a printed page and count either the number of right or left turns. It was used in pilot selection originally. Decomposition of the stimulus for each item used line length, number of turns, start position, number of upside down turns as intuitively certain variables influencing final item order in the test. Their use in a linear regression model showed that p values could be predicted from the nature of the stimulus, with a multiple R of .97. Finally, a rotated F task used in BARB (from an officer cadre with restricted range) produced p values that were predicted with R at .84, knowing stimulus characteristics. The salient quality was the number of rotated pairs of letters that were the same. The more rotations that had to be made in the item to verify the number of items that matched, the more difficult was the item. This was predicted from the work by Shepard and Metzler (1971); by Bejar (1986a, 1986b, 1986c); and by Bejar and Yocom (1991).

Dennis (1993) was able to forecast with good accuracy p values for a Directions and Distances task for navigator selection that was composed of verbal instructions. The correlation of this verbal instructions test with other spatial orientation tasks was substantial. Wright and Dennis, (1992) had equally promising results in constructing a visualization test based on cube-folding, with a single factor at six levels predicting these bands of difficulty with $R = .92$. Perhaps the most salient work in the whole field of predicting item difficulties lies in his report (Dennis et al., 1995) where the p values of verbal comprehension tasks were successfully predicted ($R = .85$) using sentence type, degree of grammatical transformation and word length in a linear model. A vocabulary test of semantic categorization, closely allied to verbal analogies, was successfully modeled using semantic theory and word frequency, with a final R of .94. A version of this involving only abstract words was modeled to produce a $R = .81$ prediction of p values. This work shows the strong influence of cognitive performance models in the approach taken by Dennis. With the same emphasis he has also

---

[2] A computerized version was developed by Nigel Barlow and David Wright, University of Plymouth.

modeled numeracy items (Dennis, 1995) with similar success in predicting difficulties with R estimated at .97. That this is no isolated phenomenon is clear from the work of Embretson (1996) who reports a multiple R of .79 in predicting Rasch model difficulties of mathematics items from a more eclectic empirical perspective.

The strength of these various approaches can be gauged from the average proportion of variance explained by the studies for which R is provided. This is .796 equal to R of .89. Moreover, the approach taken, of cognitive modeling, transfers elegantly across domains. Given such results, the construction of aptitude and achievement tests from item–generation theory principles would have two consequences. First, parallelism would be easier to achieve; and second, item response theory would have parameters that are more or less independent of contexts or domains. That is, certain cognitive parameters of items would generalize. In some contexts, particularly in mass screening where the capacity to process new information was the primary construct, item response theory could be dispensed with entirely; or reinvented to incorporate time to complete the item as another major area of concentration (see Dennis & Evans, 1996; Evans & Wright, 1993; Mislevy et al., 1991; Wright, 1990, 1992, 1993, 1997).

Item-Generative Tests and Psychometric Theory

When BARB was being constructed, Irvine et al. (1990) invoked two principles, the first of which was the ability to reference each test in the psychometric literature: the second was that a cognitive performance model for the task types within each test should be available. Once the tests were constructed, they were delivered in a fashion that Thurstone would have commended. They consisted of a number of generic item types that were consistent within each test. In this mold, five tests were produced: perceptual speed, visual orientation, transitive inference, and alphabet reconstruction. They are briefly described below with their attendant literature references.

Letter Checking Task
Psychometric factor: General Speed Gs.
Knowledge: Alphabet letters in upper and lower case.
Cognitive Model: Semantic encoding and comparison
(Hunt, Lunneborg, & Lewis, 1975; Irvine & Reuning, 1981; Irvine, Schoeman, & Prinsloo, 1988; Posner, Boies, Eichelman, & Taylor, 1969; Sternberg, 1966).

Symbol Rotation (F) Task
Psychometric Factor: General Visualization Gv.
Knowledge: Recognition of F and its mirror image.
Cognitive Model: Spatial rotation (Bejar, 1986a, 1986b, 1986c; Just & Carpenter, 1985; Shepard & Metzler, 1971).

Transitive Inference (2 and 3 term) Tasks
Psychometric Factor: Fluid General Intelligence Gf.
Knowledge: Comprehension of simple sentences; use of comparatives and negatives in assigning meaning.
Cognitive Model: decisions based on structural determinants of sentences (Clark, 1969, 1970; Clark & Chase, 1972; Evans, 1982).

Alphabet Forward and Backward Task
Psychometric Factor: General Memory Capacity Gm.
Knowledge: Alphabet letters in sequence from first to last.
Cognitive Model: Reconstructive memory task (Hockey, Maclean, & Hamilton, 1981; Hockey & Maclean, 1986; Woltz, 1987).

Number Distance Task
Psychometric Factor: General Memory Capacity (Numerical Specific) Gm.
Knowledge: Order of numbers to specified range. Number facts for one and two-digit subtraction pairs within the range specified.
Cognitive Model: Decisions based on number retrieval (Groen & Parkman, 1972; Moyer & Landauer, 1967; Parkman, 1972).

Given the wide application of these tests in their various difficulty forms since their construction in the period 1985–1990, one may enquire about their contribution, as exemplars of the item-generation theory movement in testing, to construct and predictive validities. Moreover, Lohman (1994) has been pessimistic about the attempts to discover more about the nature of intellect through decomposition methods, under which item-generation theory may be subsumed.

As far as construct validity is concerned, a number of studies have shown that the battery as listed produced, without reference frames provided by other tests, a single general factor, with highest loadings on tests depending on the attentive allocation of working memory resources. A major contribution from cognitive science has been the work of Baddeley (1968) and Baddeley and Hitch (1974) in defining working memory, a construct very much invoked in learning and retention experiments and built into key tasks in the BARB series. Until very recently, however, little use of the Baddeley and Hitch findings was made to model individual differences in gross task performance or to predict more specifically targeted learning outcomes. Working memory tasks that lend themselves to item-generation modeling have emerged strongly in the last decade (Christal, 1987; Embretson, 1995; Irvine, Dann, & Evans, 1987; Irvine et al., 1990; Kyllonen & Christal, 1988, 1989, 1990; Kyllonen & Woltz, 1988).

Kyllonen and Christal (1990) conducted the most important construct validity study during this period with working memory tasks that were inherently capable of being constructed by item-generation theory methods. They introduced a new family of computer-delivered tasks with pronounced individual differences, including more sophisticated versions of Baddeley's original sentence verification task. Their work showed reasoning tasks to be highly related to working memory capacity. In particular the Alphabet Forward and Backward reconstruction task used in BARB was singled out as so different from conventional reasoning tasks as to offer no intuitive connection between the two classes. Yet the dependence of both classes of tasks on working memory had to be the only logical conclusion. Kyllonen and Christal (1990) also suggest that the pervasiveness of working memory in the kinds of tasks that were used in the work on component definition reviewed by Lohman is an experimental artefact that accounts for the lack of success.

The results of construct validation studies using the BARB series are also unequivocal. Whenever the tasks are used alongside other tests, they define a distinct working memory factor that invariably reveals to what extent the other tests in the battery share this construct (Collis & Irvine, 1991a, 1991b, 1991c, 1991d, 1991e; 1993a, 1993b, 1993c, 1993d; Irvine et al., 1990; Irvine & Christal, 1994; Greig & Bongers, 1996; Bongers & Greig, 1997). The correlation of this factor with a second factor that holds verbal-educational domain tests requiring long-term memory information for their completion varies around a median .6 in unselected populations and in range-restricted cohorts, around .4. Table 1.4 shows recent analyses of the new T_SI series with the ASVAB tests as reference tests (Irvine, 1998a). Two-factor solutions are shown for paper and pencil analogues and computer-delivered versions scored for accuracy and latency using maximum likelihood extractions followed by direct oblimin rotations.

These results, regardless of delivery mode or scoring system (right–wrong or latency) confirm the status of working memory as a central construct in the capacity to process new information. They largely reinforce the position of Kyllonen (1996) and Kyllonen and Christal (1990), but they also underscore the dangers of interpreting the first component emerging from a test matrix as firmly representing a fundamental biological trait of a determinant nature. In conclusion, Lohman's (1994) judgment that attempts to use task elements as process markers to advance the theory of intellect

TABLE 1.4

Factorial Composition of Item-Generation Theory Tests Referenced to ASVAB
Scores

	Factors by Mode and Scoring					
Delivery Mode	Paper		Computer		Computer	
Scoring	R_W		R_W		LAT.	
Factors	V:ed	WM	WM	V:ed	WM	V:ed
ASVAB Tests						
AUTOSHOP	**.73**	-.20	-.30	**.79**	.21	**-.72**
ELECINFO	**.70**	-.07	-.13	**.78**	.09	**-.77**
GENSCI	**.80**	-.08	.03	**.64**	-.04	**-.69**
MECHCOMP	**.76**	.07	.02	**.71**	-.03	**-.68**
PARACOMP	**.50**	.11	.13	**.48**	-.13	**-.51**
WORDKNOW	**.59**	-.07	-.03	**.61**	.00	**-.62**
ARITHRES	**.36**	**.48**	**.53**	.29	**-.49**	-.31
NUMOPS	-.25	**.73**	**.61**	-.23	**-.61**	-.17
CODESPED	-.17	**.66**	**.54**	-.14	**-.48**	-.05
MATHKNOW	.18	**.54**	**.61**	.07	**-.54**	.11
Item-Gen. Tests						
ED Error Detection	-.07	**.62**	**.63**	-.10	**.64**	.09
LOC Orientation	**.32**	**.47**	**.49**	.28	**.56**	-.16
NF Number Skills	-.15	**.76**	**.83**	-.10	**.86**	.03
OE Odds Evens	.12	**.53**	**.65**	.11	**.67**	.00
RC Reasoning Categories	**.35**	**.41**	**.42**	**.39**	**.38**	.05
Correlation:	.31		.44		.39	
Subjects	235		367		367	

have been a qualified failure may have been somewhat premature as far as construct validity is concerned. The next question is what do item-generation theory tests designed for mass screening predict?

Predicting Training Outcomes. There is a voluminous literature of independent studies that validate the kinds of generative tests used for mass testing as predictors of primary and secondary stages of training in a wide spectrum of tasks that could only be followed up in military contexts. This literature includes Bongers and Greig (1996); Collis and Irvine (1991a, 1991b, 1991c, 1991d, 1991e); Collis and Irvine (1993a, 1993b, 1993c); Greig and Bongers (1996, 1997); Holroyd, Atherton, and Wright (1995a, 1995b); Jacobs (1996); Jacobs, Cape, and Lawton (1997), and Kitson and Elshaw, (1996). The overwhelming weight of the evidence reveals that individual and composite measures from the BARB series of mass-screening tests predicts the rate and efficiency with which new information given in training will be mastered. The validity coefficients vary with contexts and range from .2 at worst to .6 or more *at best*. There has been no training situation in which the BARB tests have failed to predict success. Moreover, there have been several, particularly in the exhaustive Navy studies carried out by Collis and her various co-authors, where the BARB tests have produced significant improvements over traditional tests highly saturated with educational content. Studies with USAF inductees (Irvine & Christal, 1994) and most recently with UK police applicants, Irvine (1998a, 1998b) and German conscripts (Irvine, Kutschke, & Walker, 2000) continue the trend to validity generalisation for these tests. Regardless of delivery mode, the T_SI tests of Table 1.3 parsimoniously predict Air Force Qualifying Test scores and discriminate between groups of United States Air Force Recruits, United Kingdom police applicants and German conscripts who were selected by other, independent measures.

LATENCY MODELS:
THE NEW FRONTIER FOR MASS TESTING?

In recent years there has been a revival of interest in the use of latency to complete an item as a radical element in itself. The salient literature includes Bevans (1966); Dennis and Evans (1996); Evans and Wright (1992, 1993); Jensen (1982, 1988); Kornbrot (1988, 1989, 1997); Mislevy and Sheehan (1988); Mislevy et al. (1991); Restle and Davis (1962); Tatsuoka and Tatsuoka (1978); Vernon (1993); Vernon and Jensen (1985); Weibull (1951); White (1982); and Wright (1997). An updated review of various scoring methods, with examples of how some may be used in creating latency scores and stopping rules is available in Irvine (1998a).

The work of immediate relevance for mass testing within the context of item response theory has been carried out by Mislevy and his associates and by Wright. Both have taken latencies as extra information to calibrate items using logistic methods. Indeed, far from seeing the speed–error paradigm as a problem (cf. Dennis & Evans 1996) to be resolved, Wright (1997) regards the opportunity to control the duration of stimuli as one to exploit in the estimation of latent traits; and he presents a mathematically elegant and cogent case for its inclusion.

Error Detection Latencies as Predictors of Work Rate

Outside the realms of item response theory Irvine (1998a) has applied the confidence scores of Bevans (1966) as a means of producing stopping rules based on estimating when a subject's latency for a class of item fails to produce a succession of correct answers, whose exact probability can be estimated. He uses the data supplied by Mislevy et al. (1991), for a single subject rotating triangles to congruence. Irvine also is able to illustrate that it is possible to estimate the total correct score of individuals adjusted for guessing from a small number of items whose latencies are known.

In empirical research at Lackland Air Force Base in 1997, the test with the highest correlation between the total score adjusted for guessing and the mean log latency of items attempted is the Error Detection Test mentioned in Table 1.2. The test format consists of the presentation of small samples of five items parcelled into an incomplete block design. This data allows exploration of the use of latencies from incomplete blocks of items as predictors of final score.

The Error Detection Test in its computer-delivered Mark 1 version is given in two screens, with the correct and copy versions of number plates, zip codes, and e-mails vertically opposed in center screen. The task is to detect the number of errors in the copy and to report that answer on the second screen when ready. Subjects proceed *at their own pace*. Latencies are recorded for the first screen (solution time) and the second screen (verification time), and total trial time. Each latency in milliseconds is converted to a logarithm.

Because the items are presented to the subjects in incomplete blocks, with a design for ensuring complete sampling of item types and processes in 56 items (11 blocks of 5 and one extra at random), it is instructive to regress the log latencies for each item in its block of five against the final adjusted score. Table 1.5 summarises the multiple correlation of each of the first four blocks of five items with that total score.

TABLE 1.5
Regressing Blocks of Latencies on Error Detection Test Adjusted Score ($N = 367$)

BLOCK	R	R^2	F	p
First 5	.810	.652	137.9	.000
Second 5	.837	.697	169.3	.000
Third 5	.811	.653	138.8	.000
Fourth 5	.819	.666	143.7	.000

ITEMS	R	R^2	F	p
4, 8, 12, 18	.835	.694	207.9	.000
11-20	.877	.763	119.1	.000
1-20	.894	.793	117.7	.000

The results show very high multiple R correlations of log latencies for even quite small blocks of items. The first four blocks of five items show a variance percentage accounted for between 65% and 69%.

In the lower half of the table, larger sets of items are regressed. The first set, items 4, 8, 12, and 14 were those that entered into the regression first in each of the previous four blocks. When these four are chosen, they account for 69% of the common variance. The second last row of the table shows what happens when items 11–20 are regressed. This would correspond to a strategy of ignoring the first ten items and treating them as a warm-up prior to asymptotic performance. The last row shows the consequences of regressing on the first 20 items. Although stepwise regression methods are used, the percentage of variance increases steadily, suggesting modest item intercorrelations but substantial item/adjusted score correlations. In the final model of items 1–20, stepwise regression terminated after using only 12 items. Such parsimony raises the possibility of an adaptive test paradigm derived from latencies.

This example shows that it is possible to estimate outcomes over a fixed time period using data derived from the mean log latency of items presented in the first minute or two of the test. Clearly, the shorter the time needed to estimate information-processing performance, the more versatile the test can be made to be. Moreover, this kind of result implies that the construct would not change if fewer items were presented with subjects working at their own pace. If they were presented in shorter time envelopes, however, then the question of what was being tested would need resolution. This may indeed be the question of the next quinquennium.

Subjects as Their Own Controls: The Unique Advantage of Item Generation.

Problems of measuring change in performance using test scores are not new, nor are they easily resolved. They are particularly relevant in assessing the effects of treatments in individuals or in groups. Irvine and Irvine (1996) pointed out that the results of a very large study of the administration of hypertensive drugs to elderly patients (Prince, Bird, & Blizzard, 1996), are invalidated by insufficient run-in trials; by memory effects in repeated measures using the same test; by the use of slopes that were within chance limits to estimate change, and other potential confounds. By using BARB, which provides a new test version on each occasion, it was possible to remove most of the objections raised by Irvine and Irvine in a prolonged trial by a single subject.

One patient who had undergone laparoscopic surgery agreed to undertake the BARB series of five cognitive tests for 10 successive days beginning on Day 4 after surgery, when still under the residual effects of a general anaesthetic. The patient was totally familiar with computers and with the BARB tests and reported feeling well in spite of surgery. After an interval of 19 weeks, during which no further trials at BARB were attempted, the effects of anaesthesia were judged to be absent. At that interval, 10 more trials on successive days were undertaken. Responses were made using a standard two-button mouse. Initial results on BARB Letter Checking, Number Distance, Alphabet Forward and Backward, and Symbol Rotation were analysed for Day 1 of each treatment. The treatment effect for all tests demanding a high working memory load was highly significant. Moreover, in the Number Distance test an item order effect was observed. The later items were done more slowly on both occasions.

Because the Alphabet Forward and Backward Test had been singled out by Kyllonen and Christal (1990) as a robust marker for working memory efficiency, detailed analyses of the results of this test were carried out using Days 1, 5, and 10 of each time period, immediate postoperative and 19 weeks later. From work by Woltz (1987), the number of letters encoded, the number of steps involved, and whether the steps were forward or backward in the alphabet, were assumed to affect between subject p value consistently. It was not clear how item characteristics would affect latency when the subject was very accurate (as this subject was). However, it was a reasonable hypothesis that the subject's latency to solution would be affected not only by the same between-subject item *radicals* but also by treatment and by trials within and across treatments.

Table 1.6 shows the results of the within-subject trials. Treatment and days were both significant main effects, with no interactions. The patient showed a consistent practice effect in both conditions, but was palpably slower in the immediate postoperative period.

Because predicting changes in item difficulty from item characteristics is a major focus of item-generation theory, the next step was to regress on latency to complete each item using salient attributes of the items themselves, including *radicals*. The independent variables included known item construction *radicals*: The number of letters in the stimulus set (e.g., BH, HXB); the number of steps required to make the transformation (plus or minus 1, 2, 3 e.g., BH +2, HXB -1); whether the steps were forward or backward; and in this case experimental *radicals*, the trials and treatment effects. In all, five variables were regressed against latency to correct response, with the results summary shown in Table 1.7. The predictors for each of the five stages are given, and the notes contain the standardized beta weight and the t value for each variable.

TABLE 1.6
Mean Latencies(Csec) for AFB Items by Treatment and Trials (Days)

	DAY 1	DAY 5	DAY 10	TOTAL
Post –Op	903	808	695	802
19 Weeks	744	692	631	689
Totals (214 items)	823	750	663	737

ANOVA Summary	df	F	p
Treatment	1	6.18	.01
Days	2	4.20	.02
Treatment x Days	2	0.37	.69

Each variable adds to the prediction of item–response latencies with a final r of .56 and R^2 of 31% of variance. The relative strength of the *radicals* is seen in the weight given to the number of steps to reconstruction from memory, regardless of sign. This finding appears to lend support to the experimental work of Grenzebach and McDonald (1992) who show that results of alphabetic letter-order decisions in continuous or intermittent attention modes with letter separations of 2 and 3 letters, were compatible with a symbolic-distance mechanism. Treatment and practice effects were small in comparison with stimulus set size and number of steps forward or backward.

This study, together with the current interest in the use of latencies to estimate individual differences in cognitive functions, encourages use of item-generation theory to produce tests that are robust when individuals are their own controls. Until the problems associated with repeated measures of individuals *with the same set of test items* are resolved by the introduction of multiple parallel forms, the issues raised by the Irvine and Irvine (1996) critique of the Prince et al. (1996) clinical trials on elderly patients can not be dismissed. In the work population as a whole, cognitive efficiency is a key prerequisite in occupations requiring vigilance over extended periods, whenever time zones are crossed, and whenever interventions purporting to enhance or reduce efficiency are proposed. Item-generation theory is uniquely placed to provide solutions based on multiple parallel form production.

TABLE 1.7
Alphabet Reconstruction Regression Model Summary:
Dependent Variable Response Latency

Model	R	R^2	Adj. R^2	R^2 Change	F Change	Sig. Change
1a	.35	.12	.12	.12	28.83	.00
2b	.48	.23	.22	.11	29.70	.00
3c	.52	.27	.26	.04	10.74	.00
4d	.54	.29	.28	.02	7.08	.01
5e	.56	.31	.30	.02	6.10	.01

1a Predictors: (Constant), ABSTEP (Absolute Step Number) beta .66 t 6.70
2b Predictors: (Constant), ABSTEP, and Set Size beta .43 t 6.34
3c Predictors: (Constant), ABSTEP, Set Size, Positive or Negative Step beta .30 t 3.23
4d Predictors: (Constant), ABSTEP, Set Size, Positive or Negative Step, Days beta .19 t 3.20
5e Predictors: (Constant), ABSTEP, Set Size, Positive or Negative Step, Days, Treatment beta .15 t 2.57

D-MODELS: ITEM-GENERATIVE TESTS AND LEARNING NEW MATERIAL

There is one study of the use of item-generation theory tests in operational use as mass screening devices where their efficacy as predictors of learning under strictly controlled computer-delivered conditions has been completed (Irvine & Christal, 1994). This research was carried out under a technical co-operation agreement involving the resources of The Human Assessment Laboratory, University of Plymouth, Plymouth, UK; and The Armstrong Laboratory, Brooks AFB, San Antonio, Texas. One aim of the work was to confirm, in a quasi-operational context, the findings of an earlier report by Christal (1990) later elaborated by Kyllonen (1996). Christal demonstrated that experimental, computer-delivered tests of cognitive functions could predict the initial and later stages of electronic logic gate identification with greater effectiveness than the battery of tests known as the United States Armed Services Vocational Interest Battery (ASVAB).

Replication of itself was not the prime focus of the work, useful as that might be. The function of this research was to test the hypothesis that learning novel material of a technical nature was not primarily a function of a high level of specialised classroom knowledge. For this purpose, a special set of tests was necessary. The mental processes in these tests had to be encompassed within a very low educational limit, and no specialized knowledge had to be required of the subject. BARB tests were extended in 1990–93 in two forms: A paper-and-pencil analogue version for the Navy, called The Navy Personnel Series (Collis & Irvine, 1994); and in a second modification for screening potential Army officers called the Army Regular Commissions Board Battery (ARCOM). Both modifications were based on item-generation theory so that multiple parallel forms of the tests could be generated from algorithms. Previous work with the derivatives of the BARB series had shown them to have good validities in practical settings and reliabilities in the range .84 to .92.

Given these types of tests, it was important to have available for each subject results on tests that required a high-school graduation level of education; and that assumed various kinds of technical knowledge. The ASVAB series contains just such a selection of measures, with mechanical, electrical and science knowledge tests as well as tests of mathematical knowledge and verbal comprehension. ASVAB subtests have reliabilities at least equal to those of ARCOM, and have been shown to be valid predictors of job performance in many studies of military personnel.

Finally, a criterion measure was required which involved novel learning of a technical nature, in which accuracy of a high level could be attained, so that speed of functioning could be assessed against a low error rate. Christal had used electronic logic gates in his first experiment, and it was appropriate to use this identical series again.

At Lackland Air Force Base 303 recruits were administered a computer-based version of the ARCOM Battery of seven tests, each given within its own fixed time limit. Eight Electronic Logic Gates learning trials, computer-delivered, were completed at the end of the ARCOM Battery. Test outcome variables were scores adjusted for guessing and the average latency per item in milliseconds. Logic Gates Trials (Gates) were scored for percentage correct and average time per item. In addition, the ASVAB scores for each subject were obtained from records. It was possible to normalise the Gates trials score distributions by dividing each accuracy score for each subject by the subject's own average latency per item, giving a power function of learning efficiency. These scores were called Gates 1 through Gates 8. They formed the criteria, and factor scores derived from the ARCOM and ASVAB results were the independent variables. These data compression procedures were used to produce parsimonious predictions based on as few variables as possible.

The results were uniformly acceptable, with multiple R varying narrowly between .40 and .48, with variance accounted for in the low 20% range. The most consistent finding of the regression equations is the *primacy of the working memory factor, followed by both speed of encoding and speed of working memory operations*. A specialized electrical knowledge factor derived from the ASVAB scores made only one appearance, and at the very end of an equation. Verbal comprehension contributed a little, but consistently, at the end of four trial equation series.

In summary, the accuracy and speed at which novel technical material will be learned depends not on the amount of previously learned technical knowledge, but rather the extent to which the subject can marshal mental processes of working memory effectiveness, speed of symbol encoding, speed of carrying out operations in working memory, and verbal fluency. These findings lend weight to the contention by Kyllonen (1996) and Kyllonen and Christal (1990) that general intelligence, reasoning and working memory are closely related. They also replicate the previous study carried out by Christal (1990), where experimental tests of accuracy and speed of mental processing were proven more effective than ASVAB tests in predicting logic gates learning. Most important of all, perhaps, the ARCOM tests used here were constructed from a theory of algorithm-determined item generation, and had no educational prerequisites except numeracy and literacy.

THE FOURTH ESTATE

The use of the computer in testing to add a dimension to item response theory has already been demonstrated by Tatsuoka and Tatsuoka (1978) and by Wright (1992, 1993, 1997). The speed–error problem will no doubt be resolved by suitable control of time envelopes, provided that the construct validity of the items is not altered to such an extent that the cognitive models implicit in the items are invalidated. There are signs already, however, that the subjects themselves can dispose of the models for item interpretation. Whenever latencies are collected as a matter of course, they prove invaluable as a quality control estimate of the willingness of subjects to satisfy the assumptions of the experimenter implicit in the construction and presentation of test items.

To end the empirical section of this contribution, a simple example of the use of latencies in conjunction with scores adjusted for guessing and percentage of items correct among those attempted is taken from studies conducted at Lackland Air Force Base in 1999. Subjects completed a series of six cognitive tests whose items were generated according to algorithms in the computer and delivered by the computer using a mouse interface. Table 1.8 shows the intercorrelations between scores adjusted for guessing and mean log latency per item completed when all subjects were included and when subjects were excluded if they had accuracy scores of less than 70% in each of two of the tests.

Accuracy below a certain threshold identifies those subjects whom we now call "keypressers." This describes what they do, press interface keys as quickly as possible to get to the next test. This behavior can have more than one plausible explanation. It may simply be a consequence of not understanding the test instructions; or of finding the demands of the test too much and not persisting. Persistence, however, may be allied to test context. If subjects were generally demotivated, the removal of "keypressers" in one test would result in improvement in all tests. Table 1.8 shows that different subjects were removed in the Orientation (Locations) and Reasoning Categories tests and that the improvement in latency and work-rate correlations is *specific* to performance on the tests concerned. In fact, if even only some of the subjects have not demonstrated persistence, then these results show that there is room for this, the third motivational parameter added to speed and accuracy by White's (1982) comprehensive scoring model for tests. In fact, White's is the only known full model for all three elements in test psychometrics, a situation that one hopes will not survive for much longer. In conclusion, the latency/work rate score correlation patterns in this and the factor analyses in Table 1.6 for all except the Reasoning Categories test encourage the use of time envelopes on the assumption that construct infrastructure for these items would be robust.

TABLE 1.8

Correlations of Scores Adjusted for Guessing With Mean Log latencies Under Three Different Conditions for Accuracy (Percent Correct)

TEST	N	ED	NF	RC	OR	OE	WR
ALL	367	-.97	-.88	.02*	-.54*	-.86	-.82
>70%OR	346	-.97	-.89	-.14	**-.83**	-.86	-.83
>70%RC	308	-.97	-.88	**-.62**	-.76	-.92	-.83

Notes: ED Error Detection; NF Number Fluency; RC Reasoning Categories; OR Locations; OE Odds and Evens; WR Word Rules.

*The standard error of zero r for $N = 367$ is ± .052. The correlation of -.62 is outside the 95% population limits of this correlation. Similarly, the increases in the correlations for the Locations test are significant improvements. The 95% limits of -.54 with $N = 367$ are - .64 and -.44

CONCLUSIONS

The foundations of item-generation theory for mass testing are well established. In all three contexts, using right-wrong answers, using latencies to estimate work rate and to reveal instrument sensitivity to drug influences; and in the prediction of learning outcomes, the tests that have been developed for the first assessment of individual differences among a large number of applicants for entry to a wide spectrum of occupations have proved their technical strengths and their practicalities.

As far as theory is concerned, the central role of working memory functions in the prediction of the rate and efficiency with which new information is processed and learned is a welcome departure from use of the explanatory primitive term intelligence to account for individual differences—welcome because the construct is precisely measured and because it carries with it no pejorative baggage. In the psychometric field, the use of the tests has encouraged a redefinition of the boundaries of item-response theory. At the same time it has become apparent that for mass testing contexts, there are occasions where item response theory is redundant because the forms of the tests do not need recalibration. There are also occasions when item response theory as we now understand it is inadequate to deal with the speed-error trade off and the motivational bedrock of all human performance in work contexts, persistence. Item-generation theory, through isomorphs and analogues of items for which performance models can be postulated, is a key to controlling the test. Tests have controlled psychologists for far too long, which perhaps is what Cronbach implied in 1957.

Finally, at no time in the history of test development until now has it been possible to produce as many parallel forms of tests as there are applicants, with no possibility of item-bank compromise. Moreover, as the trend to the psychometrics of inclusion rather than exclusion continues, the opportunities for item-generation theory to affirm the principles of open testing were established by Collis and Irvine (1993d) in their trial of distributing parallel form pretest booklets to all applicants. This, and similar approaches, can only serve to satisfy legitimate social and political demands for test fairness.

ACKNOWLEDGMENTS

If Dr. John D. Anderson, sometime Head of the Strategic Research Division of the Army Personnel Research Establishment in the United Kingdom, had not asked me in 1985 what tests could be like if there were no item-bank, no IRT and no money, the promise of item–generation for mass testing (through his sustained programme support to the Human Assessment Laboratory of the University of Plymouth) might never have been realized in the creation of the British Army Recruit Battery. The collaboration of many at the Air Force Laboratory in Brooks AFB, San Antonio, Texas from then onwards under a technical cooperation agreement, particularly Raymond Christal, Bill Alley, Richard Walker, Janice Hereford, was central to large-scale empirical verification of theory. The award of a Senior Fellowship by the US National Research Council during 1997–1999 to provide a daily partnership with Pat Kyllonen at Brooks AFB enabled both the synthesis in this chapter and the impetus for this volume. To all those involved, and particularly to Dr Kyllonen, I offer my thanks and warm appreciation.

REFERENCES

Armstrong, R. D., Jones, D. H., & Wang, Z. (1994). Automated parallel test construction using classical test theory. *Journal of Educational Statistics, 19,* 73–90.

Baddeley, A. D. (1968). A three-minute reasoning test based on grammatical transformation. *Psychonomic Science, 10,* 341–342.

Baddeley, A. D., & Hitch, G. (1974). Working memory. In G. H. Bower, (Ed.), *The Psychology of learning and motivation* (Vol.8, pp. 47–90).

Bartram, D. (1987). The development of an automated testing system for pilot selection: The MICROPAT project. *Applied Psychology: International Review, 36,* 279–298.

Bejar, I. I. (1986a). *The psychometrics of mental rotation (RR-86-19).* Princeton, NJ: Educational Testing Service

Bejar, I. I. (1986b). *Analysis and generation of Hidden Figure items: A cognitive approach to Psychometric Modeling (RR-86-20).* Princeton, NJ: Educational Testing Service.

Bejar, I. I. (1986c). *Final Report: Adaptive testing of spatial abilities (ONR 150 531).* Princeton, NJ: Educational Testing Service.

Bejar, I., & Yocom, P. (1991). A generative approach to the modelling of isomorphic hidden-figure items. *Applied Psychological Measurement, 15(2),* 129–137.

Bevans, H. G. (1966, April). *Probability (confidence) scoring for the Standard Progressive Matrices and the Advanced Matrices.* Unpublished paper presented to the 65th British Psychological Society Annual Conference, Swansea, Wales.

Bongers, S. H., & Greig, J. E. (1997). *An Australian trial of the British Army Recruit Battery – Part 2.* Report of The Air Force Office, Mawson ACT 2607, Australia

Bunderson, C. V., Inouye, D. K., & Olsen, J. B. (1988). *The four generations of computerised educational measurement.* Research Report (RR88-35) Princeton, NJ: Educational Testing Service.

Carroll, J. B. (1976). Psychometric tests as cognitive tasks: A new "Structure of Intellect." In L. B. Resnick (Ed.), *The nature of intelligence.* Hillsdale, NJ: Lawrence Erlbaum Associates.

Carroll, J. B. (1980). *Individual difference relations in psychometric and experimental cognitive tasks* (Report No. 163) Thurstone Psychometric Laboratory, University of North Carolina, Chapel Hill, NC.

Carroll, J. B. (1983). The difficulty of a test and its factor composition revisited. In H. Wainer & S. Messick (Eds.), *Principals of modern psychological measurement.* Hillsdale, NJ: Lawrence Erlbaum Associates.

Carroll, J. B. (1986). Defining abilities through the person characteristic function. In S. E. Newstead, S. H. Irvine, & P. L. Dann (Eds.), *Human assessment: Cognition and motivation.* Dordrecht, Netherlands: Nijhoff.

Carroll, J. B. (1987). New perspectives in the analysis of abilities. In R. R. Ronning, J. A. Glover, J. C. Conoley, & J. C. Witt (Eds.), *The influence of cognitive psychology on testing.* Hillsdale, NJ: Lawrence Erlbaum Associates.

Carroll, J. B. (1993). *Human cognitive abilities: A survey of factor-analytic studies.* New York: Cambridge University Press.

Carroll, J. B., Meade, A., & Johnson, E. S. (1991). Test analysis with the person characteristic function: implications for defining abilities. In R. E. Snow & D. E. Wiley (Eds.), *Improving inquiry in education, psychology and social science: a book in honour of Lee J. Cronbach* (pp.109–143). Hillsdale, NJ: Lawrence Erlbaum Associates.

Christal, R. E. (1984) *New cognitive tests being evaluated by TTCP services.* Report to the Technical Cooperation Program Meeting of 1984, USAF Armstrong Laboratory, Brooks AFB, San Antonio, Texas.

Christal, R. E. (1987). *A factor-analytic study of tests of working memory.* Unpublished Report; Human Resources Division, USAF Armstrong Laboratory, Brooks AFB, San Antonio, Texas.

Christal, R. E. (1990*). Comparative validities of ASVAB and LAMP tests for Logic Gates learning.* Technical Report, USAF Armstrong Laboratory, Brooks AFB San Antonio, Texas.

Clark, H. H. (1969). Linguistic processes in deductive reasoning. *Psychological Review, 76,* 387–404.

Clark, H. H (1970). Comprehending comparatives. In G. B. Flores D'Arcais & W. J. M. Levelt (Eds.), *Advances in psycholinguistics.* Amsterdam: North Holland.

Clark, H. H., & Chase, W. G. (1972). On the process of comparing sentences against pictures. *Cognitive Psychology, 3,* 472–517.

Collis, J. M., & Irvine, S. H. (1991a). *Predictive Validity and Utility of the ABC Battery with Royal Navy Officers under Training.* SP(N) Report TR 261, Office of the Senior Psychologist (Naval), Ministry of Defence, London.

Collis, J. M., & Irvine, S. H. (1991b). *The Plymouth ABC Battery for Artificer Apprentice Entrants. Validity and reliability studies.* SP(N) Report TR 265, Office of the Senior Psychologist (Naval), Ministry of Defence, London.

Collis, J. M., & Irvine, S. H. (1991c). *The Plymouth ABC Battery for RN Non-Technician Ratings under Training. Validity and reliability studies.* SP(N) Report TR 266, Office of the Senior Psychologist (Naval), Ministry of Defence, London.

Collis, J. M., & Irvine, S. H. (1991d). *The Plymouth ABC Battery for WRNS Rating Entrants. Validity and reliability studies.* SP(N) Report TR 267, Office of the Senior Psychologist (Naval), Ministry of Defence, London.

Collis, J. M., & Irvine, S. H. (1991e). *The Plymouth ABC Battery for RN/WRNS Ratings and RM other Ranks under Training. Validity and reliability studies: Summary report.* SP(N) Report TR 271, Office of the Senior Psychologist (Naval), Ministry of Defence, London.

Collis, J. M., & Irvine, S. H. (1993a). *The ABC Combined Battery for Artificer Apprentices. Further validity studies.* SP(N) Report TR 311, Office of the Senior Psychologist (Naval), Ministry of Defence, London.

Collis, J. M., & Irvine, S. H. (1993b). *The ABC Combined Battery for Royal Marine Apprentices. Further validity studies.* SP(N) Report TR 312, Office of the Senior Psychologist (Naval), Ministry of Defence, London.

Collis, J. M., & Irvine, S. H. (1993c). *The ABC Combined Battery for RN/WRNS Non-Technicians. Further validity studies.* SP(N) Report TR 313, Office of the Senior Psychologist (Naval), Ministry of Defence, London.

Collis J. M., & Irvine, S. H. (1993d). *The effects of pre-knowledge, retest and types of test administration on computer generated cognitive tasks in a group of royal navy and royal marine entrants.* SP(N) Report TR 314, Office of the Senior Psychologist (Naval), Ministry of Defence, London.

Collis, J. M., & Irvine, S. H. (1994). *A new generation of ability tests for selection and training. The Navy Personnel Series.* Technical Report 1:1994, Human Assessment Laboratory, University of Plymouth, Plymouth UK.

Collis, J. M., Tapsfield, P. G. C., Irvine, S. H., Dann, P. L., & Wright, D. (1995). The British Army Recruit Battery goes operational: From theory to practice in computer-based testing using item-generation techniques. *International Journal of Selection and Assessment, 3,* 96–103.

Cronbach, L. J. (1957). The two disciplines of scientific psychology. *American Psychologist, 12,* 671–684.

Dann, P. L., & Irvine, S. H. (1986). *Handbook of computer-based cognitive tasks.* Centre for Computer-Based Assessment, University of Plymouth, Plymouth, UK.

Dennis, I. (1993). *The development of an item generative test of spatial orientation closely related to Test SP80a.* SP(N) Report TR 307, Office of the Senior Psychologist (Naval), Ministry of Defence, London.

Dennis, I. (1995*). The structure and development of numeracy and literacy tests in the Navy Personnel Series.* Technical Report for the Office of the Senior Psychologist (Naval). Human Assessment Laboratory, University of Plymouth, Plymouth UK.

Dennis, I., Collis, J. M., & Dann, P. L. (1995 October). Extending the scope of item generation to tests of educational attainment. *Proceedings of the 37th International Military Testing Association Conference,* Toronto, Canada.

Dennis, I., & Evans, J. St. B. T. (1989). *System architecture for computerised assessment.* Report for The Army Personnel Research Establishment (Contract 2021/12). Human Assessment Laboratory, University of Plymouth, Plymouth, UK.

Dennis, I., & Evans, J. St. B. T. (1996). The speed-error trade off problem in psychometric testing. *British Journal of Psychology, 87,* 105–129.

Embretson, S. E. (1995). Working memory capacity versus general control processes in abstract reasoning. *Intelligence, 20,* 169–189.

Embretson, S. E. (1996). Multidimensional latent trait models in measuring fundamental aspects of intelligence. In I. Dennis & P. G. C. Tapsfield (Eds.) *Human abilities, their nature and measurement.* Mahwah, NJ: Lawrence Erlbaum Associates.

Evans, J. St. B. T. (1982). *The psychology of deductive reasoning.* London: Routledge.

Evans, J. St. B. T., & Wright, D. E. (1992) *The transitive inference task* (Tech. Rep. 2-1992 Army Personnel Research Establishment). Human Assessment Laboratory, University of Plymouth, Plymouth, UK.

Evans, J. St. B. T., & Wright, D .E. (1993) *The properties of fixed-time tests: A simulation study,* (Tech. Rep. 3-1993 Army Personnel Research Establishment). Human Assessment Laboratory, University of Plymouth, Plymouth, UK.

Furneaux, W. D. (1952). Some speed, error and difficulty relationships within a problem-solving situation. *Nature, 170,* 3.

Goeters, K-M, (1979). *Die anderung der psychometrischen kennewerte und der faktorenstruktur als folge der ubung von tests.* Unpublished Doctoral Dissertation, University of Hamburg, Hamburg,

Goeters, K-M., & Rathje, H. (1992). *Computer-generiete parallel-tests fur die fahigeitsmessung in der eignungsauswahl von operationellem luftfahrtpersonal.* DLR Institut fur Flugmedizin Abteilung Luft-und Raumfahrtpsychologie, Hamburg.

Greig, J. E., & Bongers, S. H. (1996). An Australian trial of the British Army Recruit Battery. *Proceedings of the 38th Annual Conference of the International Military Testing Association.* San Antonio, November, 1996.

Greig, J. E., & Bongers, S. H. (1997). *An Australian trial of the British Army Recruit Battery—Part 3: Validity coefficients and factor structure.* Report of The Air Force Office, Mawson; ACT 2607, Australia.

Grenzebach, A. P., & McDonald, J. E. (1992). Alphabetic sequence decisions for letter pairs with separations of one to three letters. *Journal of Experimental Psychology Learning, Memory, and Cognition; 18,* 865–872

Groen, G. J., & Parkman, J. M. (1972). A chronometric analysis of simple addition. *Psychological Review, 79,* 329–343.

Harris, R. L., & Tapsfield, P. G. C. (1995*). The British Army Recruit Battery Trials of Pre-Test Booklets.* Human Assessment Laboratory Technical Report 10-1995, University of Plymouth, Plymouth, UK.

Hockey, G .R. J., & Maclean, A. (1986). Direct temporal analysis of individual differences in cognitive skill. In S. E. Newstead, S. H. Irvine & P. L. Dann (Eds.), *Human assessment: cognition and motivation.* Dordrecht: Nijhoff.

Hockey, G. R. J., Maclean, A., & Hamilton, P. (1981). State changes and the temporal patterning of component resources. In J. Long & A. D. Baddeley,(Eds.), *Attention and performance, Vol. 9.* Hillsdale, NJ: Lawrence Erlbaum Associates.

Holroyd, S. R., Atherton, R. M., & Wright, D. E. (1995a October). The criterion related validity of the British Army Recruit Battery. *Proceedings of the 37th Annual Conference of the International Military Testing Association,* Toronto.

Holroyd, S. R., Atherton, R. M., & Wright, D. E. (1995b). *Validation of the British Army Recruit Battery against measures of performance in basic military training.* Centre for Human Sciences, Report DRAJCHS/liS3/CR95019/1.0. Defence Evaluation and Research Agency, Famborough.

Hornke, L. F., & Habon, M. W. (1986). Rule-based item bank construction and evaluation within the linear logistic framework. *Applied Psychological Measurement, 10,* 369–380.

Hough, P. V. C. (1962). *Method and means for recognising complex patterns.* U.S. Patent 3,069,654.

Hunt, E., Lunneborg, C., & Lewis, J. (1975). What does it mean to be high verbal? *Cognitive Psychology, 7,* 194–227.

Irvine, C. D., & Irvine, S. H. (1996). Effects of antihypertensive treatment on cognitive function of older patients: Effect is not proved. *British Medical Journal, 313,* 166.

Irvine, S. H. (1998a). *The computer-generation of ability tests for adaptive testing in selection and training: A report in the form of a technical handbook.* USAF Air Force Laboratory, Brooks AFB, San Antonio, Texas.

Irvine, S. H. (1998b). *New tests for recruitment: standardisation and validation.* Final Report for The Royal Ulster Constabulary. Inpsych Ltd. Berwick-upon-Tweed, UK.

Irvine, S. H., & Christal, R. E. (1994). *The primacy of working memory in learning to identify electronic logic gates* (Tech. Rep. 4-1994). Human Assessment Laboratory, University of Plymouth, Plymouth UK.

Irvine, S. H., Dann, P. L., & Anderson, J. D. (1990). Towards a theory of algorithm-determined cognitive test construction. *British Journal of Psychology, 81,* 173–195.

Irvine, S. H., Dann, P. L., & Evans, J. St .B. T. (1987). *Item generative approaches for computer-based testing: A prospectus for research.* Report for the Army Personnel Research Establishment. Human Assessment Laboratory, University of Plymouth, Plymouth, Devon UK.

Irvine, S. H., Dann, P. L., Evans, J. St. B. T., Dennis, I., Collis, J., Thacker, C., & Anderson, J. D. (1989). *Another generation of personnel selection tests: Stages in a new theory of computer-based test construction.* Report for the Army Personnel Research Establishment. Human Assessment Laboratory, University of Plymouth, Plymouth, UK.

Irvine, S. H., Kutschke, T., & Walker, R. F. (2000). *Screening conscripts in Germany Using Item-Generative Tests* (Report 01/00. Bundesministerium der Verteidigung: Bonn, Deutschland.

Irvine, S. H., & Reuning, H. (1981). Perceptual speed and cognitive controls. *Journal of Cross-Cultural Psychology, 12,* 425–444.

Irvine, S. H., Schoeman. A., & Prinsloo, W. (1988). Putting cognitive theory to the test: group testing reassessed using the cross-cultural method. In G. K. Verma & C. Bagley (Eds.), *Cross-cultural studies of personality, attitudes and cognition.* London: Macmillan.

Jacobs, N. R. (1996). *Validation of the British Army Recruit Battery (BARB) against phase 2 military training performance measures.* Centre for Hunan Sciences Report PLSD/CHS/fiS3/CR96049/1.0 Defence Evaluation and Research Agency, Famborough, UK.

Jacobs, N. R., Cape, L. T., & Lawton, D. H. (1997). *Validation of the British Army Recruit Battery (BARB) against phase 2 military training performance measures.* Centre for Human Sciences, Report PLSD/CHS/HS3/CR97018/1.0. Defence Evaluation and Research Agency, Famborough, UK.

Jensen, A. R. (1982). Reaction time and psychometric *g.* In H. J. Eysenck (Ed.), *A model for intelligence.* New York: Springer-Verlag.

Jensen, A. R. (1988). Speed of information-processing and population differences. In S. H. Irvine, & J. W. Berry (Eds.), *Human abilities in cultural context.* New York: Cambridge University Press.

Just, M. A., & Carpenter, P. A. (1985). Cognitive co-ordinate systems: Accounts of mental rotation and individual differences in spatial ability. *Psychological Review, 92,* 137–172.

Kirsch, H. (1971). Der Wegfiguren test als auswhlinstrument . *Aviation Psychology.* (Quoted in Goeters, K.-M. 1979, p. 125.)

Kitson, N., & Elshaw, C. C. (1996). *A comparison of the British Army Recruit Battery and the RAF Ground Trades Test Battery* (Report DRA/CHS/HS3/CR96060/1.0). Defence Research and Evaluation Agency, Farnborough, UK.

Kornbrot, D. E. (1988). Random walk models of binary choice: The effect of deadlines in the presence of asymmetric payoffs. *Acta Psychologica, 69,* 109–127.

Kornbrot, D. E. (1989). Organisation of keying skills: the effect of motor complexity and number of units. *Acta Psychologica, 70,* 19–41.

Kornbrot, D. E. (1997). *Information accrual models of cognitive processes: evidence from the shape of reaction-time distributions.* Manuscript submitted for publication, Department of Psychology, University of Hertfordshire, UK.

Kyllonen, P. C. (1996). Is working memory capacity Spearman's *g?* In I. Dennis & P. G. C. Tapsfield (Eds.), *Human abilities, their nature and measurement* (pp.49–74). Mahwah, NJ: Lawrence Erlbaum Associates.

Kyllonen, P. C., & Christal, R. E. (1988). *Cognitive modelling of learning abilities: A status report of LAMP (AFHRL-TP-87-66).* Manpower and Personnel Division, Air Force Human Resources Laboratory, Brooks AFB, Texas.

Kyllonen, P. C., & Christal, R. E. (1989). Cognitive modelling of learning abilities. In R. Dillon & J. W. Pellegrino (Eds.) *Testing: Theoretical and applied issues* (pp.143–173). San Francisco: Freeman.

Kyllonen, P. C., & Christal, R. E. (1990). Reasoning ability is (little more than) working memory capacity?! *Intelligence, 14,* 389–433.

Kyllonen, P. C., & Woltz, D. J. (1988 April). *Role of cognitive factors in the acquisition of cognitive skill.* Paper delivered at Minnesota Symposium on Learning and Individual Differences: University of Minnesota, Minneapolis.

Lohman, D. F. (1994). Component scores as residual variation (or why the intercept correlates best. *Intelligence. 19,* 1–11.

Lord, F. M. (1980). *Applications of item response theory to practical testing problems.* Hillsdale, NJ: Lawrence Erlbaum Associates.

Miller, G. A., & McKean, K. E. (1964). A chronometric study of some relations between sentences. *Quarterly Journal of Experimental Psychology, 16,* 297–308.

Mislevy, R. J., & Sheehan, K. M. (1988*). The role of collateral information about examinees in item parameter estimation.* ETS Research Report (RR-88-55-ONR). Princeton, NJ: Educational Testing Service.

Mislevy, R. J., & Wingersky, M. S., Irvine, S. H., & Dann, P. L. (1991). Resolving mixtures of strategies in spatial visualisation tasks. *British Journal of Mathematical and Statistical Psychology, 44,* 265–288.

Moyer, R. S., & Landauer, T. K. (1967). Time required for judgements of numerical inequality. *Nature, 215,* 1519–1520.

Neimark, E .D., & Estes, W. K. (1967). *Stimulus sampling theory.* San Francisco: Holder.

Parkman. J. M. (1972). Temporal aspects of simple multiplication and comparison. *Journal of Experimental Psychology, 95,* 437–444.

Posner, M. L., Boies, S. J., Eichelman, W. H., & Taylor, R. J. (1969). Retention of visual name codes of single letters. *Journal of Experimental Psychology Monographs, 79,* 1–16.

Prince, M. J., Bird, A. S., Blizzard, R. A., & Mann, A. H. (1996). Is the cognitive function of older patients affected by hypertensive treatment? *British Medical Journal, 312,* 801–808.

Restle, F., & Davis, J. H. (1962). Success and speed of problem-solving by individuals and groups. *Psychological Review, 69,* 520–536.

Royer, F. L. (1971). Information processing of visual figures in the Digit Symbol Substitution Task. *Journal of Experimental Psychology, 87,* 344–342.

Shepard, R. N., & Metzler, J. (1971). Mental rotation of three-dimensional objects. *Science, 171,* 701–703.

Sternberg, R. J. (1977). *Intelligence, information processing, and analogical reasoning: The componential analysis of human abilities.* Hillsdale, NJ: Lawrence Erlbaum Associates.

Sternberg, S. (1966). High speed scanning in human memory. *Science, 153,* 652–654.

Tapsfield, P. G. C. (1993a). *The British Army Recruit Battery: Test-retest reliability* (Tech. Rep.: 5-1993 Army Personnel Research Establishment). Human Assessment Laboratory, University of Plymouth, Plymouth, UK.

Tapsfield, P. G. C. (1993b). *The British Army Recruit Battery: 1993 applicant norms* (Tech. Rep.: 6-1993 Army Personnel Research Establishment). Human Assessment Laboratory, University of Plymouth, Plymouth, UK.

Tapsfield, P. G. C., & Wright, D. E. (1993). *A preliminary analysis of summary data arising from the operational use of the British Army Recruit Battery* (Tech. Rep.: 3-1993 Army Personnel Research Establishment). Human Assessment Laboratory, University of Plymouth, Plymouth, UK.

Tatsuoka, K. M., & Tatsuoka, M. M. (1978). *Time-score analysis in criterion-referenced tests* (CERL Report E-1). Report of the Computer-Based Education Research Laboratory, University of Illinois, Urbana, Ill.

Thurstone, L. L. (1938). *Primary mental abilities.* Chicago: University of Chicago Press and latterly as Medway Reprint (1975) Chicago: University of Chicago Press.

Vernon, P. A. (1983). Speed of information processing and general intelligence. *Intelligence, 7,* 53–70.

Vernon, P. A., & Jensen, A. R. (1985). Individual and group differences in intelligence and speed of information processing. *Personality and Individual Differences, 5,* 411–423.

Wainer H., & Messick, S. J. (Eds.), (1983). *Principals of modern psychological measurement.* Hillsdale, NJ: Lawrence Erlbaum Associates.

Weibull, W. (1951). A statistical distribution of wide application. *Journal of Applied Mechanics, 18,* 293–297.

White, P. O. (1982). Some major components in general intelligence. In H. J. Eysenck, (Ed.), *A model for intelligence.* New York: Springer-Verlag.

Woltz, D. J. (1987). *Activation and decay of semantic memory: An individual differences investigation of working memory.* Manuscript submitted for publication. Manpower and Personnel Division, Air Force Human Resources Laboratory: Brooks AFB, Texas.

Wright, D. E. (1990*). Item response and theory for item generation: Comment and developments (*Tech. Rep. 3-1990 Army Personnel Research Establishment). Human Assessment Laboratory, University of Plymouth, Plymouth, UK.

Wright, D. E. (1992). *IRT modelling using latent variable generalised linear models* (Tech. Rep.: 3-1992 Army Personnel Research Establishment). Human Assessment Laboratory, University of Plymouth, Plymouth, UK.

Wright, D. E., & Dennis, I. (1992*). Development of a test of mental cube folding for use in officer selection.* (Tech. Rep. for Science Air, 3), Ministry of defence, London. Human Assessment Laboratory, University of Plymouth, Plymouth, UK.

Wright, D. E., Irvine, S. H., & Tapsfield, P. G. C. (1992). *Test Lengths and Reliabilities.* (HAL Tech. Rep.: HAL1-1992) Army Personnel Research Establishment.

Wright, D. E. (1993). *BARB and the measurement of individual differences: Departing from traditional models.* Paper presented at the International Military Association Conference, Williamsburg, Virginia, November 1993 (also as Tech. Rep., 2-1994 (Army Personnel Research Establishment) Human Assessment Laboratory, University of Plymouth, Plymouth, UK.

Wright, D. E. (1997, October). *Exploiting the speed-accuracy trade-off.* Paper presented at a symposium on The Future of Learning and Individual Differences, University of Minnesota, Minneapolis.

2

Using the Psychology of Reasoning to Predict the Difficulty of Analytical Reasoning Problems

Stephen Newstead
Peter Bradon
Simon Handley
Jonathan Evans
Ian Dennis
University of Plymouth

In this chapter we present an overview of the methods we have used to develop a computer program which can generate reasoning items of known difficulty. The Plymouth research group was commissioned in 1997 to carry out this project by Educational Testing Services (ETS). Most of the researchers in the Plymouth group are cognitive psychologists by training and this is reflected in the methods we have employed. We believe that the methods we have used in this project may be ones that can be profitably be used in the analysis of other types of problems.

ETS asked us to focus specifically on the high level reasoning tasks known as Analytical Reasoning (AR) problems, as used in the Graduate Record Examination (GRE). A fairly simple example of an AR problem, which we refer to as the companies and floors problem, is presented in Figure 2.1. It is taken from the GRE Big Book (Educational Testing Service, 1996, p. 1039).

Our task was thus to develop a program which could generate reasoning items similar to this and to indicate how difficult each item was likely to be. We decided to approach this task from a number of different angles in the belief that together these would provide answers to the task we had been set. Our approach can be characterized as involving the following phases, although it must be borne in mind that many of these stages occurred in parallel—the sequence in which they are presented should not be interpreted as a sequential one.

In Phase 1, we ascertained what experts and problem solvers could tell us about the nature of the problems. For example, we asked participants to solve a number of AR problems while thinking out loud in an attempt to find out the process involved. We also carried out our own conceptual analysis of the problems, and drew upon the experiences of problem setters within ETS. As part of our own concepualization of the problems, we developed a computer program to encode and describe the structure of (and to solve) AR problems.

In Phase 2, we examined experimental and psychometric data to determine what insights they could provide into the sources of difficulty in AR problems. Although there is no published research on AR problems as such, a number of related problems have been studied which can provide hints as to possible factors underlying difficulty. In addition, ETS have over the years accumulated much data on performance on AR problems, much of it published in the Big Book (Educational Testing Service, 1996). These data provide both a rich source of hypotheses and potential ways of testing out hunches.

In Phase 3, we tested our predictions by conducting a series of experiments examining the psychological complexity of different tasks. We started very simply by investigating the difficulty of some of the basic rules used in AR problems, and ended up by looking at problems that were much more like actual AR problems.

In Phase 4, we developed a performance model that could predict item difficulty from the characteristics of the items themselves. This phase led to the development and refinement of our performance model and of the underlying theory.

An office building has exactly six floors, numbered 1 through 6 from bottom to top. Each of exactly six companies - F, G, I, J, K, and M - must be assigned an entire floor for office space. The floors must be assigned according to the following conditions:

F must be on a lower floor than G

I must be either on the floor immediately above M's floor or on the floor immediately below M's floor.

J can be neither on the floor immediately above M's floor nor on the floor immediately below M's floor.

K must be on floor 4.

(Continued)

1. Which of the following is an acceptable assignment of companies to floors, in order from floor 1 through floor 6?

(A) F, I, G, K, J, M
(B) G, I, M, K, F, J
(C) J, F, G, K, I, M
(D) J, M, I, K, F, G
(E) K, F, J, G, M, I

2. If G is on floor 5, which of the following must be true?

(A) F is on floor 1.
(B) F is on floor 3.
(C) I is on floor 1.
(D) J is on floor 6.
(E) M is on floor 2.

3. If M is on floor 2, any of the following could be true EXCEPT:

(A) F is on floor 3.
(B) F is on floor 5.
(C) I is on floor 1.
(D) J is on floor 5.
(E) J is on floor 6.

4. If J is on floor 3, which of the following is a pair of companies that must be on floors one of which is immediately above the other?

(A) F and G.
(B) F and K.
(C) G and J.
(D) I and J.
(E) K and M.

5. Each of the following is a pair of companies that could be on floors one of which is immediately above the other EXCEPT

(A) F and I.
(B) F and M.
(C) G and I.
(D) I and K.
(E) J and K.

6. If F is on floor 5, which of the following must be true?

(A) I is on floor 2.
(B) I is on floor 3.
(C) J is on floor 1.
(D) J is on floor 2.
(E) M is on floor 3.

7. If F and I are on floors one of which is immediately above the other, which of the following could be on floors one of which is immediately above the other?

(A) F and J.
(B) F and M.
(C) G and M.
(D) I and K.
(E) J and K.

FIG. 2.1. The companies and floors problem.

An indication of our progress in developing the predictive model is given by Dennis (chap. 3, this volume). The present chapter focuses on the earlier stages.

PHASE 1: INSIGHTS FROM SOLVERS AND EXPERTS

Analysis of Think-Aloud Protocols of People Trying to Solve AR Problems

Our first empirical study involved asking a number of people to solve AR problems while verbalizing their thought processes. This gave us a number of insights into how the problems were approached. We used just two problems, one of which was the companies and floors problem presented in Figure 2.1.

The approaches adopted by different participants were strikingly similar. Every individual we studied started out by familiarizing themselves with the problem. They then tried to familiarize themselves with the conditions in the initial rule set and formed a representation of the problem space, usually with the aid of some sort of graphical representation. For example, in solving the companies and floors problem given in Figure 2.1, everyone we tested used some form of written representation of the problem, usually a vertical list of the six floors to which offices had to be assigned. The first thing they did was to put K into floor 4, using a representation such as the following:

```
6
5
4        K
3
2
1
```

The next rule to be represented was that F is lower than G. This was usually represented as a letter G above a letter F, but without assigning these to any specific position in the vertical array.

The two adjacency rules (I must be next to M, and J cannot be next to M) were always represented last, using slightly more variable representations. Negation was usually represented either with a cross or by the word "no" in front of the letter. For example, one participant represented the two rules as follows:

```
I                          J
M                          M X
I                          J
```

Other participants produced a combined representation of the rules, for example:

I   J X
M   OR   M
J X   I

There are, of course, problems in drawing conclusions from studies using think-aloud protocols, as one can never be sure how full or accurate the verbalizations are. However, they are generally recognized to provide an accurate picture of the contents of the immediate working processes being used in solving the problem (Ericsson & Simon, 1993). We were confident that through our studies we had obtained a reasonably accurate picture of how these problems are tackled, at least in the initial stages.

However, we were not convinced we had learned a great deal about the factors contributing to problem difficulty. We did learn the importance of representation, because the information in the problems was sometimes misrepresented and this led to predictable difficulties later on. However, one of the notable things about the study was that there were relatively few individual differences: Most people did the same things, although they presumably differed in how well they did them. In addition, we were not sure how representative our task was of how people approach these problems in the GRE, as we allowed our participants unlimited time to solve the problems; the GRE proper is run under strict time limits.

Conceptual Analysis

The think-aloud protocols did guide our own analysis of the problems. We came to the conclusion that there were a small number of different types of problems requiring slightly different approaches in their solution. For example, a significant number of problems involve ordering of elements, that is placing entities into locations according to certain restriction rules. The companies and floors problem given in Figure 2.1 is an example of this. Another group of problems involved assignment, in the sense that they involved placing elements into groups according to certain restrictions. An example of one of these is given in Figure 2.2. It is taken from the GRE Big Book (Educational Testing Service, 1996). This problem is different from the ordering problems as it involves assigning people to groups according to certain selection restrictions, rather than putting them into a designated order.

In addition to ordering problems and assign problems, there are mixed problems combining elements of both, and a small number of other problems that do not fall easily into any of these categories. However, ordering, assign, and mixed problems account for the majority of the AR problems contained in the GRE Big Book.

There are almost certainly some common processes in the solution of all of these different types of problems but they are sufficiently different for us to have decided that they needed to be considered separately in the first place. This characterization of problems is essentially the same as that used by ETS's own problem generators. Because we were aware of their characterization before we conducted our own conceptual analysis we were inevitably influenced by it. However, the categorization of problems is robust and it proved quite easy to capture the differences between problem types in the computer program we developed.

From time to time, the managing director of a company appoints planning committees, each consisting of exactly three members. Eligible for appointment are three executives from Finance—F, G, and H—and three executives from Operations—K, L, and M. Any given committee is subject to the following restrictions on appointments:

At least one member must be from Finance, and at least one member must be from Operations.

If F is appointed, G cannot be appointed.

Neither H nor L can be appointed unless the other is appointed also.

If K is appointed, M must also be appointed.

FIG. 2.2. An assign problem.

Most of our work so far has been on ordering problems. We had to restrict our attentions to make the task manageable, and these problems seemed a little easier to tackle than other types. One of the main reasons for this is that, as we see in the next section, there is an existing psychological literature on problems similar to these which helped guide our approach.

Structural Analysis of Problems and Development of a Computer Program to Encode Problems

There are essentially three parts to all AR problems:

Initial scenario
Restriction rules
Test items

The initial scenario is the paragraph describing the general nature of the problem (in the companies and floors problem given in Figure 2.1, it would be the first three sentences). This is followed by a number of rules (usually 3 or 4) which narrow down the possibilities. The test items are the questions that people taking the test are required to answer. In our research we have ignored the scenarios and tried to analyze the underlying structures of problems with respect to the rules and test items used. We have conceptualized ordering problems as involving mapping X elements into Y slots. A simple example would be the companies and floors problem, in which six companies (the X elements) have to be put into six floors (the Y slots). This example involves one-to-one mapping, as each company must be assigned to a single floor. Some problems are more complex than this, containing unassigned elements or empty slots.

After the initial scenario of the companies and floors problem, there are many possible orders in which the companies can be placed (5,040 to be precise). These are reduced by the initial rule set. This particular problem uses four types of rules. The generic labels we have given to these rules are given in capitals in parentheses after each rule.

F must be on a lower floor than G. (ABOVE/BELOW RULE)

I must be either on the floor immediately above M's floor or on the floor immediately below M's floor. (ADJACENCY RULE)

J can be neither on the floor immediately above M's floor nor on the floor immediately below M's floor. (NEGATIVE ADJACENCY RULE)

K must be on floor 4. (ASSIGNMENT RULE)

A number of other rules are used with simple ordering problems. There are, for example, rules that specify that an element must be immediately above or below another (IMMEDIATELY ABOVE/BELOW RULE); and ones that specify that elements must be at a fixed distance from each other (DISTANCE RULE). There are also negated versions of some of these rules, as in the example of negative adjacency presented earlier. These rules are mostly contained in the set of rules given immediately following the scenario, but many AR problems contain what is called a stem rule, an additional rule imposing restrictions, which is placed within the test item.

Some of the rules contain conditional statements ('If G is on floor 5, then J must be on floor 6'); others contain exclusive disjunctives ('Either G is on floor 5 or J is on floor 6, but not both'). Biconditionals and inclusive disjuctions are also used.

There are four main types of test item:

Possible Model: The correct option is a possible ordering of the elements. An example is Question 1 of the companies and floors problem (see Figure 2.1):

Necessity: The correct response is true in all models. An example is Question 2 in Figure 2.1.

Possibility: The correct response is an option which holds in at least one model. An example is Question 7 in Figure 2.1.

Impossibility: The correct response can occur in none of the models, for example Question 3 in Figure 2.1.

Using this structural analysis we can give a description of all ordering problems produced by ETS. What is more, the analysis allows us to put the problems into a computer program that provides a detailed description of the properties of the problems. It will tell us, for example, what generic rules are used, how many possible orderings there are after the initial scenario description, how each rule reduces the number of possibilities, and how many of the rules need to be used to answer a specific test item correctly.

PHASE 2. INSIGHTS FROM PUBLISHED EXPERIMENTAL LITERATURE AND FROM EXISTING PSYCHOMETRIC DATA

Review of Reasoning Literature on Problems Similar to AR Problems

No one to our knowledge has actually carried out controlled experimental studies on AR problems, or at least not studies that have been published. It is, however, possible to see analogies between previous research and AR problems, and to make predictions concerning the factors contributing to the difficulty of these. A great deal of psychological research has been carried out on orderings, and this research is the main focus of this review.

This literature is usually referred to as "transitive inference" (see Evans, Newstead, & Byrne, 1993).

Two main experimental paradigms have been used to investigate reasoning with ordered information: Three-term series problems and linear ordering problems. This is an example of a three-term series problem:

> Al is taller than Bill
> Charles is shorter than Bill
> Who is tallest?

Linear orderings involve chains of statements such as these (e.g., 'A is taller than B; B is taller than C; C is taller than D; D is taller than E') from which people are asked to draw inferences. Both types of problems are relatively simple to solve. Indeed, this is one of the few areas of deductive reasoning where the main measure of difficulty is the time it takes to solve the problem rather than accuracy.

Research has looked at a number of factors relating to these problems, some of which are highly relevant to the types of AR problems involved in the GRE.

Negation. When a negative is used (e.g., A is not as tall as B instead of A is shorter than B, or B is taller than A) this leads to increased difficulty (Clark, 1969). This difficulty is measured in milliseconds but it is highly consistent. This suggests that problems containing negation are likely to be more difficult than those without.

Markedness. Dimensions often have a marked and nonmarked end. For example, the taller–shorter dimension has one marked end (short) and one nonmarked (tall). The reason for this is that one of the adjectives is used to describe the whole dimension—we would usually call it tallness rather than shortness. And if we wanted to make a neutral inquiry as to someone's height, we would ask how tall they are; asking how short they are would seem to presume that the person is short. One oft-quoted American illustration comes from the baseball fan who came to watch two stars of the time, Mickey Mantle and Willie Mays. He was heard to shout: "I came to see which of you guys was better. Instead, I'm seeing which is worse." The players were under no illusion as to the fact that they had been insulted.

Research has shown that marked adjectives are more difficult than unmarked ones—though again the differences are measured in milliseconds (Clark, 1969). AR sets often use marked adjectives such as *lower* and *after*, and this might thus be expected to contribute to problem difficulty.

However, not all dimensions have marked and unmarked ends; for example, "left of" and "right of" are *both* deemed to be marked.

Content. We know that there are content effects in many areas of reasoning (see Evans et al., 1993), but ordering problems appear to be one area where this is of minor importance. Most of the research on three-term series problems and linear orderings has used realistic but arbitrary material—for example, names of people or objects placed into arbitrary relations such as 'taller than' or 'better than'—much like the kind of material used in AR sets. Using such material, content effects are generally not found.

Furthermore, the type of relationship used also seems to have little effect on problem difficulty. It makes little difference whether the relationship is temporal (e.g., before or after), spatial (e.g., above or below) or comparative (e.g., better or worse). However, it has been claimed that people find it easier to work with vertical relationships (e.g., above or below, better or worse) than with horizontal ones (e.g., to the left of or to the right of, before or after) (Huttenlocher, 1968).

The Search for an Integrated Representation. When people are given linear ordering problems, they usually try to combine the information into a coherent, integrated representation. Given the information: A > B; B > C; C > D; D > E, people will combine this information into a single array: A > B > C > D > E (e.g., Potts, 1974).

This leads to interesting findings, for example that people find it easier to draw the inference that A > E than they do the inference that A > B — even though the latter contains information actually given in one of the premises! This is because A and E are farther apart on the integrated representation, and therefore easier to discriminate, than A and B.

At first sight such findings are not really relevant to the types of AR problems used in the GRE because these are usually ones that cannot be combined into a single representation. However, in some of them the stem rules eliminate all but one possible ordering. In addition, it is possible that some people might *try* to integrate the information into a single array even when this is not possible and waste time doing so when this proves futile. The protocol study summarized earlier showed that people often attempt to combine pairs of rules into a single representation.

Visual Versus Verbal Strategies. There has been a continuing debate in the literature as to whether people solve ordering problems using a visual or verbal strategy. A visual strategy would involve building up a mental picture or image of the information presented and using this in solving the problem. The verbal strategy would involve representing the information as abstract propositions (see Evans et al., 1993, for a review of this debate). There is some evidence that there are individual differences, in that some people tend to spontaneously use visual strategies and others verbal strategies; and also that task demands can influence the sort of strategy adopted. This alerts us to the possibility that there may be differences between people as to the problems they find the most difficult.

Number of Possible Models. There is significant research indicating that the more models that are consistent with a description, the more difficult the problem becomes. For example, Byrne and Johnson-Laird (1989) investigated single model and multiple model versions of spatial reasoning problems. The following is a single model problem:

> A is right of B
> C is left of B
> D is in front of C
> E is in front of B
> What is the relation between D and E?

There is just one way of representing this information, as follows:

> c   b   a
> d   e

compare this with the following problem:

> B is right of A
> C is left of B
> D is in front of C
> E is in front of B

This superficially very similar problem permits two quite different representations:

Model 1			Model 2		
c	a	b	a	c	b
d		e	d		e

Problems such as the first one—for which only one model is valid—are easier than those such as the second one, for which more than one model is possible. In general, the more possible models there are, the more difficult a problem will be.

This is clearly relevant to AR problems where there are initial rule sets that permit hundreds of models and initial rule sets that reduce the number of models to a manageable size. It is reasonable to suggest that the number of models possible after the initial rule set (and particularly after any stem rule) might be a determinant of problem difficulty.

Conditional Rules. There is a host of research on reasoning demonstrating that people have considerable difficulty processing conditional statements (e.g., If A then B) and frequently misunderstand them. This research has not been carried out specifically on ordering problems, but it is such a pervasive phenomenon that we can be confident that AR problems containing conditionals will lead to increased complexity. The presence of the word "if" does not necessarily mean that a rule will be conditional (see, e.g., Items 2, 3, 4, 6 and 7 in Figure 2.1). However, a genuinely conditional rule such as 'If J is on floor 2, then M is on floor 5' would contribute to difficulty.

One source of the difficulty of conditionals is that they often tend to be interpreted as biconditionals. This means that a statement such as 'If A then B' is taken to imply 'If B then A.' This implication is sometimes valid in everyday situations, for example in the statement 'If it is a right angle then it is 90 degrees.' However, there are many situations in which this implication is invalid, for example, the statement 'If this is a trout then it is a fish.' If people adopt the biconditional interpretation then they will experience problems with some AR sets, and will reach the wrong conclusion on some of them.

Disjunctive Rules. Disjunctive statements are ones containing 'either . . . or' rules. Disjunctions can be either inclusive ('A or B and possibly both') or exclusive ('A or B but not both'). Although disjunctives are not usually found to be as difficult as conditionals, they are nevertheless known to require extra psychological processing. Hence one might expect AR problems containing them to be more difficult than those that do not.

PHASE 3: EXPERIMENTAL STUDIES OF FACTORS PREDICTED TO AFFECT DIFFICULTY

We have carried out a number of studies to investigate which of these many potential sources of difficulty are important in AR sets. Not all possible sources of difficulty have been investigated. Some of those mentioned in the preceding section were so obviously relevant that it seemed pointless to demonstrate this again; for example, we were confident that conditionals would contribute to difficulty without needing to test this.

Our approach to the research was to start out with simple, reaction time studies designed to look at the difficulty of individual rules and gradually move toward more complicated situations closely resembling the way in which AR problems are actually presented.

The reaction time studies involved both inspection times and decision times. To give just one example of the kind of study we have carried out, in our first study people were presented, on a computer screen, with the scenario for the companies and floors problem followed by the further rule that "C is on a floor immediately above E." They were then asked to judge whether an ordering such as AEDCFB was possible by pressing a YES or NO key. Both reading times and decision times were measured. In this situation, it was possible to use a wide variety of different rule types to see whether this affected reaction times.

The results from the decision time analysis are presented in Figure 2.3. It can be seen that some rules are easier than others. Assignment rules (those which fix the position of an element) are especially easy, and negative rules of whatever kind are clearly the most difficult.

Follow-up studies have used combinations of two or three rules to investigate the generality of the findings. Other experiments have used scenarios that were more similar to the way in which AR problems are normally presented. For example, one study presented a scenario followed by four initial rules, exactly as would occur in a GRE presentation. However, participants were then presented not with the standard multiple-choice question but with a single statement in which they had to judge whether it was necessary (or in other conditions whether it was possible or impossible). In this way we were able to measure decision times for individual statements and determine whether there were differences between different rules used in the test item and between different types of test item (necessary, possible, impossible).

Our more recent studies have used AR sets presented in much the same way as in the GRE. This has allowed us to look at the effects of different types of distracters (i.e., the incorrect options in the multiple choice test) on overall difficulty, and at the effects of number of models possible after presentation of the rule set. An example of the kinds of findings is presented in Figure 2.4, which shows errors made as a function of number of models and rule type (assign, adjacent, or above). It can be seen that two model problems are in general the easiest, although for some reason this is less marked with adjacency rules.

For reasons of brevity only a summary of the main findings from our series of experiments is presented.

1. *Negatives are more difficult than affirmatives.* Our findings have strongly indicated that the presence of a negative increases difficulty. Many of the rules used have

both positive and negative forms, for example 'F is on floor 4' versus 'F is not on floor 4,' or 'I must be immediately adjacent to M' versus 'I cannot be adjacent to M.' In every case, the negative form of a rule proved to be more difficult than the affirmative version. What is more, negativity led both to longer latencies and to more errors.

2. *Assignment rules are the easiest of all the rules.* Assignment rules are those which indicate that an element is in a particular slot (e.g., company K is on floor 4). These seem to be easier to process than any other rules. This finding is perhaps not surprising in light of the thinking-aloud study we reported earlier. In that study, all our participants initially represented the assignment rule before any others, despite the fact that it was the last one presented to them. People seem to find these rules easy to work with, presumably because they allow an unequivocal representation of the information to be made.

3. *There are few other major differences between the rules used.* In our studies we used a variety of rule types, but these were all more or less equally difficult. It does not seem to make any difference whether the rule involves 'above,' 'below,' 'immediately above,' 'immediately below,' or 'next to'; these are all of roughly equivalent difficulty (see, e.g., Figure 2.3). On the basis of the research reviewed earlier, we were expecting rules involving marked adjectives such as 'below' to be harder than unmarked adjectives such as 'above.' In this case, the predictions based on earlier research were not confirmed. Note also that some of these rules are more informative than others; for example 'immediately above' rules eliminate more possibilities than do 'above' rules. When we look at individual rules, then, informativeness does not seem to affect difficulty.

4. *Overall informativeness has an effect.* Although the informativeness of individual rules has little effect on overall difficulty, the overall informativeness of the rule set does. Rule sets, especially stem rules, which leave few possible models tend to be easier than those which leave more possibilities. This discrepancy is quite easy to explain. Each rule individually leaves so many possibilities open that participants are unlikely to even attempt to compute these. However, when the possibilities have been narrowed down to a manageable number, participants might well try to work out all the possibilities, and hence the number of these affects the ease of this task. When the possibilities have been narrowed down, there is more opportunity to construct an integrated representation capturing all the possibilities. If, for example, four out of six elements are fixed by the rules, it is relatively easy to build up and remember a mental representation capturing this information.

5. *There is little difference between different types of test items.* In our studies we were able to investigate the relative ease of Necessity, Possibility, and Impossibility test items. We found no systematic differences between these. We did, however, find interesting interactions involving this variable. This is because, as will be seen in the next section, the difficulty of test items depends on the distracter items used.

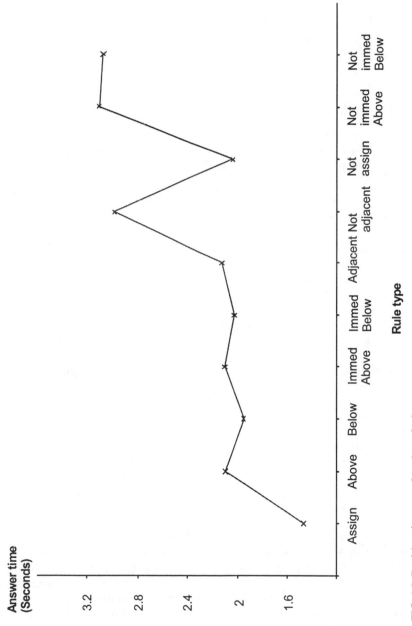

FIG. 2.3. Decision times as a function of rule type.

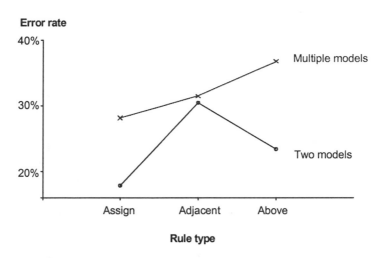

FIG. 2.4. Error rate as a function of number of models and rule type.

6. *Type of distracter affects difficulty.* We also investigated in our studies the effects of different types of distracters (i.e., the incorrect options). To illustrate, with a Necessity test item the distracters can be either possible or impossible. Consider, for example, Question 2 on the offices and floor problem in Figure 2.1. The correct choice is D, but all of the other options could be true, as there is a way of constructing the situation in which the companies could be on the floors indicated. In other AR sets, Necessity items such as this have one or more distracters that are impossible in the sense that no model can be constructed in which they are true. For example, in Question 6 in Figure 2.1, the correct answer is A—'I is on floor 2'—which clearly means that a distracter such as B—'I—is on floor 3'—is impossible.

Our research indicates that, if the distracters are impossible, then the problem tends to be easier than when the distracters are possible. This is presumably because it is easier to eliminate impossible distracters than it is possible ones. Many impossible distracters break a single rule, while with possible distracters, all rules need to be considered. As discussed in the next section, the number of rules which need to be considered is an important determinant of difficulty.

7. *Number of rules required affects difficulty.* Test items differ as to the number of rules needed to establish their truth or falsity. To give a fairly simple example, consider Question 6 in Figure 2.1. If one of the choices had been 'G is on floor 6', it would require just two rules to work out that this had to be the correct answer; combining the initial rule 'F must be on a lower floor than G' with the stem rule 'F is on floor 5' leads immediately to the conclusion that G is on floor 6. Other test items require more rules to be combined, quite often all of them. Our research has suggested that the minimum number of rules required to

accept or reject one of the options is a good predictor of difficulty: the more rules required, the more difficult it is to accept or reject that item.

PHASE 4. DEVELOPMENT OF PREDICTIVE MODEL

Armed with the foregoing, we are now in a position to develop and to test a model of item difficulty. Using the program, we can generate problems of specified structure. Based on the literature and experimental work, we can predict which problems will be easy and which difficult. These predictions can be tested both against existing ETS data and against future experimental work. The development of this program and of the difficulty model it contains is the theme of the chapter by Dennis (chap. 3, this volume).

REFERENCES

Byrne, R. M. J., & Johnson-Laird, P. N. (1989). Spatial reasoning. *Journal of Memory and Language, 28*, 564–575.

Clark, H. H. (1969). Linguistic processes in deductive reasoning. *Psychological Review, 76*, 387–404.

Educational Testing Service (1996). *GRE. Practicing to take the general test: Big Book.* Princeton, NJ: Educational Testing Service.

Ericsson, K. A., & Simon, H. A. (1993). *Protocol analysis: Verbal reports as data.* Boston, MA: MIT Press.

Evans, J. St. B. T., Newstead, S. E., & Byrne, R. M. J. (1993). *Human reasoning: The psychology of deduction.* Hove, Sussex: Lawrence Erlbaum Assocciates.

Huttenlocher, J. (1968). Constructing spatial images: A strategy in reasoning. *Psychological Review, 75*, 550–560.

Potts, G. R. (1974). Storing and retrieving information about order relationships. *Journal of Experimental Psychology, 103*, 431–439.

3

Approaches to Modeling
Item-Generative Tests

Ian Dennis
Simon Handley
Peter Bradon
Jonathan Evans
Stephen Newstead
University of Plymouth

This chapter has two purposes. The first is to provide an overview of results from three item-generation projects with which we have been involved in recent years. The second is to use these three projects to illustrate a distinction between two approaches to item generation and modeling. The first two projects—the development of the Directions and Distances test and the Numeracy and Literacy tests for the Royal Navy—both employed what we term Approach 1 to item generation. We begin with an account of the Directions and Distances project and use that to illustrate a more abstract characterization of Approach 1. Approach 2 is introduced using the Analytic Reasoning project in which we are currently engaged. After this, the contrast between the two approaches is more generally discussed.

APPROACH 1: THE DIRECTIONS AND DISTANCES TEST

The Directions and Distances test was a test developed on behalf of the Royal Navy to replace their test SP80A. SP80A was a spatial test developed by P. E. Vernon and used in officer selection. The immediate motivation for developing a replacement was that the test had been in use for a long time and no parallel forms were available. The immediate problem could have been addressed by developing new forms of the test using conventional techniques. However, those involved in initiating this project recognized a convenient opportunity to explore the applicability of item generation to power tests and the long-term possibilities which that implied. SP80A had a strong gradient of difficulty. The ability to generate items and predict their difficulty would be useful in reproducing this gradient, would offer the potential to produce new parallel forms as required, and would enable variant forms for other populations with different levels of ability to be produced.

SP80A involved multiple-choice items where the stem consisted of a few sentences that were heavily spatial in content; and the response alternatives generally related to a distance or a direction in the spatial arrangement described in the text. Many of the items fell into two categories that were labelled *Parade Ground* (PG) items and *God's Eye View* (GEV) items, respectively. PG items described a route in the plane traversed by an object and typically asked a question about the distance or direction of the start point from the endpoint. GEV items described the layout of a small set of objects on a two-dimensional plane through a series of statements each specifying the relative locations of two objects. The question was about the relative location of two objects that had not been referred to in the same statement. These two types of item are illustrated in Figure 3.1 (some amendments have been made to items that the generative algorithm could produce for reasons of test security). The test is used in a context where it can be closely proctored and candidates are not allowed to write anything other than their responses.

What makes these items suitable for item generation? Three characteristics are crucial. First we can specify an algorithm capable of generating items from a large universe of possible items. Second we can identify some features whose level can be identified for each item generated. These features alter and can be used to predict item difficulty. Third we can identify other features we suspect will not affect item difficulty.

The development of the Directions and Distances test first involved identifying the features that would vary across items and the levels of those features which would be used. Thus, with parade ground items, for example, the route traversed by the object could vary. Thus, route is one item feature and the particular routes used are the levels of that feature. All the routes used employed only 90° turns. These turns may be specified either by statements that the object "turns left" or "turns right" or by specifying the compass direction in which the object is travelling on each leg of its journey. Thus, the way in which turns are specified is a second item feature with two levels. A full list of item features for Parade Ground items is given in Figure 3.2. Obviously the division of item features into those that control item difficulty and those that do not is an empirical matter, although cognitive theory, intuition, and existing empirical work

Parade Ground

A yacht leaves its mooring, sails 10km North-East, a further 15km South-East, then another 4km North East and finally 15km North-West. In what direction does the mooring now lie from the yacht?

(a) North-West   (b) South-West   (c) North-East   (d) South-East

God's Eye View

On a certain University campus the Chemistry Department is 500 metres South-East of the Library, the Library is 800 metres West of the Registry and the Registry is 500 metres North-East of the Chapel. Which of the following pairs of buildings is closest together?

  (a) The Chemistry Department and the Chapel
  (b) The Chemistry Department and the Registry
  (c) The Library and the Chapel
  (d) The Library and the Registry

FIG. 3.1. Examples of parade ground and God's eye view items.

may all provide useful clues for this. Once the full set of item features was specified it was possible to produce an algorithm, implemented as a computer program, which produced items with specified values for each feature.

The division of the features listed in Figure 3.2 into controlling and noncontrolling features derives from experimentation with a carefully designed sample of items. The purpose of this experimentation was to establish the status of each feature as controlling or noncontrolling and to develop a model to predict item difficulty from those features that do affect it. It is important to recognize that although the universe of possible items is fully specified by the set of features and levels used only a very small proportion of that universe can be examined in developing a model for item difficulty. The sample of items used determines what feature interactions can be evaluated. In general, trying to look at very many interactions or at high order interactions is impractical. It was decided, in advance of the studies on Directions and Distances, that only the main effects of item features would be considered.

In the study from which it was developed the fit of the model for predicting the difficulty of Parade Ground items from levels of controlling features was R^2(adj) = 0.78. The model generated from God's Eye View items also produced an R^2(adj) of 0.78. A cross validation study using a 17-

---

Controlling Features

Route
How turns are specified (turns right/turns left vs. compass direction)
Use of cardinal (N,S,E,W) versus semi-cardinal (NW, NE, SE, SW) compass points
Question asked ('What direction?' versus 'How far?')

Noncontrolling Features

Scenario
Re-scaling of distances
Start direction

FIG. 3.2. Controlling and noncontrolling features for parade ground items.

item version of the Directions and Distances test given to a sample of 120 RN officers and RN Aircrew gave a correlation of 0.72 between predicted and observed item difficulty. The use of correlations between observed and predicted item difficulty as a way of assessing the satisfactoriness of our models warrants a brief comment. As item generation develops, standard ways of looking at this question will no doubt be developed with widely recognized interpretations. For the present, the advantage of quoting correlations between observed and predicted difficulties is that this provides a measure of fit which is readily understood and assimilated. It does have the disadvantage that it will depend on the spread of item difficulties in the item sample in question. However, whenever item generation is used, there will be a need to develop the capability to produce a full spectrum of item difficulties. Accordingly, the spread of item difficulties will not usually vary greatly from one context to another and this will serve to minimize the problems of interpretation arising out of variation in the spread of item difficulties.

Our attempts to manipulate and predict item difficulty should never produce a major shift in the construct measured by the test. In two studies on RN officers in training, correlations between Directions and Distances scores and SP80A scores previously obtained at the Admiralty Interview Board (A.I.B.) were 0.56 and 0.50 respectively even though the officers concerned had attended the A.I.B. at least two years prior to the study. Moreover in each of these two studies the Directions and Distances result was more successful in predicting training outcomes than was the SP80A score. Thus the ability to generate Directions and Distances items and to predict their difficulty was not achieved at the price of a major change in what the test is doing; and has not undermined its usefulness.

APPROACH 1 TO ITEM GENERATION: A GENERAL CHARACTERIZATION

The Directions and Distances test exemplifies what we shall refer to as Approach 1 to item generation. The first characteristic of Approach 1 is that the item universe is defined as the total set of items that can be produced by the factorial combination of a specified set of features and their levels. Thus, for example, in the case of Parade Ground items the features are those listed in Figure 3.2. Although the Universe of possible items is large it is also well specified and an item is fully specified once its value on each feature has been specified. In general we will design items for Approach 1 anticipating that some features will contribute to determining item difficulty while others will be irrelevant. In parallel, we can select the values of noncontrolling features at random in order to produce superficially different items of equivalent difficulty.

The successful implementation of Approach 1 relies on the execution of studies using very carefully designed sets of items. Such items make it possible to determine the impact of controlling features and to confirm the status of noncontrolling features. Inevitably the number of items involved in these studies will be small relative to the size of the item universe. This means that the effects examined are restricted to the main effects of the features under consideration along, perhaps, with a small number of low order interactions that are thought to be of particular interest. It is not possible to look at higher order interactions amongst the item features. Executing the scale of study necessary to do so would undermine the benefits obtained by an item-generative approach. In the examples of the application of Approach 1 discussed in this chapter the models used were intentionally restricted to main effects models.

The production of distracters for multiple-choice items has the potential to considerably complicate the use of Approach 1. The ways in which the impact of different distracters on difficulty combine can be complex and may not conform to the simple additive models discussed in the previous paragraph. One tempting distracter may or may not lure candidates away from another tempting distracter. This will depend on whether the confusion or bug which makes the distracter a likely response is the same or different in the two cases. Faced with this possibility one would then have to specify features for each distracter; and then consider how many of the distracters possess a particular feature. Clearly, such a scenario complicates the characterization of the item universe.

We have avoided these potential complications by not using distracters to manipulate item difficulty. In some cases the set of response options has been fixed for all items of a particular type. Thus, for example, in Directions and Distances items with a question about *direction* the response options are fixed. They are either the four cardinal points of the compass or the four semicardinal points. Similarly, with items about *distance*, the generative algorithm produces distracters in a prespecifed way by adding and subtracting various distances mentioned in the item stem. In some of the literacy items discussed in the next section the choice of distracters from a set of possibilities, which are believed to be equivalent, is treated as a noncontrolling feature. However, again, there is no attempt to use the distacters as a method for controlling item difficulty.

LITERACY AND NUMERACY TESTS FOR NAVAL RATINGS

The second example of Approach 1 is work on Literacy and Numeracy tests for the Royal Navy (Dennis, Collis, & Dann, 1995). This helps to illustrate the range of tests to which Approach 1 might be applicable: and in particular how it might be used in knowledge-rich attainment domains. This theme is developed more fully in the account given by Dennis, et al. (1995). We update this example by referring to some results that were not available at the time the previous account was prepared.

As with Directions and Distances the work on Numeracy and Literacy was carried out in order to produce an item-generative equivalent of an existing test. More specifically, the purpose of this work was to produce generative analogues for two elements of the Royal Navy's Recruiting Test (RT) which is used in selection and allocation for Ratings entry. These elements were RT2, which may be broadly characterized as a test of literacy, vocabulary, and comprehension and RT3, a numeracy test. For the purpose of illustration we discuss two item types from the literacy test—*Sentence Transformation* and *Concrete Odd Word Out*.

A number of items in RT2 ask candidates to select from a set of sentences the one that is least similar to the others in meaning. The four sentences with the same meaning are all grammatical transformations of one another whereas the odd sentence uses the same words but exchanges the grammatical roles of two words. The *Sentence Transformation* item type represented an attempt to emulate these items within a generative framework. Generation of the items is based on two components. The first of these is a number of sentence sets as shown in Figure 3.3. Each set consists of two lists of sentences in an abstracted form with symbols occupying the content word positions. The second component of the generative principle is a set of lists of words to occupy each of these positions as is illustrated in Figure 3.3. In order to provide potential controlling features two sets of words were produced for each slot. One set consisted of short (typically monosyllabic), common words and the other set consisted of longer, less common words.[1] Some of the slots in the sentence frames were for optional *modifiers* (adjectives, adverbs). In order to generate an item four sentences are chosen from one of the two lists and one sentence from the other. The words used to substitute for the symbols are either all short and common or all long and less common. The slots for modifiers are either all occupied or all empty. The controlling factors for this item type are *the sentence set used, the type of word used (short common vs. longer and less common), and whether or not modifiers are used.* Noncontrolling features for this item type are which of the two lists the odd sentence comes from, the particular sentences chosen, and the particular words used from within the relevant lists. The fit of the predictive model for this item type on the data on which it was developed was given by an adjusted R^2 of 0.73.

Odd word out items are intended to provide a test of vocabulary and single word reading similar to that provided by a number of the items in RT2. Candidates are presented with a list of five words and are told that four of them have some resemblance which the fifth lacks. They are asked to pick the odd word out. In order to provide similar scope to RT2 it was judged desirable to produce such items involving both concrete and abstract words. Separate generative frameworks for these two were constructed, but only that for concrete odd word out items is described here.

The framework used for concrete odd word out items was based on *a semantic hierarchy* reminiscent of that of Collins and Quillian (1969). This is shown in Figure 3.4. A list of words is available for each of the level three categories referred to in Figure 3.4. These words are divided into three frequency bands on the basis of the frequencies given in standard word frequency counts. Items can be generated from this framework by taking four words from one part of the hierarchy and the keyed word from elsewhere in the hierarchy. Items can vary in the degree of semantic separation of the keyed word from the remaining four words. This can be measured as the highest level in the hierarchy at which there is a distinction between the odd word out and the remaining words. For example, if an item is made up of four wild animals and one domestic animal the odd word differs from the remainder only at Level 3 of the hierarchy, whereas with four wild animals and a fish there is a distinction at Level 2 and with four wild animals and a kitchen utensil the distinction can be made at Level 1.

From the work of Collins and Quillian (and much subsequent work) in semantic memory one might predict greater semantic separation of the odd

---

[1] Obviously the effects of word frequency and word length are potentially separable. However this was not achievable within the scope of the studies it was possible to run in developing this item type.

Sentence Set 1	Sentence Set 2
It was the A X who Qed the B Y's Z.	It was the B Y who Qed the A X's Z.
It was the Z of the B Y which the A X Qed.	It was the A X's Z which the B Y Qed.
The Z Qed by the A X was that of the B Y.	The Z Qed by the B Y was that of the A X.
The B Y's Z was Qed by the A X.	The A X's Z was Qed by the B Y.
The A X Qed the B Y's Z.	The B Y Qed the A X's Z.

Items are produced by choosing either set and combining any four sentences from that set with any one sentence from the other.

There is a list of alternative word substitutions for each symbol. Thus in the above X may be substituted by any of the following words-

man, boy, girl, lady, millionaire, accountant, solicitor, librarian

---

FIG. 3.3. Illustration of the generative framework for sentence transformation items.

word out from the remaining words will produce easier items. This was what we found. The framework described can be used to manipulate the semantic homogeneity of the four nonkeyed words. For example, if the keyed item differs from the remainder at Level 2 (e.g., a plant vs. four animals) in the hierarchy, the four remaining words may all come from the same Level 3 category (e.g., all four are wild animals) or may be drawn from two different Level 3 categories (e.g., two wild animals and two domestic animals). There were indications, however, that making the nonkeyed words more diverse also made it harder to predict the difficulty of odd word out items. Putting this another way we wish, to treat the specific choice of categories and words as a noncontrolling factor for these items. This is obviously an approximation. However, it is an approximation that seems to be less satisfactory when semantic diversity is introduced among the nonkeyed words. Hence only those item types where all four non-keyed words came from the same Level 3 category were actually included in the Literacy test. For those item types that were used the controlling features were the frequency band from which the words were drawn (this was the same for all five words) and the level of the hierarchy at which the keyed word was distinguished from the remainder of the words. For these item types the adjusted R^2 from the study in which the predictive model was derived was 0.88. This would obviously be expected to fall on cross validation.

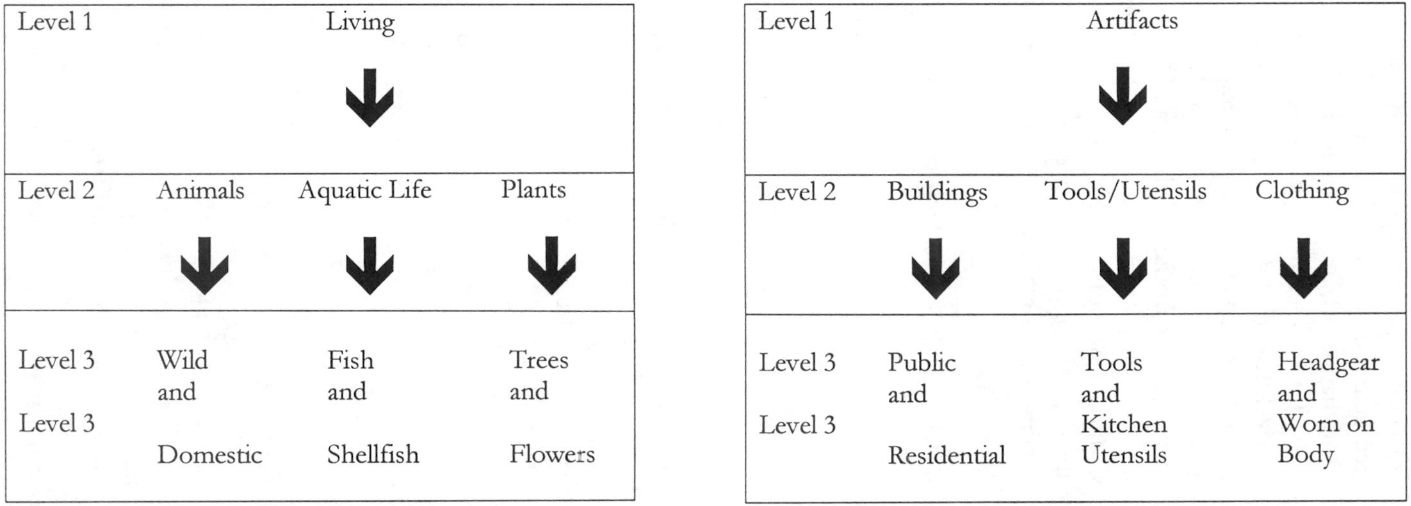

Level 1	Living		
Level 2	Animals →	Aquatic Life →	Plants →
Level 3	Wild and	Fish and	Trees and
Level 3	Domestic	Shellfish	Flowers

Level 1	Artifacts →		
Level 2	Buildings →	Tools/Utensils →	Clothing →
Level 3	Public and	Tools and	Headgear and
Level 3	Residential	Kitchen Utensils	Worn on Body

FIG. 3.4. Semantic hierarchy used in generating concrete odd word out items.

Once more we want to know if generating items and predicting their difficulty has been acquired at the expense of a change in the construct being measured. If this had happened, it would lead to a loss in the predictive value of the test. Jones, Dennis, and Collis (1995) reported correlations between the new Literacy and Numeracy tests and the RTs based on a sample of 1987 ratings applicants. The Literacy test shows a correlation of 0.75 with RT2 and the Numeracy test shows a correlation of 0.73 with RT3. A report produced by Abram, Elshaw, and Stevens (1998) examined the prediction of training performance in Air Engineering Mechanics and Royal Marines. For both trades the new Literacy and Numeracy tests predict training performance as well as the four current Recruiting Tests taken together and correct a problem of gender fairness which is evident in the RTs.

SOME CONCLUSIONS ON APPROACH 1

What then has been achieved by this work using Approach 1 and what are its limitations? Before answering these questions we describe the operational context of the research. The traditional approach to selection testing in the British Armed Forces has involved the use of tests that have been developed in a single form or a small number of forms and then used over a period of many years. This model of test use places a premium on test security; and in the way it has traditionally been applied, candidates have been given very little advance information about the tests.

Our efforts in item generation have led to the development of tests that are eminently usable in this context. The Directions and Distances test has now been in regular operational use for several years. The Literacy and Numeracy test has predictive validities that are at least as good as the tests that it was designed to replace. However, this outcome could have been achieved through traditional approaches to test development. More significant is the capability to produce new parallel forms of these tests without extensive item trialing, thus reducing the premium on test security and providing a safeguard against the erosion of validity over time.

At the present stage in the development of item generation we would not advocate the use of such forms without appropriate trialing of the form and tests for parallelism. This point is discussed further below. The approach that has been taken also yields the potential to readily produce new forms of a test with a different difficulty level for groups with different ability distributions. Again, trialing of the form but not new item trialing will be necessary. The cost of achieving this has been a program of work that is somewhat but not vastly more extensive than that which might have been necessary using traditional methods of test development. In some places a more extensive program of work would have helped to produce greater certainty or precision around aspects of the predictive models.

There is work for the statisticians to do in telling us how good our models need to become for different practical purposes. However, we can say that Approach 1 has made it possible to generate items from large universes and to predict their difficulty with sufficient accuracy to achieve the outcomes identified. This has been done without, as far as we can judge, undermining the ability of the tests to carry out the function for which they were originally created. These outcomes have been achieved for a range of item types including items oriented toward areas of educational attainment.

What of the limitations of Approach 1? The manner in which the item universe can be simply and precisely specified is the source of a number of advantages for Approach 1. It is also the source of its greatest weakness, however. The generative framework may be decoded by somebody with access to a moderately sized sample of the items that it has produced. Nevertheless, candidates can be given example items illustrating the item types they will encounter. In the trial of the Literacy and Numeracy tests from which the predictive validities were derived all candidates were given pretest booklets incorporating example items for each item type. On the other hand, if generated items were to be released into the public domain, and particularly if there were a coaching industry studying these items, there would be a serious risk of the test being fundamentally compromised.[2] The approach to item generation we characterize as Approach 2 is being used in a project that relates to a context in which these concerns are a major factor.

APPROACH 2: ANALYTICAL REASONING

This project is one in which we are currently engaged on behalf of Educational Testing Service. The work here is still in progress and the following discussion, so far as it relates to predictive models, should be regarded as very much an interim report. The purpose of the project is to generate and predict the difficulty of a subset of Analytical Reasoning (AR) Items—an item type used in the Graduate Record Exam and in the Law School's Admission Test. Our work is currently directed toward generating item types known as *order items:* these are concerned with a linear ordering of a set. An example taken from the GRE Big Book (ETS, 1996) is given in

---

[2] There is an important distinction between compromising a *generic item type*, of which there may be innumerable specific instances all different in an actual parallel from, and compromising a whole test by having all of its specific items in advance. Item generation using Approach 1 may lead to item type compromise or decoding resulting in strategy coaching, but never to whole test disclosure, because a new test collection of specific items can be generated for each individual. (Eds.)

Figure 3.5. The example is a *necessity item*. In these items candidates are asked about what *must* be true. Other forms used include *possible models* items, where the options are all orderings of the items and candidates must choose which one is compatible with the rules; *possibility* items, where candidates are asked to choose which of the options could possibly be true; and *impossibility* items, where all options except the keyed option are possible. Elements that provide the basis of the problems to be solved are presented in *sets that share a common statement of the initial rules*. Typically a set will contain one possible models item and a mixture of necessity, possibility, and impossibility items. The example shows that an additional rule is often incorporated into the stem of the item.

The theoretical background to our work on this item type is revealed by Newstead, Bradon, Handley, Evans, and Dennis (chap. 2, this volume). This chapter tries to highlight some contrasts between our approach to this item type and that adopted by Dennis and others in the projects previously considered. Our current research is built around *generating the underlying logical structure* of items. How is this different from what is described as Approach 1?

It is taken as a working assumption that any effects on item difficulty of the scenario in which the logical structure is addressed will be second-order effects. Our approach to generating items is founded on model semantics. For an order item a model is any possible ordering of the entities referred

---

An office building has six floors, numbered 1 through 6 from bottom to top. Each of exactly six companies- F, G, I, J, K, M – must be assigned an entire floor for office space. The floors must be assigned according to the following conditions:

F must be on a lower floor than G.
I must be either on the floor immediately above M's floor or on the floor immediately below M's floor.
J can be neither on the floor immediately above M's floor nor on the floor immediately below M's floor.
K must be on floor 4.

If G is on floor 5, which of the following must be true?

    (A) F is on floor 1.
    (B) F is on floor 3.
    (C) I is on floor 1.
    (D) J is on floor 6.
    (E) M is on floor 2.

FIG. 3.5. Example of an analytic reasoning item of the order type.

to in the items. Thus, with an array of n elements there are, before any rules have been applied, n! possible models. *The generative program has the capability to test whether a model is compatible with a given rule.* Moreover, as the program adds rules to a putative rule set it can delete from the set of possible models those that are incompatible with the rule. From the set of models derived in this way the *possibility and necessity* of statements relating to the possible models can be evaluated. Anything that is true in all possible models is necessary. For something to be possible it must be true in at least one of the models. Something that is true in none of the models is *impossible. The generative program's ability to produce items rests on this capability to analyze their logic.* Essentially the approach that the program takes to producing items is based on heuristically guided but otherwise random generation of candidate rule sets. These candidate rule sets and items generated from them are then tested against a number of constraints that define what constitutes an acceptable item.

The model semantic approach cannot only be used to establish what is necessary given a particular set of rules. It can also be extended to determine the minimal set of rules required to establish necessity or impossibility. This can be done by re-computing the set of possible models for all possible subsets of rules taken from the rule set. In this way the minimal subset for which the necessity or possibility of some conclusion continues to hold can be identified.

An example of an item produced by the generative program and the corresponding output is shown in Figure 3.6. This illustrates the way in which the program has been developed in order to produce from an item a number of measures that might potentially predict its difficulty. This output relates to a problem on the ordering of six elements A, B, C, D, E, F. The initial rule set may be interpreted as (1) E is somewhere above D, (2) E is adjacent to F, (3) F is not in position 3, and (4) B is adjacent to F. In the first column of figures immediately after the rules the number of models compatible with the rule is given. Thus of the 720 models that are possible for an ordering of 6 elements, 360 are compatible with Rule 1 and 240 with Rule 2. The second column of figures specifies the cumulative impact of the set of rules. Thus there are 102 models that are compatible with all of the first three rules and 20 models that are compatible with the full set of four rules. The program provides a full list of these 20 models but these have been omitted here for reasons of space. In its normal use the program generates a number of items for each initial rule set. Here we give one example of a necessity item. The stem may be read as: "if C is above B, which of the following must be true?" The output indicates that the additional rule in the stem reduces the number of possible models from 20 to 4.

X=6 Y=6
aboED   360   360
adjEF 240   120
NlatF3   600   102
adjBF   240   20

Necessity Item (4 models)
Stem Rule: aboCB

1 adjDA (4/4) [all] (correct)
2 adjBC (2/4)
3 adjFA (0/4) [2 4]
4 adjAB (1/4)
5 adjDB (1/4)

FIG. 3.6. Example of program output for a generated necessity item.

The response *options* are all statements about the adjacency of two elements. The program indicates in how many of the four models the adjacency statement is true. Thus Option 1 is the correct answer. D is adjacent to A in all four possible models and thus D must be adjacent to A. B is adjacent to C in only two of the four models and so forth. For the options that are necessary or impossible the program also specifies the set of rules that are required to establish *necessity* or *impossibility* in square brackets after the option. Thus *all* the rules in the initial rule set as well as the stem rule are required to establish that D *must* be adjacent to A. On the other hand, F cannot be next to A (Option 3) and this can be demonstrated using only Rules 2 and 4 from the initial rule set.

We have looked at the output of our generative program in some detail. The program's approach to item generation provides collateral information about item properties likely to be useful in predicting its difficulty. For example, as well as providing a rule set the program provides a measure of the *informativeness* of the rules by the number of models that they *exclude*. For *necessity* items, the program provides information on whether or not distracters are possible given the rule set. For the keyed option, the set of rules required to demonstrate necessity is provided. For response options to items that are *impossible*, the set of rules necessary to prove impossibility is provided. For options that are *possible but not necessary* the proportion of models that are true is given.

The program of experimental work that has been carried out to develop predictive models for AR Order items is significantly more extensive than that undertaken for *Directions and Distances* or *Literacy and Numeracy*. Some of this work is described by Newstead et al. (chap. 2, this volume). Useful predictive models which draw on the information produced by the generative program are possible. Separate predictive models were developed for the four different item types: *possible models, possibility, impossibility, and necessity.* Overall the combined complexity of the rules making up the initial rule set and of the stem rule turns out to be a major factor in predicting item difficulty. The pattern of difficulties associated with the different rules is discussed in the chapter by Newstead et al. However, other measures derived from the output of the generative program also make contributions to prediction.[3]

Thus a variety of measures derived from the problem itself and from collateral information produced in generating it are useful in predicting difficulty. Between them these measures produce a useful level of predictive power. In a cross-validation study using 15 AR sets with four items in each set there was a correlation of 0.83 between observed and predicted *p* values for the 60 items. The range of difficulty within each item type is more restricted and correspondingly the correlations within item type are smaller with a correlation of 0.60 for possible models items, 0.54 for possibility items, 0.80 for impossibility items, and 0.57 for necessity items.

THE CONTRAST BETWEEN THE TWO APPROACHES

At the heart of the contrast between Directions and Distances and Literacy and Numeracy on the one hand and the AR project on the other is the difference in the way the item universe is specified. In each of the former two projects it was specified through the factorial combination of a set of a predefined item features. In the AR project, however, we have simply a generative algorithm and some tests that an acceptable item must pass. We have no simple way of knowing how many acceptable items there are and our method of defining the item universe does not of itself equip us with a set of item features for use in predicting item difficulty. This difference in

---

[3] Thus, for example, for possibility items a score based on the sum over distracters of the combined difficulty of the rules necessary to demonstrate the impossibility of the distracter makes an additional contribution to the prediction of difficulty. Similarly for impossibility and necessity items the difficulty of the subset of rules needed to demonstrate the impossibility or necessity of the key provides a term in the predictive model. Properties of the set of possible models also prove to be relevant. For some initial rule sets all the possible models may be quite similar in that they all have certain elements in the same position with only one or two elements free to occupy alternative positions. For other initial rule sets the set of possible models may be more variable. It is plausible that candidates find it easier to represent the former situation and it turns out that for impossibility and necessity items a measure derived from the set of possible models which is designed to capture the extent to which they are similar to one another also contributes to the prediction of difficulty.

the method of specifying the item universe has some significant ramifications.

To a certain extent the task of developing predictive models under Approach 1 is a matter of sustained empiricism. The item features whose effect must be determined are known and discovering their effects is a matter of appropriate experimental design. Approach 2 requires an input from aspects of cognitive psychology to assist in the task of identifying measures that can be derived from items and used to predict their difficulty. As discussed in the chapter by Newstead et al., the approach we adopted for doing this for AR items drew on a variety of methods including protocol analysis and the experimental study of problems much simpler than standard AR items. The successful application of Approach 2 may prove to involve more extensive and expensive programs of experimentation than are necessary with Approach 1.

Once a predictive model is available the task of generating items of specified difficulty is also somewhat different under the two approaches. Under Approach 1 it is simply necessary to identify a combination of controlling features that produce the desired level of difficulty. Values for noncontrolling features can then be selected at random and the item defined by the selected values of both controlling and noncontrolling features can be produced. Under Approach 2, in contrast, item difficulty can only be determined once an item has been produced by deriving from that item the measures necessary to predict its difficulty. Of course, there could well be heuristics to guide the generative process toward the production of items of particular levels of difficulty but the determination of difficulty is essentially retrospective.

The important role of noncontrolling factors under Approach 1 has already been referred to. Approach 2 does not involve explicit identification of noncontrolling factors in the same way. Rather, any property of the item not reflected in the predictive model is a noncontrolling factor.

The role of distracters also tends to be different under the two approaches. Under Approach 1 we avoid the complexities that arise from making the distracters a variable feature of the items. This has been done either by designing items so that the response options are the same for all items or by having a fixed set of relationships between the item stem and the options so that the options are fully determined once the stem has been generated. Alternatively, as for example in odd word out items, the selection of distracters from a set of roughly equivalent possibilities is treated as a noncontrolling feature. Under Approach 2, in contrast, measures based on properties of the distracters may well be included amongst the predictive measures used. Thus, for example, the difficulty of the set of rules needed to prove the impossibility of the distracters is among the predictors we use for possibility items.

What Limits Our Ability to Predict Item Difficulty?

How successful do we need to be in our efforts to predict item difficulty? For example, when do the inaccuracies in estimating ability arising from errors in estimating item difficulty offset the economies that can be achieved through adaptive testing? These are statistical questions into which we would not presume to venture.[4]

However, it is worth reflecting on the considerations that determine the upper boundary on our ability to predict item difficulty under the two approaches. Under Approach 1 it is possible to be quite explicit about the possible sources of error in predictive models. Essentially these are (i) errors in estimating model parameters, (ii) terms omitted from models (e.g., interactions), and (iii) features treated as noncontrolling that do have some impact on item difficulty.

First, errors in estimating model parameters can be made as small as we wish within the constraints imposed by the resources available for running the studies on which the model is based.

Next, there is a limit to the extent to which the problem of omitted interactions can be dealt with. The value of the item-generative approach lies in the fact that we can develop a model that applies to the whole of a large item universe by investigating a relatively small sample of items from that universe. Although the sample of items can be designed to investigate particular suspected interactions it is impossible to look at all possible interactions, particularly high-order interactions. Thus, there may be quirky regions of the item universe, not explored in test development, where the predictive model fails. The implications of this failure depend on how the generative tests are being used.

Lastly, to a large extent the problem of noncontrolling factors that do indeed affect difficulty is also tractable. Once we are clear what size effect we would deem to be of practical import we can ensure that our studies have sufficient power to detect such an effect (assuming that sufficient resources are available). An exception occurs where the item structure relies on being able to treat certain influences as noncontrolling. Thus, for example, the sentence transformation item type assumes that the particular word chosen from the list of possibilities for a particular slot does not affect item difficulty. If this assumption is wrong in a particular context then the sentence transformation item type would not be useful in that context. Overall, subject to the qualifications stated earlier, it should be possible in many applications of Approach 1 to achieve whatever level of precision in prediction we believe is necessary to the application.

---

[4] Wright's chapter (chap. 10, , this volume) addresses this issue.

We cannot be so certain of how successful our prediction is likely to be under Approach 2. This depends on our ability, within the self-imposed logical constraints of the model, to identify and to capture in appropriate metrics those aspects of items that determine their difficulty. With Analytical Reasoning item types we have been reasonably successful. Our efforts have been deliberately informed by the well developed literature on the psychology of reasoning. More examples are needed before we can reach general conclusions about how successful Approach 2 is likely to be and what conditions limit its successful application.

CONCLUSIONS

The examples show that both approaches to item generation have potentially useful if somewhat different roles to play. Approach 1 will generally be cheaper to implement than Approach 2 and is applicable in situations where test forms are kept secure. In such contexts Approach 1 can produce multiple parallel forms as required, produce sample items for pretest familiarization and produce forms of varying difficulty for groups of different levels of ability. The main limitation of Approach 1 is in contexts where large numbers of items are disclosed and there is also a coaching industry. There, the principles underlying the generation of items may be discovered and exploited (but see Footnote 2, Eds.). In these situations Approach 2 is likely to prove more useful. Although it requires more extensive programs of experimentation, the higher costs of Approach 2 may be offset by the saving in item writing costs in open contexts where very large numbers of items need to be produced.

One feature common to all the projects is that the charge was to produce an item-generative version of an existing test or item type. The attachment of sponsors to tests and item types that are already proven to be effective is understandable. However, it may be that to get the best out of item generation we need to move to creating tests designed specifically with the possibility of item generation in mind. In the examples we have considered our efforts to manipulate and predict item difficulty do not appear to have undermined the ability of the tests to measure the construct that they were created to measure. However, it could be argued that this outcome was somewhat fortuitous. Starting the design of item-generative tests with a blank sheet would enable us to draw more effectively on our knowledge of cognitive psychology and to create items whose features are known to affect item difficulty through mechanisms related to the construct that the test is intended to measure. (See chap. 4, this volume by Mislevy, Steinberg, & Almond.)

REFERENCES

Abram, M., Elshaw, C. C., & Stevens, G. (1998). *An initial validation of the NPS test battery.* Defence Evaluation and Research Agency report DERA/CHS/MID/CR980193/1.0.

Collins, A. M., & Quillian, M. R. (1969). Retrieval time from semantic memory. *Journal of Verbal Learning and Verbal Behaviour, 8,* 240–247.

Dennis, I. (1993). *The development of an item generative test of spatial orientation closely related to test SP80A.* Senior Psychologist Naval Report TR307.

Dennis, I., Collis, J., & Dann, P. (1995). Extending the scope of item generation to tests of educational attainment. *Proceedings of the 37th Annual Conference of the International Military Testing Association,* Toronto.

Educational Testing Service (1996). *GRE Big Book.* Princeton, NJ: Educational Testing Service.

Jones, S. R., Dennis, I., & Collis, J. (1995). *The Naval Personnel Series: Performance of Rating Candidates and relationship to the Recruiting Test.* Defence Research Agency report DRA/CHS/HS3/CR9507/ 01.

Discussant Remarks

Len Swanson
Educational Testing Service

The chapters presented in this section raise two broad questions about the promise of automated item generation (AIG). The first question is what applications of AIG are most promising—that is, in what situations should we apply these methods? The second question is what kinds of tests these methods can or should be used for. For example, will they work with high-level reasoning tasks and, if so, which ones?

APPLICATIONS

The early literature on automated item generation suggested that it could be an important tool for reducing the cost and improving the speed of item writing. However, with the emergence of computer-delivered testing the real promise of AIG may come in addressing a larger problem—how to sustain the continuous testing that is almost implicit in computer delivery of tests. One of the two major challenges to the success of continuous testing is avoiding the effects of item preknowledge on the validity of scores. As a result of this challenge a major cost in computer-delivered testing is item writing and review. In fact, about 10%–15% of the costs of a computer test can be directly attributed to item writing costs (test administration, at 40%, is the largest factor). But even beyond cost, continuous testing exposes the test to compromise through preknowledge. As a result, our perspective is shifting from improving test development efficiency to changing the paradigm underlying computer-delivered testing. The chapters in this section serve as a rationale for this shift in perspective.

IRVINE CHAPTER

Irvine's purpose in his chapter is to review the historical and theoretical influences on the state of the art of item generation, organized around the three measurement paradigms—right/wrong models, latency models, and dynamic learning. He characterizes item-generation theory as a "bulwark against test compromise through overexposure," and a way of avoiding recalibration of tests entirely. He describes IRT as a "stop-gap response to the human inability to generate parallel tests." And he characterizes early attempts at computer-delivered testing as a "preoccupation with transferring old tests to computers to see if they will produce the same results."

How convincing is Irvine's case for automated item generation? He argues that AIG can be used to:

- create multiple parallel forms with high reliability;
- predict item difficulty from item radicals in a variety of contexts;
- develop IRT parameters that generalize across contexts and domains;
- develop fully generative tests that predict training outcomes; and
- provide repeated testing of an individual.

NEWSTEAD AND DENNIS CHAPTERS

In their chapters, Newstead, Dennis, and their colleagues extend Irvine's arguments to a high-level reasoning domain, GRE Analytical Reasoning. This is a critical, even landmark, extension because it brings the possibility of automated item generation to computer-delivered high-stakes college admissions testing, with its emphasis on strong face validity and continuous testing.

The methodology used here is also of considerable importance. Newstead et al. begin by analyzing Analytical Reasoning problems through applied cognitive theory and other methods such as protocol and structural analysis. They hypothesize sources of difficulty from the reasoning literature and from this develop and test models of difficulty. Two important aspects of these methods are the application of item-generation principles to high-level tasks, and what the results reveal about our understanding of high-level cognitive processing.

SUGGESTED DISCUSSION TOPICS RELATED TO THE METHODOLOGY

There are several topics we might discuss regarding the methodology described by Irvine and employed by Newstead and his colleagues.

- Can this methodology give us insight into construct isomorphs that better measure similar or related skills? That is, can we improve the test from this structural and empirical analysis?
- Can the methodology inform targeted item writing? A broader question is how we go about marrying automated item generation and manual item writing (Singley & Bennett).

- Can the information derived about the items help us score open-ended responses, as Bejar has suggested?
- Can this information be part of the validity evidence supporting the item type?
- When we aggregate from low-level difficulty factors, are factors such as context, situation, and test-taker beliefs a confounding influence in difficulty modeling? (See Evans and others on "bias" in reasoning.)
- Can we incorporate item-generation procedures into the test design process itself, and what would that synergy buy us? Later in this conference we'll be discussing evidence-centered test design; is it useful to think about this form of design in conjunction with principled item generation?
- Is there a useful connection between AIG and natural language processing? Can we use the methods and frameworks from item generation theory, together with emerging capabilities in natural language processing, to move us even closer to automated scoring of open-ended responses?

Suggested Discussion Topics Related to Applications and the Kinds of Test Being Developed

A second category of questions relates to the testing applications that might be appropriate for AIG.

- How convincing is the case for face validity of automatically generated tasks, and how does this vary depending on the kind of task begin generated?
- How convincing is the case for automated item generation overall, particularly for large-scale college admissions testing?
- How useful is AIG as a tool for "manually" crafting items, regardless of whether they are used in paper-and-pencil or computer-delivered tests? What does it save, in terms of time and costs?
- A more far-reaching question is under what circumstance we can generate an entire computer-delivered test totally without human intervention. In other words, can we generate a CAT "on the fly" that is unique to each individual? There are several important aspects to this notion:
  — Would such a test have the needed face validity?
  — Would the difficulty modeling be accurate enough?
  — Can we use AIG for all of the item types needed? That is, how complete can we make our item-generation tools?
To a large extent the answer to this question of fully automated testing depends on the test purpose. For example, it will be easier to generate an entire test in an instructional environment (where estimation accuracy is less important) than it is in a high-stakes college admissions environment.

Next Steps

The early work of Irvine and his colleagues left room for skepticism on most of these questions. The chapters that follow show that tremendous progress has been made in the past few years, more than many of us could have imagined. Whether automated item generation will become mainstream in future assessments is no longer in question; the only remaining question is how we will harness and develop this capability.

Organizations that wish to fully capitalize on AIG need to first decide on a strategic direction for applications. Do we want to use it only to reduce item-writing costs? Or do we want to eventually be able to deliver individualized generated tests? A research agenda that systematically addresses the purposes we have in mind for AIG and the kinds of tests we want to apply it to then needs to be developed. If appropriately applied, and based on a sound research agenda, the chapters in this section suggest that AIG can dramatically alter the testing landscape.

DISCUSSION

BRAUN:

Thank you, Len, for that thoughtful discussion. You've raised a number of issues. Let us now entertain comments and questions and discussion from the floor. Are there comments or responses to Len's discussion, or to the presentations themselves?

Questions

WAINER:

Like Len, I was blown away by the progress that has been made. I have a series of allied questions; all related to the fact that the items that each examinee receives are unique and so you must rely heavily on theory for the validity of the inferences you make. Let us consider some practical issues, generated by the world in which we have to live. Specifically, I was thinking about two contesting points: (1) that requires items after they're used to be released to the public and (2) that anyone who's taking a test must be told how that test is going to be scored, and what theoretical structure underlies it. When we have fixed forms for the tests we have generally been able to negotiate these two requirements successfully. How would this work with generated on-the-fly items? If everything must become public, that is, everyone knows the rules about how items are generated, and you move away from the kinds of g-loaded items that were mentioned, then how coachable do the items become? If somebody knows the underlying rules do they become more coachable? Are there test-taking strategies that allow people to be able to do better? If they are coachable, how do you find out?

How do you answer someone who comes to you afterwards, and sues you, because they believe that the items generated for them are more difficult than your model says? Since you have no empirical evidence from any other examinees how can you contend in court that such an examinee is wrong and that they should not have been given a much higher score? And how do you deal with things like DIF? How can you know that the items I happened to get would not have had negative DIF for my group?

When the components of each test are completely unique, how do you deal with these kinds of issues?

Coachability

DENNIS:

I have a partial response on the coachability issue. If we think about the three examples I discussed, in the first two, the things Howard mentions are potentially real problems. I don't think they were problems in the context in which those pieces of work were carried out, but they are problems in trying to translate what I call "Approach 1" to more open contexts. In the case of analytical reasoning, the items the computer is producing (within the subtype in which we're currently operating) are absolutely no different from the ones the item writers are producing. Given that, there are possibly some problems, but they are no less with the items the human item producers are writing than they are with the items the computer is producing.

Differential Item Functioning (DIF)

BRAUN:

If I could just add to that: It seems to me that the DIF issue, which is an interesting one, could be perhaps finessed by a kind of empirical Bayes approach. In other words, instead of trying to do DIF on a particular item, you do DIF on a template, which has generated the family of items. Using an empirical Bayes method, you could accumulate information across items that are in effect unique. That is, only one person gets them. But accumulating over all the variants within a family, perhaps stratified by some of these features, you might be able to come up with a different kind of DIF statistic. But it would be one that would still be responsive to the need to understand whether there were in fact unexpected differences in performance between groups.

WAINER:

I'm looking forward to test somebody who gets that! Because if you say on average there is no DIF, which is what you're essentially saying . . .

BRAUN:

On average within an item family . . .

WAINER:

. . . within an item family, yes. Then they say, "well I didn't take the average, I took my test."

BRAUN:

OK, well I hope by that time I'm a private consultant, and I can make as much money defending it!

Coachability (again)

BENNETT:

The coachability issue is a particularly interesting one because I think I can see some situations in which it becomes a nonissue.

That is, if the rules used to describe items for modeling purposes are schema based, then coaching becomes learning. There becomes no difference between the two. As long as the number of schemata is relatively large and the number of items we generate from each model is also relatively large, we should have no hesitation about making public those schemata so that examinees can learn them.

IRVINE:

When the BARB system was introduced, particularly for the Navy trials, they were able to introduce for the first time booklet testing. By that I mean each candidate had a booklet, with examples of the generic types of items that were going to be given, and in some cases, they weren't allowed to actually take the computer test until they had shown they had actually completed the booklet. So what they were encouraged to do was learn as much as they could about the generic or item family types and come ready on the day. The point of that is that if there are shifts in the item difficulties because of the introduction of study booklets, we will know it. And we will then introduce slightly more difficult versions of these same generic types of items to adjust for the fact that people are going to get themselves ready. So the notion of open testing is one that's freely discussable, given the generic types of items and isomorphs of the kind of things that we're playing with. So, it is helpful to know that other people have been able to introduce the notion of openness, and hence more fair, because educational testing is a political science. Sometimes more political than science.

LUEBKE:

I'm not sure that completely solves the problem, because education about items is differentially available to the population. So if you take a high-stakes, gateway test like the GRE or, the one I work on, the LSAT, to what extent do you then favor people who have the economic resources to gain the information they need to do better on the test? Also, the goal of that kind of test isn't strictly to further educational attainment, but also to ascertain how in this population different kinds of skills are distributed. And on that basis, admissions decisions are made. Which is a different use of the test than educational.

Interactions among item factors

ALMOND:

I had a question hitting along some of the remarks that Howard was making about trying to predict or model DIF, as well as the more mundane modeling of item difficulty. One of the assumptions coming out of this modeling work was that all these factors were more or less independent, or at least they followed an additive or generalized additive model. It was a bit worrisome to me that there might be some combination of problem story, and use of marked versus unmarked things, which would drive you up into some kind of weird corner of that distribution. That would produce either an item that was extremely difficult, or one that had some sort of bias against some particular population. I was wondering to what extent the research has been able to show that these kind of linear models, independence models, were actually wholly true.

NEWSTEAD:

It's an empirical matter, in the sense that the simplest assumption is the additive model, and that's the one we started with. It seems to be doing quite well, and what we need to find out is if it breaks down somewhere, and if it does, what kind of interaction you're talking about. That's where we have to research. But I think that all we can say is so far, so good, it seems to be working quite well. But if it doesn't, well, it won't be back to the drawing board, but it will be introducing a slightly more complicated model than the one we currently have.

WAINER:

Stephen, how do you know? If you're giving out items so local all the time, you don't have the possibility of taking a specific one, and giving it to a gazillion people, and seeing what the various characteristics of that item are. You're always working in Henry's context of a random effect. So that's what troubles me about this—that there is no way to know. You're always leaning very heavily against the model. I keep thinking of some kind of QC that has to be filled in to any kind of programming, which you would select out some items that everyone would get, and continuously check to make sure that everything is going the way it's supposed to.

BRAUN:

Well, certainly that's quite practical, in certainly the BARB system that was described, and even here. You could systematically seed items back in, and use that as a check.

DENNIS:

It can actually be more than a check. It can be a tool for constantly refining your model.

BRAUN:

Exactly. But I want to come back to Russell's point, because I wasn't sure I understood it. You were saying, Russell, that if you did some analysis, at least on the basis of the kinds of empirical work that is been done now, you would have found some very interesting interactions among these radicals. You found that a certain combination of levels of those factors produced items of extraordinary difficulty. Would that, on the face of it, in your view, be evidence against the construct validity of the items?

ALMOND:

Well, there are a couple of different things. One I was worried about was not so much interaction among radicals, but interaction among incidentals. If somehow we had a problem using AIDS, which is politically loaded, in the context of the story, then the use of a marked versus unmarked comparison terms might have radically different effects.

And, the other comes out of earlier work that I did in reliability modeling, where I'm looking at when a nuclear reactor is going to blow up. Somehow you want to look at the condition where everything is on. You want to look at this upper left-hand corner, because that's going to be where the real disasters occur, if somehow the system is nonlinear.

There's also some question in my mind, whether there is not some intelligent kind of sampling protocol, like the latin hypercube. That might help us get at some of these interaction effects, get some model checking for the presence of these interaction effects, into the pretesting phase. Then we can be sure that when we pass a family of items into the pool, or the automatically generated shell, rather than individual items that actually have some basis to believe that this statistical law we're using.

DENNIS:

Clearly, the more extensive the sampling you do of the item universe, the more opportunity you've got to detect possible interactions. But the more sampling you do, the more costly it gets. So, there's a tradeoff. And I think to some extent, we've just got to decide where we want to settle on that tradeoff. One end of it is we never, ever use anything that we have not already trialed on a zillion people. The end we're using is items that we can produce in the thousands but with minimal evidence about their properties. You know, clearly, we don't want to occupy that end. Some people might want to just sit at the safe, costly end, and some of us might want to sit somewhere in the middle.

BRAUN:

And, we're wondering where that middle really sits. . .

SWANSON:

Yes, and that will depend on the kind of testing. . .

What is learned during coaching?

HORNKE:

Well, I wanted to go back to the learning and coachability issue that Howard raised. I understand the concern in the United States. In Europe, there is not that much concern. I respond usually in the following manner: If someone learns from a preparatory course, I am happy with it. If that behavior sustains over time, so that you really learn something, then I'm very happy for them. And so, why don't you accept that notion in this country? I realize that there are learning opportunities distributed unevenly in your society. But education is unevenly distributed in your society, so teaching to a test somehow mirrors teaching kids anywhere. Sorry, I think it's no excuse, but there is no escape from the problems.

WAINER:

The issue is not are they learning the construct that we're trying to test, but are they learning some strategy that's not the construct, that allows them to get a higher score for a different reason.

HORNKE:

Well, I would be concerned if you teach a construct that is only included in a small set of items. Then people get a higher score just because they have been taught a strategy. That's fine. But if a strategy is that general, as we have seen in the item-generation program, then I wouldn't give it that much thought. We are taught strategies all the time. When you leave this conference, you hopefully have new strategies. So what? If you buy a new car, after 2 days you've got a new synergy for your life. So what?

EMBRETSON:

Actually, I'd like to follow up on that point, because I think that item generation might help to lessen the impact of differential coaching that occurs right now. If you have more items based on better principles, you can expose your pool of examinees more uniformly to what, in fact, is required by items. Right now, we know the differential distribution of preparation is really quite significant. In my university I get mainly upper-division seniors preparing to take various kinds of tests. And most of them, I can chart courses *like select set*. They wouldn't dream of taking tests without going to some kind of a coaching preparation right before it. They are very highly skilled by the time they sit down to take that test. Now if you have a more uniform distribution of preparation—and you have a possibility of it, because you have more items, and better understanding of what those items involve—I think you can move forward. That's one strategy. The other you might consider too, is actually going to a more dynamic testing format. We were coaching tests repeatedly, and looked at the improvement over the course of the testing situation.

Benefits to the practice of item writing

FIERO:

I've been writing analytical reasoning items for a long time. And so I'm listening closely to some of the methods being discussed here. I'm also trying to decide if it's possible to have a completely generative version of the Analytic Reasoning test.

The first thing I would say is that a human item writer at ETS would not use marked language. We would think that it introduced a kind of difficulty not related to the construct.

Another thing is that we would not write certain items because examinees have only so much time. There are levels of difficulty or confusion we can achieve, but we don't want to achieve unless it pays off.

So now I'm thinking about myself a little differently. I'm thinking about myself as someone whose first job is to create a radical, and whose second job is to develop some other incidentals that will allow that radical to live somewhere else. And the hard thing for us is to create the second set of items. There's got to be a bridge, somehow, from the original radical and incidental, to new incidentals, in which the radicals can be embedded. Often, an item writer will create a second set of incidentals, and will find out that the problem is that those incidentals don't behave the same way that the first incidentals do.

BRAUN:

I think that's Russell's point, that you're going to get interaction among incidentals.

FIERO:

So, we're not terribly successful yet, in getting parallel difficulties, and I think some of it has to do with the way that the items are pretested and the way the pretests are used operationally. But, anyway, that is a big problem, so I'm trying to imagine how the computer is going to be able to furnish the appropriate set of incidentals. My last vision comes from Len's notion that the test developers become meta-item writers. The incidentals take time to get right. I don't think they take more time than a radical to get right.

The last situation I'm trying to imagine is where the computer is providing the incidental and radical combinations. Natural language processing designers can create those incidentals right now. So you have to imagine that you're designing a whole array or repertoire of things that could be brought in, and fit into the radicals, and that's a tough one, but I kind of like the idea of doing that, but it isn't a simple process. In other words, to get those incidentals to behave is not a simple process, and in the long run it's not going to be a simple process either.

WALTHALL:

I like the idea of generating items on the fly, but I wouldn't overlook the possibility that with this kind of modeling there is tremendous potential even if you have a production model that requires human test developers to intervene at various stages of the process. Take DIF, for example. DIF is the result of an item operating at a different level of difficulty for different groups, which in most cases is not desirable but in some may be unavoidable and necessary. But whatever the case, you want first and foremost to understand as much as you can about why an item is functioning at a different level of difficulty for different populations. There are certainly going to be cases in which you want to minimize that effect if you can and still have an adequate measure of candidates' ability. If this modeling methodology works at predicting difficulty for a general population then while this may be a leap, it ought not to be a terribly complicated matter to take that model to a subset of that population and begin applying it there. So you might have a number of different models of difficulty for a number of different populations. That might enable you to start to get a more refined explanation about why a particular kind of item is more difficult for one population or subgroup than for another even after you match them on ability according to some common scale. And that might enable you to devise ways of measuring the skill in question that minimize DIF but still enable you to get at the construct.

If you had that capability, you could apply it either to items that are generated by hand, or to items that are generated by what I guess you could call computer-assisted generation. Now Bill (Eilfort) can speak to this much more than I can, because he is using tools developed at Plymouth to generate the logical schema for certain kinds of analytical reasoning sets. The idea here is that you get a logical schema for an analytical reasoning stimuli and the questions that go with them. Human test developers then proceed to develop verbal scaffolding around the schema, so you have real analytical reasoning items you can administer to candidates. Now if those schema come with quite accurate predictions of difficulty for both the general population and subgroups in that population, you get two big advantages. First you get help in generating the questions themselves. In the context of analytical reasoning, we don't know how valuable that is yet, because the items are not expensive, in terms of labor, to produce. But in addition we could get very robust models for predicting the difficulty of the items, which would be useful to us in a number ways of course. It could significantly reduce the number of items we have to pretest, and it could help us minimize differences in performance that appear related to group membership and that we may conclude are, finally, extraneous to the construct we are trying to measure. And you might get both of these advantages, even if you fell short of being able to generate analytical reasoning items completely on the fly, without human intervention.

Item generation & construct validity & DIF

MISLEVY:

The first item on Len Swanson's "Methodology Discussion Topics" list is to improve the test. And yes, that's a good thing, especially when we need to make it more efficient. But it is probably more exciting to think about steps that aren't yet created, steps that will have to be part of the retrofit of what was done in the past, which evolved to do the job well without item generation. But when we come to new applications, we probably say, "What are the elements that give me evidence about certain aspects of the proficiency curve? How can you systematize the way you get evidence about it?"

That leads quite naturally to thinking about principal ways of designing items, some of which may be lending themselves to generation, others which don't. But it's the right way to think about building assessments. That helps a lot with the DIF issue, because DIF is a substitute for having construct validity.

BRAUN:

The issue of construct validity seems to me to be at the heart of this. Going back to Ned's point, if we had reasonably credible models for item functioning across ranges of difficulty for different populations, we would know a lot more than we do today, of the kind of DIF analysis that we do item by item. Is that a fair statement?

WALTHALL:

Yes, absolutely. Currently, we have the ability to minimize DIF in the delivery of an assessment—perhaps less so in its design—and in either case very, very crudely. The problem now is that you pretest the item, you look at it, and you can hypothesize about what is causing the DIF, but you are never very certain and that does not get you very far. It is very difficult in an ongoing operational program to call time out and launch a study involving the systematic collection of data on every hypothesis that you formulate with regards to why one particular item is more difficult for one subgroup than another after you match for ability. So whenever you can, you throw the item out after it has been pretested. That's certainly better than nothing, but it's a crude process, and you are working in the dark most of the time. You are hacking away at your item pool, which can help, but you finally don't know what the underlying cause of the DIF is. You are treating the symptom, not the disease. If on the other hand we had very robust models of what drives DIF—and DIF is, after all, differential difficulty—we could eliminate the items we wanted to eliminate before we ever pretested them, or even wrote them. I mean there are two things that would be of tremendous use to test developers: the ability to predict how difficult an item will be for a general population, and the ability to predict how difficult it will be for various subgroups in that population. If you had that crystal ball, you could build item pools much more efficiently, and perhaps more important, you could probably develop a much more robust understanding of what factors in an item contribute to differential item function and which of those factors are really intrinsic to the construct. I guess what I am driving at is that all of these capabilities are things that test developers could use. That's true even if in the process of developing them you finally fell short of the longer term goal of generating items on the fly, without much in the way of human intervention.

IRVINE:

What I didn't say in my paper was that it begins with what Cronbach, in 1957, said about the two disciplines, the correlational and experimental. As I listen to you talking about radicals and incidentals, what I think is implicit in what the three of us are saying today, is that if you put yourself in control of the item, then every time you deliver it, you experiment with the test models, implicitly, or explicitly. So in a way, every time you deliver the test, you conduct an experiment of a very rigorous nature about how right you are. And I think that that is the kind of discipline that item generation forces upon us.

Dave Wright hasn't said anything, but I know that he has taken a hard look at some of the applied IRT technology, that he's been playing with, particularly the transitive inference rules. And he did find that some of what we thought would be incidental to the difficulty of the items, proved to have some statistically significant differences. But I believe David thought the proportion of variance was so small that it wouldn't make any difference to the final p value. Have I summarized you correctly?

WRIGHT:

If you have enough data you find everything is significant. For example, the order of the responses in the transitive inference test, if the right answer comes first it makes the answer easy. These effects are very small.

BRAUN:

But again, speaking as a statistician now, the statistical significance must be put in the context of practical significance. But I want to come back to this point. I think the point you're making, Sid, is that every time you give a test generated in this way, each item carries with it a prediction, and so you can look both across candidates for items within a certain family to see whether the model is holding up. But you can also look within a candidate, and see to what extent the candidate's performance in the aggregate seems to accord with the prediction.

IRVINE:

Absolutely correct. In that study of the effects of anaesthesia on item performance in a single patient we took what we thought the radicals were for the items and regressed them against that patient's performance. And we found that treatment and practice and the radicals (number of letters presented, number of steps, whether they had to go forward or backward in the alphabet) that entered into a regression equation predicted changes in performance over time. I think it ended up with an R-squared of about 34 or something like that. We were getting about .5 or .6 in predicting the effect of these items on the performance of single individual based on latencies. So it does seem to transfer from groups to individuals.

BRAUN:

Of course, it's just one individual at this point.

IRVINE:

There was only one individual in this particular trial.

BRAUN:

A very compliant individual!

IRVINE:

Well, it was an individual who had a vested interest in the outcome, somewhat of a mature age as well.

"g" and test specificities

GOETERS:

I've got a question concerning the validity—why is there not more concern with the g aspect? According to my observation, when I interpret the results presented by Sid Irvine, especially, you use a lot of computerized tests, and these tests were designed to cover several topics—let us say spatial orientation, reasoning, and so forth. But the result of the factor analytic research was that there is one main factor in it—working memory. And so the question is, is this an artifact of the method used? How much specific variance is there in the individual tests? Can the specific variance be used in the actual selection decision?

IRVINE:

It is a matter of fact that the specificity in these types of tests do latch on to the specificities of more traditional tests. The specificities are, as Godfrey Thomson said, wallflowers in a ball. They're waiting for a partner to come and drag some variance out of them. But remember, we have a Thurstonian model here, and we deliver the same type of item over and over again. But you have a Spearman theory, and you can infer from the working memory estimate of the individual, the rate at which the new information can be learned. And that's the purpose of mass-testing: screening large numbers of people. You just want to know how quickly they can be trained, and that constrains that whole universe. So it doesn't surprise me that I only hit one factor but the Australians and others have found more than one factor, when they've had specific variants in other tests that were given. What it does say, of course, when it is used in structural analyses with the ASVAB (Armed Services Vocational Aptitude Battery) is more about the ASVAB than it does about our tests.

BRAUN:

Could you make that statement more explicit, about the ASVAB?

IRVINE:

The ASVAB is not a *g*-loaded test in the sense that we would it understand it. It is a very highly verbally educationally loaded battery. And a large first general factor differences in the way in which education is delivered across this enormous country. But what you have is a huge declarative knowledge factor in the ASVAB, and very little in the way of working memory at all, and that has been shown in I think many, many studies we have conducted with this particular kind of battery. So I have no fear of the ASVAB as being a pejorative test held against all kinds of different ethnic groups. I don't think the research holds up that kind of inference or interpretation of the test, frankly. I mean, that's my own personal opinion. But you've waved the red flag, and I charged. Thank you very much.

Connections with natural language processing

ALMOND:

I just wanted to briefly touch on something, the last point there on Len's "Methodology Discussion Topics" list—the natural language processing. I just wanted to emphasize that the technology there works both ways. Not only are they getting very good now at understanding important features and extracting key features and schemas from a piece of found text, but they're also getting very good at generating text from schemas. As a matter of fact, on the Dilbert website, I was able to generate something that was almost indistinguishable from the ETS mission statement, *by sheer random chance*.

However, I think there's some potential here that we need to be thinking about that particular piece of technology, and how that gets into the picture.

BRAUN:

That's right, and I think also that the research agenda for NLP is in many ways parallel or analogous to the research agenda in item generation.

ALMOND:

Yeah, I think there's some real potential for synergies that could start to pay off.

More construct validity comments

BEJAR:

I want to endorse something said earlier. I'm returning to a comment Lee Cronbach made about generalizability theory. He said, that it wasn't important what answers you provide but the fact that it forced you to ask some questions. And I think in the same sense, item generation makes you ask all those questions, and in that process I think ultimately *score testing improves steadily.*

BRAUN:

I wonder if, for example, we can understand more about specific item types like analytical reasoning? Whether for a population, say the GRE-test-taking population, if we were to give them some of the BARB tests, that are heavily loaded on working memory, and these items, the analytic reasoning, with a high correlation, for example, . . .

IRVINE:

I would predict that the BARB tests would find differences in a high-stakes population. And I'll put my fearless prediction in an envelope. We could regress the GRE Analytic Reasoning score on some of the more modern tests we've been developing, and I suggest that about 3 out of the 5 would load, and our final correlation would be about .41.

BRAUN:

.41? I'll write that down.

Incidentals

NEWSTEAD:

In the work that we've been doing, incidentals depend on the scenarios that are used. The brief we've been given by ETS is to use abstract materials. It's up to the item writers to try and develop the scenarios in which they can be used. We do know from the reasoning literature that there are quite large effects based on the kind of thematic material we use in a variety of reasoning problems (so that in principle, the clothing makes a difference). But we also know that if the scenario is at a sufficiently general abstract level, then it's not going to make very much difference. So it is possible to get around some of the potential problems by being aware of the kind of clothing that is likely to make a difference to the predictability of the model. I think, in theory, that wrapping up in clothing could be done automatically. I don't think it's that much of a problem. The difficulty might be that you would be imposing restrictive scenarios on the item writer. I'm not sure whether that in it self is acceptable to the producers of these tests. But in theory (they're sufficiently constrained, so that given a scenario,), you could wrap them up relatively straightforwardly.

BRAUN:

Again, I'll just point out, it seems to me that just as we might have a factorial structure for radicals, you could have a factorial or some other structure representing the universe of incidentals. By empirical investigation, you could determine them as being on average, relatively innocuous. If I interpret what you're saying correctly, the issue is more likely to be a difficult one not so much in abstract reasoning, but more in a contextualized reasoning. It is more likely to be a difficult issue as you get into situations in which you must draw more from real word scenarios. Is that a fair thing to say?

NEWSTEAD:

I want to say that I think the current items generated are at a satisfactory level of generality, sufficiently so to avoid most of the potential problems.

ANONYMOUS:

I just wanted mention that this incidental item manipulation you're referring to. In fact, we've been doing this very kind of research just by the by, in writing variants of Arithmetic Reasoning item sets. These are "reclothings" of the same logic. We have statistics that show that in some cases the statistics come out identical—and there are many cases like that—and some cases they don't. If you wanted to do something like generative testing, you could easily take your incidentals, write your variants, do some pretesting, find out just which scenarios do and don't affect difficulty.

BRAUN:

There's a statistical issue here as well. If you test enough null hypotheses, eventually, something's going to look indicative by chance. But you have to recognize that some of these signals may in fact be misleading. You may think there's something wrong when you're just being subjected to the expected vagaries of chance, so you have to take that into account.

Parting words

BRAUN:

I want to thank the presenters, the discussant, and everyone but before you leave, I just want to remind you, as I said earlier in the morning, at 4:30, we're going to have a memorial session for Sam Messick, and I know none of us have really prepared statements, but Betty will be here, and I hope that you will let me know if you would like to say just a few words, and we're not talking here about long speeches, I don't think that's called for . . . well, of course, if you want to, that's fine, but just some personal reminiscing, something about your connection with Sam, what Sam's work, or Sam, the man, meant to you, I think would be really wonderful and would certainly be appreciated by Betty. So please don't be shy, this is an opportunity for you to say to your colleagues and to the family, something about Sam, and I think this conference is as good a place as any to have that say. Thank you.

II
CONSTRUCT-ORIENTED APPROACHES TO ITEM GENERATION

4

On the Roles of Task Model Variables in Assessment Design

Robert J. Mislevy
Linda S. Steinberg
Russell G. Almond
Educational Testing Service

> *A construct-centered approach [to assessment design] would begin by asking what complex of knowledge, skills, or other attribute should be assessed, presumably because they are tied to explicit or implicit objectives of instruction or are otherwise valued by society. Next, what behaviors or performances should reveal those constructs, and what tasks or situations should elicit those behaviors? Thus, the nature of the construct guides the selection or construction of relevant tasks as well as the rational development of construct-based scoring criteria and rubrics.*
>
> — Messick, 1992, p. 17.

Task Design and Assessment Design

Whereas most of the other chapters in this book describe features of tasks that can be systematically varied to create families of similar tasks, this chapter takes a step back to examine the question of which features we should vary and why. We contend that this question cannot be meaningfully answered except in the context of the purpose of a particular assessment. In all assessments—from a standardized final exam to an informal evaluation in a tutoring session—we must draw inferences about what the student knows and can do from a limited set of observations. The challenge for the test designer is to produce a set of tasks that will elicit the necessary observations. This chapter defines a formal evidentiary framework for linking the manipulable features of the task (task model variables) to those knowledge, skills, and abilities (KSAs) which are the targets of inference.

Tasks are properly a central focus of educational assessment, because they produce the evidence on which to base any subsequent feedback, decisions, predictions, or placements. Historically, task design has been regarded more as an art than a science. Today, however, pressures from several directions impel us to consider more principled approaches to task design. Continuous computerized testing, for example, consumes far more test items than testing at limited occasions. Research from cognitive and educational psychology is providing insights into the structure and acquisition of knowledge, and offering clues about alternative ways that knowledge can be evidenced. New technologies for simulating work environments force the question of how to make sense of the rich data they can produce.

An assessment designer in this new world must create tasks with a credible argument for how students' behaviors constitute evidence about targeted aspects of proficiency (those complexes of knowledge, skills, and abilities we wish to make claims about); and a clear structure for how the tasks will be produced, presented, and evaluated. Task design is thus an element of assessment design more broadly conceived. The present chapter discusses task design in this light. We borrow terminology and concepts from our "evidence-centered" assessment design project, "Portal," to frame the discussion. The ideas are illustrated with examples from two assessments: The Graduate Record Examination (GRE), as a prototypical large-scale standardized assessment, and HYDRIVE, a coached practice system, as a representative product constructed explicitly from a cognitive perspective and using simulation technologies. The point is to see these two seemingly quite different assessments as instances of the same underlying design elements.

Evidence-Centered Assessment Design

The first principles of evidence-centered design come from the perspective of evidentiary reasoning as it is developed in the work of David Schum (1987, 1994). Schum draws on themes and tools from centuries of scholarly research, in fields that range from philosophy and jurisprudence to statistics and expert systems. He argues that while every realm of human activity has evolved its own specialized methods for evidentiary reasoning, common underlying principles and structures can be identified to improve applied work in all of them. These foundational principles of evidentiary reasoning are especially useful for attacking new or novel problems, when standard solutions and familiar methods fall short.

Our objective is to exploit this perspective, and the principles and tools gained thereby, in the domain of educational assessment. We use the term *assessment* broadly, to include not only large-scale standardized examinations but classroom tests both formative and summative, coached practice systems and intelligent tutoring systems, even conversations between a student and a human tutor. All face the same essential problem: *drawing inferences about what a student knows, can do, or has accomplished, from limited observations of what a student says or does.* An evidentiary perspective helps sort out the relationships among what we want to infer about examinees, what we can observe that will provide evidence to back our inferences, and situations that enable us to evoke that evidence.

Evidence-centered assessment design squares well with Messick's (1992) construct-centered approach, epitomized in our introductory quote. The difference is mainly a matter of emphasis. Messick accents the importance of conceptualizing the target of inference, or just what it is about students the assessment is meant to inform. As Yogi Berra said, "If you don't know where you're going, you might end up someplace else." There are three key stages:

Identifying the aspects of skill and knowledge about which inferences are desired (the "targets of inference"). A given assessment system is meant to support inferences for some purpose, whether it be course placement, diagnostic feedback, administrative accountability, guidance for further instruction, licensing or admissions decisions, or some combination of these. In order to support a given purpose, how should we characterize examinees' knowledge?[1]

Identifying the relationships between targeted knowledge and behaviors in situations that call for their use. What are the essential characteristics of behavior or performance that demonstrate the knowledge and skills in which we are interested? What do we see in the real world that seems to distinguish people with different kinds or at different levels of proficiency in these respects?

Identifying features of situations that can evoke behavior that provides evidence about the targeted knowledge. What kinds of tasks or situations can elicit the behaviors or performances that demonstrate proficiency? The way we construe knowledge and what we consider evidence about it should guide how we construct tasks and evaluate outcomes.

Although in a familiar domain it is often possible to skip ahead quickly to the third stage, we stress the first two stages of acquiring and reasoning from evidence. In tasks with the richer data and more complex student

---

[1] We use to the term *knowledge* broadly, to encompass its declarative, strategic, and procedural aspects, and recognize that a person's knowledge is intertwined with social, cultural, and technological contexts. This latter understanding is central to argument from evidence to implication, and as such equally critical to assessment design and validity investigations.

models that are now beginning to appear in educational assessment, the field lacks off-the-shelf methodologies for structuring inference. Thus, we turn to the principles of evidence-centered design to address that lack.

Our recent research—the Portal project—has a conceptual framework and supporting software tools for designing assessments. The project has three distinguishable aspects: An evidence-centered perspective on assessment design, object definitions and data structures for assessment elements and their interrelationships, and integrated software tools to support design and implementation. In this chapter we use this approach and provide a high-level description of the central objects and interrelationships. In particular we explore aspects of the Portal "task model." We establish connections between features of tasks and various assessment functions including task construction, inference, reporting, and validity argumentation—all of which can described in terms of the roles of task model variables.

The following section sets the stage for this discussion by laying out the essential structure of the Portal "conceptual assessment framework." Following that, we consider the various and interconnected roles of task model variables.

A MODEL FOR EVIDENCE-CENTERED ASSESSMENT DESIGN

Overview of the Basic Models

Figure 4.1 is a schematic representation of the six highest-level objects, or models, in a Portal conceptual assessment framework (CAF). These models must be present, and must be coordinated, to achieve a coherent assessment. We would claim that these basic models are present, at least implicitly, and coordinated, at least functionally, in existing assessments that have evolved to serve well some inferential function (e.g., deciding which students to admit to a program, or whether or not to recommend a remedial course of study for a student). Making this structure explicit helps an assessment designer organize the issues that must be addressed in creating a new assessment. Retrospectively, it helps clarify how pervasive design issues have been managed in successful assessments in the past, or overlooked in failures.

These are the basic models:

The *Student Model* contains variables representing the aspects of proficiency that are the targets of inference in the assessment, and it is where we manage our uncertain knowledge about these variables. Student model variables thus concern characteristics of *students*.

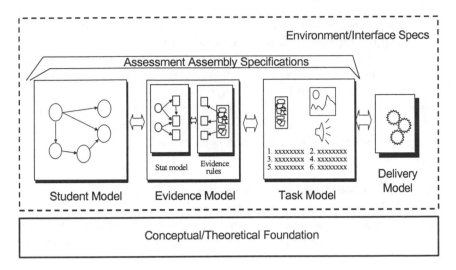

FIG. 4.1. High-level objects in the Conceptual Assessment Framework.

The *Evidence Model* describes how to extract the key items of evidence (values of "observable variables") from what a student says or does in the context of a task (the "work product"), and models the relationship of these observable variables to student-model variables. Observable variables concern characteristics of *performances*.

The *Task Model* describes the features of a task that need to be specified when a task is created. We use the term *task* in the sense proposed by Haertel and Wiley (1993), to refer to a "goal-directed human activity to be pursued in a specified manner, context, or circumstance." A task can thus include an open-ended problem in a computerized simulation, a long-term project such as a term paper, a language-proficiency interview about an examinee's family, or a familiar multiple-choice or short-answer question. We reserve the term *item*[2] for these latter cases. Task model variables concern characteristics of the *situations* by which evidence is obtained.

The *Assembly Model* describes the mixture of tasks that go into a fixed-form assessment, or the procedure for determining the mix dynamically for an adaptive assessment.

---

[2] Items are "simpler" than more general tasks only in that the form of the response is usually compact and straightforward to evaluate. The actual cognitive processes necessary to solve an item may be quite complex. The distinction between task and items is particularly useful in reading comprehension passages and similar testlets where multiple items share the same cognitive processes, context, tools, & c. Here the term "task" helps remind us that these items are best manipulated as a unit.

The *Delivery Model* describes the environment in which a particular task will run and the capabilities that are required for this to happen. A delivery model could describe a computerized or a human delivery mechanism, or a system that combines both. Four rather different examples of delivery models are the familiar, noninteractive, presentation of items in a paper-and-pencil (P&P) examination; the procedure through which a human interlocutor conducts an interview to gather evidence about an examinee's language proficiencies; the set of templates to use when presenting tasks using a web browser; and the set of specifications for a dental patient simulator.

The *Environment Model* describes the overall assessment environment. This includes specifications for whatever is needed to carry out the assessment, such as physical requirements, tools for examinees, computer hardware and software, timing requirements, security procedures, and so on.

In general, a CAF will have one operational student model, assembly model, and environment model. It may, however, have many different operational evidence, task, and delivery models.

The Student Model

The student model directly answers Messick's question, "What complex of knowledge, skills, or other attributes should be assessed?" Student-model variables describe characteristics of examinees (knowledge, skills, abilities) about which the user of the assessment wants to make inferences (decisions, reports, diagnostic feedback, advice).

Configurations of values of student-model variables are meant to approximate selected aspects of the countless skill and knowledge configurations of real students, from some perspective about how to think about skill and knowledge. This is how we want to talk about the student, although we can't observe the values directly. There could be one or hundreds of variables in a student model. They could be qualitative or numerical. They might concern tendencies in behavior, use of strategies, or ability to apply the big ideas in a domain. The factors that determine the number and the nature of the student model variables in a particular application are the conception of competence in the domain and the intended use of the assessment.[3] A test used only for selection, for

---

[3] As we shall see, task model variables play a central role in defining student-model variables operationally. The idea is for this operational definition to be the result of purposeful planning, rather than an coincidental outcome of task creation.

example, might have just one student-model variable, overall proficiency in the domain of tasks, while a diagnostic test for the same domain would have more student-model variables, defined at a finer grain-size and keyed to instructional options.

Defining student model variables specifies our target(s) of inference. The assessment will only accumulate evidence about the knowledge, skills, and abilities represented by student model variables; therefore these must always be in line with the purpose of the assessment.

At any point of time in an assessment, the student model represents our beliefs about whether or not a student has a given pattern of knowledge, skills, and abilities based on the evidence we have seen so far. At the beginning of a given student's assessment, we know little about the values of this student's variables and wish to sharpen our knowledge. We move from a state of greater uncertainty to lesser uncertainty about these unknown values by making observations which provide evidence about them, and integrating this new information into our beliefs.

In Portal, we use a Bayesian student model. This means that at any point in time the student model expresses the probability that the student has a given pattern of knowledge, skills, and abilities. In the early stages of the assessment, these distributions will be "uninformative" (based on what we expect from any student in the target population), although in an ongoing educational setting we might use information from previous assessments. At any stage the evidence models (described below) allow us to make predictions about how the student will perform on a new task. Using Bayes theorem we turn those predictions around and update our beliefs about the student's knowledge, skill, and abilities to incorporate the evidence from the student's performance. We'll say a bit more about how this is done in the following section on Evidence Models, but see Mislevy and Gitomer (1996) or Almond, Mislevy, Herskovits, and Steinberg (1999) for a more complete discussion.

We use graphical models (Whittaker, 1990) for student models because they allow us to specify the patterns of dependence and independence among the variables. (In a graphical model variables are represented by nodes in a graph and edges represent patterns of dependencies and independencies among the variables.) Our research efforts to date have centered on two important special cases: Discrete Bayesian networks, which are essentially latent class models with explicit representation of dependencies among the classes, and normal graphical models, which are essentially multivariate IRT models that can exclude specific interactions (i.e., we can set entries in the inverse covariance matrix to zero).

Example 1. Figure 4.2 graphically depicts the student model that underlies most familiar assessments: a single variable, typically denoted θ, that represents proficiency in a specified domain of tasks. We use as examples the paper and pencil (P&P) and the computer adaptive (CAT) versions of the Graduate Record Examination (GRE), which comprise domains of items for Verbal, Quantitative, and Analytic reasoning skills. Our knowledge about a particular examinee's θ before the test starts is expressed as an uninformative prior distribution. We will update it in accordance with behaviors we see the examinee make in various situations we have structured; that is, when we see her responses to some GRE Verbal test items.[4]

Example 2. Figure 4.3 is a more complex example of a student model, taken from Mislevy and Gitomer (1996). It is based on HYDRIVE (Steinberg & Gitomer, 1996), a coached practice system that ETS built to help Air Force trainees learn to troubleshoot the hydraulic systems of the F15 aircraft. Students worked their way through problems in a computer simulated environment much as they would on the flight line. The variables of the student model were used to capture regularities in the student's behavior, and their tendencies to use identified expert troubleshooting strategies.

FIG. 4.2. The student model in the GRE Verbal measure contains just one variable: the IRT ability parameter θ, which represents the tendency to make correct responses in the mix of items presented in a GRE-V.

---

[4] The simplicity of this student model is deceptive, by the way. It takes a great deal of hard work to make such a simple model work well. In order to be appropriate for capturing and expressing information from potentially thousands of different items, some very sophisticated interrelationships are posited. Much care is taken in just how and which are to be observed for a given examinee; empirical evidence is be carefully checked to avoid inferential errors that lead to certain kinds of unfair inferences. In the second half of the paper we will mention some of the considerations that are needed to ensure this simple model will suffice in the GRE.

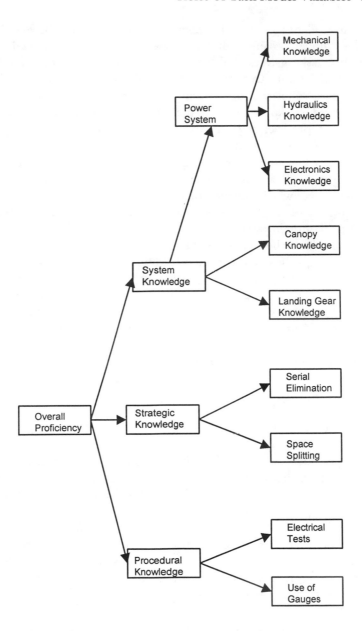

FIG. 4.3. The student model in the HYDRIVE example is a more complex Bayes net.

This student model is a fragment of a Bayes net, and these nodes are the student model variables. Student-model variables were derived in light of cognitive task analyses (CTA) of the job, the purpose of the HYDRIVE system, and the instructional approach of the system. The CTA showed that expert troubleshooting requires a conjunction of declarative, strategic, and procedural knowledge, so the student-model variables reflected key aspects of proficiency along these lines. Because the main purpose of HYDRIVE is instruction, the student model variables conform to a set of principles of instruction in the domain—in this case, troubleshooting a hierarchical physical system. The student model variables are defined at the grain-size at which instructional decisions are made—in this case, infrequent, high-level review sessions for aspects of system functionalities and troubleshooting strategies.

We can use the cognitive theory of the domain and our knowledge about a student's KSAs to make predictions about the observable features of that student's performance on a task. We can turn these predictions around (using Bayes theorem) to draw inferences about student model variables from observations. In this way, we update our belief about the people's student-model variables from what we see them do in situations that we have structured and modeled to this end. The updated distribution of student-model variables for a given person at a given point in time can be used to trigger decisions to such as to stop testing, shift focus, offer feedback, or make a placement decision.

Evidence Models

Evidence models address Messick's second question, "What behaviors or performances should reveal [the targeted] constructs?", and the natural follow-up question, "What is the connection between those behaviors and the student model variables?"

There are actually two parts of the evidence model. First, *Evidence Rules* extract the salient features of whatever the student has produced in the task situation, or the *Work Product*, and ascertain values of *Observable* Variables (Figure 4.4). This might be simple or complex, it might be done automatically or through human judgment.

Example 1, continued. This is an evidence rule in the GRE P&P test:

> IF the response selected by the examine matches the response marked as the key in the database,
> THEN the item response IS correct
> ELSE the item response IS NOT correct.

Observable Variables

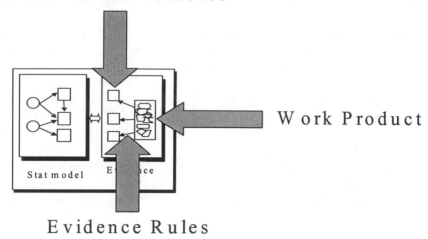

Work Product

Stat model   E   nce

Evidence Rules

FIG. 4.4. The "Evidence Rules" in the evidence model extract the salient features of the work product a student produces, and summarize them in terms of values for observable variables.

Example 2, continued. Here's the form evidence rules take in HYDRIVE. The work product is the list of actions a student takes in the course of working through the problem. As a student is working through a problem, short sequences of actions are grouped into clusters that each provide an item of information about the state of the system. These clusters are then evaluated in terms of their effect on the problem space. This rule sets the value for an observable variable that says whether or not the student has taken actions consistent with space-splitting the power path (an expert strategy):

> IF an active path which includes the failure has not been created and the student creates an active path which does not include the failure and the edges removed from the problem area are of one power class,
> THEN the student strategy IS splitting the power path
> ELSE the student strategy IS NOT splitting the power path.

A given work product may give rise to several observable variables. A single essay may be evaluated in terms of multiple aspects of language use, for example, or a science investigation may require several interdependent steps that each contribute to a composite work product. The values of a set of observable variables in such cases is a vector-valued description of the performance.

The statistical component expresses how the observable variables depend, in probability, on student model variables (Figure 4.5). Recall that the student model expresses our beliefs (in the form of a probability distribution) about the student's knowledge, skills, and abilities at any point in time. The statistical component of the evidence model takes the form of a predictive distribution for the observed features of the work product given the state of the student's knowledge, skills, and abilities. This predictive distribution combined with the current beliefs in the student model gives rise to probabilities for states of observable variables, which can be observed and as such constitute evidence about the student's state (see Haertel & Wiley, 1993, on the importance of the distinction between states of knowledge and states of performance). In Portal, we also model these relationships as Bayes net fragments. They can be attached to the student model Bayes-net fragment to absorb the evidence (Almond et al., 1990).

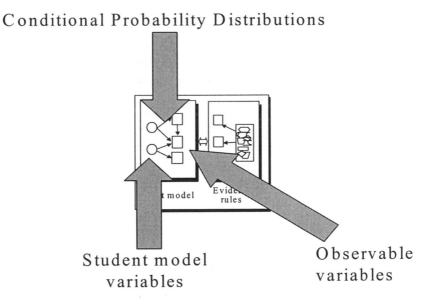

Conditional Probability Distributions

Student model variables

Observable variables

FIG. 4.5. The "Statistical Model" in the evidence model expresses the probabilistic dependence of observable variables on student-model variables.

Example 1, continued. Figure 4.6 shows the statistical portion of the evidence model used in the GRE CAT, an item response theory (IRT) model. On the left is a Bayesian inference network for updating the probability distribution of the student's proficiency parameter in accordance with her response to a particular Item *j*. On the right is a library of all items that could be given, along with the structures necessary to dock any one with the student model in order to incorporate the evidence its response contributes. In particular, previously estimated item parameters, which define the conditional probability distribution of item responses, are available. The information stored along with these fragments also informs how to select the next item so the next response will be optimally informative while retaining the balance of kinds of items that are presented and the aspects of skill that are tapped.

Example 2, continued. Figure 4.7 is the statistical part of the evidence model in the HYDRIVE example. On the left is a more complex Bayes net, in which a fragment containing two observed variables is docked with the student model, connected to the student-model variables that we posit drive their response probabilities. The structure of these fragments depends on our understanding of how mechanics troubleshoot this system and how the tasks are constructed. For example, a student does space-splitting consistently only if he is familiar with space-splitting as a strategic technique, sufficiently familiar with the system to apply the strategy, and familiar with the tests and gauges he must use to carry out the strategy in a given situation. (Note that which evidence-model fragments are used in HYDRIVE depends on the situations the student works himself into, while

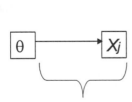

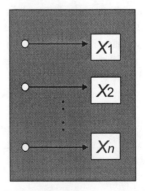

Sample Bayes net fragment
(IRT model & parameters for this item)

Library of fragments

FIG. 4.6. The "Statistical Model" in the evidence model for the GRE example.

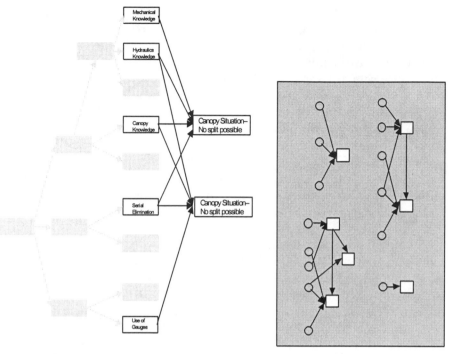

A typical Bayes net fragment   Library of fragments

FIG. 4.7. The "Statistical Model" in the evidence model for the HYDRIVE example.

in the GRE-CAT the evidence models are determined by the items we decide to administer.) When we observe a student's actions in a situation like this, we determine the values of observable variables using the evaluation rules, then in turn update our belief about the student model variables through the statistical model. The student model variables thus synthesize information across many situations.

In the GRE, the evaluation rules just extract a single observed variable from each task that summarizes how well each student has done on that task. Furthermore, our target of inference is the student's tendency to do well on tasks like these. In this case, a familiar IRT model or a classical test theory model can be used in the statistical portion of the evidence model. (This is a trivial graphical model with a single proficiency variable in the student model and a single observable variable in the evidence model.)

In more complex situations, statistical models from psychometrics can play crucial roles as building blocks—IRT models, rating scale models, latent class models, factor models, hierarchical models, and so on. These models evolved to address certain recurring issues in reasoning about students know and can do, given what we see them do in a limited number of circumscribed situations, often captured as judgments of different people who need not agree.

As mentioned earlier, there can be multiple evidence models in a CAF. This is because different configurations of kinds of evidence and interrelationships with student-model variables might be required. Reasons for having more than one evidence model include the following: (1) Different tasks produce different kinds of work products, which need distinct sets of evidence rules; (2) different statistical models are needed to relate observed variables to student model variables; (3) different tasks and associated evidence rules produce different observable variables; (4) different subsets of student-model variables in a multivariate problem are posited to drive probabilities of different observable variables; and (5) different values of task model variables qualitatively change the focus of evidence.

An example of an assessment that needs only one evidence model is a test that uses the same single-proficiency IRT model for all items, and does not model the item parameters in terms of different task variables for different tasks. A first example of an assessment that uses a single-proficiency IRT model but needs more than one evidence model is a test with a mix of multiple-choice items and performance tasks rated on a partial-credit scale. A second example is an assessment in which different task features are used to model the IRT item parameters of different types of items.

To be used operationally, an evidence model must be compatible with both the student model and a task model. Compatibility with the student model means that all knowledge, skill, and ability variables used as the basis of predictions about the observable features appear in the student model. For compatability with the task model, one necessary condition is that the evidence model and the task model share the same work-product specifications. That is, what the student produces in the task situation and what the evidence rules interrogate must be the same kind of thing. A further condition is agreement on specified ranges of a subset of task model variables called the *scope* of the evidence model (further discussed below). For example, in HYDRIVE we may restrict the scope of an evidence model to tasks involving the canopy system.

A given evidence model may be used with more than one task model, if the same scope, evidence rules, and structural relationships between observable variables and student-model variables are compatible with each of these task models. Similarly, more than one evidence model could be compatible with a given task model, if all the evidence models addressed the same work product and had a compatible scope. These evidence models could differ by applying different evaluation rules to the work product (e.g., different scoring rubrics), or modeling observable performance as a function of variables from a different student model in order to serve a different educational purpose (e.g., a finer grained student model when using the item for coached practice than when using it for selection).

Task Models

Task models address Messick's third question, "What tasks or situations should elicit those behaviors [that provide evidence about the targeted knowledge]?" A task model provides a framework for describing the situations in which examinees act (Figure 4.8). In particular, this includes specifications for the stimulus material, conditions, and affordances, or the environment in which the student will say, do, or produce something. It includes rules for determining the values of task-model variables for particular tasks. And it also includes specifications for the "work product," or the form in which what the student says, does, or produces will be captured. Altogether, task-model variables describe features of tasks that encompass task construction, management, and presentation. We discuss the several roles of task model variables more fully in the next section.

Assigning specific values to task model variables, and providing materials that suit the specifications there given, produces a particular task. Assigning values or materials to only a subset of them produces a task shell. Multiple task models are possible in a given assessment. They may be employed to provide evidence in different forms, use different representational formats, or focus evidence on different aspects of proficiency. Again we postpone to the next section the role of task model variables in making these determinations.

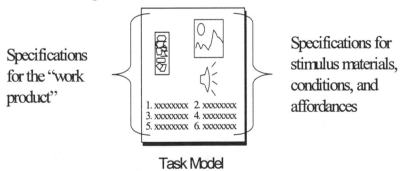

Specifications for the "work product"

Specifications for stimulus materials, conditions, and affordances

Task Model

FIG. 4.8. Elements of the task model.

A task thus describes particular circumstances meant to provide the examinee an opportunity to act in ways that produce information about what they know or can do more generally. The task itself does not describe what we should attend to in the resulting performance or how we should evaluate what we see. This is determined by the evidence model, as described earlier, which needs to match on the work product it expects and on features specified in the scope of the task and evidence models.

Distinct and possibly quite different evidence rules could be applied to the same work product from a given task. Distinct and possibly quite different student models, befitting different purposes or conceptualizations of proficiency, could be informed by data from a given task.

Example 1, continued. A task model in the GRE describes a class of test items. There is some correspondence between task models and GRE "item types" (e.g., sentence completion, passage comprehension, quantitative comparison). Different item types will generally require different task models, because different sets of variables needed to describe their distinct kinds of stimulus materials and presentation formats, and different features may be important in modeling item parameters or controlling item selection. Different task models will be required for P&P and CAT use of what is the same item from the perspective of content, because specifications for presenting and managing the item are wholly different in the two modes.

Example 2, continued. A task model in HYDRIVE contains the initial state of all the components in the simulation of the relevant aircraft system, and video and audio clips required to present the problem and to illustrate states and actions of the aircraft during solution. Further, because HYDRIVE is a coached practice system, each task model also includes links to instructional modules (which are themselves described in terms essentially the same as those of a task model) that can be activated by prespecified actions or states of the student model.

We will return to these task-model examples later, to say more about the variables they contain and their relationships with the other models in the assessment.

The Assembly Model

The models described earlier specify a domain of tasks an examinee might be presented, procedures for evaluating what is then observed, and machinery for updating beliefs about the values of the student model variables. *Assembly specifications* constrain the mix of tasks that constitute a given examinee's assessment. We observe neither the whole of the task domain nor an uncontrolled sample, but a composite purposefully assembled to meet a targeted mix of features of tasks to administer to each examinee. In IRT testing, optimal test assembly under multiple constraints has been a topic of much interest recently, both for fixed tests and CAT (Berger & Veerkamp, 1996). One can impose constraints that concern statistical characteristics of items, in order to increase measurement precision, or that concern non-statistical considerations such as content, format, timing, and cross-item dependencies.

Because student model variables represent knowledge, skills, and abilities that cannot in general be directly observed, the mix of tasks we use to obtain evidence about them is an important part of the effective definition of the student model variables. For example, if we take all of our reading passages from the *New York Times*, then the effective definition for the "reading" student model variable becomes the ability to read the *New York Times*. We explore this role of assembly models in defining the student model variables next.

The Delivery Model

The term delivery model refers to the capabilities that are needed to construct the environment and the situation in which the examinee will act, and to manage the interaction as may be required.

Example 1, continued. In the GRE CAT, the delivery model is the description of requirements for the software that manages the presentation of items and captures examinees' responses. When a particular item is selected to administer to an examinee (as determined by the assembly algorithm, informed by the current state of the student model and the identification of items presented thus far), this software must render the stimulus material on the screen, provide for and respond to examinee actions such as scrolling through a reading passage, inform the examinee of time usage, and log the selected response choice. The delivery model contains the descriptions and specifications for all of these functionalities, detailed to the extent that an external contractor could build a system that provided them.

Example 2, continued. The HYDRIVE system contains a simulation of the hydraulic systems of the F15. The delivery[5] model for HYDRIVE contains the descriptions and specifications for the simulator functionalities at a level that could be handed over to an external contractor. In particular, the simulator consists of objects that correspond to the mechanical, electrical, and hydraulic components of those systems, and can simulate the outcomes of troubleshooting actions in correctly functioning and variously malfunctioning states. The state of the system is updated as an examinee takes actions such as setting switches, supplying auxiliary power, replacing components, and manipulating controls. In addition, a component properly included in the simulation system tracks the implications of the student's sequence of troubleshooting actions on the so-called active path toward solution. In this way, the same action can be evaluated as "space-splitting" in one situation but "redundant" in another.

Task models can be written to work with more than one delivery model, if important elements of a family of tasks are the same under different modes of delivery. For example, a verbal analogy task is compatible with both a paper and pencil and a computer-based delivery model. Task model variables describing the syntax and content of such a task would apply to either delivery mode. Other task model variables, however, would take on values that applied to a particular mode of administration. It is also possible to develop special purpose delivery models; for example, a delivery model for students with limited vision. Using these delivery models to define specifications, we could envisage a marketplace of "delivery engines," each of which would support a certain delivery models and the corresponding task models.

ROLES OF TASK MODEL VARIABLES

In the preceding section, we described task model variables as a language for characterizing features of tasks and specifying how the interaction between the examinee and the task is managed. But what kinds of task model variables are needed, and what roles do they play? This section discusses how task model variables can play several roles in the assessment process outlined earlier.

---

[5] Previously we referred to delivery models as "simulator models" emphasizing those situation in which the delivery model contained specifications for a simulator. We let more conventional item delivery mechanisms be a special case. Recently, we have reversed the notation, letting simulators be a special kind of delivery model.

Task Construction

A fundamental tenet of the evidenced-centered approach to assessment design (and of Messick's construct-centered approach as well) is that the characteristics of tasks are determined by the nature of the behaviors they must produce, to constitute evidence for the targeted aspects of proficiency. This perspective stands contrary to a task-centered approach, under which the primary emphasis is on creating tasks, with the target of inference defined only implicitly as the tendency to well on those tasks. Practical experience and valuable insights inform task design under this latter approach, to be sure. But the flow of the design rationale from construct to evidence to task makes its reasoning explicit from the start—easier to communicate, easier to modify, and better suited to principled generation of tasks. It is this last connection, depicted in Figure 4.9, we now consider.

This evidentiary perspective on assessment design also conforms nicely with a cognitive perspective on knowledge and performance. A cognitive task analysis in a given domain seeks to shed light on (1) essential features of the situations; (2) internal representations of situations; (3) the relationship between problem-solving behavior and internal representation; (4) how the problems are solved; and (5) what makes problems hard (Newell & Simon, 1972). Designing an assessment from cognitive principles, therefore, focuses on the knowledge people use to carry out valued tasks in a domain at large, and abstracts the characteristics of those tasks that provoke valued aspects of that knowledge (e.g., Embretson, 1998). Those characteristics, then, become formalized as task model variables.

Irvine and his colleagues (Irvine, Dann, & Anderson, 1990, Collis et al., 1995; Dennis et al., 1995) use the term *radical* to describe those features which drive item difficulty for theoretically relevant reasons, and"incidentals" to describe those which do not. A model for creating tasks would define variables of both types. When tasks are generated automatically, values of these variables are instantiated in a predefined schema. The argument for the relevance of behavior in the resulting task situation is largely in place at this point, only to be verified empirical validation. Early work by Hively, Patterson, and Page (1968) illustrated schema-based item construction in this spirit. When individual tasks are created, the test developer may write them to meet targeted values of values of certain task model variables. The values of others may be set after stimulus material that meets certain characteristics is found and the rest of the task is written.

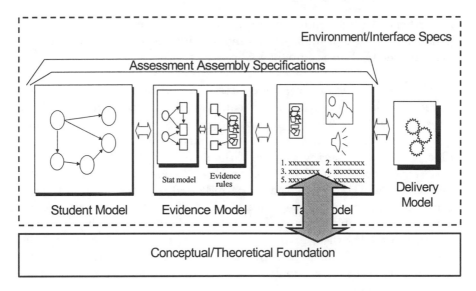

FIG. 4.9. The role of task-model variables in *task construction* connects the operational function of creating tasks with the theoretical foundation of the assessment—What situations evoke the behavior we need to see as evidence about the proficiencies we care about?

Example 1, continued. Historically, GRE items have been essentially hand-crafted. Test developers write them to meet broad specifications and to take the form of established item types, but apply their own insights and intuitions as to sources of difficulty and regions of knowledge that will be tapped. It is possible to train human test developers to write such items, by using the rich collection of accumulated examples to illustrate the reasoning behind their construction. Without a formal model, though, it is difficult to automate the process of task construction (or any of the other processes described below).

Some researchers, such as Chaffin and Peirce (1988), undertook studies that would make more explicit the definition and the structure of the domains of tasks that seemed to underlie the assessments. And sparked by the pioneering work of Carroll (1976), other researchers launched investigations into the cognition that leads to performance on traditional item types, thereby gaining psychologically grounded insights into the features that make them difficult. These strands of research work backwards from the procedurally defined assemblages of items that constitute a GRE to a principled explication of the domain of tasks that constitute evidence about "what the GRE measures," and a cognitive understanding of the skills and knowledge that seem to be required. Such an understanding provides a foundation for working forward, and indeed researchers are currently exploring how generative schemas, their parameters defined in terms of task-model variables, can be used to create items for the GRE (e.g., Enright & Sheehan, 1998).

Example 2, continued. Given the aircraft simulator in HYDRIVE, one creates a task by specifying which components are faulty, and in which ways, among the possibilities the simulator can accommodate. The relevant task model variables thus indicate initial states for all the components. (Specifying these states was not as difficult for a task creator as it might first seem, since the normal conditions for all components were defaults. Only exception conditions had to be indicated.) When video and audio clips accompany such a task, additional task model variables describe technical specifications for running them and substantive characteristics relevant to the knowledge required to solve the problem. For example, is there an obvious cue to the problem? . . . an irrelevant cue in the introductory clip? . . . multiple cues, which only together provide information about the area of the fault?

Focusing Evidence

The proficiencies defined in any assessment have many facets, and the features of tasks can be controlled to focus the evidence on some of these facets rather than others. The *scope* of an evidence model is a list of task-model variables and associated ranges of values that must be consistent with corresponding values of those variables in a task, for that evidence model to be used to extract information from the task (Figure 4.10).

Example 1, continued. The full GRE model contains three student model variables (with no modeled interaction): one each for verbal, quantitative, and analytical reasoning. Each item is assigned to one of these three scopes (and placed on an appropriate form or item pool). The "scope" of the GRE evidence model tells us which θ to update.

Example 2, continued. An evidence model constructed to extract evidence about space-splitting usage must, perforce, be used in a task situation in which it is possible to carry out space-splitting. Its scope would include the task model variable Space-splitting possible? constrained to the value Yes. Only a task model with a scope that contains Space-splitting possible? constrained to the value Yes is compatible with an evidence model that can update a "space-splitting knowledge" student-model variable.

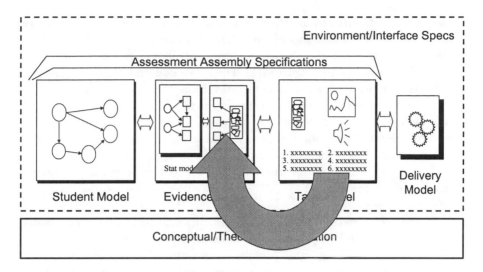

FIG. 4.10. The role of task-model variables in *focusing evidence* connects the characteristics of task situations with the kinds of evidence that can be extracted from performance in those situations, as governed by the conceptual underpinnings of the assessment.

The student model in the HYDRIVE example includes variables for knowledge about the subsystems of the hydraulics system, including the flaps and the canopy, and for knowledge about using troubleshooting strategies, including space-splitting and serial elimination. The preceding example shows how the variables on the scope of the evidence and task models serve to focus the evidentiary spotlight of tasks onto different variables within a complex student model. But the same HYDRIVE tasks could be used for in an end-of-course test with only a single overall proficiency variable in the student model. The same scope designations would still be needed, however, to ensure that an appropriate set of evidence rules was applied to extract evidence from the work product produced in response to a task. In this latter case, the variables used in the scope task serve to focus evidence-gathering on a particular region of a more broadly construed proficiency.

Assessment Assembly

Once a domain of items has been determined, test assembly specifications control the mix of tasks that constitute a given examinee's test. Constraints can be imposed with respect to statistical characteristics of tasks, such as the expected information it offers for various student model variables, and also with respect to nonmeasurement considerations such as content, format, timing, cross-item dependencies, and so on. In assessments that are adaptive, constraints can be dynamic as well as static. Many constraints are defined in terms of task model variables, so task-model variables must be defined to characterize each task in terms of all the features needed to assembling assessments (Figure 4.11). The set of constraints, in conjunction with the specification of a domain of tasks, rules of evidence, and evidence-model likelihoods (in Portal, Bayes net fragments), constitute an operational definition of the student-model variables in an assessment—that is, they implicitly define "what the assessment measures." (A key question for the assessment designer, then, is whether this implicit functional definition of student model variables accords with the explicit conceptual definitions meant to drive the design.)

Example 1, continued. In addition to information-maximizing constraints based on items' IRT parameters, the assembly specifications for the GRE CAT contain "blocking" and "overlap" constraints. Taken together, they ensure that the collection of items administered to all examinees will have similar balances of content and format, and be reasonably well modeled by the single-proficiency IRT model.

Blocking constraints ensure that even though different examinees are administered different items, usually at different levels of difficulty, they evertheless get similar mixes of content, format, modalities, skill demands, and so on. Stocking and Swanson (1993) list 41 constraints used in a prototype for the GRE CAT, including, for example, the constraint that 1 or 2 aesthetic/philosophical topics be included in the Antonym subsection.

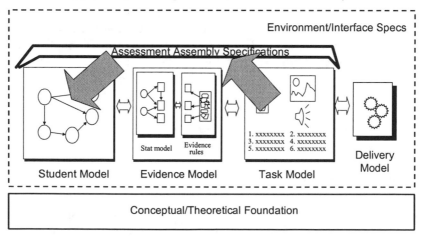

FIG. 4.11. The role of task-model variables in *assembling assessments* connects the characteristics of task situations with the mixture of tasks which, taken together, constitute an assessment—and thereby operationally define the student-model variables.

Overlap constraints concern the innumerable idiosyncratic features of items that cannot be exhaustively coded and catalogued. Sets of items that must not appear in the same test as one another are specified. They may share incidental features, give away answers to each other, or test the same concept. A task-model variable for GRE items, therefore, is the "enemies list": For a particular item, this is the set of items in the same pool which cannot concomitantly appear on an examinee's test. The notion of overlap constraints evolved through substantive lines, from the intuition that using too-similar items reduces information about examinees. Although each item is acceptable in its own right, their joint appearance causes "double counting" of evidence when a conditional-independence IRT model is used (Schum, 1994, p. 129).

IRT-CAT adapts to changing states of knowledge about the student-model variable, but the target of inference is always the same: "What is θ ?" It uses information formulas and task-based blocking and overlap constraints to select items in this context. Generalizations of these kinds of item selection procedures are required for more complex models, in which different subsets of a larger set of student model variables may shift into and out of attention. Research in the psychometric literature that leads in this direction includes the work on item selection and test assembly in the context of multivariate IRT models (Segall, 1996, van der Linden, 1997) and latent class models (Macready & Dayton, 1989).

Mediating the Relationship Between Performance and Student-Model Variables

We considered earlier the importance of cognitively or empirically relevant features of tasks during task construction, and the role of task-model variables in structuring this process. Those features characterize which aspects of the targeted proficiencies are stressed, in which ways, and to what extents. Some of these same variables can play a role in the statistical part of the evidence model for the same reasons. The conditional probability distributions of the values of observable variables, given the relevant student-model variables, can be modeled as functions of these task model variables in the evidence-model Bayes nets fragments (Figure 4.12).

In assessments that use IRT to model conditional probabilities of observable variables given a single student-model variable, this amounts to modeling item parameters as functions of task-model variables (e.g., Fischer, 1973, Mislevy, Sheehan, & Wingersky, 1993). One practical advantage of doing this is reducing the number of pretest examinees that are needed to obtain satisfactory estimates of item parameters assembling tests and for drawing inferences about examinees. This can be done by

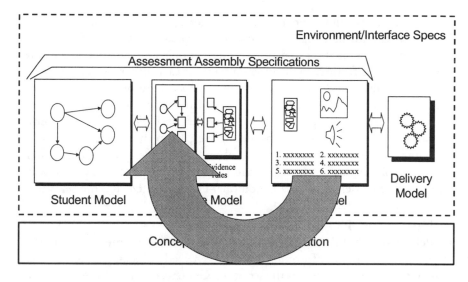

FIG. 4.12. The role of task-model variables in *meditating the relationship between performance and student-model variables* is a technical connection between values of student-model variables and conditional probabilities of observables in task situations with specified features.

characterizing items post hoc, but a more powerful approach is model conditional probabilities in terms of (perhaps a subset of) the same features that theory posits to be important and around which items are constructed (Bejar, 1990). Embretson (1998) illustrated how assessment design, task construction, and statistical modeling can thus be unified under a cognitive perspective. Collis et al. (1995) used the approach with computer-generated tasks, with the objective of creating items with operating characteristics sufficiently predictable to be used without any pretesting at all.

In assessments with a single student-model variable and conditionally independent observations, modeling item difficulty as a function of task model variables is closely related to the desired end of modeling conditional probabilities. Task model variables typically show similar relationships with IRT difficulty parameters and classical indices of difficulty such as percent-correct in the target population. Further, experience suggests that IRT difficulty parameters are at once easiest to model and most important in subsequent inference (Mislevy et al., 1993).

Example 1, continued. Many studies have been carried out on the features of GRE items that appear to account for their difficulty. Chalifour and Powers (1989) accounted for 62% of item difficulty variation and 46% of item biserial correlation variation among GRE analytical reasoning items with seven predictors, including the number of rules presented in a puzzle and the number of rules actually required to solve it. Scheuneman, Gerritz, and Embretson (1989) were able to account for about 65% of the variance in item difficulties in the GRE Psychology Achievement Test with variables built around readability, semantic content, cognitive demand, and knowledge demand.

In assessments that have more than one student model variable, though, simply modeling item difficulty in terms of task model variables is not sufficient. Two tasks can be equally difficult in the sense of percents-correct in the target population, but for different reasons. If those reasons reflect differential stress on the various student model variables that drive performance on the task, then a more complicated structure is needed to properly disambiguate the evidence about those student model variables.

Example 3. The current Test of English as a Foreign Language (TOEFL) measures Reading, Listening, and Structure in three separate single-proficiency tests with conditionally independent items in each. The TOEFL 2000 development project is investigating more complex tasks that demand the use of skills across these formally separate areas. Consider a task model for a class of tasks in which an examinee must first read a passage of prose, then construct a written response to some directive based on the passage. For simplicity, suppose that only a single aspect of performance is extracted, a holistic rating of whether or not the response is both substantively appropriate and satisfactorily constructed. Finally, suppose that student model variables for Reading and Writing are posited to drive the probabilities of this observable variable. Clearly, task features concerning both reading load and writing demand will influence the difficulty of a task in this class, in the sense of, say, proportion of satisfactory performances. But one task with a complex argument that only requires a simple phase for a response, and a second task with a simple passage that demands a formal letter, could be equivalent in this regard. The conditional probabilities for a satisfactory response to the first task would be low until reading skill is fairly high, but insensitive to writing skill once a low threshold is met. The conditional probabilities for a satisfactory response to the second task are a mirror image, low until a fairly high level of writing skill is present but insensitive to reading skill once a threshold is met.

Characterizing Proficiency

What does a value of a student-model variable mean? One way to answer this question is by describing typical performance on various tasks in the domain from students at that level. Another role for task-model variables, then, is to link values of student model variables to expected observable behaviors (Figure 4.13). This role is a corollary of the previous one, which involved modeling the conditional probabilities in evidence models in terms of task model variables. The essential idea is this: Given the values of these task model variables for a given real or hypothetical task, we can calculate expected values of the conditional probability distributions for its observable variables in the Bayes net fragment of a conformable evidence model. We can then predict what we would expect to see in the performance to a given task by a person with a given value of θ. In the context of unidimensional IRT, this interpretive approach has been called "behavioral anchoring" of scale scores.

Example 1, continued. The three-parameter IRT model is used with the GRE CAT. If we know an item's parameters, we can calculate the probability of a correct response from a student with any given θ. We can further give meaning to a value of θ by describing the kinds of items a student at that level is likely to succeed with, and those he is not. To the extent that item features account for item parameters, then, we can describe the student's proficiency in terms of substantive task characteristics and/or cognitively relevant skills. For example, Enright, Morely, and Sheehan (1999) explained about 90% of the variance in item difficulty parameters in a constructed set of GRE Quantitative word problems with the factors (i) problem-type, (ii) complexity, and (iii) number vs. variable. A student with $\theta = -1$ would have about two thirds chances of correctly answering a simple "Total cost=unit cost x units" problem presented in terms of actual numbers; a student with $\theta = 1$ would have a two thirds chance of success with a more complex "distance = rate x time" problem presented in terms of actual numbers; and a student with $\theta = 2.5$ would have about a two thirds chance with a complex cost or distance problem presented in terms of variables.

Example 2, continued. The probability distribution of any observable variable in the HYDRIVE example depends on at least three student-model variables: one for knowledge of the subsystem involved, facility with the expert-level troubleshooting strategy that can be applied, and familiarity with the tests and procedures that apply to the situation. Behavior depends on all three, so how can the idea of behavioral anchoring be applied? One approach is to identify a level of single student-model variable of particular interest and a task in which it is required, then calculate expected response probabilities for the designated level of this special student-model variable,

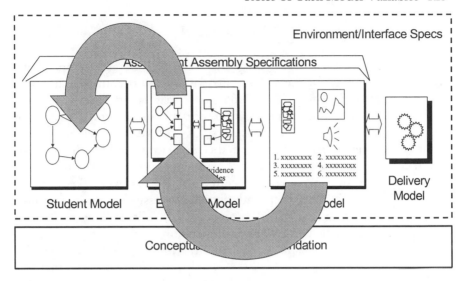

FIG. 4.13. The role of task-model variables in *characterizing proficiency* connects values of student-model variables with expected performance in task situations with specified features, to facilitate users' interpretation of scores and exemplify the theory-driven link between scores and performances.

averaging over the conditional distributions of all the other student-model variables. This is a weak prediction in HYDRIVE, though, because performance depends heavily on the other student-model variables. Even a trainee who understands space-splitting quite well is unlikely to do it on a subsystem he is not familiar with.

One alternative way to anchor a variable in a multivariate model is to give conditional interpretations. For example, being high on space-splitting means a 75% chance of applying this expert strategy *if the examinee is familiar with the subsystem*. A second alternative is to provide descriptions of expected behavior for specified vectors of student-model variables, since the resulting conditional probabilities will specify expectations more tightly. The results are meaningful to the extent that the selected vectors are interpretable profiles (e.g., typical new student, or typical expert on a different aircraft).

One elaboration of behavioral anchoring that might merit special note is the "market basket score." In market basket scoring, we define a reference collection of tasks with a well defined collection of features, as specified through values of task model variables. The student model for the examinee and the evidence models for the reference tasks contain the necessary information to make a prediction for how well the examinee would perform on the reference tasks.

CONCLUSION

Standard procedures for designing and carrying out assessments have worked satisfactorily for the assessments we have all become familiar with over the past half century. Their limits are sorely tested today. The field faces demands for more complex inferences about students, concerning finer grained and interrelated aspects of knowledge and the more complicated conditions under which this knowledge is brought to bear. Advances in technology can provide far richer samples of performances, in increasingly realistic and interactive settings. How can we make sense of this complex data? And even with familiar assessments, cost pressures from continuous testing and social pressures for validity arguments demand more principled assessment designs and operations.

Using terms and concepts from the Portal project, we have outlined a design framework to attack these challenges. We believe that an understanding of the elements and the interrelationships that are needed for evidentiary reasoning in the assessment context provides a foundation for principled task design. We have explored the roles that variables in task models play in constructing tasks, focusing evidence, assembling assessments, characterizing proficiency, and mediating the relationship between task performance and student proficiency. Even with such a framework, successfully designing a complex assessment remains a formidable task. Without one, though, it is almost impossible.

ACKNOWLEDGMENTS

This paper was presented at the conference "Generating items for cognitive tests: Theory and practice," co-sponsored by Educational Testing Service and the United States Air Force Laboratory and held at the Henry Chauncey Conference Center, Educational Testing Service, Princeton, NJ, November 5-6, 1998. The first author's work was supported in part by the Educational Research and Development Centers Program, PR/Award Number R305B60002, as administered by the Office of Educational Research and Improvement, U. S. Department of Education. The findings and opinions expressed in this report do not reflect the positions or policies of the National Institute on Student Achievement, Curriculum, and Assessment, the Office of Educational Research and Improvement, or the U. S. Department of Education.

REFERENCES

Almond, R. G., Mislevy, R. J., Herskovits, E., & Steinberg, L. (1990). Transfer of Information between System and Evidence Models. In D. Heckerman & J. Whittaker (Eds.), *Artificial intelligence and statistics 99* (pp. 181–186). San Francisco: Morgan Kaufmann.

Bejar, I. I. (1990). A generative analysis of a three-dimensional spatial task. *Applied Psychological Measurement, 14,* 237–245.

Berger, M. P. F., & Veerkamp, W. J. J. (1996). A review of selection methods for optimal test design. In G. Engelhard & M. Wilson (Eds.), *Objective measurement: Theory into practice* (Vol. 3, pp. 437–455). Norwood, NJ: Ablex.

Carroll, J. B. (1976). Psychometric tests as cognitive tasks: A new "structure of intellect." In L. B. Resnick (Ed.), *The nature of intelligence* (pp. 27–57). Hillsdale, NJ: Lawrence Erlbaum Associates.

Chaffin, R., & Peirce, L. (1988). *A taxonomy of semantic relations for the classification of GRE analogy items* (Research Report RR-87-50). Princeton, NJ: Educational Testing Service.

Chalifour, C., & Powers, D. E. (1989). The relationship of content characteristics of GRE analytical reasoning items to their difficulties and discriminations. *Journal of Educational Measurement, 26,* 120–132.

Collis, J. M., Tapsfield, P. G. C., Irvine, S. H., Dann, P. L., & Wright, D. (1995). The British Army Recruit Battery goes operational: From theory to practice in computer-based testing using item-generation techniques. *International Journal of Selection and Assessment, 3,* 96–104.

Dennis, I., Collis, J., & Dann, P. (1995, October). Extending the scope of item generation to tests of educational attainment. *Proceedings of the International Military Testing Association, Toronto.*

Embretson, S. E. (1998). A cognitive design system approach to generating valid tests: Application to abstract reasoning. *Psychological Methods, 3,* 380–396.

Enright, M. K., Morely, M., & Sheehan, K. M. 1999). *Items by design: The impact of systematic feature variation on item statistical characteristics.* (GRE Research Report No. 99-15-R). Princeton, NJ: Educational Testing Service.

Enright, M. K., & Sheehan, K. M. (1998, November). *Modeling the difficulty of quantitative reasoning items: Implications for item generation.* Paper presented at the conference "Generating items for cognitive tests: Theory and practice", co-sponsored by Educational Testing Service and the United States Air Force Laboratory, at Educational Testing Service, Princeton, NJ.

Fischer, G. H. (1973). The linear logistic test model as an instrument in educational research. *Acta Psychologica, 37,* 359–374.

Haertel, E. H., & Wiley, D. E. (1993). Representations of ability structures: Implications for testing. In N. Frederiksen, R. J. Mislevy, & I. I. Bejar (Eds.), *Test theory for a new generation of tests* (pp. 359–384). Hillsdale, NJ: Lawrence Erlbaum Associates

Hively, W., Patterson, H. L., & Page, S. H. (1968). A "universe-defined" system of arithmetic achievement tests. *Journal of Educational Measurement, 5,* 275-290.

Irvine, S. H., Dann, P. L., & Anderson, J. D. (1990). Towards a theory of algorithm-determined cognitive test construction. *British Journal of Psychology, 81,* 173–195.

Macready, G. B., & Dayton, C. M. (1989, March). *The application of latent class models in adaptive testing.* Paper presented at the annual meeting of the American Educational Research Association, San Francisco, CA.

Messick, S. (1992). The interplay of evidence and consequences in the validation of performance assessments. *Educational Researcher, 23*(2), 13-23.

Mislevy, R. J., & Gitomer, D. H. (1996). The role of probability-based inference in an intelligent tutoring system. *User-Mediated and User-Adapted Interaction, 5,* 253–282.

Mislevy, R. J., Sheehan, K. M., & Wingersky, M. S. (1993). How to equate tests with little or no data. *Journal of Educational Measurement, 30,* 55–78.

Newell, A., & Simon, H. A. (1972). *Human problem solving.* Englewood Cliffs, NJ: Prentice-Hall.

Scheuneman, J., Gerritz, K., & Embretson, S. (1989, March). *Effects of prose complexity on achievement test item difficulty.* Paper presented at the annual meeting of the American Educational Research Association, San Francisco, CA.

Schum, D. A. (1987). *Evidence and inference for the intelligence analyst.* Lanham, MD: University Press of America.

Schum, D. A. (1994). *The evidential foundations of probabilistic reasoning.* New York: Wiley.

Segall, D. (1996). Multidimensional adaptive testing. *Psychometrika, 61*(2) 331–354.

Steinberg, L. S., & Gitomer, D. G. (1996). Intelligent tutoring and assessment built on an understanding of a technical problem-solving task. *Instructional Science, 24,* 223–258.

Stocking, M. L., & Swanson, L. (1993). A method for severely constrained item selection in adaptive testing. *Applied Psychological Measurement, 17,* 277–292.

van der Linden, W. J. (1997). *Multidimensional adaptive testing with a minimum error-variance criterion* (Research Report 97-03). Enschede, the Netherlands: Department of Educational Measurement and Data Analysis, University of Twente.

Whittaker, J. (1990). *Graphical models in applied multivariate statistics.* New York: Wiley.

5

Modeling the Difficulty of Quantitative Reasoning Items: Implications for Item Generation

Mary K. Enright
Kathleen M. Sheehan
Educational Testing Service

The emergence of cognitive psychology has greatly reduced the separation between the two disciplines of scientific psychology, experimental and correlational, described by Cronbach in 1957. Cognitive psychologists have developed experimental methods to analyze the knowledge and mental processes that underlie performance on many types of items from achievement and aptitude tests (see Pellegrino & Glaser, 1979; Snow & Lohman, 1989). They also have explored which processing abilities are differentially related to levels of performance on tests. Thus the links between performance on assessment tasks and individual variation in knowledge and skills have been more clearly articulated. In turn, this type of analysis can inform item generation as illustrated in many of the chapters in this volume. However, some gaps that remain between experimental and correlational approaches are differences between depth and breath of focus, between our ability to build generative models for small sets of items, and our desire to include varied and unique items in assessments. Tensions exist between cognitive modeling of narrow sets of problems and broadly conceived assessment frameworks, between attention to a part of a system and appreciation of the complexity of the system as a whole.

The research in this chapter reflects these tensions. A series of studies is described in which difficulty modeling is used to clarify the constructs assessed by quantitative items on graduate admissions tests in order to develop a more principled basis for item generation. All of the studies focus on items from the Graduate Record Examinations (GRE) quantitative measure. The progress of this research illustrates the kinds of obstacles that face us in generating and using item variants. The purpose of the GRE quantitative measure is to assess quantitative reasoning skills defined very broadly, while it is easiest to model the difficulty of sets of items defined very narrowly. Therein lies one of the challenges in integrating applied measurement and cognitive psychology.

The motivation for difficulty modeling has become more complex over time and has included construct validation, item generation, pretest sample size reduction, and item classification. Initially, difficulty modeling was utilized as a method of construct representation as described by Embretson (1983) "Construct representation is concerned with identifying the theoretical mechanisms that underlie item responses, such as information processes, strategies, and knowledge stores" (p. 179). Subsequently, Bejar and Yocom (1991) demonstrated that the ability to explain item difficulty underlies the ability to generate items with known difficulty. More recently, methods have been developed that permit the use of collateral information about item features to supplement examinee performance data and allow reliable estimates of items' psychometric characteristics from smaller examinee pretest samples (Mislevy, Sheehan, & Wingersky, 1993). Finally, with the implementation of continuous computer-based testing and the emerging capacity to create item variants (Singley & Bennett, chapter 14, this volume), an augmented item classification system would seem desirable. Difficulty modeling can be used to develop and evaluate alternative classification systems.

Two lines of research are described in the following sections. The first line of investigation began with the analysis of the difficulty of word problems from the GRE quantitative measure. A small scale, correlational study of 20 items had resulted in the identification of a number of features that appeared to be related to item difficulty. A precise accounting of the impact of these features on item difficulty was subsequently developed by creating and pretesting sets of item variants in which the identified features were varied systematically. The second line of research concerns the development and evaluation of an augmented item classification system (a) to describe a larger part of the domain assessed by the GRE quantitative measure, (b) to predict the difficulty of a wider variety of items, and (c) to identify ways to generate item variants systematically.

CREATING SYSTEMATIC VARIANTS OF WORD PROBLEMS

Preliminary Study

Our first investigation in this area was a study of the relationship between item features and item difficulty for a set of 20 word problems from the GRE quantitative measure (Sebrechts, Enright, Bennett, & Martin, 1996). Extended written solutions to these problems had been collected from a sample of 50 college students. To evaluate potential determinants of item difficulty, both equation-based and graphical representations of the mathematical structure underlying each problem were developed. The representations were then coded in terms of features such as the number of elements and operations, the embeddedness of relations, and the number of variables. The problem statement was coded with respect to content and linguistic features. Inspection of the relationships between the coded stimulus features and measures of item difficulty suggested there were three dimensions that might prove useful for understanding performance differences—mathematical complexity, context, and "algebraicness." Complexity was reflected in characteristics of the structural problem representations such as the number of operations, the number of constraints, and the number of levels of parentheses. Context included content features such as time, money, or distance. Finally, *algebraicness* referred to whether or not the problem required the manipulation of variables. Although we had initially considered all 20 problems in our set to be "algebra" word problems, we found that problems that included more than one variable or elementary functions of a single variable were particularly difficult.

Systematic Item Generation

For word problems on many standardized tests, the kinds of item features described earlier are varied unsystematically and on an ad hoc basis so it is difficult to estimate precisely how much any particular feature contributes to variation in performance. In our next study we developed and pretested items that varied systematically on some of these features so that we could better estimate the degree to which different manipulations affected performance.

Design of Word Problems. Two families of related word problems were created. One family consisted of rate problems, the other of probability problems. For each family, a design matrix specified three item features that were crossed with each other to create eight classes of variants within the problem family. Six different items were written for each class yielding 48 variants in each family. All items were presented in a 5-option multiple-choice format.

Family 1: Rate Problems. The structure of rate problems used in this study was based on "round trip" problems in which the distances for two parts of a trip are equal while the time and rate for different parts of the trip vary (cf. Mayer, 1981). This mathematical structure also can be cast in other contexts such as unit cost. Based on the findings of Sebrechts et al. (1996), three item features—complexity, context, and using a variable—were selected for manipulation in the study. Some examples of problems similar to those created for this study are shown in Table 5.1.

The basic structure of these problems can be described in terms of three constraints that can be combined into a simple linear system:

$Rate_1$ x Unit A_1 = Unit B_1

$Rate_2$ x Unit A_2 = Unit B_2

Unit B_1 = Unit B_2

To increase problem complexity an additional constraint or step was added to half of the problems:

Unit A_1 + Unit A_2 = Total Unit A.

Thus the less complex problems (Level 1) were composed of three constraints and the more complex (Level 2) had four constraints. In addition, the problem goal was changed when the fourth constraint was added to make the scenario more plausible. Thus, the less complex problems had a goal of finding Unit A_2, given Unit A_1, $Rate_1$, and $Rate_2$. The more complex problems had givens of Unit A_1, Total Unit A, and $Rate_1$ and goals of finding Unit A_2 and $Rate_2$.

Problem context involved either cost or distance. Finally, to manipulate the algebraic content, one of the elements of the problem was changed from a quantity to a variable—"John bought 6 cans of soda" became "John bought x cans of soda." This latter manipulation led to a problem solution that was an algebraic expression rather than a quantity.

Family 2: Probability Problems. The second family consisted of variants of probability problems. Examples of problems typical of this family are shown in Table 5.2. These problems had three components—determining the number of elements in a set, determining the number of elements in a subset of that set, and calculating the proportion of the whole set that was included in the subset. Given a lack of prior research on these types of problems, hypotheses about the specific features that might affect difficulty were more speculative.

TABLE 5.1
Examples of Rate Items

| | | Item Design Features | |
| | | Use Variable | |
Context	Complexity	No	Yes
Cost	Level 1	Soda that usually costs $6.00 per case is on sale for $4.00 per case. How many cases can Jack buy for the price he usually pays for 6 cases?	Soda that usually costs $6.00 per case is on sale for $4.00 per case. How many cases can Jack buy on sale for the price he usually pays for x cases?
DRT	Level 1	Under normal circumstances, a train travels from City X to City Y in 6 hours at an average speed of 60 miles per hour. When the tracks were being repaired, this train traveled on the same tracks at an average speed of 40 miles per hour. How long did the trip take when the tracks were being repaired?	Under normal circumstances, a train travels from City X to City Y in t hours at an average speed of 60 miles per hour. When the tracks were being repaired, this train traveled on the same tracks at an average speed of 40 miles per hour. How long did the trip take when the tracks were being repaired?
Cost	Level 2	As a promotion, a store sold 90 cases of soda of the 150 cases they had in stock at $4.00 per case. To make a profit, the store needs to bring in the same total amount of money when they sell the remaining cases of soda. At what price must the store sell the remaining cases?	As a promotion, a store sold 90 cases of soda of the x cases they had in stock at $4.00 per case. To make a profit, the store needs to bring in the same total amount of money when they sell the remaining cases of soda. At what price must the store sell the remaining cases?
DRT	Level 2	A round trip by train from City X to City Y took 15 hours. The first half of the trip took 9 hours and the train traveled at an average speed of 40 miles per hour. What was the train's average speed on the return trip?	A round trip by train from City X to City Y took 15 hours. The first half of the trip took t hours and the train traveled at an average speed of 40 miles per hour. What was the train's average speed on the return trip?

Note. These are not items that actually were used in this study.

TABLE 5.2
Examples of Probability Items

Item Design Features

| Context 1 | Context 2 | Complexity | |
		Level 1	Level 2
Percent	Real	Parking stickers for employees' cars at a certain company are numbered consecutively from 100 to 999. Stickers from 200 to 399 are assigned to the sales department. What percent of the parking stickers are assigned to the sales department ?	Parking stickers for employees' cars at a certain company are numbered consecutively from 100 to 999. Stickers that begin with the digits 2 or 3 are assigned to the sales department. Stickers that end with the digits 8 or 9 belong to managers. What percent of the parking stickers are assigned to managers in the sales department ?
Percent	Pure	What percent of the integers between 100 and 999, inclusive, are between 200 and 399, inclusive?	What percent of the integers between 100 and 999, inclusive, begin with the digits 2 or 3 and end with the digits 8 or 9?
Probability	Real	Parking stickers for employees' cars at a certain company are numbered consecutively from 100 to 999. Stickers from 200 to 399 are assigned to the sales department. If a parking sticker is chosen at random what is the probability that it will belong to the sales department ?	Parking stickers for employees' cars at a certain company are numbered consecutively from 100 to 999. Stickers that begin with the digits 2 or 3 are assigned to the sales department. Stickers that end with the digits 8 or 9 belong to managers. If a parking sticker is chosen at random what is the probability that it will belong to a manager in the sales department ?
Probability	Pure	If a integer is chosen at random from the integers between 100 and 999, inclusive, what is the probability that the chosen integer will be between 200 and 399 inclusive?	If an integer is chosen at random from between 100 and 999, inclusive, what is the probability that the chosen integer will begin with the digits 2 or 3 and end with the digits 8 or 9?

Note. These are not items that actually were used in this study.

First, we decided to vary the complexity of counting the elements in the subset. The set always consisted of a number of integers within a given range. Examples of how the difficulty of the subset counting task was varied are described below:

Complexity Level 1	Complexity Level 2
Numbers in a smaller range	Numbers beginning with certain digits and ending with certain digits
Numbers ending with a certain digit	Numbers beginning with certain digits and ending with odd digits
Numbers with 3 digits the same	Numbers with 2 or 3 digits equal to 1

Second, we suspected that items cast as probability problems would be more difficult than items cast as percent problems. And third, we varied whether the cover story involved a real-life context (phone extensions, room numbers) or simply referred to sets of integers. Although this latter feature (real vs. pure) is a part of the specifications used to assemble test forms, we did not have a clear sense of how it might affect difficulty for these kinds of problems.

Data Collection and Calibration. Each variant was assigned to one of 24 different GRE pretest sections according to a design in which each section received at most one Cost problem, one DRT problem, one Percent problem and one Probability problem. Following standard test assembly conventions, items within a section were ordered according to test developers' estimates of item difficulty. The resulting pretest data was calibrated using a three parameter logistic Item Response Theory (IRT) model, estimated with the BILOG program (Mislevy & Bock, 1982). The resulting IRT parameter estimates characterize each item in terms of its difficulty, discrimination, and susceptibility to correct response through guessing.

Data Analysis. The impact of different item feature manipulations was investigated by using a tree-based regression technique to model item difficulty.[1] Like classical regression models, tree-based regression models provide a rule for estimating the value of a response variable (y), from a set of classification or predictor variables (x). In the particular application

---

[1] Tree-based techniques are often referred to as CART techniques, after the popular software product described in Breiman, Friedman, Olshen, and Stone (1984). The tree-based algorithm employed in the current analyses is described in Clark and Pregibon (1992).

described here, y is an (n X 1) vector of item difficulty estimates, and x is an (n X k) matrix of item feature classifications. As in the classical regression setting, tree-based prediction rules provide the expected value of the response for clusters of observations having similar values of the predictor variables. Clusters are formed by successively splitting the data, on the basis of the feature classification variables, into increasingly homogeneous subsets called nodes. A locally optimal sequence of splits is selected by using a recursive partitioning algorithm to evaluate all possible splits of all possible predictor variables at each stage of the analysis (Brieman, Friedman, Olshen, & Stone, 1984). Potential splits are evaluated in terms of deviance, a measure of the total difficulty variation calculated for the subset of items assigned to a particular node. At each stage of splitting, the original item subset is referred to as the parent node and the two outcome subsets are referred to as the left and right child nodes. The best split is the one that produces the largest decrease between the deviance of the parent node and the sum of the deviances in the two child nodes. The deviance of the parent node is calculated as the sum of the deviances of all of its members,

$$D(y, \hat{y}) = \Sigma(y_i - \hat{y})^2$$

where $\hat{y}$ is the mean value of item difficulty calculated from all of the items in the node. The deviance of a potential split is calculated as

$$D_{split}(y, \hat{y}_L, \hat{y}_R) = \sum_L (y_i - \hat{y}_L)^2 + \sum_R (y_i - \hat{y}_R)^2$$

where $\hat{y}_L$ is the mean value of item difficulty in the left child node and $\hat{y}_R$ is the mean value of item difficulty in the right child node. The split that maximizes the change in deviance

$$\Delta D = D(y, \hat{y}) - D_{split}(y, \hat{y}_L, \hat{y}_R)$$

is the split chosen at any given node. After each split is defined, the mean value of item difficulty within each offspring node is taken as the predicted value of item difficulty for each of the items in the node. The more homogeneous the node, the more accurate the prediction.

The resulting node definitions characterize the impact of specific item feature manipulations on item difficulty. This characterization can be corroborated by implementing the following procedure. First, the estimated tree structure is reexpressed as a linear combination of binary-coded indicator variables. Second, the indicator variable model is subjected to a classical least squares regression analysis. The resulting probabilities indicate the statistical significance of each split shown in the tree.

Results for Rate Problems. The IRT parameter estimates obtained for the 48 Rate problems are summarized in Table 5.3. The impact of each feature manipulation on resulting item difficulty is shown in Figure 5.1. The statistical significance of each split is provided in Table 5.4. As can be seen, all of the splits are highly significant and account for about 90% of the observed variation in item difficulty.

Detailed information about the impact of specific feature manipulations can be obtained by considering the individual splits shown in Figure 5.1. In this particular display each node is plotted at a horizontal location determined from its estimated difficulty value and a vertical location determined from its estimated deviance value. The item features selected to define each split are listed on the edges connecting parents to offspring. The number of items assigned to each node is plotted as the node label. The resulting display illustrates how specific manipulations lead to subsequent performance differences.

The tree begins with 48 items in the root node. The first split is defined in terms of the "Use Variable" manipulation. The 24 variants that did not require students to use variables are routed down the left branch and the 24 variants that did require students to use variables are routed down the right branch. The 24 variants routed down the left branch (UseVar = No) have an average difficulty of -1.49 (*SD* = 1.30). The 24 variants routed down the right branch (UseVar = Yes) have an average difficulty of .87 (*SD* = .63). Thus, items that required examinees to use variables were more difficult than those that did not by a large margin. The significance of this result can be seen both in the tree and in the table of least squares regression estimates given in Table 5.4. As shown in the tree, the UseVar split produced the largest decrease in deviance. As shown in the table, the UseVar effect produced the largest coefficient.

Looking further at the tree depicted in Figure 5.1, we see that, among the subset of rate problems that did not require operations on variables (UseVar = No), the 12 items with a Cost Context were significantly easier (*M* = -2.47, *SD* = .87) than the 12 items with a DRT Context (*M* = -.51, *SD* = .85). However, among the subset of problems that did require operations on variables, the 12 Cost items and the 12 DRT items were equally difficult. This interaction suggests that (a) many lower performing students employed context-sensitive solution strategies to solve the nonalgebraic problems, but (b) few higher performing students relied on context clues when attempting to solve the algebraic problems.

TABLE 5.3
IRT Item Parameters for Rate Problems With Differing Item Design Features

Item Features				IRT Parameters		
Use Variable	Complexity	Context		a	b	c
Yes	Level 2	DRT	M	.98	1.50	.24
			SD	.28	.30	.03
Yes	Level 2	Cost	M	1.03	1.15	.30
			SD	.25	.38	.06
Yes	Level 1	DRT	M	.77	.53	.27
			SD	.22	.42	.04
Yes	Level 1	Cost	M	.67	.29	.27
			SD	.18	.56	.03
No	Level 2	DRT	M	.82	.13	.24
			SD	.03	.25	.04
No	Level 2	Cost	M	.47	-1.84	.22
			SD	.14	.63	.01
No	Level 1	DRT	M	.75	-1.16	.21
			SD	.15	.72	.02
No	Level 1	Cost	M	.46	-3.09	.22
			SD	.13	.57	.01

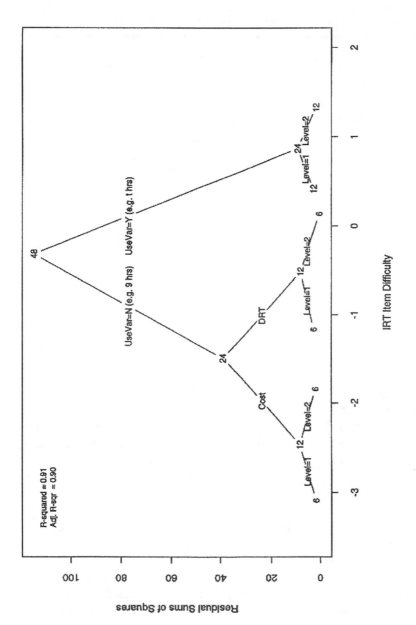

FIG. 5.1. Estimated regression tree for item difficulty for rate problem variants. Nodes are plotted as a function of the mean difficulty of items within the cluster and the sum of squares for items within the cluster.

TABLE 5.4
Regression of Experimental Item Features on IRT Item Difficulty For 48 Rate Variants

Effect	Coefficient
Intercept	-3.01***
Cost/DRT	-
Complexity	1.09***
No variable and DRT	
	1.95***
RMSE	.50
R²	.91
Adj. R²	.90

*** $p < .001$, ** $p <. 01$, * $p < .05$

To appreciate the significance of this result it is also useful to consider the effect of the Complexity manipulation. As noted previously, problem complexity was varied by adding an additional step to half of the problems. Thus, the solution process for items classified as Complexity Level = 2 involved one more step than the solution process for items classified as Complexity Level = 1. As shown in the tree, this additional step contributed to additional difficulty among all four types of problems: the nonalgebraic Cost problems, the nonalgebraic DRT problems, the algebraic Cost problems and the algebraic DRT problems. Note, however, among nonalgebraic items, the difficulty increment resulting from the Complexity manipulation is much smaller than the difficulty increment resulting from the Context manipulation. This suggests that changing the cover story of a nonalgebraic word problem will have more of an effect on the performance characteristics of the item than would changing the item's underlying mathematical structure.

The detailed information about item functioning embodied in a tree-based regression model can also be used to evaluate alternative instructional strategies. The relative positions of the terminal nodes in Figure 5.1 indicate that there were many GRE examinees who were able to solve the *more complex* nonalgebraic Cost problems but, at the same time, were *not* able to solve the *less complex* nonalgebraic DRT problems. This finding has implications for instruction because it indicates that many lower performing students were unaware of the fact that the Cost problems and the DRT problems required the *exact same* solution processes. This suggests that instructional interventions designed to acquaint students with the many structural similarities that exist between Cost problems and DRT problems may prove effective.

Results for Probability Problems. The IRT parameter estimates obtained for the Probability problems are summarized in Table 5.5. Only 44 values are listed because four of the original 48 problems turned out to be too difficult for the GRE population and therefore, were not analyzed further. The tree-based analysis of the remaining 44 items is illustrated in Figure 5.2. The significance of each split is listed in Table 5.6. Overall, the features manipulated in the study accounted for 61% of the observed variation in item difficulty.

Among the 44 Probability variants, the manipulation that had the greatest impact on item difficulty involved varying the complexity of the counting subtask. The 24 items that required a less complex counting subtask ($M = .22$, $SD = .55$) were easier than the 20 items that required a more complex counting subtask ($M = 1.51$, $SD = .59$).

For probability problems at both complexity levels, the 22 items that were cast as probability problems ($M = .98$, $SD = .78$) were slightly more difficult than the 22 that were cast as percent problems ($M = .64$, $SD = .92$). However, the difficulty of items with real cover stories did not differ substantially from similarly configured items with pure cover stories.

Summary. Two families of item variants were created and pretested to assess the impact of selected item features on item difficulty. The attempt to systematically manipulate difficulty was extremely successful for rate problems and moderately successful for probability problems. For rate problems, all of the features manipulated affected difficulty and these manipulations accounted for 90% of the variance in difficulty in the set of problems. This set of items covered a wide difficulty range. One manipulation in particular, using a variable, was very powerful. This manipulation can be thought of as changing a multistep arithmetic word problem into a multistep algebra word problem. In addition, there was a large interaction between context and using a variable. For easier items that did not involve the use of a variable, cost problems were easier than DRT problems. However, for algebraic problems that did involve the use of a variable, problem context had no discernible effect. This suggests that some aspects of context may facilitate or impede problem solution among lower performing examinees but not among higher performing examinees. The context effect also suggests that many lower performing examinees failed to recognize the mathematical similarities that exist between nonalgebraic Cost problems and nonalgebraic DRT problems. This result has important

TABLE 5.5
IRT Item Parameters for Probability Problems With Differing Item Design Features

Item Features			IRT Parameters		
Complexity	Context 1	Context 2		a	b	c
Level 2	Probability	Real	M^a	.89	1.70	.21
			SD	.13	.53	.06
Level 2	Probability	Pure	M^a	1.02	1.60	.23
			SD	.20	.29	.06
Level 2	Percent	Real	M^a	.89	1.62	.22
			SD	.36	.86	.05
Level 2	Percent	Pure	M^a	.88	1.14	.23
			SD	.15	.54	.07
Level 1	Probability	Real	M	.96	.37	.20
			SD	.13	.55	.06
Level 1	Probability	Pure	M	.95	.48	.20
			SD	.16	.53	.05
Level 1	Percent	Real	M	.84	-.05	.20
			SD	.12	.53	.04
Level 1	Percent	Pure	M	.91	.09	.08
			SD	.13	.53	.04

[a] $n = 5$, otherwise $n = 6$

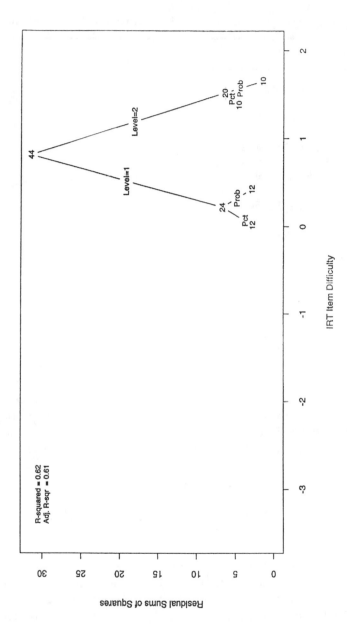

FIG. 5.2. Estimated regression tree for item difficulty for probability problem variants. Nodes are plotted as a function of the mean difficulty of items within the cluster and the sum of squares for items within the cluster.

TABLE 5.6
Regression of Experimental Item Features on IRT DifficultyFor 44 Probability Variants

Effect	Coefficient
Intercept	.05
Complexity	1.29***
Percent/Probability	.34*
Real/Pure	-
RMSE	.54
R^2	.62
Adj. R^2	.61

*** $p < .001$, ** $p < .01$, * $p < .05$

implications for instructional design because it suggests that DRT performance might be enhanced by helping students to translate their knowledge of how Cost problems are solved to the DRT domain.

In contrast with the rate problems, the probability problems were more difficult and covered a narrower difficulty range. Increasing the complexity of the counting task had the greatest impact on difficulty. One aspect of context, whether the problem was cast as a percent or probability problem, did affect difficulty but another, whether or not the problem had a real-life context, did not. However, the context interaction for the rate problems serves as a reminder not to dismiss the possibility that a real-life versus pure context contrast may be an important feature for less difficult items.

MODELING THE DIFFICULTY OF QUANTITATIVE ITEM POOLS

Although our item-generation study was highly successful as an experiment, it was much less so in practical terms. Some of the limitations apparent from a test development point of view were that (a) we created too many problems that looked like each other, and (b) the types of problems considered represent only a very small proportion of typical computer adaptive test (CAT) item pools. For example, in a sample of about 340 arithmetic and algebra items in two GRE CAT pools only 4% were classified as probability problems and 2% as rate problems.

These kinds of concerns inspired us to turn our attention to a broader sample of items and to use difficulty modeling (a) to explore the composition of item pools, (b) to determine if the kinds of features we found predictive of the difficulty of word problems were useful in predicting the difficulty of other types of items, and (c) to identify other features that might be used to systematically generate item variants.

We had two goals in mind in developing these difficulty models. The first was pragmatic—to determine the extent to which current item classification data or easily collected additional information could be used to predict item difficulty and, potentially, to reduce pretest sample size. The second goal was to augment the item classification system so that it would be more descriptive of the constructs assessed by the test and provide a basis for construct-driven item generation.

Models Using the Current Item Classification System

At present, items for the GRE quantitative measure are classified in terms of (a) general mathematical content, (b) format, (c) context, and (d) detailed mathematical content. This system was developed to describe the content domain of the test and to maintain comparability of test forms. The general content categories are arithmetic, algebra, geometry, and data analysis. The format categories are problem solving—items including five multiple-choice answers, and quantitative comparisons—items that have a fixed response format in which the examinee has to compare two expressions or statements and decide if one is greater than the other, if they are equal, or if there is not enough information to decide. The context refers to whether the item is cast in purely mathematical terms or in an everyday scenario. The detailed content classification is based on a list of approximately 70 descriptors such as "computation with fractions," "rate," "systems of equations." Only one detailed content code is assigned to an item.

Model I. To evaluate the usefulness of existing item classification information for predicting item difficulty, an empirical model was developed for a GRE quantitative CAT pool that included 339 items. The model was then cross-validated on a second pool that included 368 items. In the initial step of the analysis, a tree-based regression model was used to select a subset of 30 promising predictors. Subsequently, the "leaps" algorithm (Furnival & Wilson, 1974) was used to evaluate all possible subsets of that subset. After considering thousands of combinations of the available classification variables, only 15% of the variation in item difficulty could be accounted for.

Subsequently, a cognitive skill level classification was added to the list of item features considered. This skill level classification is routinely used to classify SAT I quantitative items and has been shown to be useful for predicting difficulty in that context. It is defined to have three levels, as follows:

1. Procedural Knowledge—Items in this category test recall of basic mathematical facts, the application of standard algorithms, and the solution of routine problems. The questions in this category are usually straightforward. That is, the examinee does NOT have to choose between alternative solution strategies.
2. Conceptual Understanding—Items in this category test comprehension of specific mathematical ideas or concepts. In most cases, the student must not only decide what to do, but also how to do it.
3. Higher Order Thinking—Items in this category test the ability to solve nonroutine mathematical problems using insight, reasoning, or analysis. Items in this category involve carrying out self-determined sequences of steps, evaluating generalizations, or drawing inferences about data sufficiency.

This new feature was coded for all of the items in both CAT pools. A tree-based analysis of the resulting classification data indicated that the cognitive skill level classification was highly correlated with item difficulty, accounting for approximately 20% of the observed variation in difficulty in both pools. A difficulty prediction model was developed that included the cognitive skill level feature in addition to existing item classification information. The results of this analysis are presented in Table 5.7. The model included the following kinds of features:

1. Specific content—items classified as computation with integers or with decimals and fractions or as linear inequalities were among the easier items; those classified as probability, percent change, and percent of percent were more difficult.
2. Cognitive skill level—procedural items were relatively easy, although procedural items with an applied (real) context were more difficult that those with a pure context. Higher order thinking items were the most difficult.
3. Format—quantitative comparison items for which there was enough information to determine if two quantities were equal or not were comparatively easy
4. General content—data analysis items were relatively easy, algebra items were more difficult.

This initial empirical model was developed to see how much information about item difficulty could be extracted from existing or readily collected item classification data. It identifies some classes of items that are particularly easy or difficult for the population of examines taking these tests but the major predictor of difficulty, cognitive skill level, like item

TABLE 5.7

Regression of Current Item Classification Features and Skill Level Features on IRT
Difficulty for Two Item Pools

Effect	Regression Statistics and Coefficients	
	Pool CP5 (n = 339)	Pool CP6 (n = 368)
Intercept	.36**	.32**
Specific Content		
Computation with Integers	-1.16***	-.66**
Comp. with Decimals/Fractions	-.57**	-.50**
Linear Inequality	-.84*	-.26
Probability	.56	.69
Percent	.43	.69*
Skill Level		
Procedural	-.81***	-.51***
Higher Order	.60***	.86***
Applied Procedural	-.52*	-1.22***
General Content		
Data Analysis	-.49**	-.35*
Algebra	.33*	.13
Quantitative Comparison –		
sufficient information	-.55***	-.48***
RMSE	.99	.96
R^2	.36	.37
Cross Validated R^2	.32	.32

*** $p < .001$, ** $p < .01$, * $p < .05$

writers' estimates of difficulty, is not very informative about item features
that might be used to systematically generate item variants.

Alternative Models

Currently, we are investigating the contribution of other kinds of item
features to item difficulty by expanding the item classification system. We
are focusing on only arithmetic and algebra items because data analysis and
geometry items often include tables and figures. A number of
considerations contributed to initial feature selection decisions. One
consideration was that we wanted features that were "articulate" in that they
might be suggestive of how item variants might be created in systematic
ways. We also wanted features that could be related to what we know about
how people solve problems and that would be more informative about
sources of item difficulty such as complexity, the kinds of reasoning
involved, or the level of mathematical knowledge needed. We planned to
use tree-based methods to develop our model because of their power in
identifying important interactions among features. We expected that
different sets of features would affect the difficulty of different types of

problems. However, we were not sure about what might be useful initial categories for dividing the pool of items into subcategories. One possibility was the procedural/conceptual/higher order distinction that had been astrong predictor of difficulty in the initial model. Another was word/nonword problems, a feature that is not included in the current classification system. On the one hand, we thought that the difficulty of word problems would be related to "complexity" or how much information the examinee had to integrate into a model of the problem situation. On the other hand, we thought that the difficulty of nonword problems was more likely to be related to the kind of procedural knowledge (e.g., arithmetic, linear algebra, nonlinear algebra) required.

The development of the MATH-TCA (Singley & Bennett, chap. 14, this volume) as well as our previous studies of word problems suggested that a description of items in terms of a set of constraints necessary to solve them might provide a basis for a coding system. Therefore we attempted to represent the 172 arithmetic and algebra problems from one pool in terms of a set of constraints that would be sufficient to solve them. We found we could readily devise these constraint-based representations for 154 of the items. In addition, we coded many features that were characteristic of the constraints and the elements in the constraints, such as their origin. For example, constraints were coded as to mathematical characteristics such as arithmetic, linear, nonlinear, or inequality. Elements were coded as to whether they were integers, fractions/decimals, or variables. A distinction was made between items with solutions expressed as quantities and items with solutions that were mathematical expressions, logical justifications, or indeterminate. The usefulness of various approaches to solving a problem such as computation, logical reasoning, estimation, or plugging in answer options was also coded. Finally a distinction was made between word and nonword problems. In nonword problems, constraints are presented in mathematically explicit form, whereas in word problems the constraints are implicit, that is, they must be constructed from background knowledge such as "Distance = Rate x Time."

Model II. The additional codes for 154 arithmetic and algebra items were added to our database and a model to predict the difficulty of these items was developed using tree-based regression. A model that accounted for about 34% of the variation in difficulty is illustrated in Figure 5.3. Again in this figure, each node is plotted at a horizontal location determined from its estimated difficulty value and a vertical location from its estimated deviance value. The first split distinguishes between items classified as procedural and those classified as conceptual or higher order. Subsequent splits among the procedural items indicate that the most difficult items in this subset are those that require processing of a nonlinear constraint. For procedural

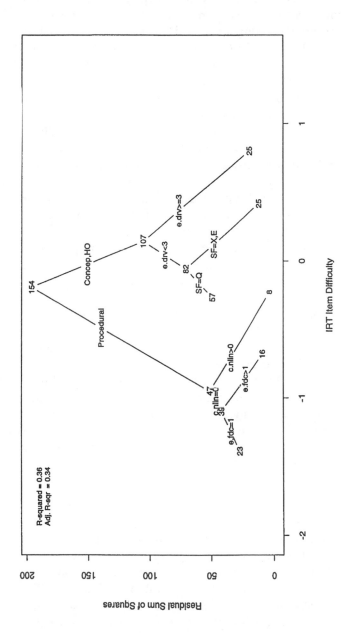

FIG. 5.3. Model II. Estimated regression tree for item difficulty for arithmetic and algebra item from one CAT pool. Nodes are plotted as a function of the mean difficulty of items within a cluster and the percent of variance explained as variables are entered into the model.

items with no nonlinear constraints, the number of fractions and decimals in the problem statement was associated with difficulty. For conceptual and higher order problems, problem complexity and the form of the problem solution affected difficulty. Problems that involved three or more computational steps were the most difficult. For those that involved less than three steps, items whose solutions were a quantity rather than an expression or logical conclusion were easier. Note that the item features that predicted the difficulty of the conceptual/higher order items are very similar to those that were useful in manipulating the difficulty of GRE item variants as previously described. We also explored a model in which the first split was between word and nonword problems, but the results were not very promising.

Encouraged by these results, we applied the coding system to a set of 171 arithmetic and algebra items from a second pool to cross-validate the results. We were able to code 163 of these items. However, preliminary inspection of the data suggested that the difficulty model for the first pool would not be a good predictor of difficulty in the second pool. We suspected that part of the problem was a difference in the type of word problem that appeared in the two pools. One thing we had noticed as we coded items in the second pool was that the items that were most difficult to code were word problems that did not have an everyday context. Rather, they concerned the properties of numbers or mathematical functions. Fourteen of the 20 items that weren't coded in the first pool were of this type. Furthermore there were more of these items in the second pool than in the first. (However, we actually coded constraints for more of these items in the second pool.) Therefore we added another feature, problem type, to the database. This feature had four categories:

1. nonword/numeric
2. nonword/algebraic
3. word/real
4. word/pure

Examples of items in each of these classes are found in Figures 5.4 through 5.7. The major difference between nonword (Figures 5.4 & 5.5) and word problems (Figures 5.6 & 5.7) is that the mathematical operations and relationships among elements are specified using symbols such as +, /, *, - < >. Many nonword problems do contain some words but most of the constraints have symbolic operators. On the other hand problems classified as word problems either do not have the operations and relations explicitly stated or they are stated in words. Numeric (Figure 5.4) and algebraic (Figure 5.5) nonword items differ in whether they include "variables" (i.e., letters instead of numbers) or not. Real word problems (Figure 5.6) have

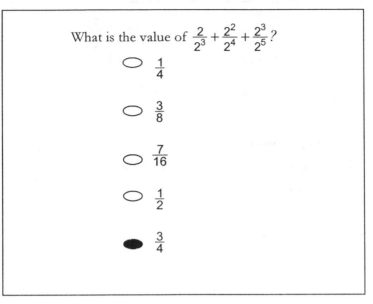

FIG. 5.4. A moderately easy numeric, nonword problem in the problem solving format.

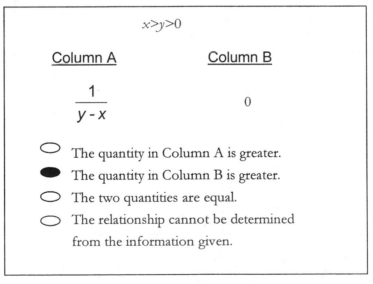

FIG. 5.5. A moderately easy algebraic nonword problem in a quantitative comparison format

Column A

Column B

The percent increase of a price
that was raised from $60 to $80

The percent decrease of a
price that was reduced
from $80 to $60

● The quantity in Column A is greater.

○ The quantity in Column B is greater.

○ The two quantities are equal.

○ The relationship cannot be determined
from the information given.

FIG. 5.6 .A real word problem of average difficulty.

If p is a prime number greater than 11, and p is the sum of the
two prime numbers x and y, then x could be which of the
following

● 2

○ 5

○ 7

○ 9

○ 13

FIG. 5.7. A fairly difficult pure word problem.

some kind of real world or everyday context while pure word problems (Figure 5.7) are about properties of numbers or mathematical functions with no real world context.

The mean difficulty of items in each of these classes for item pools CP5 and CP6 are presented in Table 5.8. The nonword arithmetic items were the easiest, the pure word problems were the most difficult and the nonword algebra and real word problems were of intermediate difficulty. These effects were consistent in the two pools. The mean difficulty of items within each category was similar for the two pools. However, as noted earlier, pool CP6 had more pure word problems than did pool CP5. Although this problem classification did not predict difficulty as well as the cognitive skill level classification ($R^2 = .10$ vs. $R^2 = .20$), it provides a basis for a more articulate model of item difficulty that can be used to relate item features to the knowledge, skills, and strategies that examinees used to solve them as well as to identify potential ways to manipulate item difficulty within classes. Therefore we identified features that predicted difficulty within the four classes of items and integrated this information into a regression model.

Model III. Our third and most current model is illustrated in Figure 5.8 for the two pools combined. The first split indicates that nonword problems are slightly easier than word problems. The second split illustrates the differences between arithmetic and algebra nonword problems and real and pure word problems. The third level of splits illustrates how different

TABLE 5.8
Mean Difficulty of Arithmetic and Algebra Problems in Four Problem Classes

| | | Problem Class | | | | |
| | | Nonword | | Word | | |
POOL		Arith	Algebra	Real	Pure	All Items
CP5	Difficulty M	-0.84	0.02	0.10	0.39	-0.11
	SD	1.27	0.83	1.26	0.83	1.13
	n	40	65	42	25	172
CP6	Difficulty M	-0.62	0.07	-0.04	0.30	-0.03
	SD	1.13	0.77	1.21	1.13	1.06
	n	34	66	31	40	171
CP5 & CP6	Difficulty M	-0.74	0.05	0.04	0.33	-0.07
	SD	1.20	0.79	1.23	1.02	1.10
	n	74	131	73	65	343

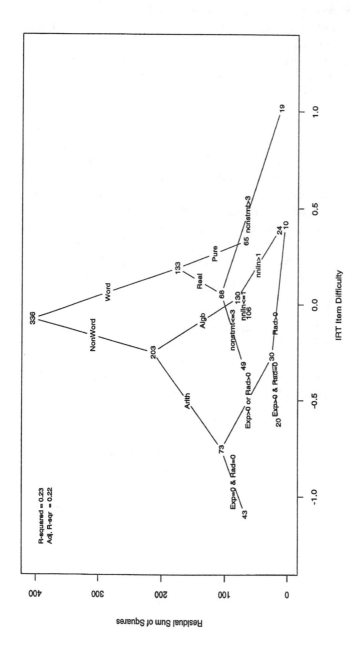

FIG. 5.8. Model III. Estimated regression tree for item difficulty for arithmetic and algebra item from two CAT pools. Nodes are plotted as a function of the mean difficulty of items within the cluster and the sum of squares for items within the cluster.

sets of features affect difficulty within the four problem classes of Level 2. For nonword arithmetic problems, types of arithmetic operations affect difficulty. The most difficult items are those that involve computations with radicals, the next most difficult include exponents, whereas the easiest items include neither exponents nor radicals. The difficulty of the nonword algebra problems was related to the number of nonlinear constraints. Those with two or more nonlinear constraints were most difficult. Among the real word problems, complexity as measured by the total number of constraints was related to difficulty. Items with more than three constraints were particularly difficult. Finally, none of the features in our set were associated with difficulty for pure word problems. In fact we were unable to code many of these items in terms of the set of features we were using. Pure word problems represent a very heterogeneous group of items that were not amenable to the way we approached item classification.

A cross-validated regression model that includes these interactions as well as main effects related to item format and cognitive skill level is presented in Table 5.9. When the models are estimated on one pool and applied to the other the amount of variance in difficulty explained is about 30%. Although this does not represent an improvement in the degree to which we can predict difficulty, we believe that this model is more

TABLE 5.9
Regression of New Item Classification Features on IRT Difficulty
for Arithmetic and Algebra Items from Two Pools

Effect	Regression Statistics and Coefficients	
	Pool CP5 (n = 166)	Pool CP6 (n = 170)
Intercept	-0.16	0.166
Nonword Arithmetic Problems		
With exponents but no radicals	-0.02	0.68*
With radicals	0.72	1.47**
Nonword Algebra Problems		
1 or no nonlinear constraints	0.36	0.66***
Nonlinear constraints > 1	0.98**	0.80**
Realword Problems with more than 3 constraints	1.29***	1.02**
Pureword Problems	0.56*	0.46*
Regular Quantitative Comparison Problems	-0.40**	-0.56***
Skill Level		
Procedural	-0.70***	-0.65***
Higher Order	0.57*	0.77**
RMSE	.91	.87
R^2	.39	.37
Cross Validated R^2	.31	.33

$*** p < .001, ** p < .01, * p < .0$

interpretable and has more potential for suggesting how to create item variants systematically. However, this model is not final. Rather it is a stage along the path to identifying smaller subclasses of items and the features that control difficulty within these subclasses.

DISCUSSION

There are a number of ways that one can expect to generate items with good estimates of item operating characteristics. One is to rely on item writers' judgments, a second is to create only close variants that inherit estimates from parent items, and a third is to generate items in accord with principles that specify how the manipulation of various features will affect item operating characteristics. The first two approaches can be implemented readily. The third approach will require more effort, particularly when applied to a large pool of diverse items, but will have greater benefits and more applications in the long term.

We have explored alternative models of item pools based on the relationship of various classification schemes to item difficulty. At present, the best predictors of item difficulty are global, undifferentiated features such as test developers' estimates of difficulty or judgments of the level of cognitive skills required. However, other criteria that can be used to evaluate these models include the usefulness of the classification system for generating item variants, and the relationship of item features to variation in the knowledge and processes needed to solve the items. We are making progress in developing models based on specific item features that will be useful for these latter purposes.

The area in which this research can make its most important contribution at present is in describing the domain of quantitative reasoning as it is currently assessed on the GRE quantitative measure. This measure has evolved over a long period of time and the constructs assessed are implicit. Our approach to articulating the constructs assessed has been to decompose the broad domain by identifying subclasses of items that are likely to require different kinds of knowledge and solution processes. We believe that we will be able to model difficulty within these subclasses and use these models for item generation. However, these item subclasses also provide us with a map of the domain as it is currently being assessed. This domain map is useful is because it allows us to ask questions about how we should integrate the item-generation capabilities into existing assessments in a thoughtful manner. Undoubtedly, we are going to find that it is easier and more economical to generate variants for some classes of items than for others. Therefore we need to evaluate the impact these emerging capabilities may have on the system of constructs assessed by the current test and whether these changes are desirable or not. An undesirable consequence would be to restrict the kinds of skills assessed because it's easier to automatically generate some types of problems than others. A desirable consequence would be to make test design specifications more explicit about the skills, processes, and strategies that are being assessed and to link these specifications to item difficulty.

If we are serious about trying to generate variants for operational tests then we need to understand how what we are doing fits into the existing system, what the effects that creating variants might have on that system, and how the system might best be changed to use variants effectively.

ACKNOWLEDGMENTS

This research was supported by the Graduate Record Examinations Board and by Educational Testing Service. We also wish to acknowledge major contributions by Mary Morley and Adisack Nhouyvanisvong.

REFERENCES

Bejar, I. I., & Yocom, P. (1991). A generative approach to the modeling of isomorphic hidden-figure items. *Applied Psychological Measurement, 15*(2), 129–137.

Brieman, L., Friedman, J. H., Olshen, R., & Stone, C. J. (1984). *Classification and regression trees.* Belmont, CA: Wadsworth International Group.

Clark, L. A., & Pregibon, D. (1992). Tree-based models. In J. M. Chambers & T. J. Hastie (Eds.), *Statistical Models in S* (pp. 337–419). Pacific Grove, CA: Wadsworth.

Cronbach, L. J. (1957). The two disciplines of scientific psychology. *American Psychologist, 12*, 671–684.

Embretson, S. (1983). Construct validity: Construct representation versus nomothetic span. *Psychological Bulletin, 93*(1), 179–197.

Furnival, G. M., & Wilson, R. W. (1974). Regressions by leaps and bounds. *Technometrics, 16*, 499–511.

Mayer, R. E. (1981). Frequency norms and structural analysis of algebra story problems into families, categories, and templates. *Instructional Science, 10*, 135–175.

Mislevy, R. J., & Bock, R. D. (1982). *Maximum likelihood item analysis and test scoring with binary logistic models.* Mooresville, IN: Scientific Software.

Mislevy, R. J., Sheehan, K. M., & Wingersky, M. (1993). How to equate tests with little or no data. *Journal of Educational Measurement, 30*(1), 55–78.

Pellegrino, J. W., & Glaser, R. (1979). Cognitive correlates and components in the analysis of individual differences. In R. J. Sternberg & D. K. Detterman (Eds.), *Human intelligence: Perspectives on its theory and measurement* (pp. 61–88). Norwood, NJ: Ablex.

Sebrechts, M. M., Enright, M., Bennett, R. E., & Martin, K. (1996). Using algebra word-problems to assess quantitative ability: Attributes, strategies, and errors. *Cognition and Instruction, 14*(3), 285–343.

Snow, R. E., & Lohman, D. F. (1989). Implications of cognitive psychology for educational measurement. In R. L. Linn (Ed.), *Educational measurement* (3rd ed., pp. 263–331). New York: Macmillan.

6

Item-Generation Models for Higher Order Cognitive Functions

Lutz F. Hornke
Aachen University of Technology

Many research questions and good research programs start with a conflict of ideas, views, and approaches. In the 1970s I, as a student, had the following conversation with my mentor LJC (Lee J. Cronbach):

> LFH: I am thinking that within a computer-based training environment it will be possible to base items strictly on their content and cognitive structure so that at least some day they may be computer generated.
> LJC: Item writing is an art!
> LFH: That shouldn't have to be true, because we should be able to incorporate all of our sound psychological knowledge into designing an item. Items should be based on theory and constructs derived from this theory. Finally any tested behavior will have to be traced back to exactly these constructs and theories!

I was a bit prejudiced, in part, by a book written by John Bormuth (1970), entitled On the Theory of Achievement Test Items that appeared two years prior to the foregoing conversation had influenced me. Bormuth wrote:

> . . . that the current procedures for constructing achievement tests are too primitive to permit achievement tests to satisfy modern demands in anything approaching the rigorous manner required [LFH: public policy and decision making]. The problem arises from the fact that, in the final analysis, the concepts and procedures traditionally employed in the construction of achievement test items are defined wholly in the private subjective life of the test writer, which makes testing little better than a dark art. At a time when most of the behavioral sciences have long since incorporated operationalism into their methods of theory building, achievement test theory—if it can be said to be a theory at all—has remained rooted in the introspective techniques of the early nineteenth century. (pp. 2–3)

I do not intend to suggest that LJC was wrong, not scientific, or that his perspective was skewed. His views were shared by Wesman (1971) who wrote:

> Item writing is essentially creative—it is an art. Just as there can be no set of formulas for producing a good story or a good painting, so there can be no set of rules that guarantees the production of good test items. Principles can be established and suggestions offered, but it is the writer's judgment in the application—and occasional disregard—of these principles and suggestions that determines whether good items or mediocre ones are produced. Each item, as it is being written, presents new problems and new opportunities. This item writing requires an uncommon combination of special abilities and is measured only through extensive and critically supervised practice. (p. 81)

On the contrary, after many years it seems that we have advanced in item writing. However, the initial idea that a computer will take psychological clauses and content and transform them automatically into appropriate items did not appear to be viable. Item writing is still an art, but one with much more theory-based reasoning. The artistic part of it reflects the creative and insightful activity that links an item to everyday behavior. This ensures that an item response will say something about a tested participant.

The following are a few more or less strict item design approaches, all of which started with the notion that there should be a (multiple) correlation between item difficulty and aspects of Item Design Rules. The fact that there is a correlation is of particular importance. However, there is a considerable difference in the item difficulty variance explained by this correlation and it is hoped that with this, in the near future we will be better able to design items.

Subsequently, some empirical results will be examined to show how we devised Item Design Rules and what correlations we found with item difficulty. The latter was based on ordinary percent correct, or in later years, on one or two parameter estimates in regard to item response theory. Item content deals with:

- Mental Rotation
- Pattern Matrices
- Verbal Analogies
- Number Problems
- Visual Analysis
- Visual Memory
- Serial Learning
- Management/work behavior and attitude scales: pro facts

Each of the item types was derived from inspection of the literature or, in the case of management/work behavior, from practical considerations. Established results from this literature were used to formulate Item Design Rules that helped human item writers create a large set of items for each item type. This was necessary to yield item banks for computerized adaptive testing. It is important to have many items in the item banks so there are enough suitable items for each individual tested at the ability level in question. Only these items can furnish sufficient information about the participant. If only these items are used in testing, the participants will be tested on fewer items than with any other broad range conventional test. It is apparent then, that tailoring items adaptively during testing requires many more items to be constructed than are required for conventional tests.

MENTAL ROTATION

In most general intelligence tests there are items with three-dimensional objects printed on paper. The participant is asked to compare two or more of them and judge whether they represent rotations of a target figure or not. Because all objects are rotated in space to different degrees, this makes it more or less difficult to discover differences among them. Metzler and Shepard (1974), Cooper and Shepard, (1973), Carpenter and Just (1986), Vandenberg and Kuse (1978), and Bejar (1990) described this kind of mental rotation task in detail.   Upon review of this research it became apparent that it might be possible to use pattern and transformational complexity in item design. This was done in the following manner (Hornke, Rettig, & Hutwelker, 1988; Rettig, Hutwelker, & Hornke, 1989). See Figures 6.1 and 6.2.

Pattern Complexity
Number of extremities (3, 4, 5 "arms")

Number of planes (1 or 2)

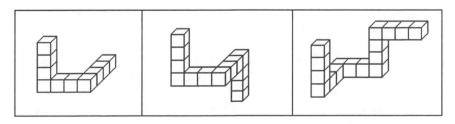

FIG. 6.1. Figural complexity.

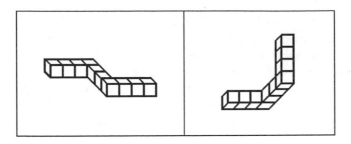

FIG. 6.2. Number of planes.

<u>Transformation Complexity</u>
Angle of rotation (45, 90, 135, 180)
Number of rotations (1 or 2) as right-left and/or front-back

Of the 720 different paired comparisons made, 478 were retained after item analysis and rigid checking for pattern idiosyncrasies as One Parameter Logistic (1PL) complying items.

The following is a possible set of four items/comparisons (See Figure 6.3):

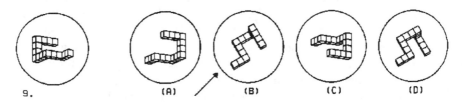

FIG. 6.3. Sample item with visual problems.

Unfortunately, the paired comparison (B) in Figure 6.3 has to be removed because one arm is not distinctly visible. This may hold for (D) as well. However, item design rules such as "pattern complexity" and "angular differences", varied in their contribution to overall item difficulty. See Table 6.1.

As seen in Table 6.2, item complexity contributes most to item difficulty followed by angular difference in the front back orientation. It is interesting to note that there are distinct main effects for angular contributions. Table 6.2 shows the degree to which angle and orientation contribute, on average, to item difficulty parameters. The aspect of these results of main interest is that item design rules correlate with 1PL item difficulties with an R of .62.

TABLE 6.1
Results of Item Design Rules as contributors to item difficulty

Variable	b	SE(b)	beta	T	Sig (t)
Complexity	.383	.030	.537	12.70	.00
Angular Difference in front-back orientation	.003	.00045	.326	6.92	.00
Angular Difference in right-left orientation	.002	.00046	.190	4.02	.00
Constant	-8.36	.0921		9.08	.00
n = 1138 males	m = 478 items		R = .62		

TABLE 6.2
Differential contributions of orientation at various angular differences (beta weights)

Angular difference in degrees .	0	45	90	135	180
Right - left orientation	.17	.40	.48	.34	.32
Front - back orientation	.16	.13	.54	.61	.41

PATTERN MATRICES

Pattern matrices, among others, are the most prominent measures of general intelligence or *g* in psychology. Due to the regularity in matrix patterns it was tempting to devise item design rules for this item type. Studies by Ward and Fitzpatrick (1973), Jacobs and Vandeventer (1972) as well as Nährer (1980) instigated a search for such rules. Hornke and Habon (1986, p. 373) reported these attempts. They used the following rule set.

 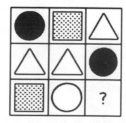 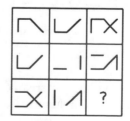

Separated Components (SC)   **Integrated components (IC)**   **Embedded Components (EC)**

FIG. 6.4. Components in Item Design (see Hornke & Habon, 1986, p. 373).

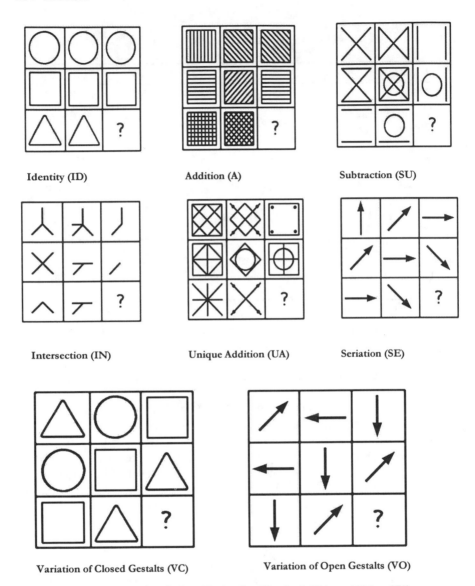

FIG. 6.5. Cognitive operations in Item Design (see Hornke & Habon, 1986, p. 373).

Within patterns components may be varied rowwise, columnswise, or row- and columnswise.

Results indicate some general trends for components, operations, and orientations:

In Figure 6.6 vertical bars indicate medians of individual contributions to item difficulty. As logic would dictate, separated components make items easier than embedded component items.

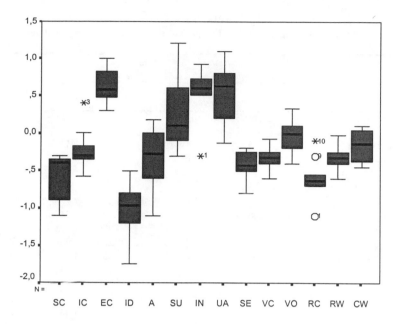

FIG. 6.6. Results from al linear logistic analysis for matrices items according to Item Design Rules (study of Hornke & Habon, 1986).

A set of 446 items was retained after item analysis and complied well with the 1PL in a 1987 study (Hornke & Rettig, 1987). However, little changed over time since Item Design Rules correlated at $R = .65$ in the first study in 1987 and still do so for the same items, $R = .66$ in 1996. For the latter study the multiple regression is given below. See Table 6.3 and Figure 6.7.

In 1987 there were $n = 7200$ participants, $m = 456$ items, and a multiple correlation of $R = .65$, and in 1996 with $n = 32222$ participants and the same set of $m = 456$ items a multiple correlation of $R = .66$ was found. All negative weights indicate that the corresponding factor makes an item less difficult, whereas positive weights indicate an Item Design Rule which makes an item more difficult. In the 1996 study 32,222 participants were tested, but due to a link design approximately some 800–900 participants contributed to each item.

For a recent study (Hornke, Etzel, & Küppers, 2000), where 272 parallel items were newly designed, individual Item Design Rule factors contribute to 1PL-item difficulty at $R = .72$ in a combined sample of 1,232 participants from Moscow, Vienna, and Katovice.

TABLE 6.3
Multiple regression weights for Item Design Rules of pattern matrices in 1996

Model	Non-standardized coefficients		Standar-dized coefficients	T	Signifi-cance
	B	Standard Error	Beta		
(CONSTANT)	-.576	.247		-2.099	.037
Separated comp.	.373	.280	.125	1.333	.184
Integrated comp.	.952	.285	.306	3.345	.001
Embedded comp.	2.697	.306	.719	8.816	.000
Identity	-1.579	.203	-.377	-7.775	.000
Addition	-.206	.165	-.068	-1.247	.214
Subtraction	-.0657	.167	-.020	-.393	.695
Disjunction	.712	.179	.203	3.968	.000
Single element Addition	.789	.166	.257	4.747	.000
Seriation	-.542	.158	-.196	-3.444	.001
Variation of closed gestalts	-.259	.155	-.093	-1.668	.097
Horizontal and Vertical	-.486	.107	-.223	-4.542	.000
Vertical	.0632	.101	.031	.626	.532

Empirically estimated 1PL item difficulties of 272 corresponding items correlate at $r = .87$ for the previous studies (1987 paper pencil and 1996 computer administered). Parallel item difficultiey for the most recent study in 1998 does correlate at $r = .73$ (with 1987 paper and pencil) and at $r = .81$ (in 1996 computer administered items). Item Design Rules contribute considerably to item difficulty and show, as do parallel item forms, stability over time, presentation mode, and geographical region.

VERBAL ANALOGIES

Verbal analogies represent another core set of items in published intelligence tests. As far as item writing is concerned, some item writers seem to use more uncommon terminology than well conceived analogical reasoning concepts. Based on the early work of Whitely (1977) and Hornke, Habon, and Mispelkamp (1984) the following were used in item writing:

- Negation/Opposition, (neg)
- Function, (fun)
- Dimensional relation, (dim)
- Class membership, (cla)
- Development/Conversion, (dev)
- Part/Whole, (p/w)

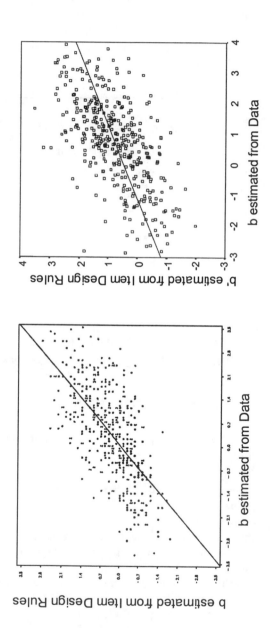

FIG. 6.7. Comparing item difficulties, b, estimated from data in 1987 and 1996 with difficulty estimates from Item Design Rules for the same items

Out of 360 written items, 257 were retained after item analysis as well as item repair and comply sufficiently with the 1PL.

A comparison of the distribution of item difficulty within and across item design in 1984 and a more recent study (Hornke & Wilding, 1996) revealed similar results. The median order of difficulty holds in both studies: Negation (function, development, and part/whole), dimension, and class. Again function, development, and part/whole lead to items of relatively similar mean difficulty (see Figure 6.8). The overall correlation of Item Design Rules is as high as $r = .969$.

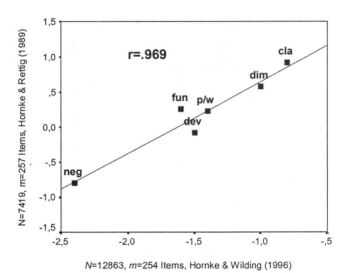

N=12863, m=254 Items, Hornke & Wilding (1996)

FIG. 6.8. Comparing Item Design Rule contributions for verbal analogy items from two independent studies.

NUMBER PROBLEMS

In order to write items for number problems some preliminary guidelines were acquired from previous approaches found in the literature:

- Psychometric approach: Individual differences are consequences of underlying mathematical ability.
- Cognitive approach: Individual differences are due to different information processing abilities. The number problems found in the experimental literature were all too simple for the target group (young adults in their early 20s).
- Curricular approach: Unfortunately there was no clear cut idea of "numerical, mathematical ability" as it is found in text books and tests published for young age groups.

For our own approach the following basic notions were employed:

Mayer, Larkin, and Kadane (1986): Structural and operational characteristics of information processing (working memory, time to access and retrieve information, declarative knowledge), organization of information, procedural knowledge (translate, comprehend, strategic planning, algorithmic execution); linguistic, strategic, and algorithmic knowledge.

Paige and Simon (1966): Transforming of text into equations, solving equations.

Loftus and Suppes (1972): Structural variables of textbased problems such as operations, steps, length, depth, sequence, verbal cues, order, and transformation; 70% of difficulty variance was predicted.

Radatz (1980): Analyses of frequent errors made by students in working on numerical problems.

Finally we were led to believe that individual differences are the result of different training and schooling in the field of mathematics and that there may be no clear cut underlying theory of mathematical ability. Mastery of any kind of relational and numerical problems should be tested on problems taught at school and would lead to curricular-based item writing. Here ideas were drawn from:

Bloom et al.'s (1956) taxonomy/hierarchy. In particular, comprehension, application, and analysis was considered.

Wilson´s (1971) hierarchy in regard to:

- Number ability: facts, terminology, algorithmic execution.
- Comprehension: knowledge of concepts, principles, structures, ability to follow. reasoning, reading and interpretation.
- Application
- Analysis
- Sequential accomplishment following established hierarchy due to schooling.

In the past it was not possible to devise clearcut well defined Item Design Rules, but item writing was based on curricular content and use. It borrowed from clerical, technical, general contents published in a variety of school books, learning materials, or training guides. The only systematic feature that was employed was the use of number problems in different ways. See Table 6.4. Items using graphs with numerical relations, arithmetic problems, and graphical representation of sets exemplify some of theses number problems.

Again, item parameter estimates of all 235 items turned out to be very similar, r = .81, in 1989 (Hornke & Rettig, 1989) and 1996 studies (Hornke & Wilding, 1996). When the Item Design Rule features are taken together and are correlated with the estimated item difficulty, they yield an R = .59. To some this may seem to indicate a low relationship. However, one has to consider the very few and low level rules which guide item writing. In this regard, the fact that a broad construct such as "basic mathematics competence" accounts for 36% of the variance in item difficulties is promising but definitely awaits further improvement

VISUAL ANALYSIS

Visual Analysis (Hornke & Kluge-Klaßen, 1991; Hornke & Storm, 1995) adopts the ideas of embedded figures tests as they are found in many test batteries. However, figure and ground consist of equilateral triangles. Some of them form a figure when laid out with their sides touching. Combining six equilateral triangles in all possible ways yields only 12 Hexiamonds (!). But they can be mirrored as well, providing 12 additional Hexiamonds. This full set of 24 figures made up the VISAN-test. (See Figure 6.9.)

TABLE 6.4
Item design features for number problems derived from curricular materials

Arithmetic		130
	Power and roots	20
	Basic operations	80
	Decimals and fractions	30
Algebra		10
	Linear equations 1 unknown	5
	Linear equations 2 unknowns	5
Everyday Calculus		40
	Percentages	25
	Interest rates	5
	Compound problems	10
Geometry		35
	Plainimetry	20
	Stereometry	15
Estimation problems		10
Number series		10

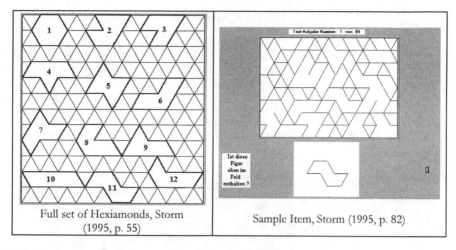

| Full set of Hexiamonds, Storm (1995, p. 55) | Sample Item, Storm (1995, p. 82) |

FIG. 6.9. Set of Hexiamonds and a sample item for visual analysis

Item Design Rules are based on an approach by Palmer (1977, 1978). He tried to describe a visual pattern by its orientation, degree of connection, and continuity of single lines. Because figure and ground follow the same rationale, the entire item is a combination of:

- ◆ Pattern simplicity (the figure in question)
  - Orientation: up-down, left-right
  - Degree of connection: lines touch at edges
  - Continuity: lines touch and have same orientation
- ◆ Background complexity (the ground pattern of lines)
  - Orientation
  - Degree of connection
  - Continuity
- ◆ Line deletions (90,100) from background pattern. In later studies, more lines (70) were deleted to decrease item difficulty in order to obtain a wider range.

As for pattern simplicity indices the original Hexiamonds' differ as in (#11) = 0.57, (#12) = 0.64, and (#10) = 1.00, for example. In addition to pattern simplicity background complexity must be added in order to yield a difficulty estimate for an entire item. By means of a computer program, 84 items were generated and tested on 74 participants. Item difficulty estimates correlated, as expected, with the Item Design Rules at $R = .63$. Reaction times were predicted even better than item difficulty correlating at $R = .98$ (see Storm, 1995, p. 151).

VISUAL MEMORY

Items for visual memory (Hornke & Etzel, 1995) are designed from the everyday competence of reading a map and remembering some of its details. A pattern of icons, like a police station, bus stop, and so forth, is presented on a computer screen. Participants are allowed to study the pattern for a fixed time to remember the location of each of these icons. They have to drag the relevant icon to that location that is supposed to fit (see Figure 6.10).

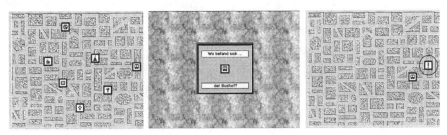

FIG. 6.10. Sample item for visual memory.

In order to moderate item difficulty three factors are used in Item Design Rules:

- Complexity: Number of icons presented (2 . . . 8).
- Homogeneity: Size of an area enclosed by a circumference around all icons in an item.
- Compactness: Pattern arrangement (good, poor Gestalt).

In total 114 1PL complying items were found after testing 560 participants. Item Design Rules accounted for a large amount of the difficulty variance. Their correlation with item difficulty reached an r of .94 (see Figure 6.11).

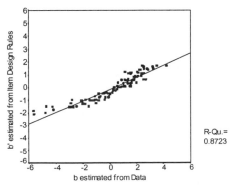

FIG. 6.11. Scattergram of Item Design Rules with item difficulties.

VERBAL MEMORY

Verbal memory items are also included in many intelligence tests. In this example verbal information is put into the everyday problem of examining a busline map and remembering all the stops (Hornke, Storm, & Etzel, 1993; Hornke & Etzel, 1995). All items are presented on a computer screen.

Sample Item: On the way from the "Start" to the "End" a virtual bus travels through a city. As it stops the stop's name is indicated for a short time on the screen. At the "End" the participant has to put all of the stop names into chronological order by picking a name from a set and dragging it to form a list (see Figure 6.12).

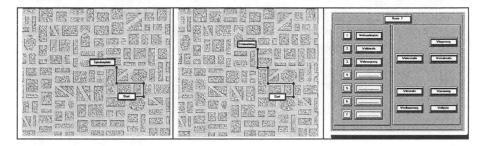

FIG. 6.12. Sample item for verbal memory.

Item Design Rules take into account:

- *Complexity:* Number of different street names to remember (3 . . . 9).

- *Imagery:* Use of street names ranging from concrete to abstract. "Lime Tree Road" is considered to provoke a concrete image and thus contributing less to difficulty than "Logic Terrace". A scaled "imagery score" from low (2.7) to high (6.0) in steps of .3 was taken from an empirical study (Wippich & Bredenkamp, 1977) yielding 11 imagery categories.
- *Inspection Time:* different time intervals (1.5 and 2.5 sec.) for each street name presented.

According to Item Design Rules, 114 items were generated and presented to 560 participants according to a link design. Again, Item Design Rules correlated at $R = .94$ with item difficulty.

PRO FACTS™

In the context of industrial personnel evaluation a series of scales were constructed (Etzel, 1999). However, item design follows more or less the radicals-incidentals-approach proposed by Irvine (see Chap. 1, this volume).

Pro facts is a system for "professional assessment for training and selection." In general, critical incidences were gathered from many interviews with insurance company employees. Their professional activities, experiences with clients, cooperation with coworkers/superiors, and work related attitudes were the focus of item writing. In that all items are cast in professional scenarios the participant should behave as if he were at work. This is thought to contribute to ecological and performance oriented validity.

For the item in Figure 6.13 the Item Design Rationale was as follows (Level 1 is intended for the item presented, see Table 6.5):

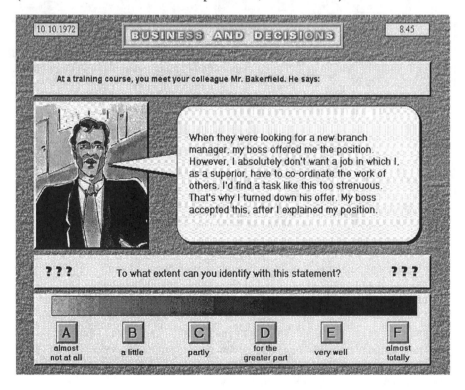

FIG. 6.13. Sample item for career orientation.

TABLE 6.5
Item Design Rationale for career orientation items

Level	Behavior The coworker...	Orientation The coworker...
1	refuses to take over positions with extended leadership demands.	regards taking over responsibility for coworkers as detrimental to his own professional life.
2	takes over leadership only when asked.	has no need to lead more coworkers and does not see it as an incentive.
3	exercises social influence on subordinate coworkers; attempts to extend his span of control.	is satisfied with his present position. To lead more coworkers does not really motivate him.
4	shows from time to time a readiness to take over enlarged leadership positions.	regards a wider span of control as a chance for personal development.
5	attempts actively to take over positions which imply larger influence on others.	is satisfied to take over more personnel responsibilities and regards this as a challenge.
6	attempts constantly to achieve positions of greater influence.	regards taking over more personnel responsibilities as a challenge and considers this the goal of his professional life.

With other test items, information was presented on one screen and the question, as well as response alternatives, on a following screen. Pictures, text, and sound are used to fully catch the participant's attention and to create a diversified job performance scenario. In the item given in Figure 6.14 the participant should identify with the man who is talking to himself. The answer choice is based on the item design rationale in that it offers different degrees of consent and relevant content references.

For career orientation the multiple correlation between Item Design Rules and the rank of classical item difficulty P reached $R = .77$.

Some validity correlations were gained for internal personnel evaluation criteria of an insurance company. In different age cohorts there were correlations of $.71 - .76$ with insurance sales and correlations of $.73 - .81$ with supervisor ratings.

CONCLUSION

Item Design Rules proved to contribute to overall 1PL-Item Difficulty which was used here, in most instances, in order to have a common ground for comparisons. However, not all constructs and scales profited in the same manner. Analogies profited least and Visual Memory items did best. Perhaps analogy terms have many degrees of freedom for interpretation.

Three terms plus five alternatives can be combined in many ways which can make sense for a participant so that the overall answer given might be considered wrong in regard to the Item Design Rules. However, there may be some truth in the answer when seen from the participant's perspective. The many associations he employs might create additional meaning so that even an incorrect alternative will make sense for him. In general, there is nothing wrong with analogy items. This is beyond control of any Item Design Rule and test interpretation, too.

The more restrictive the item content the more Item Design Rules contribute to Item Difficulty (see Table 6.6). It is promising to employ some kind of rationale for designing items that is derived from already existing knowledge. Perhaps in creating a new test, it is important to explore in depth what is already known about the construct in question., what results of previous operational attempts provide, and what can be gained from a pilot study. Telling item writers what the ingredients of an item should be, is the least common denominator. However, programming a computer to design a multitude of items according to some well defined set of rules, is a promising approach. Item writing to suit a number of constructs might oscillate between these two limits. In many cases formalizing/automating item writing will not be possible since creating additional text is far beyond what machines are able to do for the time being. However, it seems that those parts of an item which are construct related and will knowingly moderate it's difficulty should be participated to rigid rules. All additional features should be given attention, but regarded as incidentals unless better knowledge is available.

TABLE 6.6

Range of multiple correlations of Item Design Rules with estimated item difficulties for various item pools and constructs.

Item pool	Correlation of Item Difficulties (1PL) with Item Design Rules	b-1PL-Stability (1989 vs. 1996)
Verbal Analogies	.39	.90
Number Problems	.59	.81
Mental Rotation	.62	
Visual Analysis	.63	
Figural Matrices	.65, .72	.81
pro facts: Career Orientation	.77	
Visual Memory	.91 (for P-values), .88	
Verbal Memory	.88 (for P-Values), .94	

REFERENCES

Bejar. I. I. (1990). A generative analysis of a three-dimensional spatial task. *Applied Psychological Measurement, 14*, 237–245.

Bloom, B. S. (Ed.). (1956). *Taxonomy of educational objectives: The classification of educational goals.* New York: David McKay.

Bormuth, J. R. (1970). *On the theory of achievement test items.* Chicago, IL: University of Chicago Press.

Carpenter, P. A., & Just, M. A. (1986). Spatial ability: an information processing approach to psychometrics. In: R. J. Sternberg (Ed.). *Advances in psychology of human intelligence Vol. 3,* (pp. 221–253). Hilldale, NY: Lawrence Erlbaum Associates.

Cooper, L. A., & Shepard, R. N. (1973). Chronometric studies of the rotation of mental images. In W. G. Chase (Ed.), *Visual information processing.* New York: Academic Press.

Etzel, S. (1999). *Multimediale, computergestützte diagnostische Verfahren: Neue Perspektiven für die Managementdiagnostik.* Aachen: Schaker.

Hornke, L. F., & Etzel, S. (1995). Theoriegeleitete Konstruktion und Evaluation von computergestützten Tests zum Merkmalsbereich "Gedächtnis und Orientierung" (p183–296). *Untersuchungen des Psychologischen Dienstes der Bundeswehr 1993/1995,* Band 2. Bonn: Bundesministerium der Verteidigung.

Hornke, L. F., & Habon, M. W. (1986). Rule-based item bank construction and evaluation within the linear logistic framework. *Applied Psychological Measurement, 10*, 369–380.

Hornke, L. F., Habon, M. W., & Mispelkamp, H. B. (1984). Verbale Analogien als Aufgabe für eine rationale Aufgabenkonstruktion (Working paper des Psychologischen Dienstes der Bundeswehr, AL-4-84. Bonn: Ministry of Defense).

Hornke, L. F., & Kluge-Klaßen, A. (1991). *Prototypen von Items zum Merkmal Gedächtnis und Orientierung* (Working Paper, A II 61–91, Department of Psychology, Aachen University of Technology).

Hornke, L. F., Küppers, A., & Etzel, S. (2000). Konstuktion und Evaluation eines adaptiven Matrizentests. *Diagnostica, 46*, 182-188.

Hornke, L. F., & Rettig, K. (1987). *Regelgeleitete Itemkonstruktion unter Zuhilfenahme kognitionspsychologischer Überlegungen.* [Rule based item writing by means of results from cognitive psychology]. Unpublished Report (3/87) for the Psychologischen Dienst der Bundeswehr.

Hornke, L. F., & Rettig, K. (1989). Konstruktion eines Tests mit verbalen Analogien (CAT-A2): Weitere Untersuchungen. In *Untersuchungen des Psychologischen Dienstes der Bundeswehr, 24*, 49–138.

Hornke, L. F., Rettig, K., & Hutwelker, R. (1988). Theoriegeleitete Konstruktion eines Tests zur Messung des räumlichen Vorstellungsvermögens. In *Untersuchungen des Psychologischen Dienstes der Bundeswehr, 23*, 145–222.

Hornke, L. F., & Storm, G. (1995). Theoriegeleitete Konstruktion von Items zur Messung visueller. Analyseleistungen III. Untersuchungen des Psychologischen Dienstes der Bundeswehr 1993/1995, Band 2. Bonn: Bundesministerium der Verteidigung.

Hornke, L. F., Storm, G. & Etzel, S. (1993). *Theoriegeleitete Konstruktion von Items zum Merkmal Gedächtnis und Orientierung.* (Working Paper, Department of Psychology, Aachen University of Technology).

Hornke, L. F., & Wilding, U. (1996). Evaluation dreier Leistungstests mit verbalen Analogien, Matrizen und Rechenaufgaben. *Arbeitsbericht* für das Bundesministerium der Verteidigung.

Jacobs, P. J., & Vandeventer, M. (1972). Evaluating the teaching of intelligence. *Educational and Psychological Measurement, 32*, 235–248.

Loftus, E. F., & Suppes, P. (1972). Stuctural variables that determine problme-solving difficulty in computer-assisted-instruction. *Journal of Educational Psychology, 63*, 531–542.

Mayer, R. E., Larkin, J. H., & Kadane, J. B. (1986). A cognitive analysis of mathematical problem-solving-ability. In R. J. Sternberg (Ed.) *Advances in the psychology of human intelligence* (pp. 231–271). Hillsdale: Lawrence Erlbaum Associates.

Metzler, J., & Shepard, R. N. (1974). Transformational studies of the internal representation of three-dimensional objects. In R. Solso (Ed.). *Theories in cognitive psychology: The Loyola Symposium* (pp. 147–201). Potomac, MD: Lawrence Erlbaum Associates.

Nährer, W. (1980). Modellkontrollen bei der Anwendung des linearen logistischen Testmodells. *Diagnostica, 26*, 112–118.

Paige, J. M., & Simon, H. A. (1966). Cognitive processes for jugdment of numerical inequality. *Nature*, 215.

Palmer, S. E. (1977). Hierarchical structure in perceptual representation. *Cognitive Psychology, 9*, 441–474.

Palmer, S. E. (1978). Structural aspects of visual similarity. *Memory and Cognition, 6*, 9197.

Radatz, H. (1980). *Fehleranalyse im Mathematikunterricht.* Wiesbaden: Vieweg.

Rettig, K., Hutwelker, R., & Hornke, L. F. (1989). Ergebnisse zum 3D-Test. In *Untersuchungen des Psychologischen Dienstes der Bundeswehr, 24*, 145–222.

Storm, E. G. (1995). Theoriegeleitete Testkonstruktion-Erfassung visueller Analyseleistungen anhand neuartiger, computergenerierter "eingekleideter Figur-Aufgaben." *Arbeitsberichte des Psychologischen Dienstes der Bundeswehr, 1-1/95.* Bonn: Bundesminister der Verteidigung.

Vandenberg, S. G., & Kuse, A. R. (1978). Mental rotations, a group of three-dimensional spatial visualisation. *Perception and Motor Skills, 47*, 599–604.

Ward, J., & Fitzpatrick, F. (1973). Characteristics of matrices items. *Perceptual and Motor Skills, 36*, 987–993.

Wesman, A. G. (1971). Writing the test item. In R. L. Thorndike (Ed.). *Educational measurement* (2nd ed., pp 81–129). Washington, DC: American Council on Education.

Whitely, S. E. (1977). Relationships in analogies: A semantic component of a psychometric task. *Educational and Psychological Measurement, 19*, 465–476

Wilson, J. W. (1971). Evaluation of learning in secondary school mathematics. In B. S. Bloom, J. T. Hastings, & G. F. Madaus (Eds.) *Handbook on formative and summative evaluation of student learning.* New York: McGraw Hill.

Wippich, W., & Bredenkamp, J. (1977). Bestimmung der Bildhaftigkeit (I), Konkretheit (C) und der Bedeutungshaltigkeit (m') von 498 Verben und 400 Adjektiven. *Zeitschrift Experimentelle und Angewandte Psychologie, 24*, 671–680.

Discussant Remarks

Charles Lewis
Educational Testing Service

It is a great pleasure to have the opportunity to discuss three very stimulating chapters. But I think I should first make one disclaimer. If Henry Braun had given a more detailed biography, you would have noticed that I have never done research in this area. And you could have gotten a hint from the Statistics degree part. My specialty—if there is a specialty—is statistical inference, specifically Bayesian inference, and you might wonder why, given my background, I am standing here being a discussant. I feel very honored to have this opportunity, but you should legitimately ask that question.

I can think of two factors that would reduce uncertainty regarding why I would be here. The first accounts for most of the variance, but not all of it. I was fortunate enough to be a student, a colleague, and friend of Sam Messick's, and he was the one who put this conference together. I tried to convince him that I was not the appropriate person, but he was not convinced. That's one part of the variance. You might say there are other people who are students, colleagues, and friends of Sam Messick's so that obviously doesn't account for all the variance. The only other factor I could come up with was that I happen to be the administrative head of a group at ETS that includes Bob Mislevy and Kathy Sheehan, who contributed presentations. In addition, the unit involves several other people, at least half the group, who have been fairly heavily involved in research in areas very much germane to the topic of this conference. So, maybe there is some kind of reflected glory there.

Although these two factors may reduce your uncertainty regarding why I am here, you might legitimately ask whether either of these reasons is valid. I think the answer is pretty clear. These two factors may have predictive power, but that doesn't mean that there is a real sense of validity her, a "should"—should a person with these two characteristics be a discussant? No, not necessarily. Maybe if they had other qualities, but not on this basis.

So although we can provide an explanation for my presence, and we can reduce uncertainty regarding it, it doesn't necessarily mean we are very happy with the situation. I think there may be an analogy with some of the work described here. Maybe I don't have to elaborate on the analogy, maybe you already got the analogy quite clearly. The fact that we can predict or explain the difficulty of an item, doesn't necessarily mean that this is an item we want to use. Lutz Hornke was getting at some of that issue, but I think we can generalize beyond that. I think that if there is one critical theme in this discussion of what I consider three very good, very stimulating papers, the critical theme is the issue of validity, in its broadest sense. I have good precedent for this idea. Sam Messick was very good at including almost everything under the concept of validity. If there is a message here, it is that in this work we must remember validity in all its aspects, and we must never lose track of validity in what we're doing. I will illustrate that with some specifics.

MISLEVY, STEINBERG, AND ALMOND

I turn first to the Mislevy, Steinberg, and Almond chapter. I would certainly agree with them, in general, and have applauded them on numerous occasions for their insistence on the necessity of a broad, conceptual framework for talking about assessment. I would not say this to test developers or to psychologists, but I will certainly say to myself as a statistician, that we too often go about our work with blinders on. We used to pride ourselves and say we don't care what the items look like. Don't show me the text of the item, I don't want to see that, just give me the data, give me the zeros and ones, and I'll take it from there. Thank you very much.

That is not to say that the Portal framework is the first one that has ever been proposed. We're in a room where several other people have pushed this line. But the fact that it is not the first does not mean it is not important, and that it is not adding considerably to what we need. So I applaud them insisting, particularly at ETS, that we need to be thinking about assessment in a broad, conceptual framework—as broad as possible. Indeed, in that context I would say a good bit of what they are doing is making explicit things that have in general been implicit. I wouldn't say that people putting tests together never think about what goes into the test or never think about what the student is doing. But they just don't take the trouble to really examine the implication: "What if the student is doing such and such and if the intention is such and such, what does that mean about what I'm doing here in terms of writing items?" They may not be as explicit as they should be, and in that sense things may be missed. Being more explicit, I think, is always good.

One thing I wouldn't mind being more explicit in their chapters is "test use." I'd be willing to have it be pointed out to me: "No, didn't you see, it was that box right over there!" But I missed the emphasis on test use in their framework. I the context of validity, I think that the issue of test use is a critical touchstone for evaluating the rest of the system.

In addition, one has to talk about very specific validation questions that can range all the way from the context—if you stick with the authors' examples with the GRE, you say, "Ok we're using the 3 parameter logistc appropriate model? Even given what we want to do? There has to be some evaluation of that, there has to be some way of assessing that, and modifying it, and that has to be explicit. It seems to me that it should be explicit in any kind of a framework. You can say that people doing IRT pretty well know that already, but they don't. I think they may know it even less at the stage where they are constructing a Bayesian inference net. I can put together a Bayesian inference net, but how do I validate that now? How do I even calibrate that model, how do I go about getting all the conditional probabilities that go into it? And how do I go about modifying it, and cleaning it up? We don't know how to do that, but the point is, that is something that really has to be taken seriously.

Now again, when I say validate a model, I should be a little bit careful there, because we're not trying to say these models are true, for sure. We know that beforehand. They're not. Certainly in fitting 3PL or Rasch, or whatever your favorite model is, we know they are only approximations to reality, and presumably the Bayes nets are also other kinds of approximations to reality. Some statisticians, Box and Tiao, discussed this in the context of robustness, a concept near and dear to my heart as a statistician. They observed that the issue is not, "Is the model true? Yes or no?" because we know the answer is "No." The question is also not, "Is the model almost true?" The question is "Does what you dowith the model give you almost the same answer as you would have gotten if you did somehow know the true model?" So they talk about inference robustness rather than criterion robustness, and I'm going to bring that up in the context of the other chapters as well. I think that the final touchstone has to be for whatever it is we want to do with this, are our models adequate to the job? Are they doing the sort of thing we want, or are they misleading us, particularly, are they misleading us in some systematic way? So, I can make that claim without knowing anything about a lot of these models—it's a general principle to apply to these situations.

One other little thing I want to say, just to tease the authors. The term *principled assessment design*. I love that term. It reminds me of an observation that Mel Novick once made regarding the term *unbiasedness* in statistics. You say, unbiasednes is a property of a statistical estimate and, once you hear that name, he says, you must admit that was a winner of a name. Because once you hear that you think, "Well, who would ever want to have an estimate that was biased? Yikes!" In the same way, the suggestion seems to be that if you're following this particular framework then you're doing principled assessment, and presumably the alternative is doing unprincipled assessment, and who would ever want to be doing that?

Now, actually, I'll tell you, to a certain degree, I would. This goes back to a distrust of general, broad-reaching theories, and a trust in people's intuitions and common sense, so that something that is completely principled can also be dangerous. That can be in politics, or education, or in a lot of realms, We can't take our principles too seriously, we have to be very much on the alert for over application of principles. And then, another side of it is, not only should we be suing principles to some extent or other, but which principle? We just had a political election. We could say that both parties were principled politicians or we might say something else, but the issue there, even granting them that they were principled politicians, was, which principles do they represent? So, I just can't resist teasing a little bit, about the term that's made its way into the ETS lexicon recently.

ENRIGHT AND SHEEHAN

Let's turn now to the chapter of Mary Enright and Kathy Sheehan. Here we clearly take a step from a very high-level, broad view, to a very concrete, very specific application. And, in general, I tend to be a concrete sort of person, so I can relate to this very well. To me, one of the things that was really fun about this chapter was that you have this tension. On the one hand you could say that Mary and Kathy and all their coworkers are stuck with this thing, this GRE quantitative exam. Their job was not to come up with a new alternative measure of quantitative reasoning, presumably, or even to ask the question "Who needs a GRE quantitative exam?" What is the justified use of that exam? What function does such an examination serve? My understanding is that the test is somewhat easier than the corresponding mathematical test in the SAT. You say, "Well, that means that people have forgotten their math from high school to college." And if that's true, is it really important for them when they go on to graduate school? You might expect that the curve will just keep fading away, and the English PhD will say, "Boy, am I glad I didn't have to take a math course in the last five years! Why should that be relevant for deciding if I should be in graduate school or not?"

But that was not the authors' task. Their task was, given this thing, very practical—and that is one nice thing about being at ETS, you can think very practically—here is this thing that we sell, and we used to make some money selling, and maybe one day, we'll make some money again selling this. But maybe part of that will depend on what we do in terms of understanding what is going on in this test. So, as Mary pointed out, even within this very narrow, very specified context, there was this wide range of different goals you might have for studying these items, and so there was tension for me. On the one hand this is a very concrete, very specific thing, and on the other hand, very wide open in terms of what it is you would do with this sort of analysis. Of course in the context of this conference we'd say, "item generation, yes!" But that was only one application, and perhaps not even the most important one. In one study Enright and Sheehan actually did generate some items, following some rules, but the bigger study was actually trying to characterize what we've got on the test, and trying to come up with a systematic description of it. With this range of goals, I would argue that it may be—and I say *may* be because I just don't know—it may be that very different approaches might be relevant, and very different criteria of success might be relevant for these different goals. That is something that bears thinking about. Maybe it's Ok if when you're doing the research at this stage that you don't know the answer to that yet, maybe that's for other people even to say: "No, now, we want you to do it for *this* reason, we want to know *this*.

But in any event, my main point is that the wide range of goals might very well be related to different approaches and different ways of thinking about what we're doing, and that more specific question of asking, "Why are we really doing this? Why are we looking at prediction of item difficulties and discrimination?"

One thing that I found very intriguing and, again, this may be commonplace for all of you, including the authors, but for me as the statistician, I say, "Yeah, hey, I like that, that's interesting." And I think this ties back to what Bob, and Linda, and Russell were talking about in their models, that you had characteristics of items that you were using, particularly variables that the test developers had specified, such as whether it is a quantitative comparison, how many terms, or is there a variable or a number in the problem, and so on. Then there were characteristics of presumably how hard it would be to solve the problem, so that something, if I could misuse the Portal terminology, maybe the first type of characteristic is more related to a "task model," and the second is more like a "student model." Obviously both of those are relevant for predicting difficulty. Then you have the third type, which is the test developer looking at it, and saying "How hard do I think this is?" That's probably neither one nor the other. In this case, they certainly have different implications for a test writer trying to generate items, as you pointed out, never mind writing a computer program to write items. So the fact that a set of characteristics is an important predictor of difficulty may not help the test developer at all in knowing how to write an item that requires all those characteristics. It might. I mean, the characteristics that predict difficulty, and the characteristics that help a test developer certainly are not orthogonal domains. They are closely related. You know if there's a variable in there you have to do things that you don't have to do if there's a number in there. But what are those things? So, anyway, they serve different levels of discussion.

One other thing to say in this context is not only were the authors stuck—I just have to mention this again from a statistical perspective—not only were they stuck with the GRE quantitative exam, they were also stuck with the statistical model, the 3 parameter logistic model. In any kind of a discussion of what's really going on, with all these elements, the 3 parameter logistic model is totally irrelevant. The item features have nothing to do with a 3 parameter logistic model in some sense. Yet, after the fact, you're stuck. You don't have the choice of coming to GRE and saying, "Stop using the 3PL. We're going to use this thing instead—we're going to use a Bayes net, or we're going to do something or other." That's all I want to observe, that in some sense the authors have a task that is in many ways made more difficult by the constraints.

HORNKE

Now let's turn to the chapter from our visitor, not our visitor for the first time, but somebody who is very familiar at ETS. In many ways I'd say Lutz Hornke brings us a breath of fresh air. For one thing, by helping us to remember within ETS, that are not just things that look like verbal reasoning, or quantitative reasoning, but that in the outside world, people have thought more broadly about the subject of testing than we typically do here. Right away, that's a big breath of fresh air. Thank you for that.

Lutz also brings us the idea of exploring. His chapter is high on empiricism, but high on generality too, because he looks at lots of different situations, lots of different contexts and sees what happens, and sees that sometimes things work better and sometimes they don't, and tries to understand why that would be. Also, compared to Mary and Kathy, Lutz has the luxury of saying, "I'm going to make up a test on matrices, and nobody is going to stick me with a bunch of items that have already been calibrated. I'm going to make up my own and calibrate my own, and I'll see how they do. And I'll find out what happens." It's starting from scratch. Starting with principled approaches certainly gives you a big advantage over somebody who is doing what might be called archeology. So that certainly is fun.

One thing that intrigues me in general about this issue is the question of what I would call "yield." I don't know if that is a good word. It's sort of an agricultural word. But you say, "Ok, I generated x hundred times using the rule I constructed and then I fit the Rasch model and guess what? Lots of items didn't fit, or lots of items generated funny things that I didn't expect." So, in other words, the original product had so many items, and the final set had so many fewer. You could even go one step further and say, of the ones that looked Ok in terms of IRT, there were some that we could predict well using our model, and others we couldn't. We'd finally come down to the subset of items that make it through this entire process. That's the yield. And one way of evaluating any of these different approaches to item generation, would be a yield measure. A yield measure in fact is for many purposes even more interesting than an R^2 for instance. They're obviously in some sense related, but certainly if your goal is to save GRE or something like that, the yield may be more important. You could say "Well, I can generate 5,000 items, of which only 500 are finally useable." You may not be thanked for that exercise.

So anyway, that got me thinking about the issue of yield and Lutz is very good about providing lots of detail. I could see he is very honest in saying, "Guess what, we started with this many items, and when we were done there were only this many left. And here were the problems." Actually, one of my questions for Mary and Kathy was when they generated the 48 or 96 items in the first part of their study, were there any bummers there?

One other thing I want to say about Lutz's paper is something that I liked but was a bit unsure about. In the case of the Profacts, there was an explicit use described. It was that this test was specifically used for personnel assessment. Then there was a predictive validity study done that gave such and such a prediction. One of my questions for the author was, when you did that, were you using estimated item difficulties from your model? Or were you using the ones fitted from the calibration? This is the "calibrating with little or no data" story. In some sense, what you'd like would be something that generated item parameter estimates, and then, without any calibration, you apply them, and ask "Gee, how well does this test work?" In this framework when trying to predict supervisor's ratings, or whatever it might be.

So, in general, I'd come back to the issue of test use. It may be that a relatively low multiple correlation between predicted item difficulties and estimated item difficulties may still produce something that is very useful in a particular context. Whereas even a high correlation under other circumstances may produce something that is not so useful. It depends on the use, it depends on what you're trying for. In many situations, with many of these tests there was not necessarily a specific use in mind when the author constructed them. It was more of an illustration of the ability to do this sort of thing. But eventually, when we want to apply these systems in a given situation, we will want to answer the question, "How much did it help or hurt to do it this way?"

DISCUSSION

BRAUN:

Thank you Charlie. I see that you've been rather explicit in setting some challenges for our speakers, so I wonder if any of them would be interested in responding directly to some of the questions that you raised.

Portal and test use

MISLEVY:

I'll second Charlie's comments on the importance of use and validity. The theoretical conception of proficiency in some domain doesn't by any stretch of the imagination tell how you build an assessment around that. Consider the communicative competence notion, on TOEFL 2000 (a new version of the Test of English as a Foreign Language, still in development). In designing that test, you could have very different student models depending on whether you wanted to give somebody feedback for learning better or you just wanted an overall selection instrument. You have a purpose, and you have the constraints you have to work under. What you have, if you work from the theoretical conception, is some scaffolding to help you with your construct validity argument, and some of the choices you have to make. The validity checks are going to have to be from that scaffolding: How well did you actually do what it was that you hoped you were doing?

I'll thank the marketing department for the "principled assessment design" term. Having a framework can help you get started, but no one should ever think that that's really all you do—toss in a couple of research studies, and a book or two, turn the crank, and out comes the assessment.

BRAUN:

Right. Well, in fact, to make that clearer: The amount of work that goes into an application of Portal to any area is a very detailed cognitive analysis. This underscores a point Bob made. The framework is very fine to sell it, but to actually make it happen, requires all that work underneath.

MISLEVY:

Yeah, and the larger framework, certainly details of which we didn't go into, one of the important things you need to capture are the requirements for

187

the assessment you have to build. And that would include things like the purposes and the target populations and the constraints and the affordances you have to work with.

ALMOND:

Well, one thing I wanted to point out to Charlie was that if you really wanted to see more about the use of the test, you should have been reading our last year's papers. Then we were working on the student model, and we were thinking about those issues very strongly. Now we're trying to push what we're doing a little towards the task model.

The importance of good criteria in validity studies

ALMOND:

Another thing I wanted to point out was something that came up in the discussion at lunch, about predictive validity. Very often the thing we're trying to measure—ability to perform well in graduate school, ability to practice dental hygiene well, or maintain an F-15 aircraft—is pretty abstract. It's often hard to find good, reliable measures of those things we'd really like our assessment to predict. And so you have to spend a good deal of time and hard thought about what really are the knowledge, skills, and abilities you're trying to measure, and whether or not this assessment product you're making is really doing a good job of that.

HORNKE:

Well, I'm very happy that Charlie voiced a need for validation. Sid Irvine shocked my students because they believed in very cheap, everyday criteria as validation criteria, and it should be the other way around. We should have highly controlled, expensive criteria. When you go to industry—that's my field—it's hard to persuade those people to give you those data back. I would definitely love to do these studies, and then tell you a different story. As a matter of fact, I'm dreaming of the fact that you have item-generation features, and you can have a direct conceptual link to criteria behavior. If you see the features mirrored in the criterion behavior, then you could start up, and definitely design a good test, and I'm with you.

IRVINE:

I wanted to say that Cronbach's notion was like this. He said if you really want to destroy all the good work you've done in building a test, then the criterion you use should be field-based, unsupervised, and inexpensive. Russell, I think that's wherein lies the problem you articulated so well before. That you are really at the mercy of whatever information you get from very busy managers, registrars at universities, and the like. I think Howard Wainer had a sign in his office that said if you think good validity studies are expensive, try a bad one! Is that right Howard?

WAINER:

Close enough!

Validating Portal: Is Portal the right framework?

BENNETT:

What I took from Charlie's comment, about the need for validation, may be somewhat different from what he meant, or what other people understood. But, at any rate, I think that providing a framework does not absolve Portal from responsibility for validation, in the sense that it's possible to provide a framework of process and tools, that lead people down certain paths, even if the paths they take, the way they pursue those paths, and the specifics, are the responsibility of the developers of the instruments, not the developers of Portal. So what I'm saying is that maybe things you do in setting up that process that point people in certain directions may be more or less useful in the long run and that we'll only know that from result.

ALMOND:

I'm not arguing the need for validation, what I'm arguing is that validation without a framework, not necessarily a Portal framework, but a framework of some sort, is the ultimate problem. In order to think seriously about validation you first have to think about what your target measure is.

BENNETT:

I'm not sure how you separate your responsibility from the responsibility of the people who actually do the implementation of particular measures using the framework. I think that's a tough problem.

STEINBERG:

Portal deals with the domains of assessment design. Its principles, hopefully, are not that constraining that one needs to be suspicious of it, as something that's too principled. As with most tools, it was never meant to absolve people of the responsibility for the content of what it is they're doing. There's a difference between the domain of assessment design, and the domain of the assessment. So, what comes out is only going to be as good as what goes in. Hopefully what Portal does embody are the pointers, the concepts, that we feel are useful in helping guide people toward a coherent albeit still possibly misguided product.

BENNETT:

My point was that what goes out, is a function of what goes in, plus the framework—that there is some interaction between the framework and what goes in.

MISLEVY:

One analogy is that it's sort of like a CAD package for designing buildings. A CAD package may have a plumbing module, an electrical module, so that at least you're probably not going to design a house and get it all built, then think, oh, I forgot the plumbing. And what it may do is, if you have the code for the requirements of plumbing, you put in some of the requirements, and it will help you at least think about the right things to get a good approximation of what you want. You can have very ugly designs come out, but at least ones that are in accordance with the code, and the laws of physics.

LEWIS:

Randy, I like your idea. I think, that is a principle of writing—to have something that many people can interpret in many ways, and don't leave it so well specified! So I indeed meant to keep it very general, although that particular generality I hadn't thought about. But let me try to illustrate one thing I was thinking about, but I didn't put it in that framework. This is picking on you guys a little bit, and I didn't really want to do that, but since Randy brought it up: The idea of separating. Let me do it specifically in the context of the statistician, so it will be 3PL. There is the student model, the task model, and the evidence model. Now, in the student model, all you did was write a theta. As a statistician, I would say that that theta is like a platonic true-score. It has no meaning until I know a whole bunch of things—what tasks we're talking about, what items are going to be included, what model I'm assuming about the relation between the performance (Rasch, or 3PL, for instance). But it could be a lot more general than that. Other things are what population I'm going to be applying it in, how much time you give people to do it, are you playing hard rock music while they're doing it. So there's a whole setting that is necessary before I know what that theta is. The danger, that I think Randy is pointing out, is that you separate that unit out, you isolate that as a separate piece. I think it's a danger that I won't blame the Portal developers for, but it's certainly something that I see happening as a result of people learning about item response theory in a particular way. They instantiate theta in a way that is totally unjustified. And so the framework you apply can make a difference, and some frameworks are more valid than others.

MISLEVY:

Well, you're absolutely right, but that theta doesn't mean anything until you've got all the other stuff instructed. What we'd really like to avoid is doing all that other stuff, and there's a theta that happened to be whatever it is because you made a whole bunch of decisions, and then add to the fact, you try to figure out what theta measures: "What have I measured?" What you need is a validity circle. You've got some theoretical intentions of some kind of proficiency that you want to get evidence about. You think about how you want to do it, you design settings, you figure out how to get pieces of evidence. You figure out how to marshal those in various configurations through the sampling specs. When you do all that, hopefully guided by your theory, you have, in fact, operationally defined this theta. Then you've got the responsibility of saying is this anything like what I had at the outset, when I meant to do it? You can now check back and forth. You know what to do validity studies by. I think that nothing in the framework is magic. There are lots of pieces that all get done anyway, and what we would like to do is make people think about what those pieces are, why they are, and how they only come to exist in relationship to the other pieces.

Item generation used operationally

BRAUN:

Thank you. I want to exercise my prerogative as the Phil Donahue of the afternoon, and note that we're almost out of time with the discussion session. So I'd like to call on Chris Elshaw to tell us a little bit on his experience in the British Ministry of Defense, on the validity of tests based on item generation. Would you be willing to do that?

ELSHAW:

BARB (*the computerized British Army Recruit Battery*) has been operational now since 1992 and it predates my arrival at the defense evaluation and research agency, so I can't really take any credit for that. Historically, actually, it may be kind of curious in the sense that the British Army, shall we say, took a very courageous move, in the sense that they had the finances to implement computer-based testing and went ahead and did it without any validation evidence at all. There may have been 1 or 2 pilot studies, which mainly provided the validation data, but they were paper-and-pencil versions of BARB. So one could regard that as a very courageous move. We have conducted now a number of validation studies, 3, covering most of the occupational groups in the army. Generally speaking, I guess average predictive validity correlations at their lowest are about .35, but going up to about .59.

BRAUN:

What are the criteria in these studies?

ELSHAW:

They're generally school-based measures simply because they're the measures we actually can obtain. There are two kinds. Some are written examinations, some are field-based, like military knowledge, map reading, and various other things. Generally speaking, the better the criterion data, the better the predictive validities. There are also two aspects. We have been comparing what in the UK we regard as "table measures," things like verbal ability, and various other things. And there seems to be a distinction: The BARB-type measurements seem to add predictive validity when we're measuring non-book-learning type criteria. That is, the book-learning criteria, the attainment measures, like verbal reasoning, numerical reasoning, come out higher, which is not surprising really, because there's a direct correspondence between those towards the criteria. Because if you're good at maths, we test you on a maths examination. It's hardly surprising that you get high correlations between the two. But it looks like the correlations between BARB type measures—g or working memory—might be better predictors of general occupational ability. We're hoping next year to start determining predictive validities with what the army would call Phase III training—the training people are doing on the job, not schoolhouse training. I predict that BARB-type measures will give us better predictions there (with on-the-job criteria), than would things like numeracy and literacy, so I guess that's what we have to wait for.

IRVINE:

Just to recap, you're still giving a new form of BARB to every new recruit, right?

ELSHAW:

It's item generated. The other interesting thing, related to Sid's work on response latency, is that this will reduce the testing time to 16 minutes, which is remarkably efficient, to say the very least. Now, we haven't yet got the predictive validities from that, but the estimates from the experimental work is that it's not going to produce any reduction in validity. The Australian Army has adopted BARB as a common tri-service screening test, and their initial studies confirm all the ones that we found in the UK.

WAINER:

There's an ancient Confucian expression that says that the first step toward wisdom is getting the name right. I've listened to two different words that you've used, Chris, efficient and courageous. Courageous is giving a test without any validation. I guess crawling across the M1 at rush hour would be considered courageous, but some say that it was foolish.

   If you call a test "efficient" if you can administer it in 15 minutes, is it even more efficient if you can give it in 3 minutes? Or can we find a more descriptive term than "efficient"? Certainly this would be so if the success of our 3 minute test was analogous to the probable success of someone crawling across the M1 during rush hour. I suspect that the relationship between the word you chose and the phenomena it was describing could be more fully illuminated if there was a validity study. Then we would know whether the descriptor associated with a 15 minute unvalidated test should be "courageous," "efficient," "foolish," or something else. Remember St. Augustine's wise conclusion *Securus indicatorbus terrarum*.

BRAUN:

It seems to me that that was the point, that there was a validity study.

WAINER:

. . . separated by a common language.

Cost and efficiency issues

LUEBKE:

Chris, I really like what you said about the 15 minutes, I'd like to bring up the idea that . . .

BRAUN:

He's our efficiency expert, obviously!

LUEBKE:

I'm going to look at this from the marketing perspective, although I'm not in marketing, or a business perspective, or let's go back to the customer. This goes right to the validity aspect. And it goes to the point that was made earlier about how we implement it all the way through the whole system, from the validity through the actual implementation of the item development, to the presentation of this instrument, this test, if you will, to the person that's taking the test, and then the eventual customer, which may be a combination of the test taker, and whatever it is that we're trying to do about or to this test taker. I think it's really important that as we think about all this process, we think about how much value is being added to the system with our instrument, vs. how much it's costing us to develop this system. If the process is perfectly valid, and perfectly psychometrically sound, but it costs the customer more than the customer gains from it, they won't buy it very long. And the 15 minute test, for a military personnel, where you're interested in running people in, and finding out something about them, then getting them out so that you can either start to change their educational process or whatever they have to do, I think that that's very valid. We may be able to spend a lot more when we're trying to decide about a person going to college, but we really need to keep this in the back of our minds as psychometricians, and as trying to develop this Portal, how much do we need?

IRVINE:

We've always had this notion about a cost–benefit triangle. That the more people you test, the shorter you could test them if they were inexpensive to train. The more you were prepared to spend to make sure there was no failure in extended training, the more you had to actually do in the secondary phase assessment and selection. But for conscripts, 280,000 a year, which our friend here, Thomas Kutschke (*ed. note: Mr Kutschke works for the German Defence Ministry*) has to deal with, he doesn't want to spend 3 ½ hours on every person in front of a computer. The ASVAB just won't do in such contexts, bless us, even the CAT-ASVAB might prove to be too expensive. But you're quite right, people won't buy it if it costs too much, and you don't get incremental validity in the computer over what you've had already in the old paper-and-pencil tests. No point in developing an elaborate insect spray if you have somebody with a fly swatter to kill the wasp, as it were.

ELSHAW:

BARB is not the only part of military selection. You're not selected purely on BARB, scores. There are many other measures—not psychometric tests—but many other measures under consideration.

IRVINE:

How long do you take to process a recruit on the day?

ELSHAW:

There is a bit more room. I think it could be about 2 to 3 hours, in which there's a whole series of interviews, and other things.

BRAUN:

Well, thank you very much to the speakers, the discussant, and all of you in the audience who have participated. And, I guess we're going to call an end to today's session, and we'll take a 2 minute break, then we'll reconvene for the memorial session for Sam. Thank you.

III
FROM THEORY TO
IMPLEMENTATION

7

Generative Testing: From Conception to Implementation

Isaac I. Bejar
Educational Testing Service

In this chapter I discuss briefly a definition and rationale for generative testing with an emphasis on the prerequisites to implement generative testing: a thorough construct analysis that culminates in precise specifications capable of supporting generative testing. I then describe an application that led to an operational licensing exam. I conclude with some future prospects and outline some needed work to advance a generative approach. For a review of the literature, consult Bejar (1993).

DEFINITIONS AND OVERVIEW

It is useful to distinguish different meanings or levels of generativity. At one extreme we can talk about a *functional* level where the emphasis is in the generation per se but without explicit consideration of the constructs under measurement or a detailed modeling of responses. Earlier work within an educational tradition fits that description and is illustrated by the work of Hively (1974) and Bormuth (1970) among others. They proposed generative approaches whereby items were generated to measure a specific educational objective. As noted by Merwin (1977), implied in the notion of generating items for a given educational objective was the expectation that items would be of the same difficulty because they presumably measured a well-defined bit of knowledge. He concluded that, at least in the data he had examined, this expectation was not fulfilled. This early history suggests that generative testing without a concomitant theoretical analysis is not feasible.

A higher level generativity can be called *model-based*. At this level the generation of items is guided by models of performance, for example a cognitive analysis relevant to the domain under consideration. This is the level at which we are operating for the most part as illustrated by the other chapters in this book. For example, Enright and Sheehan (chap. 5, this volume) have proposed variables inspired by cognitive theory to account for variation in item difficulty, which in turn can be used to guide the generation of items. Similarly, Mislevy, Steinberg, and Almond (chap. 4, this volume) provide a framework to guide item generation by examining the many ways in which the construction of items, and more generally tasks, influence the inferences we ultimately draw from scores. They argue persuasively that without such an analysis any test design, not just a generatively oriented test design, is bound to encounter difficulties. Their framework, Portal, packages several aspects of the test design process and has immediate implications for item generation. Hornke (chap. 6, this volume) provides a model-based application to adaptive testing.

A third level of generativity can be called the grammatical. At this level the item generation and psychometric modeling are completely intertwined in such a way that it becomes possible to not only generate items but also "parse" any item to characterize its psychometric properties. That is, grammars exist for collections of items that allow the generation and parsing of items in the same fashion that a linguistics grammar (Chomsky, 1965) allows generation of sentence and parsing of sentences that belong to the grammar. Bejar and Yocom (1991) illustrated this level of generativity in a visual-spatial context. Revuelta and Ponsoda (1999) and Embretson (chap. 8, this volume) discuss examples that approach the grammatical level. The appeal of this level of generativity is undeniable. However, in practice, it may not be feasible to implement it readily for a variety of reasons. An area that seems ready for implementation is analogical reasoning (Bejar, Chaffin, & Embretson, 1991). The state of the art in computational linguistics has improved dramatically and now it seems feasible to tackle generative assessment of analogical reasoning and other verbal item types at a grammatical level. Similarly, the work on the Analytic Reasoning item type described by Newstead, Bradon, Handley, Evans, and Dennis (chap. 3, this volume), opens the door to a grammatical level of generativity for that item type. What Newstead et al. and his associates have accomplished is a deep level representation for that item type. Getting to this deep level representation, the parsing of the item, is feasible although we refer to it rather inelegantly as "back coding." The generation of items from this deep representation is also under investigation by Cédrick Fairon at ETS. The narrow scope of natural language in this item type makes it possible to write small grammars, which are implemented in INTEX (Silberzstein, 1993).

A further classification dimension of generative approaches is in terms of whether the item-generation process aims to hold difficulty constant, or to vary difficulty in a systematic fashion. Dennis' (chap. 3, this volume) distinction between "Approach 1" and "Approach 2" captures this dichotomy as well. At Educational Testing Service items generated with the constraint that they be of the same psychometric attributes have often been called *isomorphs*.[1] The term *isomorph* derives from cognitive theory (Simon & Hayes, 1976). The term was used by Bejar and Yocom (1991) to describe an approach to automated item generation where the objective is to define classes, what we later call *item models*, from which it is possible to generate or produce items *that are in all respects equivalent, isomorphic, to all other items produced by a given model.* An approach based on isomorphs is especially well suited to types of examinations, such as a licensing exam, where the objective is to make a pass–fail decision on the test taker and the challenge is to generate randomly drawn forms that are psychometrically equivalent. The approach, however, has more broad utility. In an admission context, unlike a licensing context, where the objective is to locate a student on a continuum, an optimal exam is adaptive in nature and therefore the items available to assemble a form must range in difficulty. This can be accomplished through a pool of item models that spans the difficulty spectrum. The adaptive algorithm then chooses item models, instead of items, during the adaptive process. Having chosen an item model an isomorph is then generated. The other approach identified by Dennis seems consistent with the use of the term *variant*. The term is used to refer to instances of an item model that range in difficulty or some other psychometric characterization of the items. In this case, rather than holding constant the psychometric attributes of the generated items the goal is to produce a range of difficulty. The example, presented shortly relies on isomorphs. An example using variants can be found in Bejar (1990).

In the remainder of the chapter, I discuss the role of construct analysis in generative testing. I then present an illustration of generative testing from the field of licensure testing. I conclude with some future prospects and outline some needed work to advance a generative approach to educational and psychological measurement.

CONCEPTION: CONSTRUCT ANALYSIS AND TEST DESIGN

Any assessment should begin with a very thorough analysis of the constructs intended to be measured and the circumstances under which the examination will be developed, administered, delivered, scored, and reported. This is especially true when the goal is generative modeling. In fact, taking a generative perspective forces the developer to wrestle with

---

[1] The term *clone* is often used for what we are here calling *isomorph*. The use of clone however does not seem appropriate for the intended meaning. By definition clones are both genotypically and phenotipically identical. If we equate genotype with a cognitive requirements of the item and phenotype with what the item actually looks like, it is obvious that in generating items we want them to share a cognitive representation and yet look differently to the test taker.

issues that might otherwise not need to be resolved in a non-generative context. As Bob Mislevy indicated at the conference on which this volume is based, the generation itself is not necessarily what is more important but rather the level of understanding about the construct that makes generation possible. Bennett and Bejar (1999) made a similar point with respect to automated scoring, namely that the mechanics of automated scoring are not the essence of the accomplishment. Rather, to make automated scoring possible, and to make item generation possible, it is necessary to understand the construct and the goal of the examination in far more detail that would otherwise be the case. The common thread in both of these arguments is that technological innovation in assessment should be grounded on the constructs we aim to measure rather than in technology per se.

Granted that a deep understanding of the construct and purpose of measurement are essential to designing a sound measure, there are multiple avenues to reach that understanding. A generative approach does not dictate a particular approach. Possible approaches include a "job analysis" typically carried out in conjunction with licensing exams, or a detailed cognitive analysis of the construct and response processes as exemplified by Embretson (chap. 8, this volume) or Carpenter and Just (1987). Similarly, the Portal system (see Mislevy et al., chapter 4, this volume) can be used to manage the analysis within a framework that emphasizes an evidence-centered approach to assessment. The Portal system by explicitly modeling the different "objects" (Almond, Steinberg, & Mislevy, 1999) in an assessment not only enforces their acknowledgment but also could facilitate the design of assessments and enhance the quality of their results.

A construct analysis, of course, is just a starting point. That is, at the start of the development of an assessment there may be open questions about the nature of the construct of interest. By the completion of the development those questions should have been answered and all our knowledge should have been leveraged to define a *base pool* or *base form* that is optimal for the specific *test design,* such as a linear or adaptive design, respectively, that has been adopted. A base pool or form consist of *item models or task models.* The term *item model* refers explicitly to discrete items whereas *task models* refer to larger free-response tasks. We borrow the term *item model* from (LaDuca, Templeton, Holzman, & Staples, 1986) who first used it to describe sets of "content equivalent" items. In my usage an item–task model is a set of actual items–tasks, or a mechanism for generating them, that share a common psychometric characterization, such as difficulty, for example. In some instances the set may be constructed "manually" according to specifications; in others they may be generated mechanically. Strictly speaking, the means of producing the items is not the primary defining characteristic of a generative approach. In the simplest case the test design consists of a fixed length linear exam comprised of a fixed set of item models. A slightly more complex situation arises if the exam is linear and fixed length but different test takers are assigned a set of randomly drawn item models. In the first case the base pool consists of just the few item models that appear in every form. In the second case the base pool is the collection of the different item models that can appear in a form. In both cases there is a large number of possible test forms. Similarly, for the adaptive case one defines the base pool as the set of item models from which an adaptive exam is constructed. The details of defining a base pool are necessarily more complex in the adaptive case but it is equally applicable and can be illustrated in a simple adaptive design, called the flexilevel exam (Lord, 1980). In this case item models are arranged in difficulty. Every test taker starts with an item model of medium difficulty. Then next, an easier or harder item model is administered, depending on the immediate prior response, until a fixed number has been administered. In other words, whereas traditionally we thought of items, we now think of item models that represent a collection of items sharing common psychometric characterizations. As in the traditional item-based case, a generative systems base pool consists of a set of item models and a stopping rule to achieve a given level of precision. For clarification, Figure 7.1 describes the relationship among the various terms introduced so far.

Much occurs between the time of the construct analysis, the creation of base form–pool, and the construction of item models. The process can be described as a set of iterations. For example, the initial iteration may consist of a conceptual definition of the base pool, including conceptual descriptions of the item models proposed to comprise the base pool. The attempt to create the item models from the conceptual definitions will need to satisfy several constraints and the resolution of those constraints most likely will raise question that had not been anticipated. Such questions will need to be addressed and in that process further elucidation of the construct will be achieved. In addition to the purely psychometric criteria, some of the constraints that need to be examined at each iteration of the process include questions of interface design, security, equity, cost.

For example, issues of examinee interface are critical in any computer-based exam (Bennett & Bejar, 1999). To the extent that the interface introduces variance that is irrelevant to the construct under measurement, overall quality will suffer. A possible antidote to interface effects is to introduce a tutorial to allow test takers to practice. That decision cannot be reached independently of other factors, however. If the tutorial is made

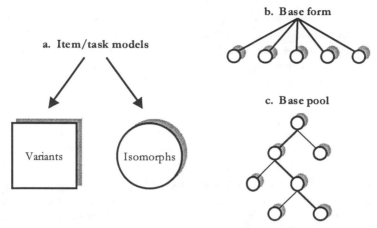

FIG. 7.1. Item and task models can take two forms. When instances of task or item model are meant to be equivalent we refer to them as isomorphs. If the instances vary in some systematic fashion we refer to them as variants. A base form is a set of task or item models. The set of models may be fixed or drawn at random. For example, the model in position 1 could be composed of a set of models of narrow scope, one of which gets selected at random. Then an instance of that item model is generated at random as well. By extension, a base pool is populated by item or task models rather than items. Also, the models could be narrow in scope and homogeneous in their psychometric properties or consists of sets of models narrow in scope but spanning a range of difficulty.

available at the test center it will necessarily consume some time. That additional time would raise the price of the examination, or if the price needs to be held constant, it will reduce the time for testing, which in turn could erode the precision of the scores. The option of using the tutorial off line may or may not be feasible. For example, the system may be so complex as to require a level of equipment that is not readily accessible to all test takers and therefore to do so would create an unfair situation for some test takers.

These issues, cost, timing, interface development, and fairness need to be kept in mind while the item models themselves are being defined. The starting point for that process is a set of specifications for the item models that covers the construct and will ultimately form the base pool or form. Some item models would cover specific aspects of performance and collectively need to represent proportionally the importance of different aspects of performance, as established, for example, as part of a job analysis, or in the educational case, in an attempt to follow mandated content standards. A likely scenario is that the prototype for such item models may already exist in the form of recognized exemplar items or tasks. In such a case, the pre-existing prototypes would be examined against the specifications to decide how well they fit as they stand and, if lack of fit is found, to introduce necessary changes. Invariably, this process will identify gaps, and new item models will need to be formulated to fill the gaps. In the end, however, there may be more candidate item models available than are feasible to use, in light, for example, of the maximum time that is available for testing as opposed to tutorials. In that case some principle would be needed to select from those the subset that will comprise the base form or pool.

The construct analysis process leading to item or task models is highly iterative as well as empirical because the psychometric attributes of an item model cannot, in general, be anticipated with certainty. As noted earlier, an item model represents a collection of items, whether already available or to be generated, that share a common psychometric characterization, for example difficulty. In practice, the common psychometric characterization needs to be estimated. For the intended common characterization to hold it must be the case that it adequately describes the set of instances of the item model. Whether this is the case or not needs to be established empirically by administering instances of the item model, that is, instances thereof, whether isomorphs or variants, to representative test takers under conditions similar to those prevailing operationally.

Assessing how well instances, whether isomorphs or variants, fit the corresponding item or task model is important but should not be seen as an all-or-none outcome. Instead it should be seen as a design parameter. For example, it may be possible to relax the fit in instances where the test can be lengthened to compensate for the relatively lesser precision that would result from such lack of fit (e.g., Bejar 1996; Revuelta, Bejar, & Stocking, 1998). However, such a decision cannot be made in isolation. If time is at a premium, then a higher degree of isomorphicity may be required. In order to achieve it, it may be necessary to better understand the response process or to constrain the item model. However, excessively constraining item models can be counterproductive if it means that the generated items are essentially identical to each other.

Scoring considerations are central to the development process in the case of free-response tasks. Whereas the task or items attempt to elicit the evidence we seek, it is through the scoring process that we obtain that evidence. Whenever the goal is to carry out scoring in an automated fashion, a natural process under computer-based testing, scorability becomes an attribute of an item or task model. Scorability in part refers to the technical feasibility of extracting from a free response by means of a computing routine the response attributes called for by the assessment. Scorability is also linked to other aspects of the assessment, most notably interface design. Typically, to make response more scorable the range of responses needs to be limited in some way. This in turn can lead to an interface that is unnatural or require some skills that are not relevant to the construct under measurement. Other things being equal, the more open ended the interface, the more natural it will be. In a generative context scorability is also linked to the fit between isomorphs or variants to their corresponding model. That is, in a generative context the automated scoring procedure must be capable of scoring equivalently all instances of a task model. To the extent that isomorphicity does not hold it could be due to some instances departing from the task model or simply because the scoring procedure has not been programmed to anticipate the idiosyncrasies of every instance of the task model. In the first case, such instances need to be modified accordingly. In the latter case, the automated scoring procedure needs to be enhanced to achieve isomorphicity. As noted by Bejar and Bennett (1999), the scoring procedure allows us to control the relationship of scores to criteria of interest by emphasizing or de-emphasizing certain response attributes as part of the scoring process. A similar procedure can be used to achieve a higher degree of fit. Of course, maintaining relationships with outside criteria and fit may be at odds with each other so a compromise mediated by expert judgment may be needed to arrive at a final scoring procedure that is most satisficing (e.g., Williamson, Bejar, & Hone, 1999).

The foregoing gives a flavor of construct analysis oriented to generative assessment and how it leads to the formulation of item and task models. Figure 7.2 is an attempt to describe the process. It appears to be a more demanding process than it might be if generative assessment were not the goal. However, the many additional benefits of a generative perspective more than compensate for any additional effort. In fact, in the long run a generative approach may be more cost effective than traditional item development. Once a generative system is in place it should be able to be used for a longer period of time than current procedures permit. Exceptions include situations where test specifications change or the security of the system becomes compromised or "wears out." At another level, and as noted by Sid Irvine at the item-generation conference, generative assessment advances our knowledge of the domain, first by forcing us as part of the design process to wrestle with design questions and second, by forcing us resolve unexpected results. That is, a task model is not unlike a hypothesis that is tested every time we administer instances derived from that item model. In that sense the pragmatic advantages of a generative approach although not trivial are not the best justification for an adaptive approach. A more important justification is the greater understanding of what we are measuring and the enhanced score meaning that follows.

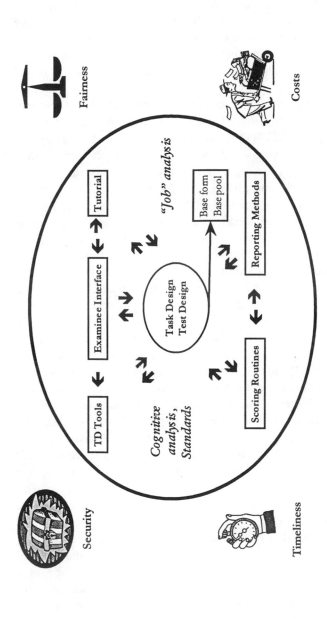

FIG. 7.2. The assessment design process is iterative and constrainted by several external factors. From a starting point of a job or cognitive analysis, a base form or pool ultimately emerges which takes into account the implications of scoring, score reporting, the background of the examinees, the possible need for tutorials, and finally the availability of test development tools. Among the external considerations that affect the process are security, costs, timeliness, and fairness (after Bennet & Bejar, 1999).

IMPLEMENTATION: AN APPLICATION TO LICENSING

ARE 97 (Bejar & Braun, 1999; Kenney, 1997) is a licensing exam for architects. It is the first national high stakes examination to rely on automated scoring operationally. It is also an example of generative modeling. A generative approach was seen as an effective means of dealing with the security considerations raised by an on-demand computer-based examination, and therefore illustrates some of the significant practical advantages of a generative perspective to assessment design.

ARE 97[2] is an example of model-based generative assessment. Cognitive theory relevant to the architectural design process was brought to bear (e.g., Akin, 1986; Katz, 1994a, 1194b) on the design of task models. However, the construct analysis for the exam was driven extensively, as is the case in most licensing examinations, by a job analysis designed to identify the knowledge, skills, and abilities (KSAs) required of a beginning architect. Such a job analysis (Stetcher, 1989) was already in existence and served as the initial round. Traditionally, the aspects of competence most suitable to free-response formats have been those of "building design" and "site design." As the name implies, building design refers to the formulation of a plan or design needed to construct a building, in this case a two-story building. Site design, on the other hand, refers to aspects of design relating to the site only, such as its topography. Because the test was transitioning from a paper exam to a computer delivered exam, this presented the opportunity to rethink the relevance of KSAs from a job analysis conducted for the paper-based exam. A new job analysis was carried out (CTB/McGraw Hill, 1994) oriented to the new delivery medium. This information was and factored into the design of the new assessment. A key goal of that design was "integrativeness," or the tapping of multiple KSAs within a free-response task. Under the original paper platform, the building design assessment consisted of a 12-hour single-item exam. On the positive side of this situation, a 12-hour exam allowed examinees to dwell on skills applied in concert to arrive at a feasible design. However, on the negative side, scoring of such massive performance presents significant logistic and cognitive challenges to the judges, which could preclude getting at the evidence being sought because in practice judging sessions impose a certain level of productivity on the part of the judges. As part of the redesign, task types were formulated that more explicitly assessed the skills the original exam had *intended* to cover but was unable to explicitly score for in a systematic fashion. In the end, two separately timed examinations were developed to meet that goal and to explicitly extract additional evidence of competence without necessarily sacrificing integrativeness.

---

[2] Information about ARE 97 can be found at *http://www.ncarb.org/are/index.html.*

A different problem was presented by the assessment for site design component. Whereas for building design new specific task types were formulated to measures important KSAs that were not being explicitly measured, for site design there were already a multitude of potential task types from previous paper examinations. The goal in this case was to select from among the different types already available. Given a set of KSAs and a set of potential types of tasks, it is natural to array them as a matrix with KSAs as columns and task types as rows in an attempt to arrive at a "blueprint" or subset of task types. This requires that subject matter experts rate the task types on each KSA (Elliot & Nelson, 1984; Raymond, 1996) in order to characterize how well a given subset of task types covers the KSAs. Such a KSA by task type matrix was maintained during the development of ARE 97 as a means of judging KSA coverage at any iteration of the assessment design process.

For the site design examination, an optimization procedure was developed to explicitly identify subsets of task types and took into account additional attributes of a task type (Bejar, 1993b). The result of such a procedure is a subset of tasks that maximizes a criterion of choice (such as the importance of the KSAs tapped by the set) and minimizes other criteria (such as the testing time consumed by the set) This proved to be a useful way to guide the discussion among subject matter experts. The set of tasks that is adopted in the end may not be optimal as a function of tangible criteria. However, the subject matter experts presumably take into account intangible criteria that are not available to an optimization procedure.

The ultimate outcome of the construct analysis process is a set of task models or a set of detailed specifications for constructing or generating a number of instances, which are the tasks (items) that are actually administered to test takers. The specifications are built around a prototypic task that is described in extensive detail. The specifications also include the interface elements specific to that task type as well as the scoring criteria. The scoring criteria cannot be done in the abstract but rather must take into account the interface that is available to test takers. By explicitly stating the allowable values of different task attributes, like the range of dimensions for sites, the number of rooms, and so forth, it becomes possible to formulate additional task instances that are isomorphic. To the extent that this objective is achieved it is possible to construct forms that are essentially equivalent to one another. To arrive at the final specification a fair amount of experimentation was carried out. For example, subgroups of test takers were suspect of being more facile with the interface, especially in the early 1990s when ARE 97 was being developed. If true, this could have introduce differential item performance into the assessment. To rule out that possibility, Bridgeman, Bejar, and Friedman (1999) studied the role of computer and other background effects. Although prior computer use and level of expertise were not major problems, the research findings pointed out the need for extensive tutoring of the interface for all examinee as a means of reducing the time limits of the exam without adverse effects. It should be noted that such tutoring would not be practical or cost effective in a secure test center environment. As a result, a decision was made to distribute the final tutorial together with the registration materials so that candidates could practice on their own prior to testing.

Although the motivation for a generative approach in ARE 97 was originally driven by issues of security, as mentioned earlier, the approach can also be justified in psychometric and cognitive terms. The inspiration from a sampling perspective in psychometrics should be evident (Osburn, 1968; Tryon, 1957). From that perspective the meaning of scores is enhanced if scores are based on tests formed from well-defined universes. Another source of inspiration was cognitive psychology, especially efforts from the perspective of understanding and controlling problem complexity and difficulty (Kotovsky, Hayes, & Simon, 1985; Simon & Hayes, 1976) as applied to architecture (Akin 1986, 1994). As such, ARE 97 qualifies as an instance of model-based generative assessment.

The task models that result from a construct analysis are not independent of the test design. Test design refers to the characteristics of the set of tasks administered to each candidate, or the procedure for choosing such a set when the design calls for it, and the conditions, such as allowed time, under which the tasks are administered. Once the characteristics of the available task models are known, it is possible to arrive at a test design that is optimal in, at least in some sense, for the purpose of the assessment. In the present context, the coverage of the KSAs along with other attributes of the task models, such as time requirements, were considered to constitute at a "blueprint" (e.g., Elliot, 1984; Raymond, 1996; Schmeiser, 1986). Among the major considerations, however, was the "sufficiency" or "optimality" of a specific set of task models, called vignette types in the ARE 97 context, with respect to the knowledge, skills, and abilities (ETS, 1993, Appendix 8; Bejar 1993b) identified by job analyses of the architecture profession (CTB/McGraw Hill, 1994; Stecher, 1989). Normally a blueprint is used to construct a single form or at most several forms of an examination. However, for ARE 97 the blueprint was used to construct a stratified pool of vignette types and task models, from which randomly chosen forms could be assembled at the test center by drawing a random instance from each vignette type called for by the test design. In such a design the primary strata are the task models or vignette types, which in this case constitute a fixed set. In practice, substrata are used to facilitate the creation, organization, and maintenance of the base pool. Specifically, the base pool is organized in terms of *scripts* and *isomorphs*. A script might refer to a particular site and building, such as a student center in a college.

Isomorphs within that script are significant variations introduced by altering the requirements, such as the views, the orientations of the building, the traffic patterns, and so forth. Figure 7.3 shows the scheme as applied to the Building Planning division. Because a fair number of test takers are repeaters, the test administration system must keep track of which scripts a candidate may have seen in earlier attempts and preclude repeated administrations of previously seen items.

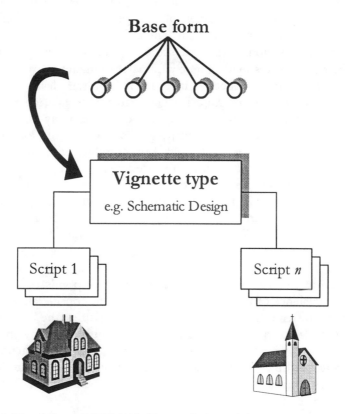

FIG. 7.3. The design of ARE 97 is illustrated. One of the tasks in the base form was Schematic Design. In this task the candidat was asked to design a two storing building according to special specifications. Each building is referred to as a *script*. The variations in the script, the actual task a candidate receives, is called an *isomorph*.

Validation of Generative Systems

The evaluation of scores derived from a generative system follows the same validation procedures (Messick, 1989) that we are already familiar with. Indeed the construct analysis phase could be viewed as a form of "preemptive construct validation." By that I mean designing the assessment mindful of the criteria that we eventually will be required to validate our use of test results. For example, what Embretson (1983) called *construct representation* would seem to be enhanced under a generative approach by virtue of requiring us to control or manipulate the difficulty. To the extent that the generative approach is successful in a given case it must be, in part, because the details of the response process have been sufficiently mastered to allow control of the psychometric characteristics of the generated items or tasks. The level of isomorphicity achieved, or in general how well we control the psychometric attributes of the generated items, feeds into reliability or precision of measurement. The contribution of an item toward reducing the imprecision of a total score is attenuated in part by the imprecision of the corresponding item parameter estimates. In practice, that effect is typically ignored, especially if relatively large samples were used to obtain the original estimates. Under a generative approach, an additional attenuating factor is the lack of psychometric homogeneity among items intended to be equivalent. The attenuating effect of lack of isomorphicity can be compensated for or moderated. For example, with free-response tasks that are scored by computer, the designer of an assessment can moderate psychometric homogeneity, to a certain extent, through the scoring algorithm (Bejar & Bennett, 1999). Thus, construct representation and precision of measurement are strongly linked under a generative design.

In the case of ARE 97, the test design calls for the administration of randomly drawn forms to each candidate. That is, for each candidate the test administration system chooses randomly one instance the vignette types called for. Because every candidate in effect responds to a different form, the equivalence of those forms is an important consideration. That is to ask, are the different forms effectively equated? During the development of ARE 97 every effort was made to ensure the equivalence of vignettes. If there were perfect vignette equivalence for each vignette type, then indeed, every form would be effectively equated. In practice, perfect equivalence is unattainable and may not even be desirable if it is obtained by reducing the scope of generated tasks.

However if the tension between scope and isomorphicity is to be resolved during the design of the assessment, an accounting of the effect of lack of isomorphicity is necessary. Bejar, Chiu, and Muraki (2001) studied the effect of lack of isomorphicity in the ARE 97 context by assessing the pass–fail consistency of randomly drawn forms. The estimate of pass–fail consistency they used required fitting an item response theory response model, namely Samejima's graded response model. Rather than a single estimate of decision consistency, the procedure produces a distribution of such indices to correspond to the situation that in practice a candidate can be administered one of many possible forms.

The second aspect of score validity that Embretson (1983) discussed, is *nomothetic span*, which refers to the relationship of scores with external criteria. When such external criteria are demographic variables (such as race and gender), nomothetic span includes what Messick (1989) called consequential validity considerations. Scores obtained through a generative assessment should undergo that evaluation just as any other assessment would be required. Ideally, the scores should strongly relate to criteria that are logically related and minimally to criteria that are less logically related. Similarly, any group differences should be manifestations of the construct under measurement and not construct irrelevant differences, such as familiarity with computers, for example. In a generative context the added twist, at least with free response scored by computer, is that the possibility of moderating homogeneity through the scoring algorithm can impact nomothetic span, not just construct representation. The scored performance of groups of interest may vary as a function of attempts to increase homogeneity. For example, a writing exam scored by computer could or could not take into account spelling. If it does it is likely there might be differences among certain groups of respondents. If spelling ability is deemed construct relevant, such group differences are appropriate manifestations of the underlying construct. If spelling ability is not deemed construct relevant, then such differences are problematic.

CONCLUSION

I have stressed the importance of construct analysis in this chapter. Such an analysis is an essential precursor to the development of any assessment but is especially important in a generative context. The example I presented illustrates how such analyses lead directly to the definition of task models, which in turn, make it possible to produce instances of the task model. In the example I presented, the generation is done "manually." In my opinion, the method of generation (mechanical or manual) is not an important distinguishing feature. The formulation of a set of task models that collectively provide data as part of some test design, whether linear or adaptive, to arrive at scores or decisions, seems a far more useful characterization of generative assessment.

My example suggests that a generative approach to assessment design is not only feasible but a natural one. It is a natural approach in the sense that it extents the sort of construct analysis that should, in any case, precede the development of an assessment. The extension is to think of *task models* whenever we used to think of items. The approach is inherently empirically driven because thinking of items as manifestation of an item or task model is tantamount to hypothesizing that test takers as a group will behave in a certain way when responding to different instances of an item model. The approach is also natural from a pragmatic perspective. The introduction of computer-based testing has presented unexpected challenges related to cost efficiency. A generative approach can be more cost effective once task models have been formulated. Admittedly, the design of task models is a relatively new endeavor and requires learning. As we shift our thinking from items and tasks to item and task models we will learn to develop them at not much higher cost that traditional items. A task or item model, however, has a longer shelf life that a single task or item. Therefore, there is a significant potential for cost savings in the long run.

Because task models are a higher order representation of actual items, hierarchical psychometric models are the appropriate enhancement to the psychometric framework of choice. Hierarchical modeling suited for generative assessment are already present in generalizability theory (Brennan, 1992; Cronback, Gleser, Nanda, & Rajaratnam, 1972) and applications exist to (Bejar & Oltman, 1999; Gao, 1996) a generative context. The practical limits of G theory in this context are due to the difficulties of dealing with missing data. That is, we can think of generative assessment as a missing data problem where a test taker takes only one from many possible instances. The missing data problem in generalizability theory is being tackled (Chiu, 1999). Similarly, Lord (1977) outlined some basic theory relevant to the case under classical test theory. The most promising framework in some sense appears to be IRT. Specifically, the expected response function idea due to Charlie Lewis and implemented in Mislevy, Sheehan, and Wingersky (1994) handles nicely the case when an adaptive algorithm administers a random instance of an item model. For dichotomously scored items, additional empirical Bayesian approaches that are oriented to generation, or can easily be oriented to generation, can be found in Bradlow, Wainer, and Wang (1999), Fox and Glas (1998), Janssen, Tuerlinckx, Meulders, and De Boeck (1999), and Wright (chap. 10, this volume). Expansions to the polytomous case are already in progress. A program, Scoreright (Wang, Bradlow, & Wainer, 2000), already exists for the three parameter and graded response case. Applications to educational surveys (e.g., Hombo & Dresher, 2001) are also under investigation. The future of generative assessment looks promising.

REFERENCES

Akin, O. (1986). *Psychology of architectural design.* London: Pion Limited.

Akin, O. (1994, May). *Calibration of problem difficulty: In architectural design problems designed for the automated licensing examination system in the United States of America.* Unpublished manuscript, Princeton, NJ.

Almond, R. G., Steinberg, L. S., & Mislevy, R. J. (1999). *A sample assessment using the four process framework.* White paper prepared for the IMS Working Group on Question and Test Interoperability. Princeton, NJ: Educational Testing Service.

Bejar, I. I. (1990). A generative analysis of a three-dimensional spatial task. *Applied Psychological Measurement, 14*(3), 237–245.

Bejar, I. I. (1993a). A generative approach to psychological and educational measurement. In N. Frederiksen, R. J. Mislevy, & I. I. Bejar (Eds.), *Test theory for a new generation of tests* (pp. 323–359). Hillsdale, NJ: Lawrence Erlbaum Associates.

Bejar, I. I. (1993b). *Optimization approach to the design of tests consisting of complex tasks.* Psychometric Society, Barcelona, Spain.

Bejar, I. I. (1996). *Generative response modeling: Leveraging the computer as a test delivery medium* (Research Report No. RR-96-13). Princeton, NJ: Educational Testing Service.

Bejar, I. I., & Bennett, R. E. (1999). La puntuación de las respuestas como un parámetro del diseño de exámenes: Implicaciones en la validez [Scoring as a test design parameter: Implications for validity]. In J. Olea, V. Ponsoda, & G. Prieto (Eds.), *Tests informatizados: Fundamentos y aplicaciones* (pp. 53–59). Madrid: Pirámide.

Bejar, I. I., & Braun, H. I. (1999). *Architectural simulations: From research to implementation.* Final report to the National Council of Architectural Registration Boards (Research Memorandum No. RM-99-2). Princeton, NJ: Educational Testing Service.

Bejar, I. I., Chaffin, R. B., & Embretson, S. (1991). *Cognitive and psychometric analysis of analogical problem solving.* New York: Springer-Verlag.

Bejar, I. I., Chiu, C. W. T., & Muraki, E. (2001). *Characterization of decision consistency under random sampling of forms:An IRT approach.* Princeton, NJ: Educational Testing Service.

Bejar, I. I., & Oltman, P. K. (1999). *Generalizability analyses of architectural design performance.* Princeton, NJ: Educational Testing Service.

Bejar, I. I., & Yocom, P. (1991). A generative approach to the modeling of isomorphic hidden-figure items. *Applied Psychological Measurement, 15*(2), 129–137.

Bennett, R. E., & Bejar, I. I. (1999). Validity and automated scoring: It's not only the scoring. *Educational Measurement: Issues and Practice, 17*(4), 9–16.

Bormuth, J. R. (1970). *On the theory of achievement test items.* Chicago, IL: University of Chicago Press.

Bradlow, E. T, Wainer, H., Wang, X. (1999). A Bayesian random effects models for testlets. *Psychometrika, 64,* 153–168.

Brennan, R. L. (1992). *Elements of generalizability theory* (2nd ed.). Iowa City, IA: ACT.

Bridgeman, B., Bejar, I. I., & Friedman, D. (1999). Fairness issues in a computer-based architectural licensure examination. *Computers in Human Behavior, 15,* 419–440.

Carpenter, P. A., & Just, M. A. (1987). *The psychology of reading and language comprehension.* Needham, MA: Allyn & Bacon.

Chiu, C. W. -T. (1999). *Scoring performance assessments based on judgements: Utilizing meta-analysis to estimate variance components in generalizability theory for unbalanced situations.* Unpublished doctoral dissertation, Michigan State University, Ann Arbor.

Chomsky, N. (1965). *Aspects of the theory of syntax.* Cambridge, MA: MIT Press.

Cronbach, L. J., Gleser, G. C., Nanda, H., & Rajaratnam, N. (1972). *The dependability of behavioral measurements: Theory of generalizability for scores and profiles.* New York: Wiley.

CTB/McGraw-Hill (1994). *National council of architectural registration boards: Comprehensive task analysis report.* Monterey, CA: Author.

Educational Testing Service. (1993). *Summary of activities for RDS subcommittee 4 (Division B) 92-93* (Summary Report). Princeton, NJ: Author.

Elliot, S. M., & Nelson, J. (1984). *Blueprinting teacher licensing tests: Developing domain specifications from job analysis results. (ERIC Document No. ED 243 936).*

Embretson, S. E. (1983). Construct validity: Construct representation versus nomothetic span. *Psychological bulletin, 93,* 179–197.

Gao, X. (1996). *Sampling variability and generalizability of work keys listening and writing scores* (Research Report No. 96-1). Iowa City, IA: The American College Testing Program.

Hively, W. (1974). Introduction to domain-reference testing. *Educational Technology, 14*(6), 5–10.

Hombo, C. M., & Dresher, A. (2001, April). *A simulation study of the impact of automatic item generation under NAEP–like data conditions.* Paper presented at the annual meeting of the National Council of Educational Measurement, Seattle, WA.

Janssen, R., Tuerlinckx, F., Meulders, M., & De Boeck, P. (1999). A hierarchical IRT model for mastery classifications. *Journal of Educational and Behavioral Statistics.* Manuscript submitted for publication.

Katz, I. R. (1994a). *Coping with the complexity of design: Avoiding conflicts and prioritizing constraints.* In A. Ram, N. Nersessian, & M. Recker (Eds)., Proceeding of the Sixteenth Annual Meeting of the Cognitive Science Society. Hillsdale, NJ: Lawrence Erlbaum Associates.

Katz, I. R. (1994b, April). *From laboratory to test booklet: Using expert-novice comparisons to guide design of performance assessments.* Paper presented at the annual meeting of the American Educational Research Association, New Orleans, LA.

Kenney, J. F. (1997). New testing methodologies for the Architect Registration Examination. *CLEAR Exam Review, 8*(2), 23–28.

Kotovsky, K., Hayes, J. R., & Simon, H. A. (1985). Why are some problems hard?: Evidence from Tower of Hanoi. *Cognitive Psychology, 17,* 248–294.

LaDuca, A., Templeton, B., Holzman, G. B., & Staples, W. I. (1986). Item-modeling procedure for constructing content-equivalent multiple-choice questions. *Medical Education, 20,* 53–56.

Lord, F. M. (1977). Some item analysis and test theory for a system of computer-assisted test construction for individualized instruction. *Applied Psychological Measuremnt, 3*(1), 447–455.

Lord, F. M. (1980). *Applications of item response theory to practical testing problems.* Hillsdale, NJ: Lawrence Erlbaum Associates.

Merwin, J. C. (1977). Considerations in exploring alternatives to standardized tests. In A. J. Nitko (Ed.), *Exploring alternatives to current standardized tests: Proceedings of the 1976 Testing Conference* (pp. 5–24). Pittsburgh, PA: University of Pittsburgh.

Messick, S. (1989). Validity. In R. L. Linn (Ed.), *Educational measurement* (pp. 13–103). New York: American Council on Education.

Mislevy, R. J., Sheehan, K. M., & Wingersky, M. (1993). How to equate tests with little or no data. *Journal of Educational Measurement, 30*(1), 55–78.

Mislevy, R. J., Wingersky, M. S., & Sheehan, K. M. (1994). *Dealing with uncertainty about item parameters: Expected response functions* (Research Report 94-28-ONR). Princeton, NJ: Educational Testing Service.

Osburn, H. G. (1968). Item sampling for achievement testing. *Educational and Psychological Measurement, 28,* 95–104.

Raymond, M. R. (1996). Establishing weights for test plans for licensure and certification examinations. *Applied Measurement in Education, 9*(3), 237–256.

Revuelta, J., Bejar, I. I., & Stocking, M. (1998). *Computerized adaptive testing with item isomorphs. Effects on the error of the test scores.* Princeton, NJ: Educational Testing Service

Revuelta, J., & Ponsoda, V. (1999). Generación automática de ítems. In J. Olea, V. Ponsoda, & G. Prieto (Eds.), *Tests informatizados: Fundamentos y aplicaciones* (pp. 227–248). Madrid: Pirámide.

Schmeiser, C. B., & Estes, C. A. (1986, April). *Translating task analysis results into test specifications: Clarity or confusion?* Paper presented at the annual conference of the National Council on Measurement in Education, San Francisco, CA.

Silberztein, M. (1993). Dictonnaires électroniques et analyse automatique de textes. Le système INTEX. Masson, Paris, France.

Simon, H. A., & Hayes, J. R. (1976). The understanding process: Problem isomorphs. *Cognitive Psychology, 8*(2), 165–190.

Stecher, B. (1989, February). *A national study of activities and knowledge/skills requirements of architects.* Unpublished report, Educational Testing Service, Pasadena, CA.

Tryon, R. C. (1957). Reliability and behavior domain validity: Reformulation and historical critique. *Psychological Bulletin, 54,* 229–249.

Wang, X., Bradlow, E. T., & Wainer, H. (2000). Users's guide to Scoright (Version 1.0): A computer program for scoring tests built from testlets. Princeton, NJ: Educational Testing Service.

Williamson, D. M., Bejar, I. I., & Hone, A. (1999). 'Mental Model' comparison of computerized and human scoring. *Journal of Educational Measurement, 36*(2), 158–184.

8

Generating Abstract Reasoning Items With Cognitive Theory

Susan E. Embretson
University of Kansas

Item generation has long been appealing to test developers. Around 1970, Wells Hively and colleagues (Hively, Patterson, & Page, 1968) proposed a system based on item forms to generate an infinitely large domain of mathematics problems. Each item form contained fixed text for a mathematics word problem, along with variable elements and replacement rules for these elements. For example, the specific numbers in the word problem were variable elements. Similarly, facet theory (see Shye, Elizur, & Hoffman, 1994), developed from Guttman (1969), postulates that rules can be specified to map specific features into an item. The other chapters in this book support the great potential of item generation in several contexts and need not be reviewed here.

Currently, item-generation is an especially important topic. Computerized adaptive testing requires large and diverse item banks to measure each person with precision and efficiency. Traditional item-writing processes are unable to keep pace with demand. Human item writers produce items rather slowly and item attrition is often high. High percentages of items either fail to meet screening criteria or fail to achieve adequate psychometric properties on empirical tryout. Further, often items are needed for specific difficulty levels. Unfortunately, item writers also have difficulty writing items for specific difficulty levels. Typically little information is available to relate stimulus content to psychometric properties. Thus, methods to generate items are currently being considered and applications are rapidly developing.

This chapter presents a generative system for abstract reasoning items that is based on cognitive theory. An item-generation system provides the means to rapidly develop many items from substitutions in a common item framework. Cognitive theory provides many potential benefits in item generation, including high levels of item validity and predictable item difficulties.

The generation system presented in this chapter is a relatively complete system that was developed from cognitive theory. The chapter begins by overviewing the potential role of cognitive theory in item generation. Then, a cognitive design system approach that includes both a conceptual and a procedural framework is described. The cognitive design system approach was applied to generate matrix completion problems. Matrix completion problems were selected for measuring abstract reasoning for two major reasons. First, matrix completion problems have been well supported as valid measures of abstract reasoning. For example, the Raven's Advanced Progressive Matrix test has been used cross-culturally for many decades. Second, matrix completion problems also have been studied by contemporary cognitive psychology methods and a promising theory was available. Third, previous research has shown matrix completion problems as amenable to generation (Hornke & Habon, 1986). The remainder of the chapter is devoted to explicating the stages involved in generating abstract reasoning items by cognitive theory. Four studies are presented on the development and psychometric evaluation of the generative system for abstract reasoning items.

ITEM GENERATION BY COGNITIVE THEORY

Importance of Cognitive Theory in Item Generation

Two important issues in item generation concern how the variable elements affect the psychometric properties of the test. These issues influence even the most simple item types and become more problematic with complex item types.

First, the *relative proportion of variable elements* in the item structures (or item forms) may influence the latent trait that is measured by the items. Using relatively few variable elements leads to highly similar items. In turn, similar items thus constrained may limit the cognitive processes that are involved in item solving and consequently narrow the latent trait that is measured. Consider, for example, mathematics word problems with constant text but varying numbers. An examinee who has been exposed to a previous mathematics word problem, but not with varied numbers, may answer the "new" item in a relatively automatic fashion. Not only is item solving much more likely, but the required processes have been narrowed to computational skills. For the first item that is attempted, however, processes such as encoding meaning and determining a problem-solving strategy may be involved in obtaining the correct solution. These processes no longer need be completed if the examinee has learned from the previous exposures to the item form.

Second, *differences between the substituted elements* may also determine the psychometric properties of the item. Even differences in the magnitude of the numbers for a mathematics word problem can change item difficulty and item correlations. Extremely large numbers, for example, can greatly increase the role of computational skills and decrease problem-solving skills.

These issues underscore the importance of a plausible cognitive theory to guide item structures and their substitutions. First, a plausible cognitive theory could provide the capacity for relatively large proportions of stimulus substitutions in item forms. High proportions of substitutions lessen the likelihood that item-solving processes are narrowed by repetitions. Further, the capacity to generate large numbers of items is increased as well. The more complete the cognitive theory, the larger the proportion of variable elements in the item structure. A complete theory would specify how each of the underlying processes involved in item solving is influenced by variations in item structures. Second, a plausible cognitive theory could also predict the impact of item structures on the psychometric properties of the generated items. If variations among the item structures represent the major processes in item solving, stronger prediction of item difficulty should be obtained as compared to variations that are unrelated to theory.

But, perhaps the most compelling reason to employ cognitive theory is obtaining construct validity at the item level. That is, the properties of the items can be explained rather than just predicted (see Embretson, 1983). Mathematical modeling, a major method for supporting cognitive theory, pinpoints the sources of cognitive complexity in items. Thus, the relative contribution of the various processes, strategies, and knowledge structures to each item can be decomposed. As shown next, item decomposition into cognitive processes is a major aspect of item construct validity. Obtaining construct validity at the item level has obvious advantages for assembling a valid test. Desired processes can be emphasized through item selection and balancing. However, another potential advantage is enhancing ability interpretations by reference to characteristic processing competencies. Sheehan (1997), for example, shows how abilities can be mapped to processes with mathematical modeling of item difficulties.

Cognitive Design System Approach

The cognitive design system approach was developed to centralize the role of cognitive theory in ability and achievement tests. Although cognitive theory has been heralded for more than two decades as a revitalizing foundation for cognitive measurement (Carroll, 1976; Sternberg, 1978), few applications in operational tests have appeared. At least two problems contribute to the sparse applications. First, the construct validity concept (Cronbach & Meehl, 1955) allows little room for cognitive theory to influence test development. Cognitive theory is most effective at the item development phase of testing. Unfortunately, the traditional construct validity concept emphasizes properties of the whole test, after it has been developed. Second, the procedures required to fully implement cognitive theory are not familiar to test developers. They are more likely to possess expertise in a basic subject matter rather than expertise in cognitive psychology.

The cognitive design system approach contains both a conceptual framework and a procedural framework to centralize cognitive theory in testing. The conceptual framework extends the construct validity concept so that theory may have a central role. This framework is briefly described here. The procedural framework is a series of stages that are required to incorporate cognitive theory in test design. More elaborated descriptions are available elsewhere (Embretson, 1983, 1995, 1998).

Conceptual Framework.

Cronbach and Meehl's (1955) conceptualization of construct validation emphasizes building empirical networks to determine what is measured by a test. The nomological network is a summary of the relationships (usually correlations) of test scores with other variables. According to Cronbach and Meehl (1955), "the vague, avowedly incomplete network gives the constructs whatever meaning they do have" (p. 289). Unfortunately, assessing correlations with external variables requires already having a developed test. If the correlations are not quite what was envisioned by the test developer, it is rare that the test will be redesigned. Test development is an expensive process involving empirical tryouts of items and many studies on test reliability and validity. So, rather than redesign the test, it is more likely that the test will be renamed or redescribed in accordance with its empirical correlates. In fact, this approach is the major route to test meaning that was anticipated in Cronbach and Meehl's (1955) framework for construct validation. The impact of theory on testing is minimal, however, because appropriate empirical results do not provide feedback for test design.

In earlier articles (Embretson, 1983, 1995), I proposed that construct representation and nomothetic span are separate aspects of construct validity that correspond to construct meaning and construct significance, respectively. These two aspects of construct validation not only have different functions, but they are supported by different types of research. Construct representation concerns the processes, strategies, and knowledge structures that are involved in item solving. Research that arises from the cognitive psychology paradigm is relevant to construct representation. Aspects of the stimuli are manipulated to vary cognitive demands in the task. Mathematical modeling of item difficulty is a major method for such research. Nomothetic span, in contrast, concerns the relationships of test scores to other measures. It consists of individual differences correlations across variables. Such correlations are the major type of data in Cronbach and Meehl's nomological network. However, nomothetic span is distinguished from Cronbach and Meehl's (1955) nomological network for two reasons. First, unlike the nomological network, nomothetic span concerns significance but not meaning. Second, a strong system of hypotheses generated from construct representation research should guide nomothetic span research.

Distinguishing construct representation from nomothetic span helps centralize cognitive theory in test development. First, construct validity may be assessed at the item level. That is, stimulus features influence processing; in turn, processing determines the construct representation of items. Second, cognitive theory can have a role in test development. Because construct representation depends on item stimulus features, items may be designed to reflect designated sources of cognitive complexity. Third, and following directly from the second point, item-generation principles can be based on features with known consequences for validity.

Procedural Framework.

Item developers typically are not trained to study an item type for construct representation. Rarely do they have the necessary expertise in cognitive psychology. Item developers often have good intuitions about item quality, as well as lists of stimulus features that vary between items. But, what they lack is an integrated and valid explanation of how these features influence item performance. The procedural framework of the cognitive design system was developed to elaborate the processes of developing an integrated and valid explanatory model of task performance.

Specify Goals of Measurement. The cognitive design system approach requires that two different types of measurement goals be specified. That is, the goals for construct representation, as well as for nomothetic span, should be distinguished.

Identify Design Features in the Task Domain. Identifying task-specific design features is more systematic and targeted in the cognitive design system approach than in the traditional approach to test development. Item features are examined for potential to manipulate the construct representation of items by altering cognitive processes, strategies, and knowledge structures. Identifying such features requires knowledge of cognitive psychology principles.

Develop Cognitive Model. Developing a cognitive model for the designated item type is essential to the cognitive design system approach. Three issues must be resolved in this stage. First, the relevant cognitive processes, strategies, and knowledge structures must be identified and organized into a unified model. A literature search is required to integrate relevant research and theory for the designated item type. Research on problem solving and thinking has often employed tasks that are similar to ability test items. However, the literature must be reviewed broadly because relevant studies are not organized around the types of tasks. Second, the stimulus features that influence processes must be operationalized. To build a cognitive model for the designated item type, these features must be quantified on existing items or newly developed items. If the goal is to generate items, the features should be manipulable as well as scoreable. Third, the effects of the cognitive features on psychometric properties should be studied empirically on existing items. The relative importance of the features on item difficulty and item discrimination will evaluate the potential of the various cognitive models for item generation.

Generate Items. In this stage, item structures and substitution rules are developed to operationalize the stimulus features into actual items. If the preceding stages are successful, the variations in item structures represent variations in processes. Now, item stimulus features are selected to fulfill the item structures and the substitution rules. The items can then be assembled into tests for empirical tryout.

Evaluate Models for Generated Tests. The models underlying item generation must be evaluated on an empirical tryout. In the cognitive design system approach, success at this stage is essential for supporting both the construct representation aspect of construct validity and for evaluating the generating system. Several important aspects of the item-generation system must be confirmed. Both cognitive models and psychometric models must be evaluated. The cognitive model is evaluated by predicting item performance. The dependent variables are mean response time and item difficulty, whereas the independent variables are the item structures and the item stimulus features that operationalize cognitive processes. The relative impact of the features assesses the relative impact of the processes, strategies, and knowledge structures that they represent. The psychometric model is evaluated by fit to the item response data.

Bank Items by Cognitive Complexity. If the generating system is effective in predicting item properties, then items may be banked by their sources of cognitive complexity. If the mathematical models provide sufficiently good prediction of item difficulty, items can be decomposed into the sources that contribute to item difficulty. The items may be designated by their patterns of cognitive complexity, as well as by their overall difficulties.

Validation: Nomothetic Span. The generated items must be evaluated for having the targeted aspects of nomothetic span. Tests are assembled from the generated items and specific predictions about the external correlates of scores are formulated from the construct representation results and from similar knowledge about the reference tests or criteria.

GENERATING ABSTRACT REASONING ITEMS

The test development process and the supporting data for generating abstract reasoning items is described in five sections. First, the measurement goals and task design features are considered. Second, in Study 1, the cognitive model for matrix completion problems is developed and evaluated for potential by mathematically modeling existing test items. Third, in Study 2, items are generated and evaluated for capacity to generate items of acceptable perceptual quality. Fourth, in Study 3, the impact of the cognitive model on psychometric properties is evaluated. Last, in Study 4, the psychometric properties of the generated items is compared to an existing test, the Raven's Advanced Progressive Matrices.

Measurement Goals and Task Design Features

Generating items to measure abstract reasoning, which is also described as fluid intelligence (Horn & Cattell, 1963), was the main goal for the project. Abstract reasoning, such as noted in Carroll (1993), is often described as involving inference which is relatively independent of specific knowledge. For construct representation, then, the goal was developing items to reflect inference processes from material that does not depend heavily on prior knowledge. For nomothetic span, on the other hand, broad correlations with a larger number of measures is desired, like other measures of fluid ability. Further, a specific pattern of correlations is also desired. Correlations with other measures of fluid ability, such as reasoning and judgment tasks, should be higher than correlations with tasks that involve crystallized ability, such as verbal comprehension or verbal knowledge.

Matrix completion problems were selected as the item type to be generated for several reasons. First, matrix completion problems have an extensive history in intelligence measurement. Matrix completion problems appeared early in intelligence measurement (Raven, 1940) and they were well connected to both Spearman's (1927) psychometric theory and Spearman's (1923) cognitive theory. Matrix completion problems reflect two of Spearman's three principles of cognition; educing relationships and educing correlates. Matrix problems are also well connected to Spearman's psychometric theory. The current version of tests developed by Raven, the Raven's Advanced Progressive Matrices, is described as highly measuring of Spearman's general intelligence factor, g (Anastasi & Urbina, 1997).

Second, matrix completion problems have potential to meet the specific measurement goals for both construct representation and the nomothetic span.

Construct representation is supported by available theories of processing on matrix completion problems. Although Spearman's (1923) cognitive theory did not survive the test of time, a recent contemporary theory of processing on matrix completion problems (Carpenter, Just, & Shell, 1990) is now available. Because the Carpenter et al. (1990) theory reflects inference processes, matrix completion problems seemingly have the desired construct representation. Further, the task design features associated with the theory, the number and type of rules, seem relatively amendable to item generation. Nomothetic span for matrix completion problems is supported by a large body of correlational studies. Matrix completion problems are heavily saturated with the fluid intelligence factor but not the crystallized intelligence factor (Carroll, 1993). Fluid intelligence is often considered synonymous with Spearman's g factor of intelligence (see Carroll, 1993).

Study 1: Developing the Cognitive Theory

To generate items effectively, a plausible cognitive model is needed. In this study, a cognitive model is developed for the generation of matrix completion problems. Carpenter et al's (1990) processing theory for matrix completion problems was supported by diverse data, but did not include mathematical modeling of item difficulty. To further develop the cognitive model, the Carpenter et al. theory was operationalized in several alternative mathematical models in this study. The alternative mathematical models operationalize the theory somewhat differently and they also specify additional features that may increase the prediction of item difficulty, such as perceptual features. The plausibility of the various postulated processes was determined by mathematically modeling item difficulty on existing test items; namely, the Raven's Advanced Progressive Matrices. Prior to presenting the study, the Carpenter et al. theory is described at length. Then operationalization of the theoretical variables into mathematical models is considered.

Carpenter, Just, and Shell's Theory of Matrix Processing.

The Carpenter et al. (1990) theory identifies two major types of processes in solving matrix completion problems: finding correspondence between figures, and inducing relationships. These two processes have striking similarity to Spearman's (1923) education of relations and education of correlates. Items vary in difficulty on these two processes due to the type of correspondence between the figures and the number of rule tokens, respectively. The two processes depend on different abilities; correspondence finding depends on abstraction capacity, whereas goal management depends on working memory capacity.

Figure 8.1 presents a matrix completion problem. Processes in solving matrix completion problems are postulated by Carpenter et al. (1990) to be executed serially and incrementally to identify each rule in each row of the matrix. The processes are encoding figures (or elements) of the first two entries in a row, determining corresponding elements, comparing the attributes of corresponding elements, inferring a rule instance, encoding the third entry, and comparing its corresponding elements with the other two entries and inferring a rule. This series of steps is repeated until all rules are identified in the first row and then is repeated on the second row, which in addition may involve mapping of the rules across rows. Last, the rules are generalized and applied to the third row. The Carpenter et al. (1990) processing theory is supported by converging operations, including protocol analysis, eye movements, computer simulations, and analyses of error rates.

Carpenter et al. (1990) implement their theory in two computer programs, FAIRAVEN and BETTERAVEN, which simulate performance for average and superior subjects, respectively. BETTERAVEN can solve even the very difficult items, whereas FAIRAVEN cannot. BETTERAVEN simulates the performance of superior subjects by recognizing more abstract types of correspondence between figures and by including a goal manager as an executive process. These are discussed, in turn.

Correspondence finding involves determining which figural elements will be governed by a rule. To simulate the performance of average subjects in solving Raven's matrices, two heuristics were embedded in FAIRAVEN: the matching-names heuristic, where objects with the same name (e.g., rectangle) have correspondence, and the matching-leftovers heuristic, in which elements that remain after applying the matching-names heuristic have correspondence. In Figure 8.1, the lines in the middle of the figures correspond in all three entries, although they vary in properties. The remaining elements (circle, square, and

$$AD_{31} \quad CD_{21} \quad BD_{11}$$
$$CD_{32} \quad BD_{22} \quad AD_{12}$$
$$BD_{38} \quad AD_{28} \quad CD_{18}$$

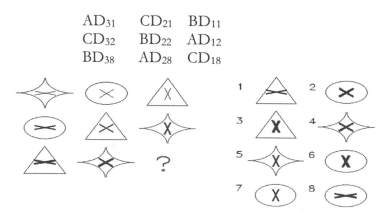

FIG. 8.1. A matrix completion item with one distribution of three relationship and two pairwise progressions.

diamond) correspond as leftovers. To simulate the performance of superior subjects, two more abstract correspondence principles were embedded in BETTERAVEN correspondence can be based on object properties (e.g., position in the entry, texture, orientation) as well as object names, and null values can correspond to real values. The latter principle permits figure addition and subtraction (where the answer is zero or null) and the distribution of two rules (see the following). Thus, BETTERAVEN does not depend on pairwise correspondence of elements as does FAIRAVEN.

The difficulty of finding rules depends on both the number of rules in the matrix and the level of the rules. Like average subjects, FAIRAVEN does not recognize many rules due to limited correspondence finding. However, like superior subjects, BETTERAVEN recognizes five rules. To resolve rule conflicts and maintain progress toward solution, Carpenter et al. postulate that the different types of rules are examined serially, according to the rule priority order which is shown in Table 8.1. Constancy is the most basic rule, so that it is examined first. Pairwise transformations are examined if constancy fails to describe the objects in a row. Then, the remaining rules are examined, in turn, until the rule is identified. Carpenter et al. (1990) present diverse data to support the postulated order of rule priority.

BETTERAVEN differs from FAIRAVEN in two aspects of rule finding. First, BETTERAVEN recognizes both the figure addition and subtraction rule and the distribution of two rule since it has correspondences based on null values. Second, BETTERAVEN has a superior goal management procedure. BETTERAVEN maintains serial order of trying rules, can resolve rule conflicts (by rule priority), remembers progress toward the goal, and can modify strategy when difficulty is encountered.

TABLE 8.1
Carpenter et al (1990) Rule Hierarchy

Level	Type	Definition
1	Constant in a Row	An element in a row is constant across columns
2	Pairwise Progressions	An element changes systematically from entry to entry across rows
3	Figure Addition/Subtraction	The first two entries in a row (or column) visually sum to the last entry
4	Distribution of Three	An object or attribute appears once and only once in each row and column (i.e., Latin square design)
5	Distribution of Two	A distribution of three relationship in which one element is a null value

To summarize, although inducing rules is a major activity in solving progressive matrices, differences between items and subjects arise primarily from executive processes and correspondence finding. That is, executive processing is needed to solve goal management problems in constructing, evaluating, and executing inference processes for a large number of rules. Further, correspondence finding involves determining which elements in the figure match.

Operationalizing the Mathematical Models.

Although Carpenter et al. presented diverse supporting data for the theory, they did not mathematically model item difficulty. Thus, it is not clear that the theory is sufficiently powerful to guide item generation. Fortunately, the two major sources of item difficulty, correspondence finding and goal management difficulty, may be readily operationalized for modeling Advanced Progressive Matrices items. Data were available to operationalize these sources of item difficulty for 36 of the 48 items in Set I and Set II of Advanced Progressive Matrices from the appendix of a technical report (Carpenter et al., 1990). The variables are described, in turn.

Correspondence finding was operationalized in a single variable, Abstract Correspondence, which was the sum of two binary variables that were scored on the items. Null Value Correspondence was scored positively if null values corresponded (i.e., as in distribution of two rules) in any relationship in the matrix problem and scored zero, otherwise. Nonsalient Correspondence was scored positively if correspondence was based on abstract properties or non-salient labels and scored zero, otherwise. The nonsalient correspondences included holistic figures that had to be conceptually segmented, elements with two different names, elements with the same name involved in two different relationships, and correspondences based on abstract properties. Goal management difficulty was represented by the number of rule tokens, which was taken directly from Carpenter et al.'s (1990) appendix.

An alternative cognitive model contained a single variable. If rules are tried serially, according to Carpenter et al.'s priority hierarchy, then the goal monitor must remember each rule that is tried. The memory load variable counts an additional memory place keeper for each (false) rule that would be tried before the correct rule is obtained. Thus, memory load was scored for each item by summing the rule levels for each rule in the item.

Two other sets of variables were also operationalized. Matrix problems differ in some basic perceptual features, even when the number and types of rules are equated. These features are also related to how items can be generated. Three perceptual variables were defined as follows: (a) Overlay, scored one if multiple objects in a matrix entry are overlaid and zero, otherwise (i.e., single objects or side-by-side objects), (b) Distortion, scored one if the shapes of corresponding objects are distorted (e.g., twisted) and zero, otherwise, and (b) Fusion, scored one if multiple objects in an entry can be perceived as one larger object and zero, otherwise. Last, a variable was constructed to represent the relative difficulty of the decision task. It was postulated that a decision task is easier if an implausible distractor exists in the problem. Distractors was scored one if at least one distractor with three or more rules failed to be realized, and zero, otherwise.

Method.

Subjects. The subjects were 191 undergraduates at a large Midwestern university. They were participating to earn credit toward grades in an introductory psychology course.

Procedure. Set I and Set II of the Advanced Progressive Matrices were administered consecutively. About 100 subjects were tested in each of two sessions. The standard instructions and timing procedures were given in each session, which was monitored by two proctors.

Results.

Descriptive Statistics. Item difficulties were estimated with both the Rasch and the two-parameter logistic (2PL) item-response theory models by marginal maximum likelihood (Program BILOG; Bock & Mislevy, 1990). The parameter estimates were anchored to a mean ability of .00 and standard deviation of 1.0. Both the full 48-item Advanced Progressive Matrices and the reduced set of 36 items studied by Carpenter et al. (1990) were calibrated.

Descriptive statistics on the cognitive stimulus features for the full Advanced Progressive Matrices indicated that the items typically involve two or more rules. Abstract correspondence was involved on 42% of the items whereas the average value for Memory Load is about 6. For perceptual features, 31% of the items involve overlay whereas less than 15% of the items involve distortion or fusion. Last, most items have one or more implausible distractors that can be eliminated by perceptual features. The reduced Advanced Progressive Matrices had similar statistics except that they had somewhat larger numbers of rules and memory load than the full Advanced Progressive Matrices. Further, the proportion of items with implausible distractors was somewhat smaller. Thus, the reduced Advanced Progressive Matrices items could be expected to demand somewhat greater processing for solution.

Mathematical Modeling. Advanced Progressive Matrices item difficulties were mathematically modeled, using the scored item features as the independent variables. The effect of these variables on Rasch item difficulty was examined by hierarchical regression analysis, with the blocks ordered successively with the cognitive variables entered first, followed by the perceptual variables and then by the distractor variable. The cognitive variables were represented by Number of Rules and Abstract Correspondence in Model I, and by Memory Load in Model II. In both models, the perceptual and distractor variables were identical. For the reduced item set, Model I ($R = .81, p < .01$) and Model II ($R = .82, p < .01$) both yielded strong prediction of item difficulty. The cognitive variables are very strong predictors ($R = .74, p < .01$ for both models). For Model I, adding the perceptual variables $\Delta R^2 = .08, p = .13$) or the distractor variable ($\Delta R^2 = .03, p = .24$) did not significantly increase prediction. For Model II, the perceptual variables did significantly increase prediction ($\Delta R^2 = .11, p < .03$), but the distractor variable did not ($\Delta R^2 = .01, p = .38$).

For the full Advanced Progressive Matrices, similar patterns of relative strength for the independent variables are found. The cognitive variables are strong predictors of item difficulty, and the perceptual variables significantly increased prediction whereas the distractor variable did not. However, the overall level of prediction was not quite as strong. The multiple correlations for the full set of independent variables were .71 and .68, respectively, for Model I and Model II.

Table 8.2 presents the standardized regression coefficients and t values for Model I and Model II on the reduced Advanced Progressive Matrices. The nonsignificant distractor variable is excluded. Also shown are the Pearson correlations for the independent variables with item difficulty. For Model I, the two cognitive variables, Number of Rules and Abstract Correspondence, both have strong positive correlations with item difficulty. Although the Pearson correlations are nearly equal for these variables, the standardized regression coefficient is somewhat lower for Number of Rules, reflecting its stronger correlation with the other independent variables. Two perceptual variables are also clearly significant in the model. Fusion is negatively related to item difficulty, which indicates that fused elements are associated with easier items. Distortion, however, is positively related to item difficulty. Overlay, in contrast, has a marginally significant and negative correlation with item difficulty, but the standardized regression coefficient was clearly not significant. For Model II, Memory Load has a strong positive correlation with item difficulty and a large standardized regression coefficient. These values are higher than the corresponding values for either Number of Rules or Abstract Correspondence from Model I. The weights for the perceptual variables are quite similar to Model I.

Psychometric Analysis. The appropriateness of a logistic item-response theory model for the data was determined by fitting successively more complex models. The fit of the Rasch model (i.e., one-parameter logistic model), two-

TABLE 8.2
Regression Estimates for Cognitive Models on Reduced APM Set

Variable	Model I (R = .79)			Model II (R = .81)	
	r	B	t	B	t
Cognitive					
Number of Rules	.69**	.27	1.58		
Abstract.Correspondence.	.71**	.42	2.48*		
Memory Load	.74**			.66	5.95**
Perceptual					
Overlay	-.24+	-.05	-0.42	.18	-1.65
Fusion	-.42*	-.17	-1.35	-.17	-1.49
Distortion	.31*	.20	1.68+	.18	1.62

$+ = p < .10, \quad * = p < .05, \quad ** = p < .01$

parameter logistic model (2PL), and the three-parameter logistic model (3PL) were a log-likelihood χ^2 test, with the degrees of freedom reflecting the number of parameters differing between the models. The value of χ^2 is given as the difference in the likelihood (obtained by -2 times the log likelihood criterion, -2lnL), between the nested models. For the full set of 48 items, the 2PL model fits significantly better than the Rasch model ($\chi^2_{48} = 96.52, p < .001$). Furthermore, although three items failed to fit the Rasch model at the .05 level of significance, no items failed to fit the 2PL model. The 3PL model, in which a lower asymptote is added, did not fit significantly better ($\chi^2_{48} = 32.80, p > .05$). No further model analysis, such as factor analysis, was attempted on the full item set because the fit of the 2PL model indicates unidimensionality.

To further compare the models, total scores, Rasch ability estimates, and 2PL ability estimates were intercorrelated for the full and reduced item set. The results indicated that the correlations of abilities estimated by the Rasch model with the abilities estimated by the 2PL model were .991 and .992 for the full and reduced item sets, respectively. However, as expected, the 2PL ability estimates have a somewhat lower correlation with total raw score than the Rasch estimates. Thus, even though the 2PL fits the data better than the Rasch model, the differences in the ability estimates between the two models is quite small. Furthermore, the Rasch ability estimates are slightly closer to the original Advanced Progressive Matrices scores than the 2PL ability estimates, because total score is the basis for the Advanced Progressive Matrices standard scores.

Discussion.

In summary, operationalizing the Carpenter et al. (1990) processing variables, goal management difficulty, and correspondence difficulty led to strong prediction of item difficulty in the Raven's Advanced Progressive Matrices items that were studied by Carpenter et al. (1990). The two variables that represented these processes, number of rules and abstract correspondence, both had significant independent influence on item difficulty, with a multiple correlation of .79 in Model I. However, equal prediction was obtained from an alternative cognitive model, Model II. This model contained a single cognitive variable, memory load, which was constructed to represent goal management difficulty. Higher level rules are postulated to involve greater goal management difficulty since lower level rules are tried first. The examinee must remember attempting the lower level rules for each relationship in the problem.

The two models differed in the role for the perceptual features, but were similar for distractor effects. In Model I, the perceptual features of the items did not significantly increase prediction. These features are highly correlated with the variable for correspondence finding. In Model II, in contrast, significant weights were found for perceptual features. For neither model was the distractor variable significant, which suggests that this variable did not sufficiently operationalize important between-item features in the distractors.

Similar results were obtained from modeling the full set of Advanced Progressive Matrices items, which includes many easier items that are holistic in nature. Somewhat lower levels of prediction were obtained although the general pattern of results was similar. The cognitive models for Model I and Model II were again equally explanatory of item difficulty. Thus, memory load predicted item difficulty as well as the two separate processes defined by number of rules and abstract correspondence. Again, the distractor variable failed to predict item difficulty. The perceptual variables had stronger impact in both Model I and Model II and prediction was significantly increased by their inclusion in both models. The increased role of perceptual features was probably due to the increased proportion of holistic items in the full set. Most importantly for the present purposes, the results support either cognitive model as a basis for item generation due to their strong prediction of item difficulty. That is, developing an adequate mathematical model of item difficulty implies that the item features that operationalize the processing variables have been identified. Structurally equivalent items can be constructed on the basis of either cognitive model. It makes little practical difference if the model contains two processing sources with no perceptual features, or one source with added predictors to represent perceptual features.

The pattern of results also has implications for the cognitive theories of processing for matrix completion problems. The results can be viewed as supporting goal management difficulty as the primary source of processing difficulty in Advanced Progressive Matrices items. The memory load model is more parsimonious than the two-source cognitive model and yet yields equally strong prediction. In contrast, the significant effect of correspondence finding in the two source model (i.e., Model I), may result from an incomplete representation of goal management difficulty by the number of rules. However, the results also can be viewed as confirming a two processing source model as well. Both processing sources proved to be significant in Model I. Furthermore, the strong influence of memory load alone in Model II may be explained by it representing a combination of the two processing sources. If so, the two-source cognitive model is favored because memory load would not be theoretically singular. Furthermore, the significant role of the perceptual features in Model II further suggests that correspondence finding was not adequately represented.

Last, the results have implications for the appropriate psychometric models for matrix completion items. The existing items on the Advanced Progressive Matrices did not fit the Rasch model very well. Significant improvement in modeling the item-response data was obtained by adding item discrimination parameters in the 2PL model. These results indicate that Advanced Progressive Matrices items are not equally discriminating. A possible source for varying item discriminations may be irrelevant or confusing features in some items. It is possible that generated items will fit for the Rasch model better due to the inclusion only of features that are supported as influencing processing.

Study 2: Item Generation

Item generation by cognitive theory contains three basic stages. First, target distributions of the sources of cognitive complexity must be specified. Second, a structure must be developed to incorporate these sources of complexity into item construction. Third, substitution rules must be applied to the structures to generate items. This study describes these three steps for generating matrix completion items, using the cognitive theory described earlier.

Sources of Cognitive Complexity.

Several combinations of the number and the types of rules were specified for the matrix completion problems. Twenty-four items duplicated the number and type of rules in problems that were studied by Carpenter et al.(1990). Six additional combinations of relationships were specified to create items of moderate memory load levels. Also specified for each item-generating structure was a set of perceptual features.

Formal Item Structure.

To implement item generation, a system must be developed with two general properties: The placement of each object and attribute in the matrix array must be specified, and the system must operationalize the cognitive design of the task. A formal structural notation system was developed to satisfy these two properties. Figure 8.1 shows a formal structure for an item that contains three relationships; a distribution-of-three relationship; and two pairwise progressions. The placement of the A, B, and C terms, which correspond to objects, defines the distribution-of-three relationship. The subscripts of the D term, which correspond to attributes of the D object, define the two pairwise progression relationships.

An item that fulfills the structure in Figure 8.1 has a memory load value of 8, which is the sum of the rules in the hierarchy in Table 8.1 (i.e., $4 + 2 + 2 = 8$). The actual item shown in Figure 8.1 corresponds to the formal structure. Furthermore, the drawing principles for the item specified no distortion or fusion of elements, and overlay of objects (the lines are inside the other figures). The star, diamond, and circle are the A, C, and B objects, respectively, in the structure. The "X" in the center is the D object. The "X" varies in a pairwise fashion in two different attributes; boldness (light, medium, dark) and girth (thin, medium, fat). Every object and attribute that is defined in the formal structure can be substituted for another object or attribute. Items that have the same formal structure, but different objects and attributes, are structurally equivalent. Structurally equivalent items have the same postulated sources and levels of processing difficulty, as well as the same predicted difficulty from the cognitive model.

Item Generation.

A list of 22 objects and 7 attributes was prepared for substitution into the 30-item structures. The same object may appear in any item structure. The attributes are also free to appear in any item structure. Five items were generated for each of the 30 structures. The position of the correct answer among the eight response alternatives was varied randomly across structurally equivalent items. The generated item bank consisted of 150 items.

A computer programmer screened the specified items for acceptable perceptual properties. Most items (i.e., 93%) were acceptable as generated. For the other items, a change of attribute or object led to acceptable quality. For example, insufficient differences in object sizes led to poor contrast in some overlay items.

Descriptive statistics on the cognitive features indicated that the generated items had very similar means on Number of Rules and Memory Load as the Advanced Progressive Matrices reduced item set, although, Abstract

Correspondence was somewhat lower. The perceptual features also were similar, except that half the generated items involved overlay.

Conclusions.

The formal structural notation was highly effective for generating a large bank of items. The system not only defined the placement of each object and attribute in the matrix, but also operationalized the cognitive model. A large bank of items was generated and only a few items were perceptually unacceptable. The few problems that were observed can be built into a set of constraints for the next generating system for the items.

Study 3: Psychometric Properties and Construct Representation of Abstract Reasoning Test Items

Although the generated items generally met the standards for perceptual quality, their substantive quality also must be evaluated. Three aspects of item quality are pertinent to evaluating a generating system in an empirical tryout. First, do the items meet standard psychometric criteria for quality? These criteria include appropriate item difficulty values, such as indicated by classical p values or item-response theory item difficulties, as well as acceptable item discriminations, such as indicated by classical biserial correlations or item-response theory model statistics. Second, do the generating item structures yield reasonably equivalent items? Structurally similar items should have highly similar item difficulties to assure interchangeability. Third, do the items represent the desired construct representation? The cognitive model that was developed must now be evaluated for plausibility on the generated items. Mathematical modeling of both item difficulty and item-response time is needed to support the items as measuring the targeted processes.

This study is a reanalysis of data reported previously in Embretson (1998). Since the article appeared, some aspects of the cognitive models were refined.

Method.

Participants. The participants were 728 young adults who were completing basic training at Lackland Air Force Base. The sample consisted of approximately 85% men and 15% women.

Tests. Five structurally equivalent forms of Abstract Reasoning Test items were prepared from the generated item bank. Each of the 30 generating structures appeared once on each form, and in the same order across forms. A different item for each structure appears on the five forms. Additionally, four common items were included on each form to link abilities across forms.

Procedure. The tests were administered by computer to each participant. The testing laboratory consisted of 40 computer stations, which were randomly assigned to a test form. Both response choices and response times were recorded.

Results.

Classical item analysis statistics were computed separately within each test form. The results were aggregated across forms, in as much as test means and standard deviations did not differ (see Embretson, 1998). Item response theory models were also fit to the data. The item parameters were estimated by marginal maximum likelihood, using the BILOG program. A major advantage of BILOG is capacity to simultaneously estimate item parameters and abilities across groups who were administered different test forms.

Psychometric Properties. Figure 8.2 presents a histogram of classical item difficulty values. It can be seen that the items are generally appropriate for the sample, although they tend to be somewhat easy. Figure 8.2 also shows the distribution of biserial correlations for the generated items. Although a few items had relatively low biserials (i.e., lower than .20), most had relatively high and acceptable values

Both the Rasch model and the 2PL item response theory models were fit to the item-response data. When the Rasch model was fit to the data, 12% of the items failed to fit the model, as indicated by a significant difference between expected and observed frequencies at the various score levels. When the 2PL model was fit to the data, less than 1% of the items (.7%) failed to fit. Thus, the generated items apparently differ somewhat in discrimination. The better fit for the 2PL model is consistent with the varying biserial correlations that were observed. The 3PL model was not fit to the data, because the 2PL model fit adequately.

Impact of Structural Equivalence. The empirical similarity of structurally equivalent items was examined by predicting item difficulties and response times on the 150 items. Item structure was treated as a fixed factor in a general linear model. Answer position was included as a control variable because it varied randomly across items. Answer position operationalized as dummy variables.

The primary analyses were on the item difficulties from the item-response theory models as the dependent variables. A multiple correlation of .89 was obtained for Rasch model item difficulties. Nearly identical results were obtained with the 2PL item difficulties as the dependent variable. A multiple correlation of .89 was also obtained. Figure 8.3 presents a scatterplot of the Rasch model item difficulties by item structure. It can be seen that scatter

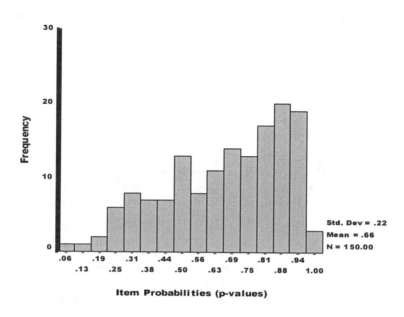

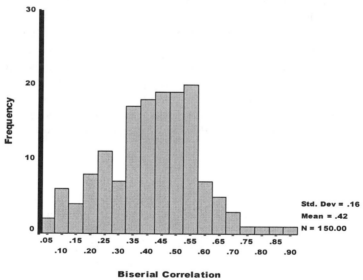

FIG. 8.2. Distribution of item properties in the generated items.

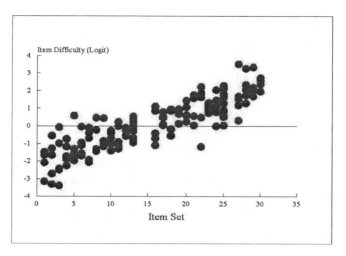

FIG. 8.3. Regression of item difficulty on item structures.

around central values for each item set was fairly uniform. Similar results were obtained with mean item-response time as the dependent variable. A multiple correlation of .91 was obtained.

Because the 2PL model was required to fit the item-response data, it was interesting to determine if item structures also influenced item discrimination. The general linear model of item structure and key position was applied to the 2PL slope parameter as the dependent variable. A multiple correlation of .82 was obtained ($p < .001$). Thus, some item structures lead to greater discrimination than other structures. Further, the homogeneity of variance test for item structures was also significant ($p = .001$), which indicates that item discriminations vary more within some structures than in other structures.

Cognitive Models. The cognitive models were examined in a hierarchical regression analysis. The cognitive variables were entered first, followed by the perceptual variables for both Model I and Model II as described earlier except that the distractor variable was omitted from the analysis. Identical analyses were repeated on three different dependent variables; the Rasch and 2PL model, item difficulties and mean item-response times. For the Rasch model item difficulties, strong prediction was obtained by both Model I ($R = .77, p < .01$) and Model II ($R = .73, p < .01$). However, Model I, with two sources of cognitive complexity, yielded somewhat stronger overall prediction than Model II. Further, the cognitive variables in Model I (Number of Rules and Abstract Correspondence) had the same contribution to prediction as the Memory Load variable alone in Model II ($R = .71, p < .01$). The perceptual variables significantly increased prediction when added to the cognitive variables in both Model I ($\Delta R^2 = .08, p < .01$) and Model II ($\Delta R^2 = .03, p < .01$). Nearly identical results were obtained with the 2PL model item difficulties as the dependent variable.

Similar patterns of prediction were observed for modeling mean item-response time for both Model I ($R = .77, p < .01$) and Model II ($R = .73, p < .01$). Furthermore, for both Model I and Model II, the perceptual variables significantly increased prediction.

Table 8.3 presents further results on Model I. The means and standard deviations for the independent variables as well as their correlations and the standardized regression coefficients for predicting item difficulty (Rasch) and response time are shown. With item difficulty as the dependent variable, it can be seen that the cognitive variables, Number of Rules and Abstract Correspondence, have nearly equal positive correlations. The standardized regression coefficients for these two variables are also nearly equal and both significant. Two perceptual variables, Overlay and Fusion, have significant regression coefficients, which indicates independent contributions to prediction. Overlay items tend to be harder, whereas Fusion items tend to be easier. With response time as the dependent variable, very similar results were obtained. Number of Rules and Abstract Correspondence have nearly equal positive correlations with response time, as well as nearly equal standardized regression coefficients. For the perceptual variables, Fusion was again strongly significant whereas Overlay was marginally significant.

Table 8.4 presents the final mathematical model for Model II on the generated items. With Rasch item difficulties as the dependent variable, Memory Load has a strong positive correlation and a strong positive standardized regression coefficient. Only one perceptual feature, Fusion, had a significant independent contribution to item difficulty, however. With response time as the dependent variable, the pattern of results and the magnitude of the estimates were nearly identical.

TABLE 8.3
Regression Estimates for Model I on Generated ART Items

Variable	Mean	SD	Item Difficulty r	Item Difficulty Beta	Response Time r	Response Time Beta
Cognitive .						
Number of Rules	2.47	.86	.55**	.43**	.47	7.40**
Abstract.Correspondence	.26	.44	.54**	.38**	.40	6.47**
Perceptual						
Overlay	.50	.50	.15*	.23**	.11	1.64+
Fusion	.23	.42	-.48**	-.14*	-.14*	-2.07*
Distortion	.13	.34	.11+	.00	-.11+	-1.73+
			R = .79		R = .77	

$+ = p < .10, \quad * = p < .05, \quad ** = p < .01$

TABLE 8.4
Regression Estimates for Model II on Generated ART Items

Variable	*Item Difficulty*		*Response Time*	
	r	Beta	r	Beta
Cognitive				
Memory Load	.68**	.56**	.68**	.60**
Perceptual				
Overlay	.15*	.07	.15*	-.06
Fusion	-.48**	-.19**	-.48*	-.21*
Distortion	.11+	.05	.11	-.06
	R = .77		R = .73	

Last, the item discriminations from the 2PL model were also predicted from both Model I and Model II. For Model I, a significant multiple correlation of .54 was obtained ($p < .001$). Table 8.5 shows that only the two variables in the cognitive model significantly predicted the biserial correlations. Items with more rules and more abstract correspondence were less discriminating. Of the perceptual variables, only Overlay had a significant Pearson correlation and a significant regression coefficient. For Model II, a significant multiple correlation of .42 was obtained ($p < .05$). Table 8.5 shows that Memory Load had a negative and significant relationship to item discrimination, but again none of the perceptual variables reached significance at the .05 level. Thus, the cognitive variables predicted item discrimination but only one perceptual variable, overlay, had any significant relationships.

TABLE 8.5
Regression Estimates of Item Discrimination for Model I and
Model II on Generated ART Items

Variable	r	*Model I*		*Model II*	
		Beta	t	Beta	t
Cognitive					
Number of Rules	-.40**	-.24	-4.18**		
Abstract Correspondence	-.31**	-.24	-2.04*		
Memory Load	-.37**			.03	-3.07**
Perceptual					
Overlay	-.23**	-.31	-3.00**	-.20	-1.86+
Fusion	.21*	-.13	-1.06	-.06	-.47
Distortion	-.04	-.09	-.59	-.14	-.86
		R = .54		R = .42	

Discussion.

The results strongly support the item-generation system for abstract reasoning items. The generation system was based on a cognitive theory for solving matrix completion problems. All three criteria of item quality for a generating system were supported. These are discussed, in turn.

First, most generated items achieved adequate psychometric properties on initial tryout. Acceptable levels of item difficulty were generally obtained. Furthermore, only a few items had item discriminations that were unacceptable. The generated items were supported as measuring a single dimension since good fit to an item-response theory model, the 2PL model, was also obtained.

Second, the generating item structures yielded items with substantially equivalent empirical properties. Item structure strongly predicted item difficulty and item-response time. Thus, the specific stimulus content of the items resulted in only minor differences in the empirical properties of the items. These results also indirectly support the cognitive model, because the item structures were derived from it. Further, item differences in discrimination also was strongly predicted from item structure. Items from structures with more rules, abstract correspondence, or greater memory load were relatively less discriminating.

A recent study suggests that even higher levels of prediction from the structural model could be obtained. Diehl (1998) found some differences in the memory load of the distractors in otherwise structurally equivalent items. The varying distractor sets probably induce empirical differences between the otherwise equivalent items. Equating the distractor sets fully should reduce the unpredictable variance in item difficulty, thus yielding even higher levels of prediction. This may be feasible by introducing further constraints on the distractor features.

Third, the generated items were supported as having the desired construct representation. Item difficulties and response times were also strongly predicted from the cognitive models. In general, the cognitive processing variables had the strongest relationships to item performance. Item difficulty was well explained by the model with two sources of cognitive complexity, goal management difficulty and correspondence finding. Item difficulty was also well explained by the alternative cognitive model with a single source of cognitive complexity, memory load. This model yielded only slightly less prediction. Item-response time was also well predicted by the two models. Although test developers generally have had less interest in these data, they are needed to establish the cognitive variables as measuring processing complexity. That is, if a variable influences processing, impact on processing response time is expected. Item-response times had about the same level and pattern of prediction as item difficulty in both cognitive models. Thus, the variables are supported as having effects on processing duration as well as on processing difficulty. The results on the cognitive models also have some theoretical implications. First, it can be concluded that either theoretical model will yield adequate prediction of item difficulty. The choice between models perhaps is best based on external considerations. For example, the model with only memory load has the desirable feature of parsimony because it has only a single variable to characterize inference complexity. The model with two sources has the desirable feature of theoretical singularity because the variables do not confound two purportedly separate sources of complexity. Second, some additional processes should be included for a more complete explanation of item solving. The cognitive model does not predict either item difficulty or item-response time as well as the structural model. Although the structural model is based on the cognitive model, apparently it provides some additional constraints that are not well represented in the cognitive model.

Some recent studies suggest what the missing variables in the cognitive model may be. First, no properties of the distractor set were included in the current models. Diehl (1998) found that the memory load of the distractor sets vary across item structures, as well as within item structures. A cognitive model of distractor plausibility may increase prediction of item difficulty. Second, examinees may vary in utilizing one type of relationship in matrix completion problems. In extending the Carpenter et al. (1990) to distractors, Diehl (1998) found that many items with high-level relationships could be solved by an easier holistic strategy; namely, the much easier figure addition relationships yielded the correct answer. Perhaps examinees vary systematically in their knowledge bases about figure addition relationships. If so, the difficulty of some items would vary over examinees. Thus, item difficulty would be not well predicted for these items from the cognitive model.

Study 4: Construct Validation: Nomothetic Span

In this study, the nomothetic span aspect of construct validity of the generated items was examined. The Abstract Reasoning Test (ART) was prepared by assembling the newly generated items into test forms. Each item structure appeared once on each test.

Nomothetic span was studied in two ways. First, the factor loadings of Abstract Reasoning Test were examined with respect to some reference tests. Because Abstract Reasoning Test was postulated to measure fluid ability but not crystallized ability, it should load only on the fluid ability factor. Second, Abstract Reasoning Test was compared to the Raven's Advanced Progressive Matrices. If the tests measure the same dimensions, they should load on the same factors. The internal consistencies of Abstract Reasoning Test and Advanced Progressive Matrices are also compared. A more complete presentation of these results appears in Embretson (1998) and so they are summarized briefly here.

A secondary purpose of this study is to further explore the construct representation of the generated items. It was noted earlier that the knowledge bases about holistic strategies for item solving may vary across examinees. Because a large sample size was planned for the nomothetic span study, it was feasible to determine if examinees differed qualitatively in their patterns of item difficulties.

Method.

Participants. Two different samples of participants were measured. Sample 1 consisted of 728 young adults who were in basic training at Lackland Air Force Base. Sample 2 consisted of 217 young adults from the same population as Sample 1.

Tests. Participants from Sample 1 were administered a 34-item test with generated Abstract Reasoning Test items. The five forms contained 30 items that were structurally matched across forms, but the stimulus content differed. Four common linking items were also included on each form. Participants from Sample 2 were administered only one form of Abstract Reasoning Test and the full Raven's Advanced Progressive Matrices. For both samples, ASVAB test scores were available from the recruitment files.

Procedure. In Sample 1, Abstract Reasoning Test items were administered in a computerized version. In Sample 2, both Abstract Reasoning Test and the Advanced Progressive Matrices were administered in paper and pencil form to match the tests for media of administration. Advanced Progressive Matrices is not available in computerized form. The order of Abstract Reasoning Test versus Advanced Progressive Matrices as the first test was randomly assigned.

Results.

Factor Loadings. For Sample 1, Moreno, Wetzel, McBride, and Weiss's (1984) factor structure for ASVAB was postulated to explain the correlations between Abstract Reasoning Test and the ASVAB tests. The Moreno et al. (1984) structure contains four factors; Quantitative, Verbal, Technical, and Speed. Their factor loading matrix was used to specify loading patterns for the ASVAB tests. Kyllonen and Christal's (1990) results suggested that the Quantitative factor is fluid intelligence whereas the Verbal factor is crystallized intelligence. Abstract Reasoning Test was hypothesized to load only on the Quantitative factor. This model fit the data well as the comparative fit index was high (CFI = .970). Although the data departed significantly from the model (χ^2_{34} = 102.57, p < .001), no further loadings for Abstract Reasoning Test improved fit significantly. The loading of Abstract Reasoning Test on the Quantitative factor was .64, which was relatively high. Thus, the hypothesis about the factor loadings for Abstract Reasoning Test was confirmed from Sample 1.

For Sample 2, the same factor structure for ASVAB was postulated as for Sample 1. Both Abstract Reasoning Test and Advanced Progressive Matrices were hypothesized to load only on the Quantitative factor. Error correlations between Abstract Reasoning Test and Advanced Progressive Matrices were specified so that they did not overly influence the Quantitative factor for ASVAB. This model fit the data well, as the comparative fit index was high (CFI = .987), and the data did not depart statistically from the model (χ^2_{43} = 53.14, p > .05). Abstract Reasoning Test and Advanced Progressive Matrices had very similar standardized factor loadings of .66 and .63, respectively.

The internal properties of Abstract Reasoning Test and Advanced Progressive Matrices were compared in the data from Sample 1. Cronbach's alpha for the 34-item Abstract Reasoning Test was .878. Cronbach's alpha for the 48-item Advanced Progressive Matrices was .881. Thus, Abstract Reasoning Test achieved the same internal consistency as Advanced Progressive Matrices but with fewer items. Further analyses of the internal properties of the two measures revealed that Advanced Progressive Matrices and Abstract Reasoning Test had about the same average item difficulty levels, but that Advanced Progressive Matrices item difficulties varied more. Thus, Advanced Progressive Matrices has many extremely easy and many extremely hard items. The biserial correlations were also compared. Relatively more items with low biserial correlations were found on Advanced Progressive Matrices than on Abstract Reasoning Test.

Qualitative Differences in Item Difficulties. The mixed Rasch model (Rost, 1990) was used to identify persons who differ qualitatively in the basis of item difficulty. The mixed Rasch model identifies latent classes from response patterns in the sample. Within each latent class, a Rasch model is applied to estimate item difficulty and ability. Solutions that extract different numbers of classes can be compared by a log likelihood goodness-of-fit test.

The mixed Rasch model was applied to data from Sample 1 because a large sample was available. In Sample 1, the linking items were excluded from the analysis so that only the 30-item structures would be represented. To provide a baseline, first a single class was extracted and the Rasch model parameters estimated. Then, a two-class solution was extracted. The goodness-of-fit test indicated that the two-class solution was signficantly better (χ^2_{60} = 556.58, p < .001) than the one-class solution. Figure 8.4 is a scatterplot of the item difficulties obtained within the two classes. Mean item difficulties are set to zero in each class. Items that are above the 45 degree line are relatively more

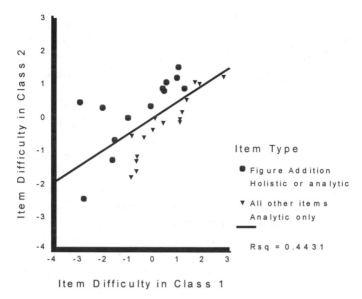

FIG. 8.4. Item difficulties in two latent classes.

difficult for Class 2. Items that fall below the 45 degree line are relatively more difficult for Class 1. The items are marked for potential to be solved by a holistic strategy or by analytic strategies only. It can be seen that the holistic items are relatively hard for Class 2 but not for Class 1.

Also estimated in the mixed Rasch model are the proportion of examinees that belong to each class. Class 1 contained 61% of the sample whereas Class 2 contained 39% of the sample. Although Class 2 is smaller than Class 1, it contains a substantial proportion of the examinees.

Discussion.

The results indicate that unselected Abstract Reasoning Test items, as generated, had the postulated nomothetic span. In the first sample, Abstract Reasoning Test scores were examined with respect to a battery of reference tests. A four-factor solution fit the data reasonably well. Unselected Abstract Reasoning Test items loaded only on a fluid ability factor, as hypothesized.Second, unselected Abstract Reasoning Test items compared very favorably with Raven's Advanced Progressive Matrices items. Their internal consistencies were nearly identical, although Abstract Reasoning Test had 30% fewer items than Advanced Progressive Matrices. Thus, Abstract Reasoning Test measures ability more efficiently. In addition, Abstract Reasoning Test factor loadings were virtuallly indistinguishable from Advanced Progressive Matrices factor loadings. Both Abstract Reasoning Test and Advanced Progressive Matrices loaded significantly only on the fluid ability factor. Thus, it can be concluded that the generated items are not only valid measures of abstract reasoning, but that they are a more efficient measure than the Advanced Progressive Matrices.

The results also suggest that the construct representation of item solving differs between classes of examinees. The mixed Rasch model identified two latent classes with different patterns of item difficulties. Differing patterns of item difficulties across examinees reduces the prediction of item difficulty from cognitive models. The mixed Rasch model results indicate that a substantially large class (i.e., 39% of the sample) find the holistic items to be difficult. These items can be solved by a relatively simple figure addition relationship or a relatively hard distribution of two relationship. Examinees who find the holistic items difficult may resort to distribution of two relationships to solve them. These examinees may not know about figure addition relationships or they may deem them inappropriate for Abstract Reasoning Test items.

The differing construct representation across latent classes may be resolved by two different approaches. First, the cognitive models could include latent classes. The mixed Rasch model identifies class membership for each examinee. Cognitive model parameters could be estimated separately within each class. Second, the knowledge bases of the two classes could be equated. That is, the appropriateness of figure addition relationships could be emphasized in more extended test instructions. If successful, the instructions could lead to more uniform difficulties of the holistic items across examinees.

Summary and General Discussion

The cognitive design approach was applied to generate matrix completion items to measure abstract reasoning. An essential aspect of the approach is building a plausible cognitive model for item solving. The cognitive model was developed by mathematically modeling the difficulty of Raven's Advanced Progressive Matrices items from an extended version of the Carpenter et al. (1990) cognitive processing theory. High levels of prediction of item difficulty were obtained from the model. Item structures were developed to incorporate key aspects of the cognitive models. Items were generated by selecting stimuli from lists of objects and attributes to fulfill the item structures. The vast majority of items were perceptually acceptable as specified. An empirical tryout indicated that the items had generally acceptable psychometric properties, empirical similarity within item structures, and the desired sources of cognitive complexity. A validity study indicated that the generated items not only had the desired factor structure, but had nearly identical correlations with other tests as the Raven's Advanced Progressive Matrices items. Furthermore, the generated items had somewhat better internal consistency than Advanced Progressive Matrices items. In summary, matrix completion items were effectively generated by the cognitive design system approach. The results support the generated items as effective measures of abstract reasoning. The success of the generating system has several general implications that extend beyond the goal of measuring abstract reasoning, however. These are considered in turn.

First, generating items to measure a high-level ability is an important demonstration of feasibility. Item generation is often thought applicable only to low level or very specific abilities. In fact, many early examples of item generation involved simple skills, such as simple arithmetic or spelling. Matrix completion problems, however, are widely acknowledged as measuring the highest level of abilities, fluid intelligence or Spearman's g. It is encouraging that these high-level items were effectively generated on the first attempt. Other high-level item types may be amendable to generation, as well.

Second, neither item difficulty nor ability were narrowed by the generating structures. The item-generation system led to a broad array of items that varied in predictable ways. Item structure was a powerful predictor of item difficulty in the current research. Although the appearance of the items varies substantially, apparently the specific stimulus content has a minor role in item difficulty. Abilities apparently were not narrowed in the generated items, either. The nomothetic span study indicated that the validity of the generated items was virtually identical to the Raven's Advanced Progressive Matrices. Maintaining a broad focus for item difficulty and ability will be important for many other item types, as well.

Third, the item parameters for the generated items were readily predicted both from the item structures and from the cognitive model. This capability suggests potential for online generation of items during adaptive testing. That is, the generating system has capacity to create items for a targeted levels of item difficulty. The capacity to predict item difficulty will be important in the success of generating many item types.

Fourth, construct validity is enhanced from a generating system that is based on cognitive theory. Item difficulty was both predicted and explained by the cognitive model. The specific source of cognitive complexity in each item may be identified. In turn, the interpretation of abilities may also be enhanced by the generating system. Abilities that are estimated in item-response theory models, as in the current studies, may be linked directly to items. If the item properties result from direct manipulation of cognitive complexity, as in the generated items here, abilities may be characterized by cognitive processing. This feature may be important in future tests as the diagnostic use becomes increasingly important.

Two caveats may be in order. First, many advantages of item generation that were just elaborated require a plausible cognitive model. Developing a cognitive model to the point of effectiveness is an unfamiliar effort for test developers. However, the advantages and eventual economies in item development may well be worth the extra initial effort. Second, although the generating system developed here was effective, it may not yet be ready for an operational test. That is, some items did fail to meet perceptual quality and desirable psychometric properties. High stakes testing may not be ready for such failures. On the other hand, the items do appear to compare favorably to a well-established test of abstract reasoning, namely the Raven's Advanced Progressive Matrices. Furthermore, some improvements to the generating system can be made. The research reported here was the first attempt to generate abstract reasoning items and improvements based on the results clearly can be made. Such improvements may eventually reduce the risk of a poor generated item to almost nothing. Any operational generating system should also include a system to identify what produces poor items, so that the system improves over time.

REFERENCE

Anastasi, A., & Urbina, S. (1997). *Psychological testing.* Upper Saddle River, NJ: Prentice Hall.

Bock, R. D., & Mislevy, R. (1990). *BILOG 3: Item analysis and test scoring with binary logistic models.* Mooresville, IN: Scientific Software.

Carpenter, P. A., Just, M. A., & Shell, P. (1990). What one intelligence test measures: A theoretical account of processing in the Raven's Progressive Matrices Test. *Psychological Review, 97,* 404-431.

Carroll, J. (1976) Psychometric tests as cognitive tasks: A new structure of intellect. In L. B. Resnick (Ed.), *The nature of intelligence* (pp. 27–56). Hillsdale, NJ: Lawrence Erlbaum Associates.

Carroll, J. B. (1993). *Human cognitive abilities: A survey of factor-analytic studies.* New York: Cambridge University Press.

Cronbach, L. J., & Meehl, P. E. (1955). Construct validity in psychological tests. *Psychological Bulletin, 52,* 281–302.

Diehl, K. A. (1998). *Using cognitive theory and item response theory to extract information from wrong responses.* Unpublished master's thesis. Lawrence, KS: University of Kansas.

Embretson, S. E. (1983). Construct validity: Construct representation versus nomothetic span. *Psychological Bulletin, 93,* 179–197.

Embretson, S. E. (1995). Developments toward a cognitive design system for psychological tests. In D. Lupinsky & R. Dawis (Eds.), *Assessing individual differences in human behavior* Palo Alto, CA: Davies-Black

Embretson, S. E. (1998). A cognitive design system approach to generating valid tests: Application to abstract reasoning. *Psychological Methods, 3,* 380–396.

Guttman, L. (1969). *Integration of test design and analysis.* Proceedings of the 1969 invitational conference on testing problems. Princeton, NJ: Educational Testing Service.

Hively, W., Patterson, H. L., & Page, S. (1968). A "universe-defined" system of arithmetic achievement tests. *Journal of Educational Measurement, 5,* 275–290.

Horn, J. L., & Cattell, R. B. (1967). Age differences in fluid and crystallized intelligence. *Acta Psychologica, 26,* 107–129.

Hornke, L. F., & Habon, M. W. (1986). Rule-based item bank construction and evaluation within the linear logistic framework. *Applied Psychological Measurement, 10,* 369–380.

Kyllonen, P., & Christal, R. (1990). Reasoning ability is (little more than) working memory capacity? *Intelligence, 14,* 389–434.

Moreno, K. E., Wetzel, C. D., McBride, J. R., & Weiss, D. J. (1984). Relationship between corresponding Armed Services Vocational Aptitude Battery (ASVAB) and computerized adaptive testing (CAT). *Applied Psychological Measurement, 8,* 155–163.

Raven, J. C. (1940). Matrix tests. *Mental Health, 1*, 10–18.

Rost, J. (1990). Rasch models in latent classes: An integration of two approaches to item analysis. *Applied Psychological Measurement, 3*, 271–282.

Sheehan, K. M. (1997). A tree-based approach to proficiency scaling and diagnostic assessment. *Journal of Educational Measurement, 34*, 333–354.

Shye, S., Elizur, D., & Hoffman, M. (1994). *Introduction to facet theory*. Thousand Oaks, CA: Sage.

Spearman, C. (1923). *The nature of intelligence and the principles of cognition*. London: MacMillan.

Spearman, C. (1927). *The abilities of man: Their nature and measurement*. London: MacMillan.

Sternberg, R. J. (1977). Component processes in analogical reasoning. *Psychological Review, 31*, 356–378.

9
Item Generation for Repeated Testing of Human Performance

Patrick C. Kyllonen
Air Force Research Laboratory and
Educational Testing Service

Drugs, fatigue, illness, shift-work, noise, depression, stress, and unusual environments such as space or the deep sea affect one's ability to think, learn, remember, decide, and react. More succinctly, environmental and physiological stressors, such as these, affect cognition. We know this from anecdotes: Coffee makes us alert; alcohol slows us down; noise makes it difficult to focus. We also know this from controlled studies in which individuals are repeatedly tested on a battery of behavioral measures (e.g., Kennedy, Turnage, Wilkes, & Dunlap, 1993). In such studies, changes in performance on the battery coincide with changes in the level of the stressors. For example, the reaction time of deep-sea divers slows with the air mixture (Logie & Baddeley, 1983). Fatigue leads to increased memory lapses, and a general slowing down (Koslowsky & Babkoff, 1993).

Item-generation methods can be helpful in stressor studies. Such studies require repeated testing of individuals. In repeated testing (sometimes called "repeated-measures testing"), generally speaking, it is not a good idea to re-administer the same test items over and over again. Such a protocol would permit item recognition, which could mask stressor effects. That is, participants could recognize specific items, and therefore do better and better on that particular item. At the same time, the stressor could be having an effect, which could cause performance to decline. The two effects, running in the opposite direction, could partially, or completely, neutralize each other. This could lead to an underestimate of the effect of the stressor on performance. Besides item effects, there are test familiarity and warm-up effects, and these, too, could mask stressor effects. But these effects are generally short lived, and can be eliminated with baseline or pretesting to asymptote. Item learning effects can be much longer lasting, and harder to eliminate with pretesting. But they also can be entirely eliminated through the use of multiple parallel forms in which items are not re-used. Item generation can be used to create multiple parallel forms.

Some of the critical difficulties in using item generation for high-stakes selection testing, which is the use discussed in most of the chapters in this book, are simply not applicable to the use of item generation for repeated-performance testing. For one, repeated-performance testing is typically a research, rather than an operational enterprise. There are no test preparation manuals to coach an individual on how to perform better as a participant in a research study. For another, the purpose of repeated-performance testing is typically to draw conclusions about the effects of the environmental stressor on people in general, rather than on a particular person. Consequently, such testing is not high-stakes from the standpoint of the individual test taker. There is no need to be concerned with issues such as fairness, or differential item functioning, or even, for that matter, individual item validity. Items with low validity do not result in decisions potentially unfair to the individual test taker. At worst, such items simply contribute noise to an assessment about the effects of the stressor being examined.[1]

Item generation contributes more than inexpensive items to the business of developing performance tests. Item generation focuses attention on the construct. By that I mean that to do item generation, it is necessary to think about what the factors are that contribute to task difficulty. Ideally, those factors are psychologically meaningful, and related to the construct being measured. For example, consider making a working-memory task more difficult by increasing working-memory load (e.g., by asking the examinee to remember more things). Such a task-difficulty manipulation would be construct-related.

The purpose of this chapter is to outline the issues and procedures for developing a generative performance battery, with an emphasis on the use for repeated testing in environmental and physiological stressor studies. I begin with a discussion of a particular application of such a battery to measure the effects of sleep manipulations on performance. Throughout the chapter I discuss issues associated with generative testing, relating them to the fatigue study to make it more concrete.

---

[1] There is potentially a category of high-stakes environmental performance tests that could be used operationally. These would be tests that are used to judge an individual's "cognitive fitness" to perform some task, such as drive a car, or fly a plane (e.g., Kennedy, Turnage, & Lanham, 1995). These might be called cognitive "sobriety tests." If such tests were developed, and used operationally, the concerns of high-stakes testing, such as fairness, and DIF, would be relevant for this use.

THE SLEEP STUDY

Research conducted by my colleagues and I in the Learning Abilities Measurement Program since 1985 focused on assessing cognitive abilities for applications in personnel selection and training. In our laboratory we administered numerous cognitive tests in hundreds of different studies to approximately 24,000 Air Force basic trainees every year. Through large-sample correlational studies, we developed a battery of tests designed to serve as a supplement or replacement to traditional aptitude tests. The site where we conducted the research, the Air Force Research Laboratory at Brooks Air Force Base, Texas, hosted numerous other behavioral sciences projects in human factors, medicine, toxicology, and an area known as chronobiology, the study of time effects on biological systems. As a result of several cross-disciplinary seminars, and in the spirit of interdisciplinary collaboration, we teamed with a group of chronobiology researchers led by Michael Rea. We sought to explore whether our research in developing cognitive test batteries could be applied to some of their concerns, such as the effects of fatigue and circadian rhythms on performance.

Our first study was concerned with the effects of an artificial dawn simulation lamp on restorative sleep. The dawn simulation lamp presents a very gradual increase in light intensity, in the way the rising sun does, and in contrast to the abrupt dark to light transition one typically experiences when getting out of bed in the morning. With some anecdotes and clinical evidence for beneficial effects of the dawn simulator on sleep and mood, Rea and his team were interested in whether the light could be used to reset one's internal clock, the system responsible for telling you when you're sleepy and when you're bright and alert. Such resetting is notoriously difficult (e.g., jet lag), and Rea was interested in seeing whether simulating dawn might be a more powerful resetting agent than simply turning on the light earlier.

Conducting these kinds of studies turns out to be very costly. For one thing, participants must spend many hours at the sleep laboratory, including meal times, and participation payments are therefore high. Second, finding participants who both can afford the time and satisfy various screening criteria (good health, nonsmokers, etc.) is tricky, and therefore recruiting costs are high. And finally, given this kind of investment in participants by the researcher, the marginal cost of collecting additional measurements, behavior and physiological (e.g., blood and saliva samples) is relatively low, and therefore researchers tend to develop a pile-it-on kind of attitude, and collect lots of data, under lots of manipulations, using lots of specialized equipment. All this goes to reinforce the importance of casting the wide net so that no effect goes undetected. But it also highlights a particular demand put on the performance battery—the one of replication.

Figure 9.1 shows the description of events participants went through. On the first day, they arrived at 7:00 PM to stay at the sleep lab overnight, with lights out at 11:00 PM. The next day, they woke up at 7:00 AM, then took our 30 min. cognitive test battery, twice, separated by a 1-hour break between sessions. They left the lab shortly after that, typically to go to their day job, and returned that same evening. For the next 7 days, they continued to take the test battery, a total of 37 times (!), while experiencing early wakening (Days 4–8), sleep deprivation (Day 4 and Days 8 and 9), and numerous brain wave (technically,) and saliva (technically,) tests, and sleeping under a dawn simulation lamp (there was also a control group that did not get the lamp, but was instead woken abruptly).

Our charter was clear. We were to develop the 30 minute (or so) battery to be both comprehensive and sensitive enough to detect any effects on participants' cognitive abilities (we also examined mood) due to induced fatigue, circadian rhythms, and sleep inertia (the feeling of grogginess upon waking). We anticipated that the frequent measurements Rea's group conducted of participants' physiological systems (the brainwave and saliva tests) would be the most sensitive to any sleep manipulations. But we thought of the question of any concomitant behavioral effect as potentially even more important: Even if there are physiological effects, do they affect people's performance?

CREATING THE IDEAL PERFORMANCE BATTERY

Studies of the effects of stressors on cognition fall into two categories: those in which specific hypotheses are being tested (e.g., does fatigue decrease short-term memory span?) and more exploratory studies. Given the state of the science, exploratory studies—addressing how a stressor might affect any cognitive function—are more common. This of course was our orientation in the sleep study. What is needed in exploratory studies is a fairly comprehensive battery—if the stressor affects cognition, it is important to cast a wide net so that one is assured of detecting that effect. This is especially true because data collection from stressor manipulations are typically rare or expensive (e.g., collecting data from astronauts on a space mission, divers on a deep-sea mission, or "live-in" participants in a sleep study). This makes the cost of Type II errors (failing to detect stressor effects) especially worrisome. To cast a wide net, instead of administering just a test or two (such as reaction time, and memory span), many stressor studies have used one of several more comprehensive "performance assessment batteries." These include the older Performance Evaluation Tests for Environmental Research battery (PETER; Bittner, Carter, Kennedy, Harbeson, & Krause, 1986), and Walter Reed Performance Assessment Battery (WRPAB), and their successors, the Delta

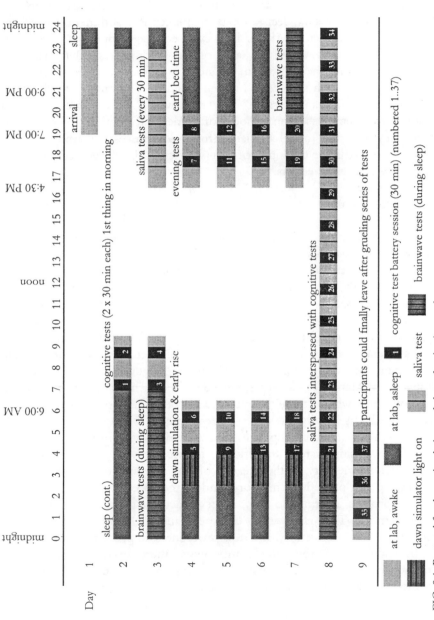

FIG. 9.1. Protocol for dawn-simulation and sleep-deprivation study.

(Turnage & Kennedy, 1992), and the United Tri-Services Cognitive Performance Assessment Battery (UTC-PAB; Englund, et al. 1987).

These batteries are intended to provide wide coverage of cognitive functions. For example, the 25-test UTC-PAB includes tests of "information processing, decision making, perception, and mental workload capacity" (Englund et al., 1987). However, coverage appears to be rather informal. Coverage is based primarily on the kinds of tests that, from the stressor literature, have proven sensitive to stressor effects, and the categories into which such tests happen to fall. An alternative to this kind of bottom-up "literature-driven" coverage would be a more top-down taxonomic scheme based on a model of human information processing. In such a system, the model human information-processing system would serve as the basis for the kinds of tests that could be developed to ensure sensitivity to stressor effects.

CAM Framework

One such taxonomic scheme based on this kind of top-down analysis is the cognitive abilities measurement (CAM) framework (Kyllonen, 1995). The CAM framework is built around what might be called a consensus information-processing model, similar to what is found in prominent cognitive psychological theories such as Anderson's (1983, 1993) Adaptive Control of Thought (ACT) theory. In such theories, the human cognitive system is said to consist of a working memory, the locus of current thinking and awareness, and two long-term memories, declarative and procedural, containing knowledge of concepts and procedures (e.g., strategies), respectively. Memories, concepts, and ideas, move into and out of working memory, and while "there" connect with other memories to constitute learning. All this activity takes place in real time.

The CAM framework stipulates that individuals vary in the components of this processing system. Specifically, individuals vary in the capacity of their working memory, in the breadth of and accessibility to knowledge in declarative and procedural memory, and in the speed with which they are able to process information (e.g., retrieve facts or procedures from long-term memory). They also vary in the speed and likelihood of learning new facts, in declarative memory, and new procedures, in procedural memory.

In addition to processing components, there needs to be content components. There is considerable research from a variety of methodological perspectives justifying a verbal–spatial distinction. Furthermore, analyses of correlation matrices of ability test batteries justify the positing of a quantitative content factor in addition to verbal and spatial factors (Snow, Kyllonen, & Marshalek, 1984). The CAM taxonomy crosses process and content components. Thus, for example, there are verbal, quantitative, and spatial working-memory components; verbal, quantitative, and spatial procedural-learning components, and so on.

We have recently extended the CAM taxonomy to include psychomotor abilities (Chaiken, Kyllonen, & Tirre, 2000). Despite a literature suggesting many psychomotor factors, we identified a single general psychomotor ability. In addition, we found that most of the variance in that ability could be explained by two factors: working memory capacity, and a timing, or "temporal processing" factor. Thus we have added a temporal-processing factor to the CAM taxonomy.

CAM Battery

It is possible to create tests that measure each of these attributes in individuals. Such a battery has been assembled, based on definitions of the various processing elements from the literature, and tasks administered in different experimental investigations to measure them (Kyllonen, 1995). For example, four different types of tests, or "paradigms" have been developed to measure working-memory capacity. These are four-term ordering (following Baddeley, 1968), operation span (following Daneman & Carpenter, 1980; and Turner & Engle, 1989), XYZ Assignment (based on Christal, 1989), and Continuous Opposites (Woltz, 1988). Three kinds of paradigms are used to measure declarative learning: free-recall, paired-associates, and implicit learning. Three more are used for procedural learning: an "if–then" procedure; a pattern-matching test, and a speeded classification test.

Figure 9.2 presents the CAM taxonomy, with the seven processing factors (processing speed, working memory, declarative and procedural learning, declarative and procedural knowledge, and timing) listed down the side, and the three content domains (verbal, quantitative, spatial) listed across the top. This 7 x 3 matrix is further subdivided into several (3 or 4) paradigms for each of the processing factors. Each entry in this matrix is a particular test, indicated by italics. For example, under working-memory capacity, there are four paradigms, the first one being "Four-term Order." There are then three four-term order tests, one in the verbal realm, called *Furniture-Animals,* one in the quantitative realm, called *10..90,* and one in the spatial realm, called *Blocks.* There are a few missing tests, for example, there are no verbal time-estimation tasks; and there are no paradigms under Declarative Knowledge.

Altogether, there are 57 tests. On average, each of the CAM tests takes about 5 to 10 minutes, and thus, the entire battery takes about 300–500 minutes to complete (about 5–8 hours). Clearly, this is too much testing for typical repeated performance studies. For that matter, it is too much testing for just about any conceivable application. The battery was constructed

	Content		
Processing Component / Paradigm	Verbal	Quantitative	Spatial
Processing Speed			
Two-term Ordering	Furniture-Animals	(10 .. 90)	Cigars
Verification	Silly Sentences	3-Number-Facts	Synthesis-Add
X Assignment	Common Category	Hard Number-Facts	Synthesis-Add-Subtract
Single Opposites	Up-Down	10-minus-n	Opposite Matrix Square
Working-Memory Capacity			
Four-term Ordering	Furniture-Animals	(10 .. 90)	Blocks
Verification Span	Silly-Sent+Words	3-Number-Facts+Digits	Synthesis-Add+Matrix
XYZ Assignment	Categories	Hard Number-Facts	Synthesis-Add-Subtract
Continuous Opposites	Up-Down	10-minus-n	Opposite Matrix Square
Declarative Learning			
Block, Old-New	Word Blocks	2-digit Blocks	Bruce-Figure Blocks
Pairs, Cued-Recall	Word Pairs	2-digit Pairs	Palmer-Figure Pairs
Symbol Pairs	Noun-Pair Lookup	Digit-Pair Lookup	Figure-Pair Lookup
Procedural Learning			
Rapid Serial Classification	Subj-Verb-Adverb	Hi-Lo Number Patterns	Four-square
Reduction	Future-Past-Present	Odd-Even	Circles
If-then	Edible-Living	Odd-Big	Shaded Square
Declarative Knowledge *No Paradigms*	Nelson-Nairns	Dates	Spatial Facts
	Abstract Facts	Counts	City Directions
	ASVAB GS	Probabilities	Lengths & Angles
	ASVAB WK	Measurements	Colors
Procedural Knowledge			
Sets	Word Sets	Number Sets	Figure Sets
Series	Word Series	Number Series	Figure Series
Matrices	Word Matrices	Number Matrices	Figure Matrices
Timing			
Time Estimation (5 - 15 s)		Timer hits 100	Horse reaches finish
Time Estimation (1 -3 s)		Successive taps	
Comparing 2 velocities		Which timer wins?	Which horse wins?

FIG. 9.2. Cognitive Abilities Measurement (CAM) taxonomy.

primarily to test hypotheses about the structure of human abilities, rather than with particular applications in mind. Thus, in application studies a subset of tests are typically administered. It is possible to sample from rows and columns to create a reduced battery that still guarantees coverage of key cognitive components.

There are two other key points about the CAM taxonomy to make when considering how it can be used in application studies. First, using analysis of variance terminology, the process and content dimensions of the CAM taxonomy can be considered fixed factors, but paradigm ought to be considered a random factor. That is, to construct a test battery covering the major cognitive factors, one would ideally include tests in each of the 7 x 3 cells to ensure full coverage. However, the paradigms in the CAM battery are simply samples from a larger universe of possible paradigms. There are perfectly good working-memory tests other than four-term order, XYZ assignment, and the other two CAM working-memory paradigms.

Furthermore, the CAM battery was intentionally designed to separate out, not completely, but to a certain extent, content factors, and specific processing factors. But in application studies, it may not be that important to make certain distinctions and thus it may be acceptable to use mixed tests. Mixed tests are ones that combine contents (e.g., verbal and spatial) or processes. For example, a psychomotor test combines working memory and time estimation components. It is still possible to separate out the components of a mixed test using a statistical (or psychometric) model, of course (which is the basis for the information processing analysis of intelligence tests, e.g., Kyllonen, 1994).

For the fatigue study, we selected tests measuring processing speed, working-memory capacity, and time estimation, with verbal and spatial content (3 x 2). We also selected tests of psychomotor ability (mixed tests). Although much of the variance in psychomotor performance can be accounted for by working-memory capacity and timing (Chaiken et al. 2000), there is nevertheless some unique variance. And few studies have looked at sleep effects on psychomotor task performance. Hence, we thought it would be useful to include psychomotor tasks in our "sleep battery."

TEST FACETS AND GENERATIVITY

In traditional test theory, items are considered random samples from a universe of possible items. The test theory model reflects the spirit in which tests are actually created—pretty much from the ground up. Researchers developed items around a general idea (e.g., verbal analogies), administered them to lots of examinees, then threw out "bad items," those that did not correlate highly with the rest of the items. The focus in this approach is on the test score, and bad items decrease the reliability of the test score.

In contrast, much of the research on information-processing analysis of cognitive abilities, beginning with Sternberg (1977), has treated test items as conditions in an experimental design. In these analyses the focus has been less on the total test score, and more on the effects of the factors of the design, and the contrasts between measurement conditions of these factors. At one time, there was hope that these contrasts, with evocative labels such as "encoding," "retrieval," "mapping," and "justification," would be the new ability constructs and would revolutionize our conception of human intelligence (Pellegrino & Glaser, 1979; Sternberg, 1984). The sobering reality has been that these contrasts have been for the most part either highly intercorrelated and highly correlated with total test score (overall performance score), or, if not, then unreliable (Ippel, 1986; Kyllonen, 1994;

Lohman, 1994). That is, these contrasts have not proven to redefine our conceptions of intelligence, but instead have proven to be old wine in new wineskins (Lohman, 1994).

Of course, as the market attests, old wine is not necessarily bad wine, and much of the research effort on reconceptualizing ability tests as being generated from conditions in an experimental design has not necessarily been wasted. Specifically, as many of the chapters in this book demonstrate, conceiving of tests as factorial designs is the basis for a certain approach to item generation. Put another way, what once were thought to be the new components of intelligence have now proven to be simply sources of item difficulty and variation, or in Irvine's terms, radicals and incidentals, respectively (Ippel, 1986).

Radicals and Incidentals: A Case Study—The Four-Term Order Test

To illustrate, let us consider one of the CAM verbal working memory tests, *Four-term Order*. On this test, examinees are presented a sequence of linear ordering statements, such as "the cat comes before the dog," "the chair comes before the table," and "the furniture comes before the animals." The examinee is then asked which of eight possible orders of the four terms (cat, dog, chair, table) is consistent with the three statements. For this example, the correct ordering is chair, table, cat, dog.

From the linear ordering literature in cognitive psychology (e.g., Clark & Chase, 1972; Johnson-Laird, 1985), we know several factors that affect the difficulty of this kind of task. These include the presence of a negation (e.g., "the chair does not come before the table") and whether the order in which the words are presented matches the list generated (e.g., "the chair comes before the table" is easier than "the chair comes after the table"). We also discovered from pilot testing that the location of the category statement ("the furniture comes before the animals") is important: Items are easier if the category statement comes first. We can use these three factors (negation, match, category position) to control the difficulty level of a particular item, and these three factors therefore may be called radicals (Irvine's terminology) or controlling factors (Dennis, Handley, Bradon, Evans, & Newstead's terminology). In contrast to these difficulty-controlling factors, we also can specify factors that do not affect difficulty, such as the specific terms used in the linguistic frames. Rather than cat, dog, chair, and table, and rather than the categories furniture and animals, we could easily plug in guitar, piano, apples, and oranges, and the categories instruments and fruit, without affecting item difficulty. Term, therefore, can be called an incidental (Irvine), noncontrolling (Dennis), or nuisance factor. Another incidental factor in this test is the position of the key (correct answer) in the list of eight choices.

Once an analysis is made of the radical and incidental factors underlying a test, it is straightforward to generate a template for a test in a process much the same as generating a design for an experiment. The template simply specifies the radical and incidental factors, and an appropriate experimental design for those. Then, depending on the constraints of available testing time versus test reliability requirements, one can decide on an optimal number of replications to include in the cells of the design. Or, alternatively, one can avoid exact replications by using a random factor, such as *term*, to create additional items.

We can illustrate how this works with the Four-Term Order test. The *negation* (present or absent), *matching* (match vs. doesn't match), and *category order* (category first vs. last) factors can be fully crossed for a 2 x 2 x 2 = 8 cell design. All three of these are fixed factors. The fourth factor, *term*, can be considered a random factor because there are many possible categories and instances that could be used in test items. For example, Battig and Montague (1969) provided lists of instances from 56 different categories (along with data on how strongly associated the instances were with the categories). (*Category* and *instance* could also be considered separate random factors, with *instance* nested within *category*.)

A common design for generating parallel forms is a randomized block factorial. In this design, the radical factors, fully crossed, form a set of item templates and the incidental factor is used to complete the template to make an item. For example, Figure 9.3 shows the eight item templates for the 4-Term Order task. The variables *ab* and *xy* are category names (e.g., furniture, animals), and the variables *a*, *b*, *x*, and *y* are associated category instances (e.g., table, chair, dog, and cat, respectively). An 8-item test could be created from two "category plus 2-instances" sets such as *furniture–chair–table*, and *animals–cat–dog*, as shown in Panel b of Figure 9.3. A parallel-form of that test (not shown) could be created from another two "category plus 2-instances sets" such as *fruit–apple–orange* and *instrument–guitar–piano*. Or, a parallel form could be created by simply varying the position of the key.

This example clearly illustrates the different roles radicals and incidentals play in item generation. *A design of the radicals (e.g., fully crossed) defines the item templates; and a design of the incidentals populates the templates and enables the creation of parallel forms.*

Which brings up several questions. First, how is that we know which factors are radical and which incidental? One approach, and it seems the most common one, is to designate certain item factors *incidentals* a priori. These would include the specific terms used (e.g., apple, orange, or 6, 8), the context in which a problem was embedded (e.g., the words and situations in an algebra word problem), and the position of the key in a multiple-choice test. The problem is that these a priori incidentals could turn out to be important determinants of item difficulty. For example, the

a) Templates

	First statement	Second Statement	Last Statement	cat. order	neg.	match
1	<ab's> come before <xy's>	<a> comes before <b>	<x> comes before <y>	first	no	yes
2	<ab's> come after <xy's>	<a> comes after <b>	<x> comes after <y>	first	no	no
3	<ab's> do not come after <xy's>	<a> does not come after <b>	<x> does not come after <y>	first	yes	yes
4	<ab's> do not come before <xy's>	<a> does not come before <b>	<x> does not come before <y>	first	yes	no
5	<a> comes before <b>	<x> comes before <y>	<ab's> come before <xy's>	last	no	yes
6	<a> comes after <b>	<x> comes after <y>	<ab's> come after <xy's>	last	no	no
7	<a> does not come after <b>	<x> does not come after <y>	<ab's> do not come after <xy's>	last	yes	yes
8	<a> does not come before <b>	<x> does not come before <y>	<ab's> do not come before <xy's>	last	yes	no

b) Actual Items

	First statement	Second Statement	Last Statement	cat. order	neg.	match
1	Furniture comes before Animals	chair comes before desk	dog comes before cat	first	no	yes
2	Furniture comes after Animals	chair comes after desk	dog comes after cat	first	no	no
3	Furniture does not after Animals	chair does not come after desk	dog does not come after cat	first	yes	yes
4	Furniture does not come before Animals	chair does not come before desk	dog does not come before cat	first	yes	no
5	chair comes before desk	dog comes before cat	Furniture comes before Animals	last	no	yes
6	chair comes after desk	dog comes after cat	Furniture comes after Animals	last	no	no
7	chair does not come after desk	dog does not come after cat	Furniture does not after Animals	last	yes	yes
8	chair does not come before desk	dog does not come before cat	Furniture does not come before Animals	last	yes	no

FIG. 9.3. Item templates for the Four-Term Order task.

use of category–instance combinations that are more abstract (e.g., party–Republican–Democrat) or less well known (e.g., drugs–Amoxil–Premarin) would likely increase the difficulty of the Four-Term Order task. And there could be significant key position effects, such as the 3rd item in a 4-alternative multiple-choice test is favored. This suggests that the radical–incidental distinction could at least be partly empirically determined. An incidental factor is defined as one that does not affect item difficulty very much, and a radical is a factor that affects item difficulty. Given that the generative test framework outlined here is based on an experimental design of items, an analysis of variance on the empirical difficulty of items from the design would enable statistical tests to determine the radical–incidental distinction. An even better alternative, given that such a test is sensitive to sample size, would be a variance component analysis to determine the relative magnitude of the effects of the various design factors. Factors that accounted for less than 5% of the variance could be determined incidentals, regardless of statistical significance. Obviously, this approach would necessitate a pretest, which can be costly, and that is perhaps the reason for the popularity of the a priori approach.

Another issue is, how do we know which incidentals ought to be used to create variants, or parallel forms, and which ones ought not to be? For example, it would seem more sensible, in the foregoing example, to create a parallel form with different categories than with simply a change in the key position. The reason is that a parallel form with different categories would seem more dissimilar to the original than a parallel form with different key positions. Such dissimilarity would be especially desirable in the case of repeated testing, when the point of creating parallel forms is to avoid item learning effects. It would seem that a considerable amount of item learning could still occur if the only change from one form to the next would be a change in the position of the key. Thus it would seem that the principle being espoused here is one of *choosing incidentals that simultaneously minimize the similarity of parallel items while not affecting item difficulty.*

How do we know how similar two items are? There are two approaches. A quick and dirty approach would be to have a handful of judges rate item similarity, based on a simple inspection of the items. A more elaborate approach would be to examine transfer or carryover (i.e., learning) effects between parallel items in a pretest. Suppose there were two incidental factors that could be used to create parallel items, incidental factor 1 (e.g., terms) and incidental factor 2 (e.g., key position). Parallel forms 1A and 1B could be created by varying factor 1 (using furniture–table–chairs and animals–dog–cat for Form 1A, and instruments–piano–guitar and fruits–apple–orange for Form 1B). Parallel forms 2A and 2B could be created by varying factor 2 (using one set of key positions such as 1, 2, 3, 4, 1, 2, 3, 4, for Form 2A, and 2, 4, 1, 3, 2, 4, 1, 3 for Form 2B). Then one group of pretest examinees could be given Forms 1A and 1B (in counterbalanced order), and another group could be given Forms 2A and 2B. The issue would be which group performed better on the second (parallel) test given. We would expect here that the group given forms 2A and 2B would perform better because the only difference between forms would be the difference in the answer key. Thus we would conclude that incidental factor 2 was less useful as a variant-producing factor because of the similarity of the forms it produced, which made them more susceptible to carryover effects. (Note the similarities here to Cronbach's "bandwidth-fidelity" dilemma).

Two Kinds of Radicals: Ippel's Model

In addition to the radical–incidental distinction, and the generated-form-similarity principle, there is another potentially important issue in identifying and using factors for item generation. That is the difference between factors that produce construct-relevant difficulty, and factors that produce construct-irrelevant difficulty. An example of the latter type of factor would be the frequency (rarity) of vocabulary used in arithmetic word problems. One could imagine increasing the difficulty of arithmetic word problems by increasing the vocabulary level. For example, compare these two problems:

1. Johnny was given $30. At the sporting goods store, baseballs cost $5 and bats cost $7. How much money would he have to spend if he wanted to buy as many baseballs as he could, and also buy 2 bats?
2. Surriander was bequethed assets with a surrender value of $30. At the exclusive bistro he frequented, libations were valuated at $5, and comestibles $7. What would be the volume of holdings surrendered upon a choice of maximizing libation count while depleting 2 comestibles?

At some level, the two problems have an equivalent format, and the equation underlying the problem is the same ($30 - [\text{mod}[[30 - (2 \times 7)] / 5]]$) However, the second one seems more difficult due to the more esoteric vocabulary and the more complex sentence constructions. But given that this is a test of math knowledge, it seems inappropriate to manipulate item difficulty by changing vocabulary. It would seem more appropriate to change problem difficulty by changing the equation or the numbers that appear in the story.

Ippel (1998) developed a scheme for formalizing this distinction between the two kinds of difficulty manipulation factors. In his method, Ippel first split the sample variance of the item accuracy values (i.e., p values) into a component that can be predicted from the variance in construct-related difficulty, operationalized as the discrimination parameter values of an IRT analysis (i.e., *b* values), and a residual variance component. Subsequently, he determined which task factors predicted the b values and which the residual component of item accuracy.

In applying the method to the Four-Term Order task, Ippel defined construct variance as that associated with a Verbal working memory factor, indicated by the three other CAM verbal working memory tests. Ippel found that the negation factor was construct related, while the matching and category position factors were not. The problem with using non-construct-related variance to manipulate item difficulty is that one reduces the discriminability of the item (the item-total correlation, or the discrimination parameter in an item-response theory analysis). Thus, ideally one would like to use primarily, if not exclusively, construct-related difficulty factors in item-generation applications.

SPEED–ACCURACY TRADEOFF

We included several processing speed tests in the sleep battery, and anticipated that these could prove sensitive to some of the study manipulations. However, not only are these tests quite different from the working-memory tests we have discussed to this point, but they present problems with respect to the item-generation framework we have been discussing. For one thing, by definition, items from speeded tests are not supposed to be difficult, if difficulty is defined as correctness in responding. Thus, the idea of a difficulty-controlling factor does not fit well with the concept of a speeded test. Difficulty can be defined as time taken to complete an item, which does make room for difficulty-controlling factors, but that introduces the problem of speed-accuracy tradeoff, the concept that one can get through an item at a faster rate by simply choosing to reduce one's accuracy. Figure 9.4 illustrates the problem, using data we collected from a pilot study involving several hundred participants.

The task yielding the data for Figure 9.4 was a fairly simple "count the dots" task in which participants were presented a 3 x 3 matrix of dots, approximately half colored white, and half colored black. The task was to count the number of white dots, which was either three, four, or five. If there were four, then the participant was to press the "L" key on a standard keyboard, and if there were three or five, to press the "D" key. We continued presenting different items to participants for a total of 135, one after another, and recorded how many they completed, and how many they responded to correctly.

As can be seen from Figure 9.4, participants tended to respond very rapidly, with the range of median item response times running from about one tenth of a second to a little over one half second. Except for a few

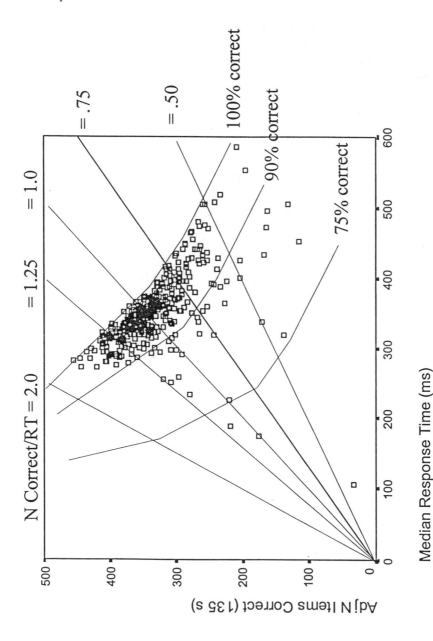

FIG. 9.4. Speed-accuracy tradeoff plot for "Count-the-Dots" task.

outliers, participants' average accuracy was also very high, in the 90%–100% range. However, one can see that within a given accuracy band, let's say those scoring at or close to 100%, there is a tremendous range in response time. Some participants were able to achieve essentially perfect accuracy while moving along at a very fast rate, while others were able to do so only by going relatively slowly. The data here are fairly typical of a wide variety of processing speed tests.

The problem these data present in the context of thinking about item generation is that the process must begin with a score. But the question is, which score? Some participants achieve 100% accuracy, but take 600 ms per item, whereas others achieve 90% accuracy, but only take 400 ms per item. Who is doing better?

Ratio Score Approach

One solution to the problem is to take the ratio of number correct/time, which is interpretable as a rate measure. However, if number correct is not adjusted for guessing, then this score would encourage rapid, "mindless," button pressing. Hence, a better score is adjusted number correct/time (where the adjustment can be the standard number right—number wrong/[the number of response alternatives—1]). Adjusted correct is what is plotted on the abscissa in Figure 9.4. (The lines emanating from the 0, 0 origin are ratio score projections for the values 2.00, 1.25, 1.00, .75, and .50.)

One problem[2] with the ratio score (correct/time) is that it is difficult to communicate to participants how their responses are being scored, and therefore participants can adopt a range of positions along the speed–accuracy tradeoff continuum without knowing which is the optimal position for them. Simply telling participants how they will be scored is not sufficient because translating that knowledge into an optimal position requires experience, and probably varied amounts of experience according to participant. The problem is not simply one of fairness, particularly in repeated-performance studies where fairness is not a concern because decisions about individuals are not being made. Rather, the problem is one of the meaning and stability of the scores that arise from the task. If participants can capriciously change their scores by simply choosing to adopt a different position along the speed–accuracy tradeoff continuum, then the scores reflect both their "ability" in the task and their somewhat arbitrary position–adoption decision. Because this decision is fairly easy to change (one can easily respond faster at the cost of more errors, if one

---

[2] Another problem is that the score rewards quick-inaccurate responding (Dennis & Evans, 1996).

experiences a motive to do so) the stability and meaning of scores is questionable.

Test Time Limit Approach

An approach we settled on for the sleep battery was to place a time limit on the test, in the same way as paper-and-pencil speeded tests have historically been administered. That is, we present items one after another until time expires. A participant's score is adjusted number correct within the time limit. A primary benefit of this task is that it is easy to communicate to the examinee what the scoring rules are, for example: "You have 2 minutes. Get as many as you can correct. For every one you get wrong, your score goes down by 1" (for the two-choice task, 1 is the correction factor, from $R - W / [k - 1]$, where k is 2).

How does this scheme mesh with item-generation principles? Because a time limit rather than the experimental design on items determines test length, in general, participants will receive different tests and their scores therefore will not be strictly comparable. This could be a problem. On the other hand, there is typically not variability between items in speeded tests. Just about any manipulation that increases variability in response time increases error rates, and therefore tends to change the nature of the test from a speeded test. Thus, many speeded tests, such as the numerical visual search task described earlier, can be characterized as having underlying them a design of several incidental factors, but no radical factors. For example, the search task includes the incidentals *terms* (the particular two-digit numbers used), whether an item is a *match or no match* item, and *position of the match* (1..9). With no radicals in the design, constructing parallel forms is straightforward in that every item is approximately equal in difficulty.

In conclusion, setting a time limit is particularly desirable for speeded tests, because it communicates effectively the "rules of the game" to participants, and therefore is likely to result in a reduction of capricious speed–accuracy tradeoff criterion setting, and therefore more stable scores. However, setting a time limit amounts to a relinquishing of control over the test design, and leads to differences between tests taken by examinees, and loss of comparability of test scores. This can be a problem for item generation. Fortunately, variability due to items is small in speeded tests, and therefore, for the most part items can be considered interchangeable with respect to difficulty, which reduces the importance of test-to-test variability.

TEST TYPES AND GENERATIVITY

Thus far we have discussed two types of test in the CAM battery, working memory tests and processing speed tests. As we have discussed, the differences between test types have implications for item generation. It may be useful to review other test types in the CAM battery, to determine any other item generation implications.

Timing and Psychomotor Tests

We included three psychomotor tests and three types of timing tests in the Sleep Battery. The psychomotor tests present moving objects on a display screen, which the examinee is expected to track continuously using the mouse. In the rotary pursuit test, the examinee tracks an object moving in a circle. In the arc pursuit test, the examinee tracks an object moving back and forth along an arc. In the pop the balloons test, the examinee tracks a sequence of balloons, "popping" them by pressing the mouse button as soon as the cursor is positioned over the balloon. The score on these kinds of tests is typically some summary of the average deviation between where the mouse should be positioned and where the examinee actually has it positioned, sampled every so often (typically many times per second). Low deviation scores are desirable, obviously. Radicals on these kinds of tests are factors such as the regularity of the movement of the tracked object (the more irregular the movement, the harder the object is to track), the speed of the movement of the tracked object (faster moving objects are harder to track), and the amount of distracting or extraneous information on the display screen. For example, on "pop the balloons" the balloons being tracked are mixed together with ones that are to be ignored, but the presence of more extraneous balloons turns out to make the tracking task more difficult. An example of a non-construct-related radical can also be found in the pop the balloons test, where participants are asked to pop a sequence of balloons, in order (e.g., first pop the yellow one, then the green one, then the red one). Varying the length of the to-be-popped sequence increases task difficulty, but probably by increasing memory load rather than by making the test more challenging as a psychomotor test. Incidentals on these kinds of tasks can include such factors as the color and shape of the tracking pointer and the tracked objects, the background display, and the particular paths the tracked objects traverse across the display screen.

Three types of timing tests are included in the Sleep Battery. A spatial timing task requires examinees to indicate when a regularly moving object will reach a particular point. The examinee views the object at the beginning of its movement, but the object then disappears, and the examinee has to imagine when it will reach its destination. A numerical-counter timing task requires examinees to indicate when a regularly incrementing counter will reach "100." The examinee observes the counter when it starts out at "1" and at some point (e.g., "50"), the counter goes blanks, and the examinee is to imagine when it would have reached 100 if it continued incrementing at the same rate. As in the psychomotor tests, the score for these tasks is some measure of the amount of deviation between when an examinee responds and when he or she should have responded. For these two tasks, radicals are the rate at which the object is changing (either moving or incrementing), and the amount of time examinees have to view the changing object before it disappears. (There is another paradigm in the CAM battery, not included in the Sleep Battery, in which examinees compare two changing objects, which at some point go blank, and try to predict which will reach the destination first. An additional radical in this paradigm is the closeness of the "race.") A third type of timing test asks examinees to initiate a clock, then to estimate, by pressing a button, when a certain amount of time will have elapsed. The radical in this task is simply the length of the interval (.86, 1.33, or 2.33 sec.).

Knowledge Tests

We did not include knowledge tests in the Sleep Battery because we conjectured that these would be the least sensitive to sleep manipulations. Given the limited time available for the battery (30 min.) we decided to leave these out.

There are two types of knowledge tests in the CAM battery, declarative and procedural. Declarative knowledge tests present a question to an examinee and the examinee either types in a response, or selects one from a set of alternatives. Examples of questions in the verbal realm are "What is the name of the process by which plants make food from sunlight?" and "What is a synonym for perspicacious?" Examples in the quantitative realm are "What is the distance from the Earth to the Sun?" and "In what year did Genghis Khan die?" Examples in the spatial realm are "In what direction would you travel if you went from St. Louis to Atlanta?" and "How many lines is a tic-tac-toe game drawn with?"

Although items vary in difficulty in knowledge tests, there are no radicals per se underlying the design of any of the different measures. Response format (free response vs. multiple choice) could be one, but it seems that the major source of difficulty is simply the cultural availability of the knowledge implied by the question. One could imagine taxonomizing knowledge domain in some kind of fashion, but such a taxonomy would go more toward the issue of coverage than of difficulty. New natural language processing methods, such as latent semantic analysis (Landauer & Dumais, 1997), might be exploited to help develop such taxonomies, but at this point it seems fair to say that item generation methods are immature to nonexistent in the knowledge testing area.

The CAM battery also includes procedural knowledge tests, which are very different from the declarative knowledge tests. A principle of procedural knowledge is that it is implicit and revealed through use, rather than explicit and revealable through a direct query as declarative knowledge is. Therefore, in the CAM battery, procedural knowledge is indicated by performance on what are sometimes referred to as inductive reasoning tests, such as sets, series, and matrices tests. The idea is that the availability of general procedural knowledge (i.e., general problem-solving heuristics) can be revealed through having examinees solve problems that call upon the use of general procedural knowledge. The structure of these tests with respect to item-generation issues is similar to that of working memory tests. For a good discussion of a design for a spatial matrices test, see Embretson's chapter 8 (this volume).

Learning Tests

We did not include learning tests in the Sleep Battery, because of a problem mentioned in the introduction to this chapter. Specifically, by design, performance on learning tests improves with practice over time, and that makes it tricky to separate learning effects from treatment effects, which are also changing over time. Nevertheless it is worth reviewing the various CAM tests that measure declarative and procedural learning. In the traditional declarative learning tests, examinees study a display for a fixed period of time, then are asked to recognize or recall items from the display. In these paradigms, study time is controlled, and varying the study time is a design radical, as is the recognition versus recall response requirement. Another radical is the complexity or amount of material that has to be memorized. The particular terms to be memorized is the incidental factor.

In the procedural learning tests, subjects are asked to categorize stimuli according to some classification rules they study. For example, in a verbal categorization task, examinees are shown three words in rapid succession (e.g., "doctors," "breathe," "quickly"). They are then asked to determine the syntactic order of the words, which are arbitrarily assigned into two classes (e.g., Noun-verb-adverb; and Adverb-noun-verb, could be considered one class, while Noun-adverb-verb, and Adverb-verb-noun would be considered another class). Radicals in this kind of task could include the rate at which the three words are presented, and the number of instances making up the class (the previous example gives two instances per class, but that could be changed to 1 or 3, since there are six possible orders of the three words). However, in the actual CAM test we do not use these radicals, because, as with speeded tests, we are interested in reducing the amount of item to item variability in difficulty, primarily so that it is possible to get a more regular learning curve. The insertion of difficulty producing factors into the design would cause bumps and depressions in the learning curve, and make it more difficult to examine learning per se. We do employ incidentals in this design, which are the particular terms (e.g., doctors, lawyers, patients, plumbers, etc. as "nouns") presented in a particular item.

Another point to be made about this kind of task is that unlike speeded tests, where the stimulus remains on the screen until a response is given, in these learning tests both the stimulus and response time is tightly controlled. For example, in the rapid serial classification test, terms are displayed for only about one half second, and a response must be made within 1 second. Early on in the learning session, examinees often respond too slowly as they are just learning the classification rules. This represents an alternative way to control speed–accuracy tradeoff, because the score is simply the number correct, without regard to response time, but the window in which to respond is very short. But the main point of administering the task this way is simply to control one's exposure to the materials presented, and to thereby control the amount of learning that can occur on every item. If participants were given unlimited time to respond, some could spend more time studying an item, thereby increasing their learning opportunity compared to others, and this would then become an uncontrolled factor.

SUMMARY

The primary benefit of item generation in repeated-testing studies is the ability to create parallel forms of a test. The use of parallel forms, as opposed to repeating a particular test over and over, eliminates item learning effects, and therefore reduces a potential confounding factor in studying the effects of various experimental manipulations in the repeated-testing study.

There are other benefits to item generation. One is item security, the importance of which is discussed by Wainer (chapter 11, this volume). Item security is not important for many typical repeated-testing applications. Such applications are primarily research studies, rather than high-stakes testing situations. Still, there are applications of performance battery assessment, such as sobriety or readiness tests, and neurological examinations, where item security is desirable, even if not absolutely essential.

However, perhaps the most important benefit of item-generation is that it puts the attention on the construct being measured, and away from the particular items being used to measure that construct. Conceiving of a test as a set of item specifications, rather than as a set of items, is a productive orientation. Devising an item generation scheme for a particular test forces the researcher to consider the radicals and incidentals underlying test items. Further, thinking about construct-related versus construct-unrelated radicals puts construct validity at the forefront of test design.

In this regard, we have identified three principles that capture our use of item generation in repeated-testing applications, and to some extent, are relevant to other applications.

1. *The Item-Generation-Design Principle.* A design of the radicals defines the item templates; and a design of the incidentals populates the templates and enables the creation of parallel forms.
2. *The Item Variability Principle.* It is important to employ incidentals that simultaneously minimize the similarity of parallel items while not affecting item difficulty. For repeated testing applications this is particularly important because it is desirable to minimize carryover effects, and items that are less similar are less likely to induce carryover.
3. *The Not-All-Tests-Are-Alike Principle.* Test types differ in the degree to which difficulty-modifying radicals ought to be employed. For many of the more complex tests, such as working-memory and procedural knowledge tests, item variability is an important feature of the test. But for others, such as processing speed and many of the learning tests, it is desirable, for different reasons, to minimize item variability. For some kinds of tests, in particular the declarative knowledge tests, we simply do not yet have a scheme for item difficulty, other than a purely empirically based one.

Relative to other psychometric methods, such as test theory, and item response theory, item generation theory is in its infancy. We can expect developments in both the range of tests to which item generation methods can be applied, and the range in applications for which such an effort will be warranted. Knowledge tests are prime candidates for future theoretical work, and applications such as medical (e.g., neurological), and readiness (e.g., "cognitive sobriety tests") batteries could benefit from the item generation approach. In any event, further developments in item generation, both theoretical and applied, will move us closer to achieving Sam Messick's vision of a science of test design centered on construct validity.

ACKNOWLEDGMENTS

This chapter is based on a talk given at the Conference, Generating Items for Cognitive Tests: Theory and Practice, Sponsored by the Air Force Research Laboratory, Air Force Office of Scientific Research, and Educational Testing Service, November 5-6, 1998, at the Chauncey Conference Center (Educational Testing Service), Princeton, NJ 08541. I am indebted to Scott Chaiken who worked with me on the construction of the "sleep" performance battery and provided access to the pilot data which stimulated many of the ideas expressed here. I would particularly like to thank him for our discussions on the speed-accuracy trade-off problem.

REFERENCES

Anderson, J. R. (1983). *The architecture of cognition.* Cambridge, MA: Harvard University Press.

Anderson, J. R. (1993). *Rules of the mind.* Hillsdale, NJ: Lawrence Erlbaum Associates.

Baddeley, A. D. (1968). A three minute reasoning test based on grammatical transformation. *Psychonomic Science, 10,* 341–342.

Battig, W. F., & Montague, W. E. (1969). Category norms of verbal items in 56 categories: A replication and extension of the Connecticut category norms. *Journal of Experimental Psychology Monographs, 80,* (3, Pt. 2).

Bittner, A. C., Jr., Carter, R. C., Kennedy, R. S., Harbeson, M. M., & Krause, M. (1986). Performance Evaluation Tests for Environmental Research (PETER): Evaluation of 114 measures. *Perceptual and Motor Skills, 63,* 683–708.

Chaiken, S. R., Kyllonen, P. C., & Tirre, W. (2000). Organization and components of psychomotor ability. *Cognitive Psychology, 40,* 198-226.

Christal, R. E. (1989). *Estimating the contribution of experimental tests to the Armed Services Vocational Aptitude Battery* (Tech. Paper No. AFHRL-TP-89-30). Brooks AFB, TX: Manpower and Personnel Division, Air Force Human Resources Laboratory.

Clark, H., & Chase, W. (1972). On the process of comparing sentences against pictures. *Cognitive Psychology, 3,* 472–517.

Daneman, M., & Carpenter, P. A. (1980). Individual differences in working memory and reading. *Journal of Verbal Learning and Verbal Behavior, 19,* 450–466.

Dennis, I., & Evans, J. St. B. T. (1996). The speed-error trade-off problem in psychometric testing. *British Journal of Psychology, 87,* 105–129.

Englund, C. E., Reeves D. L., Shingledecker, C. A., Thorne, D. R., Wilson, K. P., & Hegge F. W. (1987). *Unified Tri-service Cognitive Performance Assessment Battery (UTC-PAB) 1. Design and Specification of the Battery* (Tech. Rep. Number 87-10). San Diego, CA: Naval Health Research Center. DTIC ADA182480 (*http://www.nhrc.navy.mil/Pubs/Abstract/87/10.html*).

Ippel, M. J. (1986a). An information processing approach towards a structural theory of item equivalence. In S. E. Newstead, S. H. Irvine, & P. Dann (Eds.), *Human assessment: Cognition and motivation* (pp. 403–404). Dordrecht: Kluwer.

Ippel, M. J. (1986). *Component tests: A theory of cognitive aptitude measurement.* Amsterdam: Free University Press.

Ippel, M. J. (1998). *A method for separating construct-related and construct-unrelated variance in a faceted test.* Unpublished manuscript. Brooks Air Force Base, Texas: Air Force Research Laboratory.

Johnson-Laird, P. N. (1985). Deductive reasoning. In R. J. Sternberg (Ed.), *Human abilities: An information-processing approach.* San Francisco: Freeman.

Kennedy, R. S., Turnage, J. J, & Lanham, D. S. (1995). Criteria for evaluating tests intended to assess driver fitness. In the 13th International Conference on Alcohol, Drugs and Traffic Safety (T'95), Adelaide, Australia (*http://raru.adelaide.edu.au/T95/paper/s23p4.html*)

Kennedy, R. S., Turnage, J. J., Wilkes, R. L., & Dunlap, W. P. (1993). Effects of graded dosages of alcohol on nine computerized repeated-measures tests. *Ergonomics, 36,* 1195–1222.

Koslowsky M., & Babkoff, H. (1992). Meta-analysis of the relationship between total sleep deprivation and performance. *Chronobiology International, 9,* 132–136.

Kyllonen, P. C. (1994). Information processing. In R. J. Sternberg (Ed.), *Encyclopedia of human intelligence*. New York: Macmillan.

Kyllonen, P. C. (1995). CAM: A theoretical framework for cognitive abilities measurement. In D. Detterman (Ed.), *Current topics in human intelligence: Volume IV, Theories of intelligence*. Norwood, NJ: Ablex.

Landauer, T. K., & Dumais, S. T. (1997). A solution to Plato's problem: The latent semantic analysis theory of acquisition, induction, and representation of knowledge. *Psychological Review, 104*(2), 211–240.

Logie, R. H., & Baddeley, A. D. (1983). A Trimix saturation dive to 660 m: Studies of cognitive performance, mood and sleep quality. *Ergonomics, 26,* 359–374.

Lohman, D. F. (1994). Implications of cognitive psychology for ability testing: Three critical assumptions. In M. G. Rumsey, C. B. Walker, & J. H. Harris (Eds.), *Personnel selection and classification* (pp. 145–172). Hillsdale, NJ: Lawrence Erlbaum Associates.

Pellegrino, J. W., & Glaser, R. (1979). Cognitive correlates and components in the analysis of individual differences. In R. J. Sternberg & D. K. Detterman (Eds.), *Human intelligence: Perspectives on its theory and measurement* (pp. 61–88). Norwood, NJ: Ablex.

Snow, R. E., Kyllonen, P. C., & Marshalek, B. (1984). The topography of ability and learning correlations. In R. J. Sternberg (Ed.), *Advances in the psychology of human intelligence, Volume 2* (pp. 47-103). Hillsdale, NJ: Lawrence Erlbaum Associates.

Sternberg, R. J. (1977). *Intelligence, information processing, and analogical reasoning: The componential analysis of human abilities*. Hillsdale, NJ: Lawrence Erlbaum Associates.

Sternberg, R. J. (1984). Testing and cognitive psychology. *American Psychologist, 36,* 1181–1189.

Turnage, J. J., & Kennedy, R. S. (1992). The development and use of a computerized human performance test battery for repeated-measures applications. *Human Performance, 5*(4), 265–301.

Turner, M. L., & Engle, R. W. (1989). Is working-memory capacity task dependent? *Journal of Memory and Language, 28,* 27–154.

Woltz, D. J. (1988). An investigation of the role of working memory in procedural skill acquisition. *Journal of Experimental Psychology: General, 117,* 319–331.

10
Scoring Tests When Items Have Been Generated

David Wright
University of Plymouth

An inevitable feature of item generation, as considered here, is the delivery of items that have not been trialed. Another is the inability to make perfect predictions of item response characteristics for these items. Successful implementation of item generation requires a defensible methodological framework for dealing with these challenges.

This chapter presents some initial work on statistical models for use in test generation. These models have applications in the design of test-generation algorithms, in adaptive item generation and scoring. Particular emphasis is placed on models that take explicit account of the inability to predict the item-response characteristics in test generation. Techniques for fitting models using the Expectation Maximisation (EM) algorithm and Markov chain Monte Carlo (MCMC) methods are discussed. The ideas are illustrated using data from a timed-item two-term transitive inference test.

The generation of items can usefully be characterized as the process of sampling items from some notional universe according to some well-defined algorithm. Typically the item universes involved are indexed by a number of factors that uniquely define the items. These factors can be used to define classes of items with equivalent or at least approximately equivalent item-response characteristics. The ability to model the characteristics of the item universe from training data on a sample from the universe is fundamental to the process of computerized test generation.

As an illustration consider items from the two-term transitive inference task in the British Army Recruit Battery (BARB). (Irvine, Dann, & Anderson, 1990). Combining a problem form with a comparative and two names as shown in Table 10.1 generates an item. The item universe comprises $8 \times 8 \times 240 = 15,360$ items corresponding to eight problem forms, eight comparatives and $16 \times 15 = 240$ ordered pairs of names. In the BARB test it is assumed that the item response characteristics are

TABLE 10.1
Problem Form and Content Used in the BARB Transitive Inference Task

	Problem Forms	
1	A is better than B	Who is better?
2	A is better than B	Who is worse?
3	A is worse than B	Who is better?
4	A is worse than B	Who is worse?
5	A is not as bad as B	Who is better?
6	A is not as bad as B	Who is worse?
7	A is not as good as B	Who is better?
8	A is not as good as B	Who is worse?

Comparatives

taller - shorter
better - worse
stronger - weaker
heavier - lighter
happier - sadder
older - younger
brighter - dimmer
faster - slower

Names

Fred, Bill, Tom, John, George, Paul, Mike, Steve, Bob, Phil, Ian, Dave, Sid, Pete, Joe, Chris

determined by problem form, defining eight classes of $8 \times 240 = 1920$ items. Wright and Dennis (1999) described a modified transitive inference task in which subjects were shown the question for a time, t, and then requested to respond in a short time window. The time t was also considered to be a determinant of the item response characteristics. Since t can be varied continuously the universe of items then becomes infinite as and can be represented as illustrated in Figure 10.1. The crosses shown in Figure 10.1 show the times and problem form combinations trialed in the timed item version of the BARB transitive inference test described in Wright and Dennis (1999). Items were generated covering the $4 \times 8 = 32$ points shown in Figure 10.1. Some items were replicated leading to a total of 44 items. The choice being dictated by the total time limit available for the experiment. These 44 items were trialed on 1,273 British army applicants over the period July 1996 to November 1996.

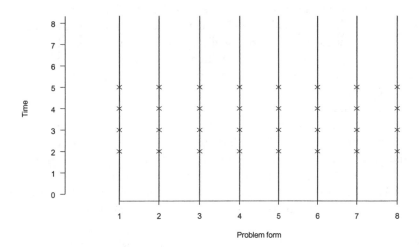

FIG. 10.1. Item universe for the timed-item two-term transitive inference test. (Dimensions for names and comparatives are excluded from this graph.). The crosses represent points at which training data were collected.

REGRESSION MODELS FOR ITEM DIFFICULTY AND DISCRIMINATION

Multiple Regression

To date much of the work on item generation has focused on the prediction of proportion correct using multiple regression models with item proportions correct as the response (dependent) variable and item radicals as the explanatory (independent) variables. The coefficient of determination R^2 has been used as a measure of the success in the ability to predict item characteristics. Although this approach is easily implemented it is limited in two ways. First, any analysis of discrimination is excluded. This means that the models cannot be used in the conventional approach to adaptive testing. Second, R^2 is inappropriate as a measure of how well item characteristics can be predicted. The problem with the use of R^2 is that the range of difficulties, as well the ability to predict them, determines R^2. This is illustrated using a computer simulation described next.

Data were simulated from two item-response theory (IRT) models involving a 20-item test presented to 200 subjects. In each case a two-parameter IRT model with a common discrimination parameter of unity was used. Item difficulties were chosen to fix the proportions correct as follows.

The first simulation demonstrates that moderate values of R^2 can result in cases where the covariate information predicts the population proportion correct perfectly. The difficulty parameters were chosen so that the population proportions correct were equally spaced over the interval 0.4 to 0.6. A single explanatory variable, which predicted this population proportion correct perfectly, was created. In repeated samples, the mean value of R^2 was 0.72.

The second simulation demonstrates that very high values of R^2 can result when there is considerable error in the prediction of population proportion correct. In this simulation the difficulty parameters were chosen so that the population proportions correct were equally spaced over the interval 0.1 to 0.9. A single explanatory variable was obtained by adding a random variable, uniformly distributed over the interval -0.1 to 0.1, to each of the populations correct. In repeated samples the mean value of R^2 was 0.94.

The message from these simulations is that unadjusted values of R^2 should not be used as an absolute measure of how well item difficulty can be predicted. However, in cases where the population proportions correct can be assumed similar, R^2 may still serve as a good way of comparing models for difficulty prediction.

Item-Response Theory

We consider here item-response theory (IRT) models of the form

$$P_i(\theta) = \alpha_i + (1 - \alpha_i)\Gamma(\beta_i\theta - \gamma_i). \tag{1}$$

where Γ denotes a cumulative distribution function. In this model θ is a latent ability drawn from a standard normal distribution. This is the standard three-parameter IRT model (see, for example, Hambleton & Swaminithan 1985). The term three-parameter refers to the three parameters per item. In a test with n items the model has $3n$ parameters. For applications in item generation we consider structured versions of the model in which the item difficulty and discrimination are predicted from item radicals. This extends the Linear Logistic Test Model of Fischer (1973). Training data from a suitably chosen subset of items from the item universe can be used to fit models that can be used to predict the item characteristics for the whole item universe. These models can also be used to represent psychological theories concerning item characteristics and provide a formal basis for comparison of competing theories. Another benefit is the parsimony achieved through the reduced number of parameters.

MODEL FITTING

IRT models have received much attention in the literature over recent years and established software packages are now available for fitting these models using the EM algorithm (see Mislevy & Bock, 1993). More recently Bayesian methodology using MCMC has been developed. See Gilks, Richardson, and Spiegelhalter (1996) for a general treatment of MCMC and Albert (1992) for an application of MCMC in IRT. The work presented in this article is based on software for fitting models of the form (1) in which the difficulty parameters γ_i and discrimination parameters β_i are determined according to a linear model on radicals. Methodology has been implemented for maximum likelihood estimation for the logistic model using the EM algorithm (Dempster, Laird, & Rubin, 1977) and for Bayesian analysis using MCMC for the probit model. This has been programed in S-PLUS (MathSoft, 1996). Copies of the S-PLUS functions are available from the author. To date the software has been restricted to the case where the guessing parameters α_i are assumed known. This article presents maximum likelihood results for the logistic model obtained using the EM algorithm. A Bayesian analysis using MCMC is given in Wright and Dennis (1999). The guessing parameters have been fixed at 0.5.

Maximum Likelihood Estimation Using EM

For the data on the timed item two term transitive inference test the sequence of models shown in Table 10.2 were considered. The term (1) in Table 10.2 is used to denote the null model. This corresponds to the situation where the difficulty/discrimination parameters are the same for all items. Significance tests for terms dropped as we proceed down the rows of the table can be based on the increase in the –2 log likelihood statistic. Under the null hypotheses that the term has no effect this statistic is approximately chi-squared distributed. The degrees of freedom are given by the change in the number of parameters. For example to test for a difference in discrimination parameters Model II is compared with Model I. The increase in –2 log likelihood is given by 39665.7-39538.9 = 126.8. Under the null hypothesis of a common discriminating parameter, this statistic is distributed approximately as χ^2 with $88 - 45 = 43$ degrees of freedom. This gives $P < 0.0001$ providing overwhelming evidence of a difference in discrimination. This P value, however, is misleading in the sense that with such large samples almost every null hypothesis will be rejected. Effects that are of no practical significance turn out to be highly

TABLE 10.2
IRT Models and −2 Log Likelihood Statistics

Model	Difficulty	Discrimination	Fit	No. of parameters
I	Item	Item	39538.9	88
II	Item	(1)	39665.7	45
III	Problem + Time	(1)	40407.9	12
IV	Problem + 1/t	(1)	40431.2	10
V	Problem	(1)	42620.7	9
VI	Time	(1)	41430.0	5
VII	(1)	(1)	44552.1	2

statistically significant. This problem arises in many other areas notably in structural equation modeling where a number of fit indices have been developed to provide measures of practical significance.

For the purposes of item generation, the ten-parameter Model IV can be used to predict the item characteristics for the item-universe. The fitted model parameters are given in Table 10.3. For example, the predicted item characteristic function for an item involving problem form 3 presented for a time of 3.5 seconds is

$$P(\theta) = 0.5 + \frac{0.5}{1 + \exp\{-[1.31293\theta - (-4.0348 + 8.4293/3.5)]\}}$$

.

It would of course be unreasonable to use the fitted model to extrapolate far outside the time limits 2 to 5 seconds.

RANDOM EFFECTS

Models With Random Effects

In principle, the models described earlier could be used as a basis for tailored testing or adaptive item generation. However, these models are inevitably imperfect and there will be variations in item characteristics that are not captured by these simple models. An appealing approach is that taken by Mislevy (1988) where random effects are used to model imperfections in the prediction of item characteristics. Within the context of item generation, where item features assumed not to affect item characteristics are assigned at random, this is a very natural approach that has many parallels in experimental design and ANOVA. This section describes some initial work on fitting models with random difficulty effects and the implications for ability estimation.

Continuing with the example of the timed-item two-term transitive inference test, the random effects Model (2) is considered. In this model, ε is assumed to be a random effect on item difficulty drawn independently from a normal distribution with mean zero and variance σ^2.

$$Difficulty = Problem\ Form + 1/t + \varepsilon \tag{2}$$

Estimates of the ε's for the 44 items in the test can be obtained by subtracting the fitted item difficulties from the reduced model (*Difficulty = Problem Form +1/t, Discrimination = (1)*) from those of the full model(*Difficulty = Item, Discrimination = (1)*). These predicted difficulties shown in Figure 10.2. This illustrates how the reduced model captures the variation in difficulty levels. Figure 10.3 shows the estimated ε's or residuals

TABLE 10.3
Maximum Likelihood Estimates

Coefficient	Estimate
Difficulty	
Problem form 1	-4.4610
Problem form 2	-4.0602
Problem form 3	-4.0348
Problem form 4	-4.7771
Problem form 5	-2.5427
Problem form 6	-3.4989
Problem form 7	-3.7278
Problem form 8	-3.4273
1/t	8.4293
Discrimination	
(1)	1.31293

with the fitted normal distribution superimposed. The maximum likelihood estimate of standard deviation σ is 0.5325.

Implications for Ability Estimation

The random effect present in Model 2 means that the process of item generation involves sampling from a distribution of item characteristics. Figure 10.4 illustrates this with a sample of 10 item characteristic curves generated from problem form 1 with a time of 3 seconds. This section deals with the problem of ability estimation in situations from data on tests involving this form of random effect.

For a subject who has completed a specific sequence of items resulting in a vector of responses $y = (y_1, y_2, \ldots, y_n)^T$, the posterior distribution of ability given the model parameters is obtained from Bayes theorem as

$$p(\theta | \underline{y}, \underline{\alpha}, \underline{\beta}, \underline{\gamma}, \sigma^2) \propto p(\theta) \prod_j \int_{-\infty}^{\infty} p(y_j | \theta, \alpha_j, \beta_j, \varepsilon_j) p(\varepsilon_j | \sigma^2). \quad (3)$$

Substituting estimates for the unknown parameter values and using quadrature to compute the integrals, the posterior distributions of ability for a subject from the training sample is shown in Figure 10.5. With a standard

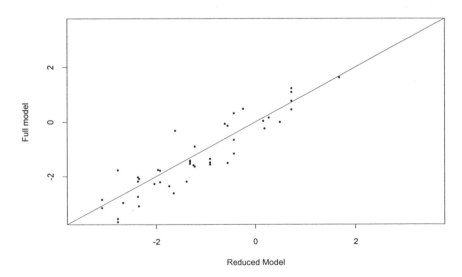

FIG 10.2. Item difficulty γ estimates obtained from the full and reduced model.

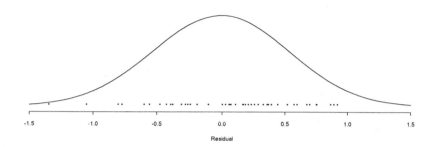

FIG. 10.3. Residuals for item difficulties obtained for the model *Difficulty* = *Problem Form* *+1/t.*

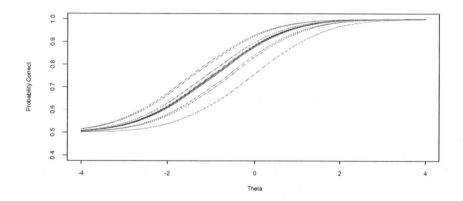

FIG. 10.4. Different item characteristic curves obtained by sampling from the distribution of random effects. (Problem form 1 with a 3 second time limit, s.d. = 0.5325).

deviation (SD) of 0.5325 the posterior distribution is close to that with an SD of zero (no random effect). With SDs of 1.0 or higher the random effects have a marked effect on inferences about ability with the posterior distribution moving closer to the prior distribution of ability as the standard deviation increases.

Intuitively we would expect random effects to cancel with large numbers of items. However, with small samples of items, for example in the early stages of an adaptive test, the random would be expected to have a greater impact on the posterior distribution of ability.

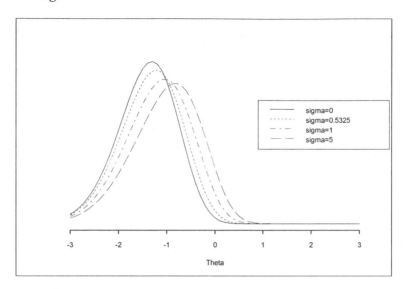

FIG. 10.5. This graph shows the different posterior distributions obtained for a subject from the training sample with 30 items correct. On the basis of this number correct the subject is on the 10th percentile of the ability distribution.

REFERENCES

Albert, J. H. (1992). Bayesian estimation of normal ogive item response curves using Gibbs sampling. *Journal of Educational Statistics, 17,* 251-269.

Dempster, A. P., Laird, N. M., & Rubin, D. B. (1977). Maximum likelihood from incomplete data via the EM algorithm (with discussion). *Journal of the Royal Statistical Society, Series B, 39,* 1-38.

Fischer, G. H. (1973). Linear logistic test model as an instrument in educational research. *Acta Psychologica, 37,* 459-374.

Hambleton, R. K., & Swaminanthan, H. (1985*). Item response theory: Principles and applications.* Boston: Kluwer-Nijhoff Publishing.

Irvine, S. H., Dann, P. L., & Anderson, J. D. (1990). Towards a theory of algorithm-determined cognitive test construction. *British Journal of Psychology, 81,* 173-195.

MathSoft (1996). *S-PLUS, Version 3.4.* MathSoft.

Mislevy, R. J. (1988). Exploiting auxiliary information about items in the estimation Rasch item difficulty parameters. *Applied Psychological Measurement, 12,* 281-296.

Mislevy, R. J., & Bock, R. D. (1983). BILOG: Item analysis and test scoring with binary logistic models [Computer program]. Mooresville, IN: Scientific Software.

Wright, D. E., & Dennis, I. (1999). Exploiting the speed-accuracy trade-off. In P. L. Ackerman, P. C. Kyllonen, & R. D. Roberts (Eds.), *Learning and individual differences* (pp 231-248). Washington, DC: American Psychological Association.

11

On the Automatic Generation of Test Items: Some Whens, Whys, and Hows

Howard Wainer
Educational Testing Service

OVERVIEW

This chapter examines those circumstances when automatic item generation (AIG) would be useful and when it would not be. Because AIG is so tightly bound to computerized testing, those circumstances when computerized testing is sensible are examined. In addition some problems with computerized testing are discussed, as are some plausible solutions. These solutions are tied to Zipf's Law which is illustrated in several situations ranging from the use of verbal items on the computerized version of Graduate Record Exam to the number of deaths due to horsekicks in the Prussian army between 1875 and 1894. I conclude with reflections on the wisdom of the Talmud.

The reaction of a child when handed a hammer for the first time is completely predictable; through the child's eyes everything looks like it could use a good whack. Clearly a reaction to the possibility of whacking precedes a deep analysis of what really requires such a response. Humans never seem to outgrow this propensity. The Industrial Revolution provided an unended stream of tools and devices for human use. We are likely to use them before asking if such use is a sensible idea. Long-term planning does not seem to be an innate talent of the human species. The proliferation of Wal-Marts, chainsaws, sport utility vehicles, and nuclear missiles are only four obvious examples; there are many others. In the course of this chapter I discuss another of these—the use of the computer in mental testing.

This discussion is guided by two principles:

The first principle was well expressed by a Talmudic *midrash*, attributed to Rabban Yohanan ben Zakkai: *"If there be a plant in your hand when they say to you, Behold the Messiah!, go and plant the plant, and afterward go out to greet him."* The educational establishment regularly discovers new sources of redemption. Today's promise is that computer-based testing abetted by computer generated tests will save us all; but one suspects that the Lord is best served by those in the testing business who continue to find salvation in the routine transactions of their daily work.

The second principle has been stated in many ways, by many people, but the clearest version was by Mae West: *"Anything worth doing is worth doing slow."*

How do these two principles apply to the topic of automatic generation of test items? I focus first on two aspects of the general topic of implementation of such procedures. These aspects are *why* and *when*.

WHY DO WE NEED AUTOMATIC ITEM GENERATION?

When tests are administered via computer, economic constraints eliminate the current practice of scheduling those tests only several times each year. To make efficient use of the expensive infrastructure required for computerized administration the tests must be administered continuously over the course of the year. But continuous administration of exams yields several knotty security problems. One of these was highlighted by the 1994 conflict between the Educational Testing Service (ETS) and Kaplan Educational Centers (Jacobson, 1995). That conflict had, as its basis, the following scenario: Kaplan tasked several of its employees to take the Graduate Record Exam (GRE) over a period of several weeks. They were asked to remember as many of the items they had seen as they could. After each administration the remembered items were written down and shown to the next exam taker. In this way duplication of effort was minimized. Kaplan discovered that after a very short time their employees were finding that they had already seen a very high proportion of the items that subsequently appeared on their tests.[1]

Why was it so easy to steal a large proportion of the test? One obvious answer could be that the pool of items that the selection algorithm had at its disposal was too small. It was too small, but, as we demonstrate shortly, simply enlarging it in the usual way (i.e., having item writers write many more items) is not a viable long-term solution. If, instead, items could be generated automatically there could be a potentially infinite pool of items whose marginal cost is practically nothing.

---

[1] Kaplan told ETS of this exercise and suggested that security of the test was inadequate. ETS sued Kaplan for copyright infringement. On January 20, 1998, prior to trial, it was settled with Kaplan agreeing that what they had done was "inappropriate" and that they would not do it again. Kaplan also paid ETS $150,000.

Thus, it appears that maintaining test security, when there is computerized administration, is a powerful practical reason for developing automatic item-generation methods. Without it, it is uncertain whether the sorts of continuous testing that is required for computerized test administration can ever compete effectively with the well developed, and spectacularly efficient, paper-and-pencil procedures that have been in use for most of the past century. But, regardless of the test administration method, having test items automatically generated has the advantages (and disadvantages) of assembly-line mass production. There could be a substantial cost saving in test production (about 10% of testing costs is item writing) as well as a uniformity of structure and quality that is not possible with hand-built items. When the goal is standardized measurement, uniformity is an often much desired characteristic.

In addition to these practical reasons, there is a theoretical one, for if we can generate items that produce acceptable evidence about a particular mental trait, it suggests that we are really beginning to understand that trait. Further, if we can accurately predict the difficulty of those items we have made an important breakthrough.

But can we? As of this moment I remain in agreement with Bob Thorndike's (1983) conclusion that "we really don't yet know what makes an item hard (p. 360)." Sure, we have broad notions. We know that

$$2 + 7 = ? \tag{1}$$

is easier than

$$\int \sec(x)dx = ? \tag{2}$$

but how does (2)'s difficulty compare with that of

$$\frac{d}{dx}\log|\sec(x) + \tan(x)| = ? \tag{3}$$

Although there have been impressive advances in our ability to manufacture items on the fly, nothing that I have learned about these advances suggests that we can accurately provide an estimate of the relative difficulty of problems (2) and (3). At least not yet.

A More Compelling Argument

Earlier I made the strong statement that without automated item generation "it is uncertain whether the sorts of continuous testing that is required for computerized test administration can ever compete effectively with paper-and-pencil procedures." I now support that statement with some evidence.

Edward Albee, in his one act play "Zoo Story" said, "Sometimes you must go a long way out of the way in order to come back a short distance correctly." This is one of those times; bear with me.

Example 1. Horse Kicks in the Prussian Army

In 1898, Bortkewitsch reported that in the 20 years between 1875 and 1894 there were 196 deaths among members of 14 corps in the Prussian Army due to horse kicks. The annual frequency of deaths Bortkewitsch reported were:

TABLE 11.1
Deaths Due to Horse Kicks in the Prussian Army From 1875 to 1894

Year	1875	1876	1877	1878	1879	1880	1881	1882	1883	1884
No. Deaths	3	5	7	9	10	18	6	14	11	9

Year	1885	1886	1887	1888	1889	1890	1891	1892	1893	1894
No. Deaths	5	11	15	6	11	17	12	15	8	4

If we reorder the years by the number of deaths (x) and rank them (with ranks i) we obtain the ordered frequency of deaths $(x_{(i)})$:

TABLE 11.2
Deaths Due to Horse Kicks in the Prussian Army From 1875 to 1894, With Years Ordered by Number of Deaths

Year	1880	1890	1887	1892	1882	1891	1883	1886	1889	1879
No. Deaths	18	17	15	15	14	12	11	11	11	10
Rank	1	2	3	4	5	6	7	8	9	10

Year	1878	1884	1893	1877	1881	1888	1876	1885	1894	1875
No. Deaths	9	9	8	7	6	6	5	5	4	3
Rank	11	12	13	14	15	16	17	18	19	20

If we then plot these ranks on the horizontal axis and the log of the number of deaths on the vertical axis we note (Figure 11.1) that the observed relationship is very nearly linear.

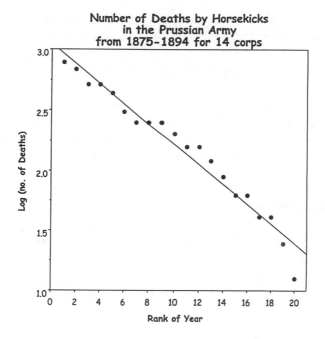

FIG. 11.1. Classic data from Bortkewitsch (1898) that are usually used to illustrate the Poisson distribution.

The finding of the linearity of the relationship between the rank of an observation and the log of its frequency, did not go unnoticed. In 1949 George Kingsley Zipf described it as a widespread quantitative phenomenon that has come to be called Zipf's Law in his honor. Zipf's original version of the phenomena can be described formally as follows:
        Consider a set of ordered data values

$$x_{(1)} \geq x_{(2)} \geq \ldots \geq x_{(n)}$$

where r is the rank of the $x_{(r)}$ data value in the ordered set. Zipf noticed that the relation

$$r\,x_{(r)} = \text{constant} \tag{4}$$

seemed to hold reasonably well for many sorts of data including words in an essay by their frequency of occurrence, books by number of pages, and cities by their population. The graph of (4) is a rectangular hyperbola. Zipf's Law, as it was originally stated has been criticized for a number of reasons and alternative formulations have been proposed to describe the empirical relationship that appears remarkably often. One version that emerges directly from the often Poisson nature of frequency data[2] is

$$\log(x_{(r)}) = \beta_1 r + \beta_0 \tag{5}$$

Equation (5) states that the relationship between the log of the frequency of an event and its rank among other events is linear. Or, stated in another way, that increasing rank linearly means increasing the frequency of occurrence exponentially. This relationship holds so often that it is disquieting.

Example 2. Sunspots

Houghton, Munster, and Viola (1978) examined the relationship between malignant melanoma and peaks of sunspot activity in data from 1950 through 1972. If we plot the log of the number of sunspots as a function of the rank of the year we again see a strong linear component (see Figure 11.2).

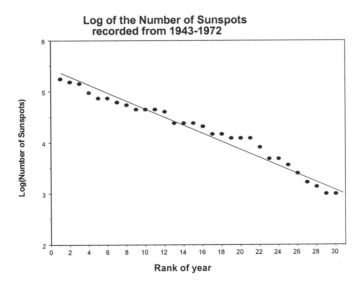

FIG. 11.2. Sunspot data from Houghton et al. (1978) also follow log-linear result.

---

[2]The Poisson distribution of the probability of a variable X taking the specific value x is $P(X = x) = e^{-\lambda}\lambda^x/x!$, where the parameter λ is the mean. Note that the function of interest, $\log(P)$ which equals $x\log(\lambda) - (\sum\log(x) + \lambda)$, is linear in x.

Example 3. Popularity of College Majors

In the 1990s college students were often majoring in health and allied fields as well as business and commerce. Mathematics and home economics were much less popular. If we rank order the 23 majors reported in the College Board's *1994 Profile of SAT and Achievement Test Takers* by their popularity and plot their rank against the log of their popularity we see equation (5) holds again (see Figure 11.3).

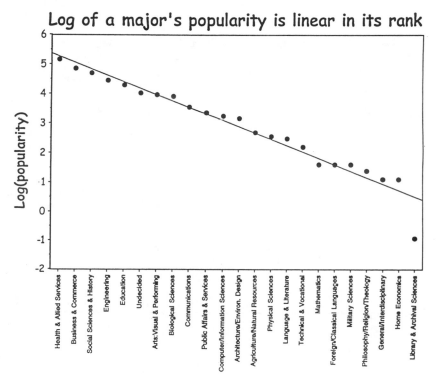

FIG. 11.3. Popularity of college majors follows Zipf's Law.

Zipf's Law holds in an enormously broad set of circumstances. Item usage data in an adaptive test is not immune. Figure 11.4 is a plot of the log of the frequency of usage of 150 of the most frequently used verbal items in the computerized adaptive Graduate Record Examination (GRE). This plot shows a substantial linear component. This linear structure also holds if we decompose the items in Figure 11.4 by item type. In Figures 11.5, 11.6, and 11.7 are the associated plots of the log of the frequency of usage of the 50 most frequently used analogy, antonym and sentence completion items that make up the 150 items in Figure 11.4.

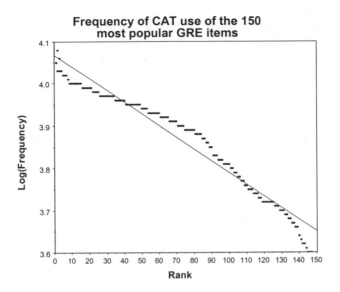

FIG. 11.4. The same general effect holds for the 150 most frequently used verbal items in the initial versions of the computerized adaptive version of the GRE (1996 data from ETS).

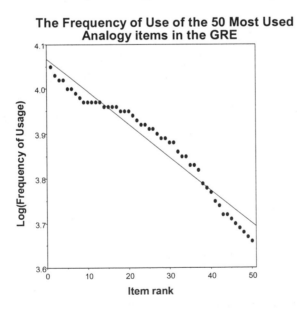

FIG. 11.5. Zipf's Law holds for the 50 most frequently used analogy items on the CAT GRE.

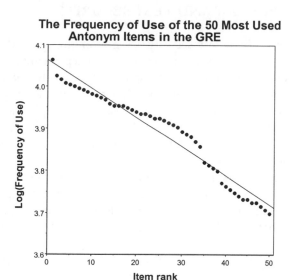

FIG. 11.6. Zipf's Law holds for the 50 most frequently used antonym items on the CAT GRE.

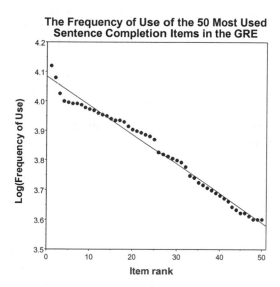

FIG. 11.7. Zipf's Law holds for the 50 most frequently used sentence completion items on the CAT GRE.

ZIPF'S LAW AND TEST SECURITY

What does this mean about test security? A notion that pervades all of testing is that the test items that are presented are a representative sample of the corpus of knowledge or abilities that are of interest. It is commonly assumed that a score of 50% on a test implies that the examinee knows about half of the material from which the test has been sampled; a score of 75% implies a knowledge of about three fourths, and so on. But if an examinee needs to know only, say 10%–20% of the material to get 50% correct this inference will be amiss.

To understand the consequences of this result more concretely let us consider the 4,937 analytic items that made up the GRE-Analytic CAT pool. After administering CATs to approximately 150 thousand examinees the usage of items matches what we would expect from Zipf's Law and is summarized in Table 11.3.

To build Table 11.3 we kept track of the number of times an item was presented to an examinee, what we might call an item-by-examinee interaction. *We found that most of these interactions are accounted for by a small minority of the items in the pool.* Note that 967 items (20% of the pool) accounts for 50% of all item–examinee interactions and that 2,028 items (41% of the pool) accounts for 80%. One way to think about this result that clarifies the intuition is to consider the situation of a fixed format test in which all examinees received the same 100 items. A cheater would have to steal 50 items to get 50% of the operational test. If the pool is expanded by a factor of five to 500 items but the test is made adaptive, the item burglar needs to steal a few less than twice as many to yield the same advantage.[3]

This is our principal result and implies that without profoundly changing the current item selection procedures *in order for an item pool's security to increase linearly the size of that pool must increase exponentially.*

"But," you might ask, "stealing and then learning 1,000 or 2,000 items is still a pretty big task. Once the item pool is this large isn't reasonable

---

[3] The item selection algorithm used that generated these data is described by Stocking and Swanson (1992) and uses the item exposure controls advocated by Hetter and Sympson (1997). Since this time, a new security algorithm has been implemented that focuses on conditional exposure control (conditional on the ability estimate). Although extensive GRE data are not yet available to examine the efficacy of this new approach, a preliminary analysis we ran on an experimental SAT CAT pool that uses this approach shows essentially the same effect we report here for the GRE under the Hetter and Sympson method.

security assured? Is the outlook for producing a secure test under the conditions of continuous testing really this bleak?" Actually, it is bleaker; much bleaker. Let us consider how a sensible item burglar would operate. It isn't sensible to steal easy items, since (by definition) most examinees would be able to get these right without preknowledge. The items that would be of greatest potential value are the hard items. But hard items are hard to write, because an item writer cannot write an item that is more difficult than the writer is able[4]. In columns 3, 4 and 5 of Table 11.3 are the frequencies of use for items of various difficulty levels; moderately difficult, difficult, and very difficult). Thus we see that only 35 very difficult items (out of a total of 4,937) need be stolen in order for the recipient to have seen half of the hardest ones he or she is likely to face. Moreover, these 35 are the easiest ones to steal, because they show up with the greatest frequency.

For all of the operational CAT item pools we have examined (three GRE pools and two experimental SAT pools) a typical result is that only 12% of the items account for 50% of the person–item interaction.

Thus if the use of these item selection algorithms continues, the strategy of trying to obtain a secure item pool by merely increasing the pool's size will not be practical. A fivefold increase in item pool size can be compromised with only a doubling of effort; instead of two weeks it might take three, instead of using 20 burglars they might need 30. In any case, it means that the increased cost of stealing is tiny compared to the increased cost of item pool development. It also means that to maintain the same level of security of a test over time there must be exponentially more items added to the pool. This implies an exponential increase in the cost of test development. It is startling and discouraging to compare the economics of CAT with those of traditional paper-and-pencil testing. In the latter linear increases in test volume yield *linear reductions* in the per examinee cost; in the former they yield *exponential increases*.

How much does it cost to write a usable test item? There is no simple answer to this. At ETS an estimate of the average cost of a new operational item (including writing, editing, pretesting and calibration) is upwards of $1,000. But all items are not of equal cost. In Figure 11.8 is a rough transcription of the relative cost of writing and reviewing several different kinds of items.

---

[4] If an algorithm can automatically generate difficult items, this may be one area of real contribution for AIG.

TABLE 11.3
A Summary of Item Usage for the GRE-Analytic CAT Item Pool

Item Usage on the GRE-A CAT				
Percent of Item-Examinee Interactions	All Items	Hard Items		
		$b{\geq}1$	$b{\geq}1.5$	$b{\geq}2$
10%	128	32	14	5
20%	294	72	33	10
30%	486	121	55	17
40%	710	176	81	26
50%	967	239	110	35
60%	1,259	313	144	47
70%	1,601	396	182	60
80%	2,028	498	230	77
90%	2,615	646	300	103
95%	3,046	758	352	120
99%	3,972	921	433	148
100%	4,455	1,134	544	182
TOTAL	4,937	1,296	645	229

Faced with these facts it is no wonder that anyone contemplating computerized (hence continuous) testing would be seriously examining various strategies for generating items faster and cheaper. Automatic item generation would obviously be an enormous help. But the help yielded is not uniform across item types. There would be 10 times more value for money if we could generate logical reasoning items automatically than if all we could do are verbal analogies.

There are other kinds of testing situations for which automated item generation would be helpful, but they all share one characteristic—they are situations in which many comparable test forms must be generated. With continuous testing one needs many forms to assure test security. But sometimes the same person is tested repeatedly over a short time period (i.e., an experiment on the effects of sleeplessness on cognitive ability might require four to six parallel forms of the same test each day) and being able to generate such test forms on the fly could surely ease at least one aspect of a complicated experiment (Kyllonen, chap. 9, this volume).

Unit Cost of Item Writing & Reviewing

$$$$
    GRE Logical Reasoning

    GMAT Critical Reasoning

$$$
    GRE Reading Comprehension

    TOEFL Reading Comp, GMAT Reading Comp

$$ **TOEFL Listening, GRE Quantitative**
GMAT Quantitative

    TOEFL WRITING, GMAT Writing

$ **GRE Verbal Discretes, GRE Analytical Reasoning**

FIG. 11.8. Unit cost of item writing and reviewing at ETS.

I hope that this adequately addresses at least some of the reasons why one would want to employ automatic item generation methods. Let us now move on to when.

WHEN DO WE NEED AUTOMATIC ITEM GENERATION?

Although the use of automatic item generation is not restricted to any particular medium for test administration, the hopes for its future have certainly focused principally on computer administered tests. This is primarily because that is where there is the most desperate need. Also, if the items are already being administered by computer it requires no great operational nor intuitive leap to imagine having the same computer generate them. Thus a major part of the question of when we need automatic item generation devolves to when do we need computerized test administration. Returning to the theme that began this chapter, this seems like a worthwhile question to explore.

Let us take a reverse attack and start with three situations in which continuous over the year test administrations (the *sine qua non* of computerized testing) are not sensible.

1. Large-Scale Achievement Tests of Coursework. Courses are usually begun at some fixed times during the year; traditionally fall, spring, and, to a lesser extent, summer. Students usually want to take the associated exam immediately after completing the course. If, because of limitations of access, some students cannot be accommodated at this time, the testing administration is putting those students at a disadvantage. Thus, achievement tests such as the college board's Advanced Placement or SAT II programs are unsuitable for continuous testing.

2. Tests Whose Scores Are Only Needed Once a Year. Typically, admissions to selective academic programs are only done once a year. If tests are given (and their scores reported) continuously it requires more careful record keeping and hence increases the possibility of error. If an institution must store a score for 6 months or longer, loss or confusion about exactly when the student is requesting admission, becomes a larger possibility. In addition, students usually prefer to take these exams at the last possible moment to assure that they have had the most opportunity to learn whatever will be on the test. College admissions officers typically advise that, "A traditional pattern would be for the student to take the SAT IIs in June of 11th grade and then take the SAT I in fall of 12th, but it is worth getting something closer to the actual application deadline—12th grade. This pattern usually will produce the most current results, which for most people means the highest scoring range." (Durso-Finley, personal communication, 1998). Thus tests such as the college Board's SAT, the GRE, TOEFL, ACT, GMAT, LSAT, or any other admissions test seem poorly suited for continuous testing.

3. Large-Scale Performance Assessments. Large test items (e.g. essay prompts) are expensive to pretest on a large scale; they take a long time to administer and are expensive to score. Hence they are rarely subjected to the same level of pretest scrutiny as multiple-choice items, which are so much cheaper to administer and score. In addition, because of the tremendous expenses involved, few large test items are subjected to even this very limited pretesting. Hence security of large items used continuously would be extremely problematic at best.

WHEN ARE COMPUTERIZED TESTS SENSIBLE?

1. **When it is in the best interests of all concerned to get the right answer.** No one would cheat on an eye test. Cheating on placement tests is also a low likelihood event. This being the case, item security is not an issue and hence having a small (i.e., economically feasible) item pool is perfectly acceptable. The

success of such computerized instruments as ETS's AccuPlacer attests to the truth of this.

2. **When the test results are needed year round,** (e.g., licensing tests) and delays in testing yield concomitant delays in the examinee being able to earn a living. Another example of when results are needed continuously are classroom diagnostic tests in which there are immediate instructional consequences. ETS's decade old Computerized Placement Test (CPT) is a wildly successful example of the use of this technology in the right situation.

3. **When the nature of the construct of interest is such that any test that measures it must be administered by computer.** At present, I don't know of any situations for which this is true. There are some tests (a licensing test for architects that uses a simulation task within a CAD–CAM environment is one that jumps immediately to mind) that use computer-based tasks effectively. Before the computerized test was available licenses were issued on the basis of a paper-and-pencil test. I don't know of any validity studies that have shown how much better the computer-based approach turned out to be. I believe that the results of the two tests are highly related.

HOW TO USE AUTOMATIC ITEM GENERATION (AIG): SOME HOPEFULLY HELPING HINTS

Obviously, if items were to be generated automatically and used within traditional printed test forms we could scrutinize the items in the traditional way. But subjecting them to content and sensitivity review as well as pretesting would mean that very little of the $1000+ cost per item would be saved. The savings would accrue only if all of those steps could be omitted without worrying about the quality of the item. Those steps would have to be omitted if AIG methods were used to generate items on-the-fly for computerized tests. So that clearly is the direction we must go in developing really worthwhile procedures. I don't know how automatic sensitivity review could take place, or, indeed how AIG methods could generate objectionable items, so I will omit further discussion of that issue. Instead, let us focus on the strictly psychometric issue of IRT parameter estimation.

To use items in a CAT efficiently we need reasonably accurate estimates of their parameters (at least their difficulty). How precisely can we now generate items to a particular set of psychometric criteria? Let us assume that the AIG algorithm has magically built into it something that allows it to produce items at a specified level of difficulty. How can we know that it is working?

There are at least three strategies:

1. Hope that the generated items are OK but never check.
    But remember Richard Feynman's (1986) warning that "for a successful technology, reality must take precedence over public relations, *for Nature cannot be fooled*" (p. F5).
2. Extend test length 50% so that errors in parameters do not matter so much (but then why are we bothering with CAT?).
3. a hybrid approach:
    a. generate items automatically but use the same ones for everybody; holding off on final scoring until enough people have taken them to calibrate the items online, or
    b. mix some newly generated items with some older (calibrated) items and equate.

AIG seems very well suited for diagnostic testing. What other method is practical for generating items that can probe deeply into a student's weaknesses? When one considers the range of areas where weaknesses can occur it is easy to see that developing an item bank sufficient for such a daunting task may be beyond the budget of even well-endowed programs. AIG seems just right. But even with AIG and CAT, zeroing in, by obtaining valid subscores, on specific areas of weakness still takes time. Any time we make a decision based on a subscore, that subscore must be reliable enough to justify that decision. Reliability is determined largely by test length. Hence making a sequence of consequential decisions about a student's weaknesses requires a long test. Can anything be done to help this?

Happily we can boost reliabilities of subscores with empirical Bayes techniques (Wainer, Sheehan, & Wang, 2000) that borrow stability for the subscore from other items on the test. In Table 11.4 we show the extent to which this sort of statistical magic can work. In the column labeled α are the values for the stand-alone reliability of the subtest. The column labeled "Empirical Bayes" are the estimates of the reliability of subscores that included the rest of the test items to the extent that the information they provide projects onto the dimension of interest. This test was very unidimensional and hence all subscores, regardless of how short, were almost as reliable as the entire test.

TABLE 11.4

The reliability of subscore measures of specific aspects of the test domain based on only those items of that domain (third column) and a weighted subscore of all items on the test, in which the weights were chosen as a function of the extent to which each item has information about that specific aspect.

	Number of items	a	Empirical Bayes
Overall	100	0.88	
APICS Subscores			
I. Concepts	12	0.39	0.87
II. Human Resources	12	0.44	0.88
III. Total QC	17	0.58	0.87
IV. Techniques	23	0.64	0.88
V. Integration	14	0.49	0.87
VI. Implementation	22	0.62	0.88
Average	17	0.55	0.87

Conclusions

1. Automatic item generation (AIG) procedures may provide some help for operational computer-based testing programs some time in the future. But not yet; probably not for a considerable time. Remember Mae West's advice.

2. The amount of financial help AIG will provide is likely to be modest—both because of the kinds of items they can produce (and the kind they can't), and because item production is not the principal expense in CBT (test administration is).

3. But AIG may provide help of a different sort—making possible certain kinds of highly interactive diagnostic testing that is just not practical without it. Thus I believe that the greatest contribution for AIG will lie in areas like diagnostic testing as part of the classroom experience; a testing circumstances where it is to everyone's benefit to get the right answer. Indeed, AIG and CAT go hand in hand. Each will be most valuable in the same areas. Neither is likely to be of much use in "once a year" testing (e.g., admissions) but rather as an integral part of an ongoing instructional program.

4. **A caveat!** We have seen that good progress has been made in automatically generating certain kinds of items (items tapping working memory–"g"), but considerably less progress on items that measure higher processes (that seem to be in vogue nowadays). The danger we must beware of is the overly narrow focusing of our tests on the things we can do cheaply rather than on the constructs we want to measure. Once again, we must always keep the purpose of the test front and center in our minds.

A Final Mystery: An Obiter Dictum

As I contemplate the potential of AIG a mystery emerges for which I have no resolution. Specifically, why is the Educational Testing Service committing resources toward the development of AIG? To understand the full extent of this mystery we need to first understand what it is that ETS can do that made it the preeminent testing organization in the world. The short answer is that ETS can administer and score millions of tests in a reasonably secure manner in a very short period of time, and promptly get the scores to those who need them for decision making. ETS also can make up high-quality tests, but that is a capacity of much smaller import. Truth be told, many of ETS's tests are far better than they need to be for the purposes they are put. It is easy to make up mediocre tests (Jim Ramsay's analyses of typical classroom tests showed that most ranged in quality from mediocre to poor) and, in many circumstance they work well enough.[5]

The fact that mediocre tests can work would suggest that ETS should have lots of competitors who can produce much cheaper tests. Indeed they would except that the capacity to deliver those tests in a timely and secure manner is a very big deal. Hence my point about what makes ETS unique and powerful. But now, with the press toward computerized tests, ETS has relinquished its control of the delivery system to Sylvan Learning Systems and has contracted with Sylvan to deliver ETS's computerized tests. The fundamental deal is that ETS makes up the tests and Sylvan delivers them.

Already this begins to suggest that ETS's dominance in testing is beginning to wane. But now we move on to AIG. The goal of AIG researchers is to develop algorithms that will generate items after the user specifies such details as the construct of interest and the difficulty level.

---

[5] Tests of lower than typical reliability and validity can still work when:

(i) the job is easy—if the test merely has to identify the very able or the very incompetent, almost anything will work (e.g., minimal competency tests, problems used in "mathlete" competitions)

(ii) the consequences are minor—obviously if the test doesn't count much it doesn't matter how well it works (e.g., classroom quizzes that are used by the teacher as a quick indicant of class comprehension or the results of a college admissions test when the college admits everyone who applies)

(iii) when the results are only used in the aggregate—a measure that is unreliable for a single examinee can still yield useful information when aggregated over many individuals (e.g., items in educational surveys (i.e., NAEP) that are used to make inferences only about large populations).

(iv) when the selection ratio is gigantic—if the test's job is to pick one "winner" from a million applicants any test with even just a little validity will work (e.g., the ancient Chinese civil service testing program described in Wainer (2000, chapter 1), or the Merit Scholarship exams that choose 1,500 winners from almost 2 million applicants).

Once such algorithms are perfected all a test giver would have to do is to lay out what kind of test was desired and they, the algorithms, would produce it. Once such a set of algorithms were completed why would Sylvan need ETS? This is the nub of the mystery. Why is ETS committing resources to the development of a technology that will, if successful, make ETS's expertise irrelevant? The only answer that makes any sense to me is that ETS views computerized testing as a passing fad, unrelated to its core competencies. Thus ETS believes its future remains in paper-and-pencil tests. Recent decisions to restore pencil-and-paper administrations for TOEFL and GRE reinforce this interpretation.

This brings me back to the Talmudic *midrash* that inspired this chapter. Perhaps CAT and AIG will indeed eventually become our salvation, but so far, it seems to me, we should continue planting our plants.

REFERENCES

1994 Profile of SAT and Achievement Test Takers (1994). New York: The College Board.

Bortkewitsch, L. von (1898). *Das Gesetz der kleinen Zahlen*. Leipzig: Teubner.

Feynman, R. P. (1986). Appendix F: Personal Observations on the Reliability of the Shuttle, in Vol. II, p. F5 of the *Report of the Presidential Commission on the Space Shuttle Challenger Accident*. Washington, DC: US Government Printing Office.

Hetter, R. D., & Sympson, J. B. (1997). Item exposure controls. In W. A. Sands, B. K. Waters, & J. R. McBride (Eds.), *Computerized adaptive testing: From inquiry to operation* (pp. 141–144). Washington, DC: American Psychological Association.

Houghton, A., Munster, E. W., & Viola, M. V. (1978). Increased incidence of malignant melanoma after peaks of sunspot activity. *The Lancet,* April 8, 759–760.

Jacobson, R. L. (January 6, 1995). "Shortfall of questions curbs use of computerized graduate exam." *The Chronicle of Higher Education,* January 6, p. A23.

Stocking, M., & Swanson, L. (1992). *A method for severely constrained item selection in adaptive testing*. (Research Report 92-37): Princeton, NJ: Educational Testing Service.

Thorndike, R. L. (1983). How can we practice what we preach? In H. Wainer & S. Messick (Eds.), *Principals of modern psychological measurement* (pp. 357–364). Hillsdale, NJ: Lawrence Erlbaum Associates.

Wainer, H. (2000). Introduction and history. In H. Wainer et al., *Computerized adaptive testing: A primer* (2nd ed.). Hillsdale, NJ: Lawrence Erlbaum Associates.

Wainer, H., Sheehan, K., & Wang, X. (2000). Some paths toward making PRAXIS scores more useful. *Journal of Educational Measurement, 37,* 113-141.

Zipf, G. K. (1949). *Human behavior and the principle of least effort*. Cambridge, MA: Addison-Wesley.

DISCUSSION

WAINER:

My comments should be interpreted with the understanding that they were prepared on the basis of the papers' titles (very much akin to judging a book by its cover) with modifications after my having heard them at the same time as everyone else in the room. I am delighted to have had the opportunity to finally hear all of these papers, and now I'm truly looking forward to being able to read them slowly and carefully. This backward approach—discuss first, read later—was necessary because of the complex and busy lives that are led by the conference participants.

Now it's time for audience commentary; both from the speakers as well as from anyone else.

Weeding out poor items in item generation

EMBRETSON:

This is the first tryout of my generative system. A person learns from the tryout what further constraints are needed for a workable system. The fact that there were a few items with poor psychometric properties, I think I can trace that back to some problems in the perceptual displays. So what can be done subsequently is to put some constraints on the system, and not allow those specific combinations, and then you get a system that's more effective. Now, it has to be self-correcting; this is the first attempt, and I think the next attempt will be better. But I think any system of generation is probably going to have to have a self-correcting feature built in it. And I think your (Howard Wainer's) idea of a mixture of online and fixed items, might be a good one to get those estimates on a regular basis of the new items, and to start correcting the system for that.

ALMOND:

There was a kind of a practical comment that I didn't get to make yesterday, in response to one of Lutz's (Hornke) papers, but it also came up today, with your (Howard Wainer's) paper. I'm looking at these graphs of the predicted vs. actual item difficulties. Now, Lutz's problem, if you remember, was that there were a couple of rotations that turned out to have some odd properties, where things were hidden. And when he included the full model in there, he said the correlation dropped way down, but he didn't show that graph. I was wondering if there are any outliers in that graph. I was also looking at one of Susan's (Embretson) graphs, and I think this was the one for the 2PL (two-parameter logistic) model. Now there was a fair amount of heteroscedasticity, which I think some of David's techniques might have addressed. But there also were maybe 8 points that had higher difficulties than were predicted by the regression line. I'm wondering if some sort of predictive methodology like this, where we're using our models to predict what's going on, doing a relatively limited amount of pretesting, we can pretty quickly screen out the ones that have the problem. Because while I agree that we can go back and find the specific problems that were in these cases, I think any time we get this automatic item-generation schema, any time we start introducing new, supposedly incidental variability in the problem, we're going to discover that some of that is radical. And we're going to need some sort of screening procedures to figure that out very rapidly.

The relationship between item generation and adaptive testing

MORLEY:

There are many different ways people can actually do an item. I'm worried about millions and millions of people madly writing items as quick as possible with less and less training. I don't see that that's better for ETS than to sit down with me. I discuss things with Jeff Watkins, and I discuss things with Jackie Chorney, and I find out what they check for in an item of this type and I encode that in the computer. That's quicker than trying to do lots and lots of weekend workshops trying to tell people by the time you get trained, you're going to put us out as item writers. You're (Howard Wainer) blaming generating items for computerized testing. It goes the other way around. You can improve things, but it involves programing, it involves mathematics, it involves psychology. And when I do something like that, I use all of those things very heavily. The alternative unfortunately is not going back to spending an hour thinking about a problem, which would be nice if it worked.

WAINER:

Well, don't misunderstand me, I'm not quite the Luddite I appear to be. I think what happened was a number of years ago, when we did the CAT book, we were too subtle. Now, I've never been accused of being subtle before, but in fact, we were too subtle about the probable kinds of difficulties that operationalizing these kinds of procedures were going to run into. And so I thought I'm not going to make that mistake again, and so I chose not to be particularly subtle today. Did anybody miss my point?

Testing and the march of progress

MORLEY:

Also, there's the problem that if you look at software for math, and you look at math textbooks, which often come with tests, if you read the small print carefully, these are all computer generated. I mean, that's standard. So part of the problem is that around 1600 Japan decided not to use the gun, and that was probably a really good decision within Japan, but unfortunately, the rest of the world existed, so you can't count on everybody else making the same mistakes ETS does.

LUEBKE:

I like your last comment there about the airplanes, Howard (Wainer). There were a lot of people that died, and a lot of people that failed trying to make flight a reality for human beings, in heavier-than-air-ships. And we haven't gotten there yet, to the point where I think we will be in the future. But I think our ability to develop the technologies and the infrastructure necessary, and the benefits that come from heavier-than-air-flight, far outweigh the efforts that humans put into it in trying to develop that. And I think that testing, and its ability to change the educational trajectory of society, and get people into the right track where they can maximize their education so that they can make positive contributions back to society is far more valuable than air transport. And so far, as far as I know, nobody's been killed by CAT. There are some people that aren't happy with it, and there are probably going to be a lot of people at ETS that may not be here in the future because of it. But it is still a valuable investment.

The history of item generation — & difficulty modeling

SIDNEY IRVINE

I wonder if I could change the tack a little bit. Because the criteria for successful testing as we all know, is that first it should be technically sound, second, it should be administratively convenient, and third, it should be politically defensible. But if you try to sell the test to an outsider, the criteria suddenly flip right out the door. First of all, they want to know if they can defend it in terms of policy. Second, they want to know how cheap it is, and whether it's going to prove anything, and last of all, they're concerned with whether it's reliable and valid, so they cannot be sued. A factor score, got x standard deviations, and whatever—That they just do not want to know.

So, what I'm interested in, is moving back to technical soundness so that one may become that more politically defensible with a story. About Raven's matrices. You see, Raven's Matrices was produced by John Raven in his masters thesis in 1936, under the supervision of Cyril Burt, and a mathematician called Penrose. And Penrose believed in matrices. And when they sat down to construct the item, they thought that the simplest form of item (this, Susan [Embretson] and Lutz [Hornke] and others would know), would be pattern matching type with a matrix of rank 1. Where the item with rank 1 was so obvious that everybody knew what the answer was. By adding a second layer, say an isoclynal latin square to change the pattern on the problem, you had a matrix of rank 2, and so on and so forth.

In other words, in 1936, they were trying to predict the difficulty of the item from the characteristics of the item. And to that extent, they were technically sound, if not avante garde. But of course the political problem is that Raven's Matrices has a large specificity. It is not a pure measure of g or anything close to it. It has an inordinately large specificity. And for one, I don't think we're ever going to make the mistake through item generation, and the way we're going about with Raven's matrices, of claiming as others have done before us it's as pure a measure of g as you're likely to get. And make inferences about populations based on that one test score, do you see my point?

So coming back to the story, what I'm really saying is, that we're coming at the same problem again, 50 years later, but we're never going to make those kinds of errors, because we have a far better cognitive theory for the way in which we characterize human experience. Raven and Penrose did not have this. What I find interesting about ETS math items in SAT and GRE is that they're not cognitive enough. You see, there are perfectly good models for the GRE math items, and the literature is there. But two or three papers by such people as Meyers, Groen, and Parkman throw an enormous light on the kind of mathematical problems people have been illustrating in their presentations. Frankly, they're essentially working memory tasks, given that people can fluently perform the operations, because you're saying do this sum, do that sum, compare them, and tell them whether the product is larger, smaller, or the same. And that's exactly the type of item that I have on my own forms of test, involving very small, very simple arithmetic calculations.

I'm not asking ETS personnel to defend what they're doing. I'm simply saying the basis upon which we constructed the items is a firm cognitive model of how these could be constructed. We knew what the performance was, and we knew from the outset what the probable classes of difficulty were, but we didn't have to use, as John Raven did, pieces of paper, and, as legend would have it, with snowflakes in windows. We had a big jumpstart from the main effects in the cognitive literature on how we would reconstruct the problem. And that, I think, is what we're talking about. I want tests to be more politically defensible just because the items produced have ironcast performance models that ensures their technical qualities. I'm not the H. L. Mencken of the ETS system, as Howard (Wainer) is, but he's valuable, for the iconoclastic sort of statement that brings out a story and a statement of where I think we're going. So thank you Howard, thank you very much.

WAINER:

No need to thank me. I'm always grateful for an appreciative audience.

MORLEY:

There's a little bit of difference, and I think you're right in that we should look more in the literature. In these kinds of questions, you have 45 minutes to do 28 questions, and you're given scrap paper, which makes a big difference in how people can do it. Also, something that I think a lot of people don't realize, that has been put in the background, that I think is hurting the ability of the current classification to predict difficulty. And that's because in the background, test developers are working extremely hard to make sure they don't. And that's because that's what they're told to. So when you have a CAT test, you have specifications, and specifications as written currently do not take the person's ability into account. So the specifications say that people get one computation-with-a-radical question. That means you must write extremely easy computation-with-radical questions, and it also means that you must write extremely hard computation-with-integer questions. And as long as you have the specifications that were written irrespective of the ability level, you're going to have people in the background that are working very hard to make sure what you think should predict, and should predict, computation-with-integers should be easier than computation-with-a-radical. But as long as we have that kind of thing, no matter how good the research is, if you don't change that, you're going to be shooting yourself in the foot in the background. And that was just a technical point I wanted to point out that most people don't realize.

New directions in testing

MISLEVY:

Much of the conversation has focused on how we can use item-generation modeling difficulty, and all of that, with the target being the existing large-scale, high-stakes test that ETS does now. And I guess as an ETS employee, I think that's important to look at. As the researcher in the field, though, I really don't think that's the place that I'm most excited about. I don't think that doing 10%–15% better using technology that didn't exist 50 years ago, at targets, purposes, under constraints that the GRE was created for 50 years ago. That's not where the big payoff is. The big payoff is doing things that aren't done at all now, because they weren't possible to do until now. (The) NCARB (exam, an architectural licensing exam that includes innovative item types) might be a better example of what I think is a lot more interesting. Now, it would be nice to have ETS remain solvent, and probably using ideas such as these to reduce costs, and make more efficient the things that have traditionally made it possible to work on (the) NCARB (exam), is worth thinking about. But, surviving is one thing, and having fun is another. I'd like to do both!

BENNETT:

Well, I think there may be a way. I think that in part because I don't think ETS's future is in admissions testing. I think the big part of the future is going to be in the kinds of things that are going to be fun—in developing measures that are more relevant and more helpful to what people have to do in educational environments and educational settings. I think the future is in developing measures that are more helpful to institutions in certifying that people have the kinds of knowledge they need to have, or are supposed to have after taking courses of various types. I think that individuals will generate their own program of courses, to take from the variety of institutions, and that they will be able to take courses by electronic means. So maybe all will work out for the best.

Cost savings for item generation

ALMOND:

I wanted to comment on one of the numbers in Howard's (Wainer) talk, especially as I am partially to blame for him having them. He was talking about item writing being 10%–15% of the cost. But also, when he was looking at those numbers, he was one of the first to point out that one of the costs that wasn't in there was the seed time for pretesting, that those numbers didn't include any of the pretesting costs.

WAINER:

No actually, Linda Cook (an ETS officer in charge of the test creation process) gave me those numbers yesterday. I'm appealing to a higher authority at this point.

ALMOND:

So anyway, what I wanted to say was that I was actually very encouraged that along with this emphasis on item generation there is also an emphasis on using the same models to generate the items and predict their difficulty. Because I think that's going to be an important part, and I think that might make Howard's figures a little bit pessimistic about how much we can save. It's still a big percentage of the cost of administration.

Templates & random effects

ALMOND:

The other question I had for the speakers concerns Isaac's notions of template, items that are very close together. And David's notion of random effects. It occurs to me that there's a very natural system of random effects, a hierarchical modeling of random effects, that might fit very well with the template model. I was wondering if any of the speakers had thought at all about those particular ideas.

BEJAR:

I've realized that, and that's one reason why we are using the *expected response function* technology from Charlie (Lewis) and Bob (Mislevy). So, yes, I think that in the future, as we learn to construct these item pools with richer hierarchies, we'll model that. For example, right now, the templates we have generate items that are very similar. So we are fairly confident that the bounds, the standard deviations on those difficulties, will be small. But for practical purposes, they may be so similar, that it may defeat the purpose that we're also trying to achieve in terms of dissipating security concerns. So we need to study this in terms of "compound templates" as we do in the NCARB (an architecture licensing) exam where we go into one of several buildings, and then even within the building, we have different rotations. So that we disguise, as much as possible, the underlying item. But I agree there is much work that remains to be done psychometrically to do this, as well as it can be done.

IV
APPLICATIONS OF ITEM-GENERATIVE PRINCIPLES

12

The MICROPAT Pilot Selection Battery: Applications of Generative Techniques for Item-Based and Task-Based Tests

Dave Bartram
SHL Group

Work on the development of the MICROPAT test battery began in the late 1970s. The tests were designed to improve prediction of training outcome for those entering military pilot training with no previous flying experience (*ab initio* trainees). The battery was one of the earliest sets of tests for occupational assessment designed specifically to make use of computer technology (Burke et al., 1995). Its focus on the prediction of very complex criteria (i.e., the later stages of operational flying training) led to a test design approach that had more in common with work/job sample approaches than those focusing on the assessment of assumed underlying abilities.

This chapter describes the development and design principles of the Micropat tests. Further details regarding the validation of the tests are presented in Bartram (1987, 1995a).

THE DEVELOPMENT OF THE MICROPAT BATTERY

The Micropat project was initially funded by the UK Army Personnel Research Establishment (APRE) with the objective of developing a battery of pilot selection tests for use by the UK Army Air Corps. In 1980, H. C. A. Dale and the present author were asked to examine the validity of the RAF Officer and Aircrew Selection Centre (OASC) tests for the prediction of success in Army Air Corps training. The Army Air Corps train army personnel to fly helicopters in a number of operational (e.g., antitank) and support (e.g, air taxi and med-evac) roles. Prior to our work, a battery of three tests were used to construct a P-score,[1] which was then used as the basis for initial selection. An Army Air Corps Selection Board then assessed those "passing" the aptitude tests. The three tests, which date from the 1940s, included two electromechanical psychomotor tests, known as the Sensori-Motor Apparatus (SMA) and Control of Velocity Test (CVT), and an *instrument comprehension test* (INS-B) based on a USAF spatial orientation test. Analyses of the available data showed that these tests were moderately predictive of outcome for the initial stage of Army Air Corps flying training (Basic Fixed Wing) but not for later stages (Basic and Advanced Rotary Wing).

In addition to analyzing the available selection data and assessing validity against training outcome criteria, a proposal was put forward to develop a new battery of tests aimed at improving the prediction of late failures in training. To this end, the Army Air Corps flying training syllabus was examined and flight instructors interviewed to identify critical facets of aptitude. From this training analysis and an analysis of the relevant literature on pilot selection, a number of new tests were proposed. There was no initial intention to develop computer-based as opposed to paper-and-pencil tests. Indeed, in 1980 the use of computer-based testing was not a "soft-option." It posed considerable technical problems in relation to the limitations then obtaining in relation to machine capacity, processor speeds, and display technology. The lack of standardization of software and hardware interfaces, and the need to program in machine code to achieve the speeds needed for dynamic tasks all added to the difficulties faced by taking a computer-based testing approach.

However, the nature of the tasks that we defined as being appropriate for the new tests necessitated the use of computer-based techniques for their delivery. Most important were the need for online real-time scoring and the potential for tasks to be dynamic and adaptive to the test taker's performance.

In 1985, the Royal Navy took over the funding to extend the development and validation work to pilot and observer selection into the Fleet Air Arm. During this period two new tests were developed: NAVOR—Test of Navigational Orientation and NAVCALC—Test of Navigational Calculations. However, apart from changes associated with changing computer hardware and software, the test design and development process had been completed by the mid-1980s. The main changes since then have involved adaptation work to check the equivalence of new software versions of the original tests. As originally designed, Micropat used a two-screen interface. One screen was used to present

---

[1] For the RAF, the composite test-battery score is referred to as the pilot index. Unlike the Royal Navy and Army Air Corps P-scores, the RAF P-score includes both test battery and biodata variables.

graphical information (a 2-plane 256 x 256 monochrome Matrox graphics card) and the other for text (a standard 80 column by 25 line text display). This arrangement was dictated by limitations in computer technology (because the early systems could not display animated graphics and standard text on the same VDU). The current version of Micropat operates in Windows, using a single screen display and much higher resolution graphics than were possible in 1980. Such changes create major problems for dynamic tests (such as tracking tasks) as one has to ensure that the critical features of the test are not lost when it is moved from one platform to another.

In 1987 work began with one of the major international airlines to incorporate Micropat tests into their cadet pilot selection process. Subsequently, the battery has been adopted by a number of commercial airlines and military organizations, and a range of validation studies have been undertaken (e.g., Bartram & Baxter, 1995, 1996). Extensive technical documentation on the Micropat tests and the various research studies carried out for the UK Ministry of Defence are presented in a series of Technical Reports and other publications (reviewed in Bartram, 1991).

THE TEST DESIGN PHILOSOPHY

The rationale behind the development of the Micropat tests was that the best chance of obtaining some substantive increment in validity, without incurring the costs associated with flight simulator or grading tests, was to develop new forms of task-based test rather than look for other conventional unidimensional tests. As flying training progresses, so there is an increasing emphasis on the management of flight systems and operational use of the aircraft. By developing tasks that assessed both the fundamental aptitudes required for early training (psychomotor co-ordination, spatial ability, and so on) and more complex task-management and information-management skills, it was hoped to improve prediction of late failures in training while also maintaining a good level of prediction for early failures.

The development of these new types of test grew out of an approach that was more eclectic than that underlying work in the United States (e.g., Carretta, 1991) and the subsequent development in the UK of the RAF Navigator and Air Traffic and Fighter Controller Batteries (Burke, 1991). Both of these adopted what may be characterized as the "discrete cognitive components" approach. Micropat, on the other hand, focused on the measurement of task-based aspects of criterion performance. Although some of these tasks can be characterized as tests of discrete components, others are more complex and multidimensional.

The *discrete cognitive components approach* assumes that criterion performance is a function of a number of discrete cognitive components each of which can be measured in terms of conventional "abilities" (e.g., spatial orientation, numerical reasoning, verbal fluency, etc.). If these abilities underlie successful criterion performance, then scores from a series of discrete tests, when combined appropriately, should provide a good prediction of such performance.

The discrete approach focuses on unidimensionality within tests, with each test being designed to provide as pure a measure of a single latent trait as possible. Although psychometrically elegant, this may have a practical weakness. It entails an assumption that optimal predictions of performance in complex tasks can be obtained through the addition of measures of component abilities. To the extent that meta-componential factors (task strategy, opportunities to trade-off weakness in certain areas for strengths in others, etc.) are important, a simple additive componential approach may tend to underpredict.

Furthermore, the link between criterion performance and underlying cognitive components is not always self-evident. As a consequence, one either has to trial a very large number of potential instruments in order to identify those with the highest predictive validities or one needs a very good model of the relationships between abilities and performance. The former is very costly in terms of numbers of people required, and was not an option for the Army Air Corps, where intake numbers were low. The latter was also not possible, because the well-articulated model did not exist. Indeed, the problem we were being asked to solve arose because the long-standing view, that prediction should be based on psychomotor co-ordination, spatial ability, and a higher level of general ability, did not seem to be sustained for the later stages of training. Apart from that, there was no well-articulated model available to us.

Hence the decision to produce a battery that contained both some conventional measures and some that appeared more like job sample measures was taken to optimize the chances of producing a successful outcome in conditions where development time and resources were severely limited. The more traditional tracking tasks were there to ensure we picked up on the same variance as the existing batteries, whereas the newer design of test was introduced in an endeavor to find measures that would predict further on down the training pipeline. For those who are not familiar with military pilot training programes, the UK Royal Navy training pipeline, for example, spans a period of about 2 ½ years from grading trials through to the completion of operational training. Some of the difficulties associated with the validating tests in situations where the training pipelines are very long, attrition rates are high and initial input samples are small, are discussed in Bartram (1995a).

A secondary consequence of the "loose-coupling" between unidimensional measures of ability and criterion performance is that the test content of such tests tends to have low face validity. The importance of face validity for ensuring good rapport and sustained motivation on the part of the test taker is often underestimated. Good face validity is also an important factor in determining whether or not those who make the decisions will select such tests for executive use (as such people are rarely sophisticated test users).

The Micropat *task-based test approach* attempted to retain certain aspects of the complexity of criterion performance within at least some of the tests. Rather than breaking criterion performance down into constituent component abilities, it is broken down into constituent tasks (each of which may involve a number of abilities and hence be multi-dimensional). Tests are devised which can be carried out *ab initio* yet which simulate essential properties of these criterion tasks. Because of their close-coupling with criterion performance, such tests tend to have good face validity. Feedback from candidates taking the Micropat tests was generally very positive: they enjoyed taking the tests and regarded them as "very appropriate" for pilot selection.

An example of this approach is the attempt to provide a measure that taps into "situational awareness." This is a complex construct used by pilots to describe the maintenance of an up-to-date knowledge of what is happening inside and outside the cockpit. It relies on both the need to monitor information systematically and regularly and an understanding of what the critical parameters are. LANDING—Landing Approach Test was designed specifically to assess this process.

However, although the relationship between test content and criterion performance may be relatively direct for such tests, their construct validity is less clear. Given the nature of the construction of many of the Micropat tests, it is as difficult to analyze the component abilities underlying them, as it is to analyze the component abilities underlying good criterion performance. On the other hand, it is far easier to set up construct validation studies relating the Micropat tests to unidimensional marker tests, than it is to investigate the constructs underlying the criterion measures.

In practice, there is considerable overlap between the tests produced by these approaches. The Micropat battery in fact is an eclectic one, containing tests that fall into both camps. For example, Micropat tests such as COMP2D—Compensatory Two-dimensional Tracking Test, ADTRACK—One-dimensional Adaptive Pursuit Tracking Test, SUBTRACT—Test of Speeded Mental Arithmetic and MANIKIN—Test of Spatial Orientation are all relatively simple single-ability measures. However, tests like the Landing Approach Test, SCHEDULE—Test of Scheduling Ability, and the

Test Of Navigational Calculations represent an approach to test development that is not within the conventional tradition of uni-dimensional measures. It falls somewhere along a dimension that has "pure" unidimensional ability tests at one end and multidimensional work samples (e.g., flight simulation or grading trials) at the other.

Apart from the general difference in approach to test design, the Micropat tests differed from conventional paper-and-pencil and from electromechanical tests in three main respects:

1. Some of them were adaptive to the performance of test taker (One-dimensional Adaptive Pursuit Tracking, Test of Scheduling Ability, Adaptive Digit-span Test).
2. Some of them were dynamic, continuous tasks rather than discrete item-based tests (One-dimensional Adaptive Pursuit Tracking, Compensatory Two- and Four-dimensional Tracking Tests, Landing Approach Test, Test of Scheduling Ability).
3. For all of them, the test content was generated from rules rather than being predefined.

For the adaptive tests, a range of different adaptation mechanisms were developed. For example, in the one-dimensional tracking tests, a series of difficulty levels were defined in terms of forcing function frequency (i.e., track speed) and input control law complexity. Each difficulty level was then tested as a fixed-difficulty task to provide empirical support for the predicted sequential ordering of conditions. In the adaptive version, conditions were then changed in response to the test taker's performance, becoming more difficult if tracking error was small and easier if tracking error was large. The adaptation criteria (the error criterion for increasing difficulty level and the error criterion for decreasing difficulty level) were identified through empirical study and set to ensure that difficulty levels changed in a smooth and progressive fashion. It was found that if these criteria were set incorrectly, the task would either become unstable or adaptation would not occur quickly enough to enable reliable estimates of ability to be obtained with short test durations.

In all cases, the use of computer technology was essential for implementing adaptive tests. The key characteristic of all these tests was that the computer program was constructed in the form of two components. One was concerned with running the test, whereas the second assessed the candidate's performance. These components ran in parallel with the latter continually adjusting the values of key parameters being used by the test administration program component.

A modification of this two-component design concept was used in tests like the Test of Scheduling Ability. Here the second component, running in parallel with the administration component, was an optimal performer model against which the actual performance of the candidate could be compared.

ITEM AND TASK GENERATION

Conventional test administration involves the presentation to candidates of items that were written prior to the assessment procedure. Computer-based assessment makes it possible not only to decide which item to present as the test proceeds but also to write the items as well. This same notion can also be applied to more complex tasks, where the dynamics of the task, the content of the task scenario, and so on can all be determined at the time of administration using rules.

The traditional method of producing test items is to rely on people who are able to interpret what is required for a test and generate items to meet this need. This can lead to bias and idiosyncrasies in the item pool and the utility of the test becomes highly dependent on the quality of the person who writes the items (Bormuth, 1970). Generative techniques are based on the notion that each test item represents a sample from a universe of potential items (cf. Tryon, 1957). The rules that are used to generate the items explicitly define the universe by setting constraints on the type and difficulty of the items that may be generated. The rules may be such as to define a very large universe or a very restricted one.

Objections to Tryon's item sampling model were based on the difficulty of specifying the nature of the universe in operational terms (Loevinger, 1965; Osburn, 1968). The development of computer-based item-generation techniques, however, has enabled us to provide very precise operational specifications of item universes. It is only by making the definitions sufficiently precise, that the computer is able to generate items. The algorithms contained within the program *are* the universe specifications. A key psychometric issue is that of the degree to which the sets of items generated using a particular rule set are internally consistent and uniform in terms of difficulty. The more tightly the rules define the universe of items, the more consistent the generated items will be and the narrower the construct being measured. Item variety may be determined by factors other than those determining difficulty or dimensionality. For example, in the Test of Navigational Calculations, scenarios are generated that are constrained in terms of both the complexity and type of content (factors affecting difficulty) but free to vary in content (i.e., the selection of actual text samples included in each scenario is random).

Algorithms may define small or large universes of items. Large universes may be finite or infinite. The size will depend on the constraints imposed on the range of item content and the spread of item difficulties and the degree of variety that can be introduced by parameters that produce incidental variation.

Irvine, Dann, and Anderson (1990) described an item-generation procedure that builds on Carroll's (1987) work on predictors of item difficulty. They developed four parallel versions of five tests using an item-generation technique whereby those aspects of the task that contribute to item difficulty are varied systemically within tightly defined parameters, whereas other components of the task are allowed to vary randomly. They refer to the former as item radicals and the latter as item incidentals. Their results showed that this approach does produce parallel tests with statistically invariant properties.

USES OF ITEM GENERATION IN MICROPAT

For all the item-based tests developed for Micropat, there are no prewritten sets of items. Each test contains a set of rules and constraints from which items are generated. These rules can either specify that the same set of items be generated every time, or that different (but equivalent) sets be generated for each candidate. The following section provides an outline description of each of the tests and illustrates how generative techniques were applied.

ITEM-BASED TESTS

Dualtask Test (duration 20 min.). The candidate is first presented with 30 arithmetic (subtraction) problems to check as either correct or incorrect. This component of the Dualtask Test is also used as a stand-alone test (Test of Speeded Mental Arithmetic, duration 5 minutes). This is followed by a two-dimensional step-tracking task with laterally inverted position control. Finally the two tasks are linked and the candidate has to complete pairs of track jumps and arithmetic problems in parallel. Performance on the arithmetic problems is assessed by two measures: percentage of accuracy and a latency measure that is adjusted for accuracy. For the step-tracking, the average time per step is assessed. The dualtask measures compare the speed and accuracy on performance in the combined task with that demonstrated during each task on its own.

For the Test of Speeded Mental Arithmetic component, all the problems have the same format: $A - B = C$. The values A and B can take are constrained by rules, as is the difference between the correct answer and the value of C for "wrong" items. Within these constraints, values are generated at random.

For the step-tracking task, the size of the target and the time for which the cursor has to be held on target are fixed (as these determine task difficulty), and the minimum and maximum extents of target movement from one position to the next are constrained.

In the Spatial Orientation Test (5 min.), the computer displays a manikin figure holding an object in one hand: The figure may be upright, inverted, or lying on its side; it may have either its face or back toward the candidate. The candidate has to decide whether the object is in the manikin's right or left hand. The primary measure is the overall time taken divided by the number of correct responses. The universe of items is here limited to 16 (2 hands, by 8 orientations of the figure). However the same generative principle applies whether the set is limited or infinite. The items are constructed from rules, with constraints placed on number of items and numbers of each condition. For the *Spatial Orientation Test*, difficulty is affected by figure orientation, and so three measures are taken (upright, inverted and lateral). For practical purposes these are combined into a single overall score, since the three are highly correlated.

Speeded Decision-making Test (10 min.). The test is an application of signal detection theory. On each trial, one of two possible aircraft silhouettes is displayed (the two differ slightly in wingspan). Candidates have to decide which of the two is being displayed (long or short wingspan) within a time limit of 1.5 seconds. Difficulty of discrimination is varied across three sets each of 50 trials. Measures obtained include mean decision latency, hit rate, and false alarm rate. From the latter two measures, d prime (a measure of discriminative sensitivity) and log likelihood ratio (a measure of response bias) are also derived.

For this test, difficulty is manipulated by the difference in wingspan between the two silhouettes. Incidentals are the interstimulus interval and the location at which the stimulus appears on screen. These are randomly selected from within predetermined limits.

The Attitude to Risk Test (15 min.) is a "gambling" task in which the candidate can, on each trial, select between 0 and 8 items. Items are selected by pressing a key on the Micropat keyboard. Each of the eight keys represents a location at which information is held. However, one key (selected at random on each trial) is a penalty key. If selected, this results in the loss of all points for that trial. Blocks of trials vary in terms of whether there is a penalty key present on all trials or on just half the trials. The test was designed to provide an objective measure of risk-seeking/caution.

Various scenarios have been used to present the test:

1. as a simple gambling task;
2. as a task involving sending a team out to gather information from 8 locations one of which may have an ambush set at it;
3. as a set of eight computer tapes, one of which may contain a virus.

The primary measures are the average number of key pressed under two different conditions: penalty present on every trial, and penalty present on 50% of the trials. These two conditions are presented in an ABBA design of four blocks each of 20 trials.

Test of Navigational Orientation (25 min.) involves dead-reckoning: Candidates have to mentally fly a journey and then indicate the heading and distance of their home base. The journeys are flown as a sequence of legs, each leg being given as a distance and heading. In addition to latency measures, the main measures are the final distance and heading errors. Examples of the sort of instructions generated are: "Fly 25 miles North," "Fly 30 miles NNW." Difficulty is affected by the number of compass directions and the number of legs in each flight. Initial studies explored using 4, 8, and 16 compass directions, but found that 16 made the task too difficult to use even with only two legs to a flight. Current versions of the test are restricted to generating flights of 4 legs using either 4 or 8 compass directions (10 test trials of each condition).

Test of Navigational Calculations (25 min.) is a work-sample test that involves producing and updating a flight log. The initial log is computer generated and contains a number of locations on a flight plan, their radio frequency, departure times, turnaround times, and flight times between locations. As the test progresses, the computer asks the candidate questions about the flight plan and presents information updates, which the candidate has to incorporate into it. The two primary measures of performance are the accuracy of the answers and the time taken to perform the task (adjusted for accuracy).

Adaptive Digit-span Test (5 min.) is a simple forward digit span test using item-generation and a stopping rule rather than a conventional fixed set of items of increasing difficulty. Digit sequences are displayed one digit at a time. After a fixed delay, the candidate then has to key in the sequence. The length of the sequence is increased progressively until performance drops below a preset accuracy criterion.

TASK GENERATION

Generation techniques are not confined to item-based tests. Micropat uses generation algorithms for performance tasks as well as for tests containing discrete sets of items. The tasks range from relatively simple ones (Two-dimensional compensatory tracking test, One-dimensional Adaptive Pursuit Tracking) to more complex ones (Landing Approach Test, Test of Scheduling Ability).

There is a set of two- and four-dimensional compensatory tracking tasks using position control laws. The former each last 10 minutes, while the latter lasts for 20 minutes. Control is exercised either by hand (Y axis) and feet (X axis) or by one hand (X and Y axis). The four-dimensional tracking task is an experimental test using both hands (two axes for one hand and one for the other) and the feet (for the fourth axis of control). For the two-dimensional tasks, three 2-minute trials are presented and error scores for each axis recorded. The primary score is the composite mean radial error across trials. The tracks are generated from the addition of three sine wave components. Task difficulty is fixed in terms of the frequency and amplitude parameters of the sine wave mixtures, but can be varied by changing the amplitude (extent of movement) and frequency (rate of movement) of one or more of the components. Changing the number of components can also be used to affect difficulty.

Other factors affecting difficulty that have to be controlled are lead or lag on controls, the mapping of control motion to screen motion (e.g., direct or inverted, augmented, or diminished), and control law (position, velocity, acceleration). For the Micropat compensatory tracking tests, these parameters are all fixed, providing a conventional fixed difficulty test. The critical difference is that the track is not predefined (as on the old electromechanical tracking tests like SMA or CVT) but is computer generated and can therefore be varied from trial to trial.

One-dimensional Adaptive Pursuit Tracking Versions 2 and 3 (each lasts for 10 min.) are one-dimensional pursuit tracking tasks with joystick control. As for the Compensatory Tracking Tests, they employ a forcing function derived from the addition of three sine wave components. The program contains a rule defining how the three sine waves may be generated and mixed to form the track forcing function. Difficulty is manipulated in this test by varying the input control law and or the speed of the track (the forcing function frequency). There are 17 difficulty levels defined in terms of increasing control-law complexity and 13 levels for speed. For control law, these levels are constructed from an ordered sequence of different mixtures of position, velocity, and acceleration components. The mapping of the sequence order to difficulty levels was investigated early on in the development of the Micropat battery (Flynn, 1981).

Based on continual monitoring of the candidate's performance the computer increases, decreases, or maintains the level of difficulty. The adaptation criteria are set to maintain the modulus mean error within prescribed limits. Performance is assessed in terms of the difficulty levels attained by the candidate over a series of fixed duration trials.

One-dimensional Adaptive Pursuit Tracking Version 1 used speed as the difficulty parameter, holding control law constant. For One-dimensional Adaptive Pursuit Tracking Version 2, track speed was held constant, and control law varied as the adaptive parameter. In both cases, a constant tracking error level is maintained by varying the difficulty level of the task as a function of the test taker's performance. This enables better discrimination over a wider ability range than conventional fixed-difficulty tracking tasks. Research with these tests showed Versions 1 and 2 to be highly correlated, with the latter giving better discrimination. As a result, One-dimensional Adaptive Pursuit Tracking Version 1 was dropped and is no longer supported in current versions of Micropat. However, the One-dimensional Adaptive Pursuit Tracking program is a general purpose one that is configured in terms of fixed and variable parameters from a simple text-based parameter file.

One-dimensional Adaptive Pursuit Tracking Version 3 is similar to Version 2, but the test candidate is given control of the difficulty level. They can choose if and when to increase or decrease it by pressing a key. This was intended to provide a measure of "error tolerance," that is the degree to which people are happy to trade off accuracy of performance against other demands. Measurement of this sort of construct posed a number of problems. In particular, such *tolerance* needs to be measured against individual performance baselines where error level is not under the control of the individual. Together, One-dimensional Adaptive Pursuit Tracking Versions 2 and 3 provide the necessary information, with Version 2 giving an individual baseline for Version 3 performance.

The Test of Scheduling Ability (15 min.) was devised to simulate tasks in which multiple displays have to be scanned and checked, with time-critical decisions being made as to whether the current situation should be allowed to continue (i.e., the candidate should monitor but do nothing) or whether actions should be initiated. The task involves the novel feature of scoring the test-taker's performance against an internal model of an optimal operator. As each action taken by the candidate affects the possible future states of the system, it is not possible to predefine an optimal set of actions. Instead, it is necessary for the program to continually inspect the current state of the system and then model what the best action would be (i.e., do nothing, or initiate some specific change). At each loop in the program, the test-taker's behavior is scored by comparing it against that of the internal optimal model. Like the tracking task, the initial state of the system and subsequent changes are generated by rules rather than being predefined.

A display of five columns is presented (see Figure 12.1), each column containing a target box with a random value (between 1 and 5) indicated in it. When a column is selected, by pressing the relevant key, a line begins to grow from the top of the column towards the target box. Only one line canbe growing at any one time (in the currently activated column). Boxes have a limited life and lines grow at different rates in different columns. If the line reaches the box in the column before the box's "life" expires, the candidate gains the points in the box. If the box's life expires before the line reaches it, both box and line are erased and a new target box appears in

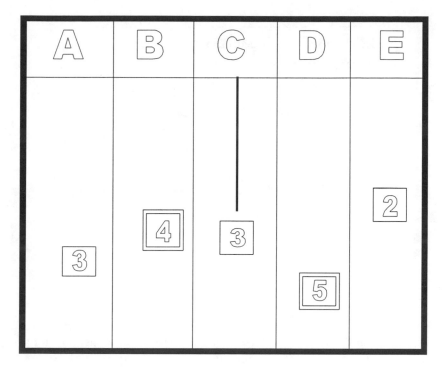

FIG. 12.1. Test of Scheduling Ability simulated screen display (see text for explanation).

the column. Candidates have to obtain as high a score as possible. This required continual monitoring of the changing status of each column and an ongoing evaluation of whether to select a new column or stay with the currently active one. The primary measure is based on a comparison between the candidate's performance and that of an optimal strategy algorithm.

A number of parameters are treated as incidentals: the location in the column of each box, the value in the box, and whether or not the box is a single or double value box (double boxes score twice the points indicated, but only remain on screen for half the time of single boxes). These are determined by random selection from constrained sets. As a consequence, the actual score obtained by each candidate (i.e., the sum of the points obtained by catching boxes) is partly determined by random variations in values of boxes and where they occur in columns. Comparisons between the point score defined in this way, and the internally generated fit to optimal model score show that the latter has higher internal consistency, but the two scores are very highly correlated.

The Landing Approach Test (15 min.) is a complex tracking task with features of a simple aircraft landing simulator (see Figure 12.2). The candidate "flies" an aircraft symbol onto a landing threshold point using a

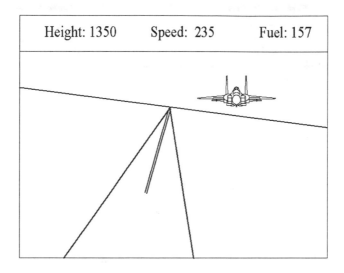

FIG. 12.2. Landing Approach Test simulated screen display (see text for explanation).

two-axis joystick and sliding power controller. Digital information about height, speed, and fuel is displayed together with continuous positional information (described to the candidate as an in-cockpit blind landing approach display). The test is designed to examine division of attention between "within-cockpit" (digital information) and analogues of "external" visual information about attitude and position. One practice and five scored approaches are performed.

Successful completion of the task is not just a function of tracking skill. Critical to the task is good forward-planning and scheduling of actions in order to arrive at the end point (i.e., the runway threshold) at the right time, height, and speed. In addition to its real-time dynamic nature, it also incorporates a novel scoring system. For the Test of Scheduling Ability it was possible to define utility functions that the computer could use to see if the candidate was following an optimal path. For the Landing Approach Test, this was not possible. A task like this generates large quantities of data relating to inputs and display/control status across time. Transforming these data into scores that are psychometrically sound and meaningful is not a trivial task.

The method adopted (see Bartram, 1987, for more detail) was to ask human experts to rate the quality of landing approaches (replayed to them without the test taker present). Equations were then developed which enable the expert ratings to be predicted from display/control status data. It was found that three relatively simple measures could be produced which well explained the variance in expert rating. The main one of these was a measure of the accuracy of the final status on the display (a composite measure based on final height, horizontal alignment, and proximity to the end of the runway center line). Two other measures are also used: Rate of descent and Speed control. The equations defining these scores are now built into the program and have been assessed for reliability and validity in a number of studies.

Information on norms, reliability (see Table 12.1) and validity for each of the tests described earlier are presented in Jones and Abram (1991) and Bartram (1995b). Reliability and sample data are summarized here in Table 12.1. Furthermore, recent discussion of the Micropat tests and other computer-based approaches to military testing is presented in a series of papers in Burke and Van Raay (1993), and summarized in Burke et al. (1995). A full list of the tests is given in Table 12.2.

Given the task-based nature of some of the MICROPAT tests, normal procedures (e.g., Spearman-Brown corrected average intertrial correlations) for estimating reliability are of uncertain merit. Although some data are available on test–retest correlations, such correlations are not appropriate as estimates of reliability as these tests were designed to be taken once only. In general, "alpha"-type measures of internal consistency are reasonable to high. There are exceptions (such as the Log Likelihood Ratio measure from the Speeded Decision-making Test and the Final Distance Error measure from the Test of Navigational Orientation). For executive use in selection, only a very restricted set of measures is used to produce an overall weighted composite (typically 10 measures from six tests), the reliability of which can be estimated using Mosier's (1943) equation.

CONCLUSIONS

Prior to Micropat there had been a number of attempts to produce equivalent computer versions of traditional paper-and-pencil or electromechanical tests and one or two 'novel' stand-alone computer-based tests—such as the Perceptual Maze Test (Elithorn, Jones, & Kerr, 1963). Early reviews of the developing role of computer-based testing in occupational assessment (e.g., Bartram & Bayliss, 1984) showed there was surprisingly little use of the potential provided by computers for the development of new forms of test. Bartram (1994) noted that until relatively recently the main exception to this failure to take advantage of what new technology had to offer the test developer had been in the development of adaptive item-based tests. Even computer-adaptive testing, despite important and substantial developments in item response theory over the past 20 years, has failed to make a very great impact on testing practice. Although there have been interesting and exciting developments in other areas, such as item generation (e.g., Bejar, 1991; Irvine, Dann, &

TABLE 12.1

Internal Consistency Estimates of Reliability Taken From UK Services and Commercial Pilot Applicant Samples Relatively Free From Range Restriction

Test	Variable	Alpha	Notes	Number of samples	Sample sizes range
One-dimensional Adaptive Tracking Version 2	TL456	0.82–0.93	Mean difficulty level	5	164 - 365
One-dimensional Adaptive Tracking Version 3	TL78	0.84–0.87	Mean difficulty level	5	93 – 357
	TTE	0.80–0.84	Mean error level		
Two-dimensional Compensatory Tracking	CT	0.92–0.99	Mean error level	3	245 - 310
Landing Approach Test	ACC	0.73–0.86	Mean final accuracy level	6	108 - 367
	SC	0.48–0.79	Speed control		
	ROD	0.71–0.74	Rate of descent		
Test of Scheduling Ability	MPC	0.77–0.89	Mean percent of optimal performance	6	55 - 269
Speeded Decision-making Test	RT	0.80–0.93	Decision speed	3	130 - 311
	DPRIME	0.64–0.71	d-prime		
	LLR	0.25–0.56	Log-likelihood ratio		
Attitude to Risk Test	NK1	0.78–0.89	Mean keys pressed condition 1	4	42 - 214
	NK2	0.91–0.94	Mean keys pressed condition 2		
Spatial Orientation Test	MTPCI	0.91	Mean time per correct response	1	133
Test of Navigational Orientation	NOFHE	0.64–0.76	Final heading error	2	80 - 133
	NOFDE	0.45–0.50	Final distance error		
Test of Navigational Calculations	NCCT	0.75	Preparation time	2	81 - 130
	NCTPCI	0.86	Time per correct response		

Note. Further details are presented in Jones and Abram (1991) and Bartram (1995b).

TABLE 12.2

List of Micropat Tests With Short Names and Descriptive Titles

Short name	Descriptive title
ADTRACK1	One-dimensional Adaptive Tracking Version 2: Speed adaptation
ADTRACK2	One-dimensional Adaptive Tracking Version 2: Control law adaptation
ADTRACK3	One-dimensional Adaptive Tracking Version 3: Candidate controlled adaptation
COMP2D	Two-dimensional Compensatory Tracking: Hand-Foot co-ordination
COMP2JJ	Two-dimensional Compensatory Tracking: Hand-Hand co-ordination
COMP4D	Four-dimensional Compensatory Tracking: Hand-Hand-Foot co-ordination
LANDING	Landing Approach Test
SCHEDULE	Test of Scheduling Ability
PLANE	Speeded Decision-making Test
RISK	Attitude to Risk Test
SUBTRACT	Test of Speeded Mental Arithmetic
DUALTASK	Dualtask Test: Tracking with mental arithmetic
DIGISPAN	Adaptive Digit Span Test
MANIKIN	Spatial Orientation Test
NAVOR	Test of Navigational Orientation
NAVCALC	Test of Navigational Calculations

Anderson, 1990), test publishers have tended to stick to the old tried-and-trusted paper-based technologies. It is hoped that the lessons learned from the experience gained from projects like Micropat will provide the means of developing new more robust measuring tools that take full advantage of the opportunities offered by new technology. Non-paper media do not require the precise preformulation of items, the use of fixed item sets, or of fixed sequences of items. They also provide the potential to present more complex tasks with on-line scoring of performance.

Rule-based item generation, whether carried out on-line or off-line, has a number of obvious advantages over the use of predefined test items.

1. It does away with the need for many hours of work in writing items.
2. One can rapidly produce multiple equivalent versions of a test.

Less obvious is the fact that the psychometric properties of the test (assessed using samples of items from the domain defined by the rules) are universe-specific rather than item-specific. For conventional tests, "items" is a fixed factor—even though the items included in a test may be intended to provide a random sample of some domain. For item generation, items can be a genuinely random factor for analysis purposes. Once the psychometric properties of the item-generation rules have been estimated, item pretesting is no longer needed to establish item parameters. The properties of the test are defined by the rule parameters not the properties of any particular item sample.

This last point is important. In principle, one could generate random samples of items from the domain defined by the item-generation rules, and then use data from those samples to estimate the properties of the domain independently of the item content of any one particular test.

There is a range of difficulties, however, with item generation. Not the least of these is being able to specify items or tasks in terms of the rules for generating those items or task. For some item types this is easy (e.g., tests like the Test of Speeded Mental-Arithmetic), for others it may be extremely complex (e.g. for tests of high level verbal reasoning). A related issue is that of knowing what, in Irvine et al.'s (1990) terminology, is radical and what is incidental. We need to ensure that the incidental variations between the items or tasks presented to a person or to different people do not affect the difficulty of the task or distort the construct being measured in any unexpected or unpredictable fashion. It is generally fairly easy to identify the parameters that are likely to make a task easier or harder. It is less easy to find those that have no effect on difficulty. Apparent "incidentals" may have effects that are unpredicted. For the Micropat tests, many of the preliminary studies carried out during design and construction, were directed toward checking that the incidentals were really incidental. For example, Fleck (1991) explored the relationship between repeated testing with Test of Navigational Calculations using either the same or different scenarios to see if the scenario is incidental to what the test measures.

Departures from traditional item-based approaches to test construction (whether using item generation or fixed-item sets) pose additional problems. Laboratory research on the Landing Approach Test and on the Four-dimensional Compensatory Tracking Test indicated that as task complexity increases so does the degree to which individual differences in task strategy influence performance. The Four-dimensional Compensatory Tracking Test, for example, requires the candidate to co-ordinate two two-dimensional tracking tasks. One involves maintaining the alignment of a vertical and horizontal bar in the form of a cross, whereas the other involves maintaining the location of the cross inside a box. Each part of the task is practised separately and then tested in combination. Detailed analysis of performance protocols (Banerji, 1982) showed that subjects could obtain very similar overall error scores with very different strategies (e.g., some people would switch back and forth between the two task components whereas others would attempt to minimize both sources of error at the same time).

However, developing measures to capture this type of complexity was seen as one of the key challenges when constructing the Micropat tests. Differences in the efficacy with which individuals could apply strategies to complex tasks under high levels of demand was thought to be one of the critical factors discriminating those who failed late in training from those who were able to cope. The extent to which it is possible to measure such complexity using short, relatively simple tasks, however, remains unresolved.

The Micropat approach to test design was pragmatic (Irvine et al., 1989, characterized it as an "ergonomic approach"). As a consequence, the battery of tests contains a wide range of types of task. The authors drew on a wide variety of psychological models and other sources in developing the battery, but were mainly influenced by their backgrounds in aviation and in experimental and cognitive psychology. Many of the psychometric implications of the work were not fully realized at the time of construction. It is quite possible that had they been, a different more traditional approach would have been taken. In that sense, approaching the problem of test design from a cognitive psychology rather than a psychometric tradition provided the impetus to try out new ideas that psychometrically more sophisticated colleagues might have fought shy of. Nevertheless, the data we have accumulated from a large number of different sources has tended to support the view that the main (so-called primary) measures are reliable and have good distributional properties. The tests are very positively rated as relevant and interesting by test takers. The validations studies carried out in a range of different settings (military and commercial) have supported the validity of a composite test score based on six of the tests from the battery. This composite has been demonstrated to have good generalizability across all the *ab initio* training course studied to date (see Bartram, 1995a).

Many of the tests developed during the Micropat program never saw the light of day. In some cases, computer technology was not adequate for the task, in others, it was not possible to devise reliable scoring protocols or constrain generation appropriately. However, as a result of the lessons learned from work on projects like this we are now in a much better position as psychologists and test designers, to make effective use of the enormous freedoms offered us by new technology in the advance of measurement techniques.

ACKNOWLEDGMENTS

The work reported in this paper was carried out under a number of MoD Research Agreements initially from the Army Personnel Research Establishment and subsequently the Royal Navy SP(N). The author is grateful to all those, both psychologists and non psychologists within the Services who contributed to this work. All the initial research and development work on Micropat was carried out in collaboration with H. C. A. Dale, who was responsible for the training analyses and many of the ideas behind the tests. The views expressed in this paper are those of the author and do not necessarily reflect those of the MoD.

REFERENCES

Banerji, N. (1982). *A study to investigate intra-individual differences in performance on tracking tasks used in pilot selection.* Unpublished masters thesis, University of Hull, Hull, England.

Bartram, D. (1987). The development of an automated pilot testing system for pilot selection: The MICROPAT project. *Applied Psychology: An international review, 36,* 279–298.

Bartram, D. (1991). The Development and Validation of Micropat for Royal Navy Aircrew Selection: 1985–1991. *Ministry of Defence SP(N) Report R 163.* London: Ministry of Defence.

Bartram, D. (1994). Computer based assessment. *International Review of Industrial and Organizational Psychology, 9,* 31–69.

Bartram, D. (1995a). Validation of the Micropat Battery. *International Journal of Selection and Assessment, 3,* 84–95.

Bartram, D. (1995b). *Software Documentation for MICROPAT Version 6.0.* Hull, England: Bartdale Ltd.

Bartram, D., & Baxter, P. (1995). Cathay Pacific Airways pilot selection validation. In N. Johnston, R. Fuller, & N. McDonald, (Eds.), *Aviation psychology: Training and selectio* (pp. 194–202). Aldershot: Avebury Aviation.

Bartram, D., & Baxter, P. (1996). Validation of the Cathay Pacific Airways Pilot Selection Programme. *The International Journal of Aviation Psychology, 6,* 149–170.

Bartram, D., & Bayliss, R. (1984). Automated testing: past, present and future. *Journal of Occupational Psychology, 57*, 221–237.

Bejar, I. (1991). A generative approach to psychological and educational measurement. *ETS Research Report.* Princeton, NJ: Educational Testing Service.

Bormuth, J. R. (1970). *On the theory of achievement test items.* Chicago: University of Chicago Press.

Burke, E. (1991). Computer-based testing in the Royal Air Force. NATO Panel VIII Research Study Group 15 *Workshop on computer-based assessment of military personnel,* Brussels.

Burke, E., Kokorian, A., Lescreve, F., Martin, C. J., Van Raay, P., & Weber, W. (1995). Computer-based assessment: A NATO survey. *International Journal of Selection and Assessment, 3,* 75–83.

Burke, E F, & Van Raay, P. B. (1993). *Computer-based assessment in NATO: Final Report RSG 15.* AC/243(Panel 8)TR/12. Brussels: NATO Headquarters.

Carretta, T. R. (1991). Computer-based assessment of US Air Force Pilot Training Candidates. NATO Panel VIII Research Study Group 15 *Workshop on computer-based assessment of military personnel,* Brussels.

Carroll, J. B. (1987). New perspectives in the analysis of abilities. In R. R. Ronning, J. A. Glover, J. C. Conoley, & J. C. Witt (Eds.), *The influence of cognitive psychology on testing* (pp. 267-284). Hillsdale, NJ: Lawrence Erlbaum Associates.

Elithorn, A., Jones, D., & Kerr, M. O. (1963). A binary perceptual maze. *American Journal of Psychology, 76,* 506–508.

Fleck, D. (1991). *The reliability of two versions of the NAVCALC test.* Unpublished masters thesis, Hull University, Hull, England.

Flynn, I. N. (1981). *A preliminary study in the development of an adaptive tracking task as a selection test for helicopter pilots.* Unpublished masters thesis, Hull University, Hull, England.

Irvine, S. H., Dann, P. L, & Anderson, J. (1990). Towards a theory of algorithm-determined cognitive test construction. *British Journal of Psychology, 81,* 173–196.

Irvine, S. H., Dann, P. L., Evans, J. St. B. T., Dennis, I., Collis, J., Thacker, C., & Anderson, J. (1989). Another generation of personnel selection tests: Stages in a new theory of computer-based test construction. *UK Army Personnel Research Establishment draft report.*

Jones, A., & Abram, M. (1991). Micropat Data Book: Issue Three. *Ministry of Defence SP(N) Report TR 280.* London: Ministry of Defence.

Loevinger, J. (1965). Person and population as psychometric concepts. *Psychological Review, 72,* 143–155.

Mosier, C. I. (1943). On the reliability of a weighted composite. *Psychometrika, 8,* 161–168.

Osburn, H. G. (1968). Item sampling for achievement testing. *Educational and Psychological Measurement, 28,* 95–104.

Tryon, R. C. (1957). Reliability and behaviour domain validity: Reformulation and historical critique. *Psychological Bulletin, 54,* 229–249.

13

On the Implementation of Item-Generation Principles for the Design of Aptitude Testing in Aviation

Klaus-Martin Goeters
Bernd Lorenz
DLR German Aerospace Center

The DLR Department of Aviation and Space Psychology in Hamburg specializes in the selection of operational personnel such as pilots, air traffic controllers, and astronauts. In the DLR selection programs full-scale testing includes cognitive, psychomotor, and personality assessment (Goeters, Hörmann, & Maschke 1989). With the exception of projective tests nearly all kinds of psychodiagnostic tools are used: mental tests (paper-pencil or computerized versions); apparatus tests including simulator-like work samples; biographical data; personality questionnaires, and assessment center techniques. Apart from selection tests DLR has also developed and applied test batteries for human performance monitoring in extreme environments such as deep-sea diving (Lorenz, Wenzel, Lorenz, & Heineke, 1993), long-term confinement (Lorenz, Lorenz, & Manzey, 1996; Manzey & Lorenz, 1998a), and space (Manzey, Lorenz, Schiewe, Finell, & Thiele, 1993; Manzey, Lorenz, Schiewe, Finell, & Thiele, 1995; Manzey, Lorenz, & Polyakov, 1998; see Manzey & Lorenz, 1998b for a review).

The majority of tests used at DLR for the selection of operational personnel are in-house developments because methods from the general test market are not appropriate for various reasons: specific combination of job demands, testees only of a higher educational level, nonclinical application, required confidentiality of test material. The DLR test construction usually is conducted in accordance with the principles of classical test theory. Traditionally, the outcomes were fixed version tests which followed classical factor-analytic concepts. For example, in the cognitive domain measurements derived from psychometric factors are basic selection criteria for aerospace operators: General Reasoning R, Numerical Facility N, Associative Memory Ma,

Perceptual Speed P, Spatial Orientation S, and Visualization Vz. These terms are chosen according to the well-known "ETS-Kit of Reference Tests for Cognitive Factors" (French, Ekstrom, & Price 1963), which guided for many years the structural concepts of DLR's test development in the cognitive area. The listed factors are also partially reflected in the coming European criteria for the psychological evaluation of pilots (JAA, 1996). Apart from biographical and personality factors the following aptitudes are included in this set of criteria: Logical reasoning; mental arithmetic; memory function; attention; perception; spatial comprehension; psychomotor function; multiple task abilities.

This criterion list indicates a broad factorial structure. Each individual complex (e.g., attention) can be divided into more precise subfactors or elements that are described in an appendix to the criterion list. Paper and pencil tests place important restrictions on what may be measured. They deal, in the main, with the processing of visually presented material, whereas in pilot selection also the auditory component is highly relevant (due to radio communication with Air Traffic Control). Therefore, the above mentioned performance criteria require in some cases the testing of both sensory channels (e.g., visual as well as auditory attention).

NEED FOR ITEM GENERATION

In about 1990, new demands arose in the area of selection and in experimental field studies. Specifications called for the easy construction of parallel tests from basic item material. The problems to be overcome by the introduction of parallel forms included repeated applicant assessment; commercial test coaching; international groups of applicants; single-subject human performance monitoring in extreme environments. These are discussed in turn.

Repeated Applicant Assessment. Due to the success of the DLR selection concept which has been proven by several validity studies (Maschke & Hörmann, 1988, 1989; Eißfeldt & Maschke, 1991; Goeters, 1998) DLR became responsible for the psychological selection of pilots (mainly Lufthansa group), air traffic controllers (Deutsche Flugsicherung & EUROCONTROL), and astronauts (DLR & European Space Agency). Quite often applicants took part in various selection programs (e.g., first being tested as pilot and later as controller applicant). Because various types of practice effects most likely lead to an overestimation of true aptitudes a need to remove any advantage became evident.

Commercial Test Coaching. More serious than repeated applicant assessments was the undermining of psychodiagnostic measures by systematic coaching. Commercial coaching emerged when in the 1980s mass testing was introduced due to a very high demand for new pilots. Because of the ongoing job attractiveness up to now many young applicants have been willing to pay a considerable amount of money for coaching to prepare for the psychological selection program. For DLR this created an urgent demand for tests that could be changed in short periods of time: and stimulated test development: fundamentally.

International Groups of Applicants. In Europe, companies and organizations increasingly have to hire personnel of different nationalities from the common European labor market. Therefore selection requires the administration of tests which enable a fair treatment of applicants independent of their national background. Here, international equivalence for all persons who have to be assessed with regard to their capacity or competence is an important additional criterion for the psychometric quality of the evaluation tools.

Single-Subject Human Performance Monitoring in Extreme Environments. Studies investigating the impact of extreme and hazardous environments on human performance such as deep-sea diving (Lorenz, 1994), long-term confinement (Lorenz, Lorenz, & Manzey, 1996), or space missions (Manzey, et al., 1993; Manzey, et al., 1995) typically involve few subjects. Most often a single-subject experimental design is the only feasible approach (see Manzey et al., 1995 for a detailed description of the statistical methodology). In a recently completed space study Manzey, Lorenz, and Polyakov (1998) applied a performance monitoring battery 61 times to a single cosmonaut over an overall period of two years, including preflight training and baseline data collection; inflight assessments during the 438-day world record stay onboard the orbital station MIR; and a 6-month postflight period. The computerized tests were developed according to a recommended standard for research with environmental stressors (AGARD, 1989) and were completely generative. Figure 13.1 depicts the time course of speed (response rate) and accuracy (percentage of error) in two cognitve tests, Sternberg memory search using two different memory sets and grammatical reasoning (see AGARD, 1989 for a description of these tests). For a third test, a psychomotor task (Unstable Tracking Task), the time course of root mean squared error (RMSE) is shown in Figure 13.1. For all three tests the upper and lower confidence levels are indicated. It became evident that basic cognitive performance remained consistently stable on MIR-station. If any, the pre- and the postflight period appeared critical in this regard. However, psychomotor efficiency was markedly disturbed during adaptation to the space environment and, again, during re-adaptation to normal Earth conditions.

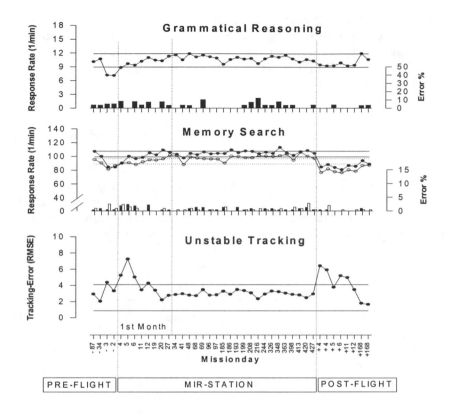

FIG. 13.1. Performance of a single cosmonaut in a computerized task battery as a function of mission day during a 14-month long-duration spaceflight. For the Grammatical Resoning Task (top panel) and the Sternberg Memory Search Task (mid panel) the time courses of mean response rates (line graphs) and error rates (bar graphs) are shown. The Sternberg data are presented separately for two different levels of memory load: two-letter-set (open circles/bars), four-letter-set (filled circles/bars). The bottom panel shows the time course of the mean root-mean squared tracking error (RMSE). Horizontal lines indicate the upper and lower levels of confidence (95%) for comparisons of in-flight and postflight sessions with preflight baseline sessions (days –87 and -34 before launch).

PARAT TESTS: FROM COMPUTER-GENERATED PAPER AND PENCIL TESTS TO FULL COMPUTERIZATION

In selection the major goal was to develop item-writing principles in order to generate a sufficient number of parallel tests for the relevant cognitive factors. The test versions were also to be directly transferable from one European nationality/language area to another. The solution in the PARAT (PARAllel Testing) program (Goeters & Rathje, 1992) was that homogenous item material was chosen which ideally would allow for an infinite task multiplication.

Language impacts and aspects of the item with an obvious cultural relation were avoided as far as possible. Item difficulties were controlled by factors such as speed, complexity, distractors, and so forth.

The first generation of PARAT tests were multiple forms of cognitive paper-and-pencil tests synthesized by computer programs. The outline of the rules that were implemented in the item construction software principally aimed at controlling item difficulty. These rules were initially derived by the test developer from careful examination of the item difficulties according to his experience and were cross-checked by empirical data on item equivalence. Taking difficulty related constraints into account the specific composition of the items in one test version was randomly chosen. Overall this method worked very well. Applicants always could be confronted with new test versions. This was a basic but still limited strategy against test coaching. Based on the availability of a sufficient number of parallel tests the most efficient countermeasure was a pre-information booklet, which was distributed to the applicants before being tested. In this booklet the test principles of the PARAT tests were described and miniature tests for exercise were presented. Thus, a certain degree of pretraining could be standardized for all applicants.

Most of the test versions generated within the PARAT frame became sufficiently parallel according to the criteria of classical test theory. Table 13.1 shows means and standard deviations of three different computer-generated versions of the PARAT-battery derived from three different applicant samples (see the following test descriptions). Except for the ROT (rotation of dice) all differences were negligible (Cohen's d < .15). In the ROT, version A was found more difficult. On the level of paper-and-pencil tests these differences usually could not easily be traced back to differences on item level because most of the tests were speeded and used sum scores as the test raw scores (e.g., number of correct items per elapsed time). Item evaluation only became possible with the second generation of PARAT tests, which were transfered into a complete Computer Assisted Testing (CAT) environment (Lorenz, Rathje, Goeters, Finell, & Lamschus, 1996). After an experimental phase where DLR received support from the Human Assessment Laboratory at the

TABLE 13.1

Means and SD of Raw Scores for Three Different Computer-Generated Versions of the PARAT-Battery Which Is Applied in Aptitude Testing of Applicants for *ab initio* Pilot Training

| Test | A-Version | | | B-Version | | | C-Version | | |
	Mean	Std.Dev.	N	Mean	Std.Dev.	N	Mean	Std.Dev	N
CLE	259.06	23.48	1318	262.44	22.49	1462	258.20	22.22	1243
MSN	18.73	8.96	1318	18.25	8.32	1428	19.26	8.98	1244
FPT	44.11	13.71	1322	42.24	14.53	1475	43.76	13.88	1252
ROT	24.36	9.24	1318	27.34	8.31	1463	26.33	8.87	1243
KBP	66.99	13.69	1321	67.34	13.17	1474	70.28	14.04	1251

University of Plymouth the level of full computerization was reached in November 1997, when the new fully computerized Phase-1 selection for the Lufthansa ab-initio pilot training courses came into operation (Phase-1: First stage of selection by classroom group testing; Phase-2: second stage with individual apparatus testing and assessment center scenarios). The rationale for the development of the CAT battery had to meet two main requirements:

1. Tests of the PARAT-Program should be transfered to full computerization and existing item-generation rules should be further refined by experimental analyses of item-response times with regard to determinants of item difficulty.
2. Aptitudes that used to be assessed during Phase-2 selection such as psychomotor ability, time sharing, and selective attention should already be tapped in Phase-1.

The first requirement ensures continuity to the former paper-and-pencil Phase-1 selection, keeps a reasonable level of familiarity with the battery among test instructors and Lufthansa members of the selection board, and ensures that the test pre-info booklet for the applicants will still be valid. Regarding the second requirement, the new Phase-1 battery should take advantage of the computer technology enabling new access to typical Phase-2 aptitude constructs. The importance of time sharing ability and selective attention has recently been confirmed by studies investigating the ability requirements of air traffic controllers (Eißfeldt, 1998) and pilots (Goeters, Maschke, & Klamm, 1998) using the Fleishman Job Analysis Survey (Fleishman, 1992). According to these two requirements a twofold specification strategy for a new Phase-1 CAT battery was adopted: On the one hand existing aptitude tests in the transfer from paper-and-pencil to computerized tests were subjected to experimental analysis in order to elucidate task characteristics influencing item difficulty. This strategy referred to as *radical identification* preceding the empirical a-posterior determination of item parameters can efficiently reduce costs in the development of parallel test forms as Irvine, Dann, and Anderson (1990) have convincingly demonstrated. On the other hand validated information-processing models can guide test development by composing tests along cognitive requirements structured by these models. The former strategy was followed in the second generation of the PARAT tests. The latter strategy was emphasized in the attempt to evaluate relevant basic abilities within the frame of an information-processing model like the well-validated Sternberg memory-scanning model. The major aim here was to develop a more theoretically sound route to the assessment of abilities with special emphasis on timesharing and selective attention. For that purpose a series of subtests based on the Sternberg memory-scanning paradigm (Sternberg, 1966) was implemented into the CAT-battery. Knowledge about task variables with a substantial impact on the difficulty of item recognition, (i.e., radicals sensu Irvine, Dann, & Anderson, 1990), could be inferred from the wide body of literature about this task. The attractiveness for a Phase-1 selection tool was twofold: First, the item-generation software has already proven useful in numerous applications in our environmental stress research program (e.g., see Figure 13.1). Second, a composition of task variables were chosen in order to cover ability requirements in the domain of perceptual processing (visual vs. auditory probe presentation), short-term memory capacity (high vs. low levels of memory-load), selective attention (degraded vs. not degraded probe stimuli), and timesharing ability (single vs. dual task operation with a concurrent tracking task).

THE COMPUTER-ASSISTED TEST BATTERY FOR AB-INITIO PILOT SELECTION (PHASE-1)

The CAT battery developed for the Phase-1 selection of ab-initio student pilots are implemented on the new DLR CAT-facility that hosts at present 30 computer workstations. These are based on 6.86 processors interconnected by a Novell™ network but behave during testing as stand-alone machines in order to ensure accurate response timing. Standard input devices are flat TFT touch screens (MicroTouch™), mouse and joystick. All power tests of the multiple-choice nature are written on the Microsoft-Windows™ 3.11 platform using a self-developed VisualBasic toolkit called CONQUEST (CONstruction of QUESTionaires) to enable easy item editing, item coding, manipulation of graphical material, and control of optional procedural features (e.g., allowing to turn through screen pages, correcting responses, etc.). All timed and speeded tests including the Sternberg subtests are written on the Microsoft-DOS™ platform using the commercially available code generating system ERTS™ (Beringer, 1993), which has proven processor independent response timing qualities with millisecond accuracy (Beringer, 1993). A Microsoft-Windows™ based test management software implemented on the supervisor's workstation supports the compilation of tests to batteries, applicant assignment to workstations, downloading testware modules to the workstations, monitoring of assessments at the workstations during testing, controlling the transfer of applicant data collected at the workstation to the server host, and some features for off-nominal situations. The Phase-1 battery contains five PARAT-tests and eight other performance tests. All tests are described next. Except for the PARAT-tests and the Sternberg memory search tests all other tests are still fixed version tests. The whole battery is accomplished by an English language test and a personality questionnaire not described here.

TASK DESCRIPTIONS: PARAT-TESTS

Memory Test (MEK). This is a test of visual associative memory. The applicants are presented screens containing 40 memorization items presented in two series with 20 items each. Memorization items are pairs of pictures taken from CorelDraw™ clipart libaries and a two-digit number. After the first two screens, that is, after the first 8 memorization items, recall items (picture only, number has to be recalled) are added to the screen. An example of such a screen is presented in Figure 13.2. Half of the items were easy the other half difficult to verbalize (see Figure 13.2). The difficulty of number retrieval varies solely as a function of the item location within the series which, first, determines the time interval between memorization items and recall items of the respective picture-number-pair, and which is, second, influenced by primacy- as well as recency-effects. A simple item-generation algorithm applied to both series separately allows for random combinations of the same picture and number set within a constant memorization-recall time protocol. Contrary to our expectation ease of verbalization had no influence on item difficulty, nor the interaction of item location by ease of verbalization. Cronbach's alpha for the first series was .86 and for the second series .85, respectively (n = 330). The between-series correlation was .86, which yielded an overall reliability of .92 after Spearman-Brown correction.

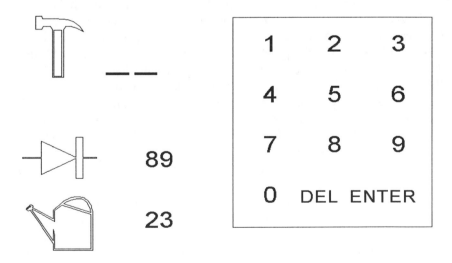

FIG. 13.2. Item example of the associate memory test (Merkfähigkeit MEK): In the blank field a previously memorized two-digit number has to be recalled and typed in by using the touch-sensitive numerical keypad on the screen. Then, two new items have to be memorized.

Clearance (CLE). The Clearance test assesses auditory short-term memory. The applicants are presented a target item (e.g., E7-Q4) via headphone followed by a sequence of four probe items which may be (1) completely different (7E-4Q), (2) identical (E7-Q4), or (3) partly different (E7-4Q). The applicants have to indicate the identical parts of the probe items by touching corresponding fields on the screen. Item difficulty varies as a function of target size with regard to number of parts (two parts as in the earlier example or three parts) and number of items within parts (1 digit - 1 letter or combinations of three parts, e.g., 1 digit - 1 letter - 1 digit). Furthermore, the serial position within the probe sequence had a strong and almost linear influence on item difficulty. Thus, the probe that immediately followed the target message was easiest to recognize and recognition accuracy decreased with each subsequent probe. This is apparently due to interference between target rehearsal and recognition of very similar distractor probes. The item generation ensures that targets and probes using phonetically equivalent letters in the German language are generated (e.g., TF - KB and CS - HG). The odd-even Spearman-Brown corrected split-half reliability was .91 ($n = 330$).

Mental Concentration Test (KBT). The quite complex and demanding rule of this task is illustrated and explained in Figure 13.3. Basically, the applicants continuously have to perform a series of subtasks: visual search, symbol-digit-substitution, simple mental arithmetic, and continuous memory. The item-generation program provides randomization of symbols in both the task and the search row keeping constant for each applicant (a) the target position in the search field, since this affects the difficulty of the visual scanning component, (b) the difficulty of arithmetic operation (carry vs. non carry, i.e., whether or not addition resulted in a number greater than 10), and (c) equal probability across the three response categories within each bottom row. Cronbach's alpha of the 8 screen scores (number correct) was .91 ($n = 330$).

Airplane-Position Test (FPT). The Airplane-Position Test is a spatial orientation test and was a new development within the frame of the PARAT-project (Goeters & Rathje, 1992). The test is described and illustrated in Figure 13.4. The test is self-paced and timed, and, therefore, involves a strong work-rate component as well. This is the only PARAT test where currently no item-generation principle was implemented, because already the paper-and-pencil version already exhibited some conceptual deficiencies with regard to its construct validity. Experienced applicants apply simplifying rules, for example, looking for a rotation pattern that results in an overall 360 degree turn and exclude these turns from mental rotation. This changes the demand to a test of rapid pattern recognition rather than spatial orientation. At present conceptual changes are under development that circumvents this deficiency. The split-half reliability (split by time and Spearman-Brown corrected) is .96 ($n = 330$).

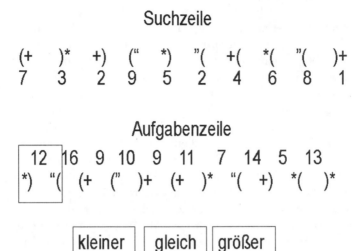

FIG. 13.3. Item example of the Mental Concentration Test (Konzentrations-Belastungs-Test KBT): The top of the screen contains a *search row* (Suchzeile) of symbol-digit-pairs. The bottom contains a *task row* (Aufgabenzeile). The applicants have to search the framed symbols of the task row in the search row and to add the associated digits (5 plus 2 in this example item). The sum may be either less (kleiner), equal (gleich) or greater (größer) than the framed number and the corresponding key-field has to be touched. Next, the frame moves one symbol forward, thus frames the second and third symbol and a new number. Therefore, only one new symbol has to be searched for digit substitution while one digit of the previous search has to be kept in mind. This procedure continues until the end of the task row is reached or 45 seconds have elapsed. Then the screen changes and a new search and task row appear.

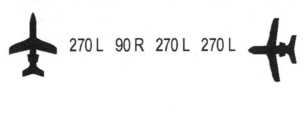

FIG. 13.4. Item example of the Aircraft-Position-Test (Flugzeug-Positions-Test FPT): It consists of two airplane symbols having one of four different headings (0, 90, 180, or 270 degrees). Between both aircraft symbols information is given as to a series of four heading changes to be performed mentally on the first aircraft. (E.g. the item above demands heading changes of, first, 270 degrees to the left, second, 90 degrees to the right, third, 270 degrees to the left, and finally, again 270 degrees to the left). Next, the applicants are required to indicate which additional rotation would be necessary to match the final heading of the first aircraft with the heading of the second aircraft by touching the corresponding key-fields on the screen (90L in the item above).

Rotation of Dices (ROT). In this test the applicants are asked to imagine a dice having a cross on one of its six planes, which is announced via headphone. Next, a series of tilting instructions (left, right, forward, leftward, see Figure 13.5) are given via headphone to be performed on the dice in mind. The applicant has to indicate the final location of the plane with the cross by touching a corresponding field on the screen. In the original PARAT version item difficulty was altered by increasing (a) the pace and (b) the number of tilting instructions from 5 to 7, and finally to 9. The algorithm used for generating parallel forms took precautions that the number of tilting instructions leaving the position of the cross unchanged (e.g., tilting forward when the cross is left) was constant across parallel forms as these were found easier than other tilting instructions (Ortmüller, 1990).

The CAT-version of the ROT was changed to a self-paced and timed test, that is, that the applicants touch a specified field to pace a new tilting instruction. The number of correct responses performed in a limited time yields the score. Recording the response times of self-pacing enabled a more detailed analysis of item difficulties. This revealed the following results: (1) The number of tilting instructions had no influence anymore on the difficulty (i.e., the pacing latency time did not vary as a function of the length of the instruction series). Thus, the length of the instruction series turned out to become an incidental rather than a radical. (2) The type of tilting instructions had a significant influence on the pacing latency. This latter finding is illustrated in Figure 13.6. It depicts the latency time of self-pacing as a function of all 24 possible tilting operations to be performed by the applicant. These 24 categories were sorted by increasing latency. The fastest pacing times were

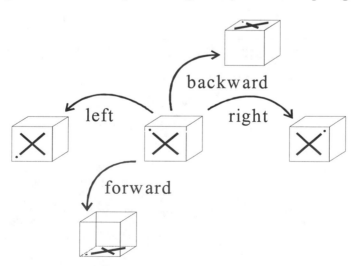

FIG. 13.5 Tilting instructions to be performed mentally in the Dice-Rotation test (ROT).

found in instructions leaving the position of the cross unchanged (see filled circles), which confirmed the above mentioned radical dimension already controlled by the item-generation algorithm used in the paper-and-pencil PARAT version of this test. Moreover, there was one class of tilting instructions that caused distinctively higher pacing times. These were all four tilting instructions to be performed on the bottom position of the cross. In these cases the position to be generated by the applicant is essentially an inversion of the instruction given, which obviously produced a Stroop-like interference with the tilting instruction (tilting forward results in the back position, leftward in the right position, etc.). Counting the number of instructions per tilting category for each of the three PARAT versions of the ROT test revealed that the A-version contained significantly more instructions of the inversion type. Therefore, the A-version turned out to be more difficult than the B- and the C-version (see Table 13.1). The algorithm used in the CAT battery was modified accordingly. This finding underlines the importance of empirically testing a-priori notions about item radicals and incidentals to properly refine the item generation algorithm.

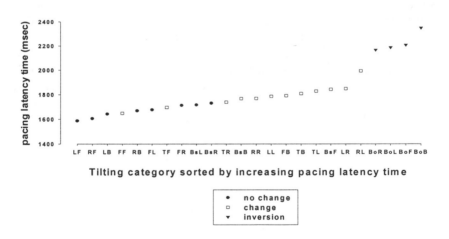

FIG. 13.6. Mean latency of self-pacing the next tilting instruction in the Dice-Rotation test (ROT) as a function of the type of tilting to be followed. All 24 possible tilting categories (6 positions of the cross x 4 tilting instructions) are sorted by increasing latency. Tilting categories are labelled by a two-letter code: first letter: position of the cross (T: top; Bo: Bottom; L: Left; R: Right; F: Front; Bs: Backside); second letter: tilting instruction (F: forward; B: backward; L: leftward; R: rightward). For example LF means: position of the cross is left and the instruction to be followed is "tilt forward," the position to be generated is "left" (no change). The latency until the applicant paces the next instruction is measured in msec.

FIXED-VERSION TESTS

Mechanical Comprehension Test (TVT); Reliability: Cronbach's alpha = .75. The Mechanical Comprehension Test consists of multiple-choice questions concerning technical problems that are illustrated by technical drawings. The test does not assess specific mechanical knowledge but rather asks for the understanding of mechanical, technical, and physical principles. Responses are given by touching the optional fields at the screen.

Physics Knowledge Test (TQ); Reliability: Cronbach's alpha = .95. This test comprises a range of multiple-choice questions across several areas in mid-level physics such as simple technical systems, mechanics, electrics, fluid mechanics, and wave theory. Responses are given by touching the optional fields on the screen.

Mathematical–Logical Reasoning (RAG); Reliability: Cronbach's alpha = .79. This test contains multiple-choice questions in the domain of more complex logical reasoning including arithmetical problems. This demands, for example, the application of the rule of three, judging the integral size of complex geometrical planes, etc. Thus, the test is actually a mixture of basic mathematical knowledge and logical reasoning. Responses are given by touching the optional fields on the screen.

Mental Arithmetic-Acoustic (KRN); Reliability: Cronbach's alpha = .81. This test consists of 20 arithmetical problems of different complexity which are presented via headphones. The time available for solving an individual item is 30s. Answers are given by touching a numerical keypad presented on the screen.

Visual Perception Test (OWT); Reliability: Cronbach's alpha = .83. In this test the applicant is presented for quite a brief period of time (2 s) rather complex displays consisting of two dials surrounded by varying numbers of squares and triangles. Next, he as she is requested to type in the indicator values read out from both dials and alternatively either the number of squares or the number of triangles counted. This has to be accomplished by inputs on the touch-sensitive numerical keypad before a new item is displayed.

Unstable Tracking Test (UTT); Reliability: Retest = .87. In this manual control task a fixed target is centered on the screen. A cursor moves horizontally either to the left or to the right from the center of the screen. The applicants are instructed to keep the cursor over the target by means of a joystick. The system dynamics is first-order including a divergent element-lambda- rendering the tracking loop unstable in that the error induced by the applicant is magnified by the system. If the applicant loses control, the cursor will be reset to the center of the screen and tracking continues. This dynamics is derived from the critical tracking paradigm developed by Jex, McDonnell, and Phatak (1966), however, a constant subcritical lambda = 2 is used. Moreover, a system induced disturbance input (forcing functions) is introduced consisting of the sum of five sine waves taken from Jex and Allen (1970). Generally, disturbance inputs are not necessary for this type of tracking because the error induced by the applicant is sufficient to keep the task running. However, our experience has shown that the distribution properties and the reliability of the root mean square error are improved significantly by superimposing such a quasi-random disturbance. The retest reliability given earlier was derived from the correlation between the two 2-minute single trials of the Unstable Tracking Task completed before and after the Sternberg subtests. A Cronbach's alpha estimate across all 10 trials including the eight dual task trials (UTT plus Sternberg memory search, see below) yielded a reliability of .97. The correlation between the last two dual task trials was .90. This is higher than the differential stability estimates of the original critical tracking task after a much more extended practice reported by Bittner, Carter, Kennedy, Harbeson, and Krause (1986). The test is attractive because the lambda value and the bandwidth of the disturbance input provide good means to alter the difficulty of the task according to the ability level of the target population.

THE STERNBERG FACTORIAL BATTERY

The Sternberg Memory Search Tests. For this task, based on Sternberg's (1966) paradigm, a set of letters (consonants only)—the memory set—is presented to the applicants to memorize. Next, a 2-minute series of letters (probes) is presented one at a time. Applicants press the "yes" key (left mouse button) if the probe belongs to the memory set and the "no" key (right mouse button) if the probe does not belong to the memory set. "Yes" and "no" probes have equal probability. Applicants are instructed to respond as fast and as accurate as possible. The tests is self-paced and as soon as the applicant responds the screen is erased for 1s and a new probe presented.

The task difficulty was varied along four dimensions:

1. *Perceptual Modality:* probes were presented either visually or auditory.
2. *Memory Load:* corresponding to memory sets of five or seven letters.
3. *Probe Quality:* by using normal or degraded probes. In the visual modality probe quality was degraded by hiding a probe at different positions within a string of the four letters X, Q, W, T. These four letters never became targets in the whole subtests and precautions were taken that all five positions of the fifth letter, a target or nontarget probe, were equally probable. In the auditory subtests the memory set presentation was not changed, only the probes were digitalized letters of a male

speaker presented via headphone. Probe degradation was achieved by the dichotic stimulation technique. Thus, different probe series were given to the left and right side of the headphone. An indicator tone at the beginning and after blocks of 10 probes presented either to the left or to the right ear instructs the applicant to switch the ear he as she should attend to. Item generation with regard to the left/right composition of probes ensures that no target/target probe occurs but also no nontarget/non target probe occurs. Hence, each error is an intrusion error (i.e., either an erroneous acceptance of a target or an erroneous rejection of a nontarget coming in both cases from the nonrelevant ear).

4. *Task Load*: was varied by requiring the applicants to perform the Sternberg test concurrently with the Unstable Tracking Task with equal emphasis on both components of the dual-task. Sternberg probes were presented above the target area of the Unstable Tracking Task. Their vertical separation of about 2.5 degrees generally enables concurrent performance while keeping both tracking cursor and Sternberg probe within foveal vision.

The version of this test is in many aspects similar to the AGARD-STRES version (AGARD, 1989), which has been used extensively in a series of studies monitoring the influence of long-term exposure to environmental stress on human performance (see studies cited earlier). Complete factorial variation of the four dimensions resulted in 16 subtests. From each subtest separate scores (mean reaction times and percentage of errors) for yes- and no-responses were derived yielding a total of 64 individual scores, 32 reaction times plus 32 percentage of errors values.

In a first step, Lorenz and Goeters (2000) investigated to what extent the four task variables, radicals sensu Irvine et al. (1990), influence the difficulty of an item in terms of changes in response latency and accuracy. Along the logic of Sternberg's additive factor method (Sternberg, 1969) the observed effects of radicals including their pattern of interaction are open to interpretation in terms of cognitive functioning. Lorenz and Goeters (2000) investigated this by computing ANOVA models separately for visual and auditory subtests and for the tracking subtests based on the data of 396 applicants (356 males, 40 females). Two major results were obtained: (1) In the performance of the Sternberg task, Memory Load and Probe Quality, but not Task Load were strong radicals. The effect of Task Load was primarily reflected in the tracking component which deteriorated markedly from single to dual task operation. (2) Distinctive differences between modalities were found in the patterns of interaction effects involving Probe Quality in both the RT and the percentage of error data. It is suggested that the type of stimulus degradation used in both modalities most likely tap qualitively different aspects of selective attention. In the visual subtests stimulus degradation induced some sort of visual search, in the auditory subtests the dichotic technique of stimulus degradation requires ignoring information from the irrelevant ear. This irrelevant information has a high potential to interfere with internal rehearsal mechanisms.

It is important to mention that the randomization technique took enough precaution over the control of *radical* dimensions to ensure equal means and standard deviations in subsamples. This was proven by comparing the descriptives of two random seeds of the whole sample. Thus, the influence of differences in the specific memory sets used and/or differences in the sequences of probes automatically generated did not affect performance so that these characteristics can be regarded as *incidentals* sensu Irvine et al. (1990).

FACTORIAL ANALYSES

A series of principal component analyses (PCA) was performed on the new Phase-1 CBT battery. A PCA was performed on all aptitude tests excluding the 16 Sternberg subtests and the Unstable Tracking (2 single plus 8 levels of dual-task) which were analyzed separately.

Table 13.2 shows the four-factor solution for the aptitude tests obtained by using the Kaiser-Guttman criterion (eigenvalue > 1) and subsequent orthogonal varimax rotation. The statistics (eigenvalues, % variance, cumulative % variance) were taken from the rotation sums of squared loadings. The first factor accounting for 22% of the variance is best described as *Quantative Reasoning* (RQ according to Carroll, 1993, p. 213, N/R according to French et al., 1963) because of the salient loadings of the tests KRN and RAG. The fact that tests of more complex attention (KBT, OWT) or auditory memory (CLE) have additional loadings on that factor is not surprising and provides an indication of the link between mental arithmetic and working memory ability (Hitch, 1978). The second factor is a mixture of *spatial orientation* (SO according to Carroll, 1993, p. 308, or S according to French et al., 1963) because of the loadings from FPT and ROT, and *perceptual speed* (P according to Carroll, 1993, p. 308 and French et al., 1963) suggested by the loading of the KBT on this factor. The third factor is easily described as a factor of *Mechanical/Technical Comprehension/Knowledge (MK)* (Carroll, 1993, p. 525) because it is solely defined by the tests TVT and TQ. The fourth factor is Associative Memory (MA according to Carroll, 1993, p. 266 & French et al., 1963) marked by the test MEK with substantial loadings also from the other auditory memory test CLE.

Lorenz and Goeters (2000) further investigated the question as to how the task variables of the Sternberg subtests can be related to abilities in terms of an individual susceptibility to the respective task demand. Because in the total of 32 RTs or error percentages, respectively, each level of a given task variable is replicated 16 times, good conditions for the emergence of an ability factor related to the task demands are given. The emergence of perceptual factors, for example, could take the form of consistently higher intercorrelations within rather than across both modalities. A memory factor could be substantiated by

TABLE 13.2
Four-Factor Matrix Loadings (varimax rotated) of the CAT-Aptitude Test Battery[a]

Test	Factor 1 N/R	Factor 2 S/P	Factor 3 MK	Factor 4 MA	H^2
KRN	.86				.77
RAG	.72				.69
OWT	.58	.46			.58
FPT		.85			.77
ROT		.82			.74
KBT	.51	.60			.62
TVT			.89		.80
TQ			.82		.75
MEK				.89	.84
CLE	.52			.58	.66
Eigenvalue	2.20	2.08	1.69	1.24	
% variance	21.96	20.83	16.91	12.42	
Cumulative % variance	21.96	42.79	59.79	72.12	

[a]loadings < .40 omitted.

an intercorrelation pattern that contrasts low against high levels of memory load, a timesharing factor, and a selective attention factor by a respective pattern of intercorrelation. Table 13.3 illustrates this reasoning of a joint analysis of task- and ability-components. Thus, the task variables (radicals) tap a range of cognitive abilities critical for pilot tasks: (a) Abilities in visual and auditory perception related to probe modality, (b) short-term memory efficiency related to memory load varied by the size of the memory set, (c) timesharing ability related to task load (single vs. dual), and (d) selective attention related to probe quality. Factor analyses were performed to address this issue.

TABLE 13.3
Rationale of a Joint Task Components and Ability Components Analysis of the Sternberg Memory Search Task

Task Requirements	Ability Requirements
Task Variables (Radicals)	Abilities
• Modality	• Visual and Auditory Perception
• Memory Load	• Short-Term Memory
• Task Load	• Timesharing
• Probe Quality	• Selective Attention

A PCA (direct oblimin) on both sets of the Sternberg variables, the 32 average response times and the 16 false rejections converge to a quite similar three-factor pattern (see Lorenz & Goeters, 2000, for a more detailed presentation of results): Visual subtests demanding visual search and auditory subtests demanding dichotic listening clustered on separate factors. The other systematically varied task variables, that is memory load, task load, and response type did not establish a source of individual differences significant enough to show up as an ability factor. The correlations in the 10 x 10 matrix of tracking scores (2 single and 8 dual trials) ranged from .68 to .91. This is important to note as there was a strong learning progress from the first to the last tracking trial upon which task effects were superimposed. Apparently, this learning did not affect individual differences. Although not stationary, the score was differentially stable, which is also expressed in the high value of Cronbach's alpha mentioned earlier. This property makes this task a valuable tool for repeated measurements in environmental stress research according to criteria described by Bittner et al. (1986). The high degree of homogeneity is confirmed by the PCA. This revealed a single factor (eigenvalue 8.43) explaining 85% of the variance with score communalities ranging from .76 to .89.

The low success in the construct validation of timesharing ability is contrasted by findings that multiple task scenarios such as work sample tests, nevertheless, are good predictors of pilot performance (North & Gopher, 1976; Damos, 1993; Hörmann, 1998). Lorenz, Eißfeldt, and Pecena (1999) could demonstrate that performance in an auditory task to be performed at the applicant's own request and as a secondary task to a complex air traffic control primary task were among the best selection predictors against criteria of late ATC field training soon before the students became fully qualified controllers. The efficient accomplishment of this task was much more a result of proper planning, coordinating, and priority managing strategies which cannot be invoked by simple dual tasks. Therefore, Lorenz and Goeters (2000) conclude that other approaches to assess timesharing efficiency has to be developed allowing more strategical space with regard to priority and time management.

Whereas no support for the existence of a timesharing factor could be found the Sternberg data provide evidence for distinct abilities in the domain of visual and auditory attention. In a study that also aimed and failed at the identification of timesharing ability reported by Lansman, Poltrock, and Hunt (1983), the emergence of a perceptual modality factor was also found in a set of visual and auditory detection tasks. Moreover, in the Sternberg subtests examined here abilities were formed in the perception of degraded stimuli in both modalities. This suggests a link between separate perceptual abilities and the encoding stage of the Sternberg memory-scanning model (Sternberg, 1975). One factor is linked to visual search the other to dichotic listening. As for the definition of a selective attention ability in the domain of auditory perception, evidence has accumulated that the Dichotic Listening Task (DLT) originally developed by Gopher and Kahneman (1971) is predictive against criteria of pilot training success (Gopher, 1982; Gopher & Kahneman, 1971) and air traffic controllers (Boer, Harsveld, & Hermans, 1997). Boer and Ruzius (1985) found rather low correlations between the classical dichotic listening task of Gopher and Kahneman (1971) and the rapid serial visual presentation task (RSVP) adopted from Sperling and Reeves (1980), which in some sense can be regarded as a visual analogue of dichotic listening. This task required subjects to detect targets in either the left or the right of two streams of letters presented simultaneously on a screen. Similar to the DLT, indicators instructed the subjects when to switch over to the stream that was relevant to attend to. Correlations varied between .21 and .41. Because they do not range much beyond correlations between any pair of information-processing tasks, the authors question whether RSVP measures selective attention. The findings of Lorenz and Goeters (2000) support the notion that the lack of substantial correlations resulted from different underlying abilities.

Results of the construct validation study of the Sternberg subtests had initiated the development of a new complex task scenario, the Multiple Task Coordination test (MTC), involving the simultaneous performance of manual tracking, display monitoring for specified events (critical system state or system malfunction), and auditory monitoring of dichotically presented call-signs for specified targets. Thus, the composition of this task draws on the dimensions of individual differences found in the Sternberg study and integrates these dimensions into a coherent complex scenario. This development is an attempt to achieve the predictive validity of complex work-sample tests, however, with a more sound construct validity.

FUTURE DIRECTIONS

Item-generation principles have proven to work well with comparatively simple item concepts as being used in Phase-1 ab-initio pilot aptitude testing in order to control for item difficulty. Moreover, theoretical knowledge about radicals that influence test performance provide a better understanding of underlying abilities. Modality-specific ability factors in the domain of selective attention could be described that are most likely to be identified with the encoding stage of Sternberg's model (Sternberg, 1966). However, adequate procedures to derive individual stage-related test scores, do not exist. As Irvine (chap. 1, this volume) notes, this is a crucial deficiency of latency-derived models, which he refers to as L-models. These are experimentally validated structure models, like that of Sternberg's memory-scanning model (Sternberg, 1966), which are based on reaction times. In the future, attempts of a joint task component (radical) and ability component analysis should be extended to more complex simulator-like tasks, which have proven a better predictive power, but often suffer from little knowledge regarding their construct validity. This is the basic idea of the current development of a complex multiple task scenario to supplement the Phase-1 CAT battery for pilot applicants. The work of Ackerman (1988, 1992) has demonstrated the benefits of a joint task component and ability component analysis in pinpointing the ability determinants of individual differences in complex skill aquisition. Thus, from an applied perspective, it seems promising that this kind of aptitude research will contribute significantly to the development of better selection instruments.

REFERENCES

Ackerman, P. L. (1988). Determinant of individual differences during skill acquisition: Cognitive abilities and information processing. *Journal of Experimental Psychology: General, 117*, 288–318.

Ackerman, P. L. (1992). Predicting individual differences in complex skill acquisition: Dynamics of ability determinants. *Journal of Applied Psychology, 77*, 598–614.

Advisory Group for Aerospace Research and Development, Aerospace Medical Panel Working Group 12. (1989). *Human performance assessment methods (AGARDograph 308)*. Neuilly-sur-Seine, France: Author.

Beringer, J. (1993). Entwurf einer Anwendersprache zur Steuerung psychologischer Reaktionszeitexperimente [Concept of a code generating language for the development of psychological reaction time experiments]. In *Europäische Hochschulschriften, Reihe 41, Informatik (Vol. 8)*. Frankfurt a.M.: Lang.

Bittner, A. C., Carter, R. C., Kennedy, R. S., Harbeson, M. M., & Krause, M. (1986). Performance evaluation tests for environmental research (PETER): Evaluation of 114 measures. *Perceptual and Motor Skills, 63*, 683–708.

Boer, L. C., Harsveld, M., & Hermans, P. H. (1997). The selective-listening task as a test for pilots and air traffic controllers. *Military Psychology, 9*, 137–149.

Boer, L. C., & Ruzius, M. H. B. (1985). *Auditory versus visual selective-attention tasks* (Tech. Rep. No. IZF 1985-19). Soesterberg: TNO-Institute for Perception.

Carroll, J. B. (1993). *Human cognitive abilities: A survey of factor analytic studies*. New York: Cambridge University Press.

Damos, D. L. (1993). Using meta-analysis to compare the predictive validity of single- and multiple-task measures to flight performance. *Human Factors, 35*, 615–628.

Eißfeldt, H. (1998). The selection of air traffic controllers. In K. M. Goeters (Ed.), *Aviation psychology: A science and a profession* (pp. 73–80). Aldershot: Ashgate.

Eißfeldt, H., & Maschke, P. (1991). *Bewährungskontrolle eines psychologischen Auswahlverfahrens für den Flugverkehrskontroldienst anhand von Kriterien der Berufsausbildung* [Study on the predictive validity of a psychological selection procedure for air traffic controllers based on training criteria]. DLR-FB 91-11 (in German, English abstract). Cologne: DLR.

Fleishman, E. A. (1992). *Fleishman Job Analysis Survey. Rating Scale booklet*. Palo Alto: Consulting Psychologists Press.

French, J. W., Ekstrom, R. B., & Price, L. A. (1963). *Manual for kit of reference tests for cognitive factors*. Princeton, NJ: Educational Testing Service.

Goeters, K. M. (1998). General standards of selection: Validity and utility analysis. In K. M. Goeters (Ed.), *Aviation psychology: A science and a profession* (pp. 103–112). Aldershot: Ashgate.

Goeters, K. M., Hörmann, H. J., & Maschke, P. (1989). The DLR test system for ab-initio pilot selection. *Proceedings of the Fifth International Symposium on Aviation Psychology* (pp. 663–668). Columbus, OH: OSU.

Goeters, K. M., Maschke, P., & Klamm, A. (1998). An extended job analysis technique, the professional demands of airline pilots and implications for selection. *Proceedings of the 23rd Conference of the European Association for Aviation Psychology.* Vienna.

Goeters, K. M., & Rathje, H. (1992). *Computer-generierte Parallel-Tests für die Fähigkeitsmessung in der Eignungsauswahl von operationellem Luftfahrtpersonal* [Computer-generated parallel tests for aptitude measurements in the selection of aviation operators]. DLR-FB 92-29 (in German, English abstract). Cologne: DLR.

Gopher, D. (1982). A selective attention task as a predictor of success in flight training. *Human Factors, 24,* 173–183.

Gopher, D., & Kahneman, D. (1971). Individual differences in attention and the prediction of flight criteria. *Perceptual and Motor Skills, 33,* 1335–1342.

Hitch, G. J. (1978). The role of short-term memory in mental arithmetic. *Cognitive Psychology, 10,* 302–323.

Hörmann, H. J. (1998). Selection: Basic concepts. In K. M. Goeters (Ed.), *Aviation psychology: A science and a profession* (pp. 46–54). Aldershot: Ashgate.

Irvine, S. H., Dann, P. L., & Anderson, J. D. (1990). Towards a theory of algorithm-determined cognitive test construction. *British Journal of Psychology, 81,* 173–195.

JAA-Joint Aviation Authorities (1996). Joint aviation requirements—flight crew licensing part 3 (Medical): Aviation psychology. *Manual of Civil Aviation Medicine,* 170–179.

Jex, H. R., & Allen, R. W. (1970). Research on a new human dynamic response test battery. *Proceedings of the Sixth Annual Conference on Manual Control,* 743–777. Wright-Patterson AFB.

Jex, H. R., McDonnell, J. D., & Phatak, A. V. (1966). A "critical" tracking task for manual control research. *IEEE Transactions on Human Factors in Electronics, 7,* 138–144.

Lansman, M., Poltrock, S. E., & Hunt, E. (1983). Individual differences in the ability to focus and divide attention. *Intelligence, 7,* 299–312.

Lorenz, B. (1994). *Cognitive and psychomotor performance of divers under simulated deep-sea conditions: Methodology and results of human performance monitoring based on single-case analyses.* DLR-FB 94-07 (in German, English abstract). Cologne: DLR

Lorenz, B., & Goeters, K. M. (2000). *Stage and ability structure of Sternberg's Memory Search Test under varied task conditions.* DLR-FB 2000-13, Cologne: DLR

Lorenz, B., Lorenz, J., & Manzey, D. (1996). Performance and brain electrical activity during prolonged confinement. In S. L. Bonting (Ed.), *Advances in space biology and medicine* (Vol. 5, pp. 157–183). Greenwich, CT: JAI.

Lorenz, B., Eißfeldt, H., & Pecena, Y. (1999). *Selection of ab-initio air traffic control applicants for EUROCONTROL: Validation of the DLR - battery against training effectiveness.* DLR-FB 99-05. Cologne: DLR

Lorenz, B., Rathje, H., Goeters, K. M., Finell, G., & Lamschus, D. (1996). *Empirical comparison of full-scale selection methods (DLR) and computer assisted testing (HAL).* DLR-FB 96-02. Cologne: DLR

Lorenz, B., Wenzel, J., Lorenz, J., & Heineke, M. (1993) Longitudinal performance observations in 4 divers during a series of 5 experimental dives in 3.5 years. In R. E. Reinertsen, A. O. Brubakk, & G. Bolstad (Eds.), *Proceedings of the XIX Annual Meeting of the European Undersea Biomedical Society,* (pp. 308–320), Sintef Unimed, Trondheim.

Manzey, D., Lorenz, B., Schiewe, A., Finell, G., & Thiele, G. (1993). Behavioral aspects of human adaptation to space: Analyses of cognitive and psychomotor performance in space during an 8-day space mission. *Clinical Investigator, 71,* 725–731.

Manzey, D., Lorenz, B., Schiewe, A., Finell, G., & Thiele, G. (1995). Dual-task performance in space: Results from a single-case study during a short-term space mission. *Human Factors, 37,* 667–681.

Manzey, D., & Lorenz, B. (1998a). Effects of chronically elevated CO_2 on mental performance during 26 days of confinement. *Aviation, Space, and Environmental Medicine, 69*, 506–514.

Manzey, D., & Lorenz, B. (1998b). Mental performance during short-term and long-term spaceflight. *Brain Research Reviews, 28*, 215–221.

Manzey, D., Lorenz, B., & Polyakov, V. V. (1998). Mental performance in extreme environments: Results from a performance monitoring study during a 438-day space mission. *Ergonomics, 41*, 537–559.

Maschke, P., & Hörmann, H. J. (1988). Zur Bewährung psychologischer Auswahlverfahren für operationelle Berufe in der Luft- und Raumfahrt. *Zeitschrift für Flugwissenschaften und Weltraumforschung, 12*, 181–186.

Maschke, P., & Hörmann, H. J. (1989). *Vorhersage der Berufsbewährung bei lizensierten Flugzeugführern: Die Validität von fliegerischer Vorerfahrung im Vergleich zu standardisierten psychologischen Eignungstests* [Prediction of professional success of licensed pilots: Validation of flight experience in comparison to standardized psychological aptitude tests. DLR-FB 89-53 (in German, English abstract). Cologne: DLR

North, R. A., & Gopher, D. (1976). Measures of attention as predictors of flight performance. *Human Factors, 18*, 1–14.

Ortmüller, S. (1990). Konstruktion eines dreidimensionalen Raumvorstellungstest [Construction of a three-dimensional spatial orientation test]. *Unveröffentlichte Diplomarbeit am Fachbereich Psychologie der Universität Hamburg* (unpublished diploma thesis).

Sperling, G., & Reeves, A. (1980). Measuring the reaction time of a shift of visual attention. In R. S. Nickerson (Ed.), *Attention and Performance VIII* (pp. 347–360). Hillsdale, NJ: Lawrence Erlbaum Associates.

Sternberg, S. (1966). High speed scanning in human memory. *Science, 153*, 652–654.

Sternberg, S. (1969). The discovery of processing stages: Extensions of Donder's method. *Acta Psychologica, 30*, 276–315.

Sternberg, S. (1975). Memory scanning: New findings and current controversies. *Quarterly Journal of Experimental Psychology, 27*, 1–32.

14

Item Generation and Beyond: Applications of Schema Theory to Mathematics Assessment

Mark K. Singley
IBM T. J. Watson Research Center

Randy E. Bennett
Educational Testing Service

In this chapter, we attempt to show how schema theory can be applied to the automatic generation of items, the scoring of more complex test responses, and to intelligent tutoring. When attempting to develop algorithms for automatic item generation in mathematics, one necessarily learns a lot about the underlying structure of the problems. This knowledge of problem structure is indispensable to making progress in item generation, but it may also be useful for other applications. In particular, it may be useful for either assigning partial credit scores or offering remediation in instructional settings. We report here on a particular theory of problem structure, schema theory. Schema theory is applied to the automatic generation and variation of items, the analysis of multiple-line solutions, and the delivery of instruction.

The key to our analysis is the basic assertion that math problems can be characterized (and categorized) in terms of the underlying set of equations that relate the entities of the problem to one another. According to this analysis, problems that superficially appear quite distinct may in fact be instances of the same underlying problem structure, or *schema*. An interesting property of schemas is that, for any particular problem type, not all of the underlying primitive equations may be required for solution. This is what gives the schemas psychological content and differentiates them from purely structural descriptions of problems.

Given a schematic description, a wide spectrum of item generation and variation possibilities exists, ranging from the deep to the superficial. We describe a tool we have built that is currently being used at ETS, the Math

Test Creation Assistant, that can be used for schema-based item generation and variation. Using the system involves defining item models that include the schema equations and variables as well as other linguistic and numeric constraints. We also describe two new analytical engines, the Schema Prover and the Schema Compiler, that take this same definition of a problem schema and apply it to the analysis of multiline examinee responses.

SCHEMA THEORY AS A CONCEPTUAL AND PRACTICAL BASIS

In mathematics, there is a large class of problems that can be construed as involving linear systems of equations. Many standard algebra word problems fall into this category. For example, here is an algebra word problem that appeared on a recent test in multiple-choice format:

> *Excluding rest stops, it took Juanita a total of 10 hours to hike from the base of a mountain to the top and back down again by the same path. If while hiking she averaged 2 kilometers per hour going up and 3 kilometers per hour coming down, how many kilometers was it from the base to the top of the mountain?*

The key to our use of schema theory is the assertion that word problems can be characterized (and categorized) in terms of the underlying set of equations that relate the entities of the problem to one another. According to this analysis, problems that superficially appear quite distinct may in fact be instances of the same underlying problem structure, or *schema* (Marshall, 1995; Mayer, 1981). The *Juanita* problem is an instance of the *round-trip* schema. The round-trip schema involves the following equations:

(1) $d_t = d_u + d_d$
(2) $t_t = t_u + t_d$
(3) $d_u = r_u * t_u$
(4) $d_d = r_d * t_d$
(5) $d_t = r_t * t_t$
(6) $d_u = d_d$

This set of variables and primitive equations defines an entire class of problems. Given a set of variables and equations such as this, a particular problem within the class is represented as a set of variable assignments and a goal. Table 14.1 defines the schema variables and gives their values in the context of the *Juanita* problem. Table 14.2 organizes the schema equations into a table. One of the relationships in the table, $r_u + r_d = r_t$, does not hold. However, the other relationships are correct.

TABLE 14.1
Variables, Their Meanings, and Their Values

Variable	Meaning	Value
d_u	distance up	x (goal)
d_d	distance down	unknown
d_t	distance total	unknown
t_u	time up	unknown
t_d	time down	unknown
t_t	time total	10 h
r_u	rate up	2 km/h
r_d	rate down	3 km/h
r_t	rate total	unknown

TABLE 14.2
Round-trip Schema Equation Table

		part	+	part	=	whole
distance	=	d_u		d_d		d_t
rate	*	r_u		r_d		r_t
time		t_u		t_d		t_t

An interesting property of schemas is that, for any example of a particular problem type, not all of the underlying primitive equations may be needed, or indeed used, to find the right answer. This is what gives the schemas psychological content. In a purely structural description, only the equations required for solution are included. However, in a schematic description, the entire set of relationships that model the situation are included. In essence, the schema position states that certain sets of relationships tend to co-occur in the world and therefore tend to cohere in a person's head. When someone is confronted with such a situation (e.g., when someone is asked to solve an algebra word problem), the entire set of relationships is activated and brought to bear to try to understand the situation. One large part of the problem is determining which subset of the equations contained in the schema is actually relevant for solving the current problem (Singley, 1995).

For example, in the sample problem (p. 362), equations (2), (3), (4), and (6) are required, but equations (1) and (5) are not. However, this is impossible to determine a *priori*. To solve the problem, the relevant equations first must be identified, then mapped directly on to the given information, and finally composed together to create an equation that contains only the goal variable:

$$\frac{d}{2} + \frac{d}{3} = 10 \qquad \text{where } d = d_u \text{ or } d_d$$

Using algebra, one can determine from this equation that $d = 12$, and the problem is solved.

In summary, the schematic account of algebra word problem solving involves the following steps:

- activation (generation or retrieval) of the appropriate schema based on comprehension of the problem statement,
- identification of the relevant equations from that schema for the current problem,
- choosing those equations that match the information given in any single problem
- composition of relevant equations into a solvable equation,
- algebraic solution.

We do not wish to imply that examinees actually go through these steps in the exact order or granularity just shown. Particular problem-solving strategies may combine and/or interleave the above solution in a variety of ways.

In the remainder of the chapter, we report our efforts to apply this basic analysis to (1) generate items automatically and/or semiautomatically, (2) make predictions concerning item difficulty, (3) support analysis of multiple-line responses and partial-credit scoring, and (4) build instructional applications that can provide immediate feedback and remediation for emerging problem solutions.

TOOLS FOR AUTOMATIC ITEM GENERATION

As mentioned earlier, the cornerstone underlying our thinking with respect to item generation is the notion of a problem schema, a set of variables and constraints that defines a problem's deep structure. Given this notion of a schema, a wide spectrum of item-generation possibilities exists, ranging from the deep to the superficial:

- Given a set of primitive equations (e.g., distance = rate * time, part + part = whole), generate a set of interesting problem schemas. These schemas could be arranged into a taxonomy of sorts, and could serve as a repository of ideas for test developers.
- Given a particular schema (e.g., the round-trip schema defined earlier), generate interesting structural elaborations. This involves adding one or more constraints. For example, in the round-trip schema, one could add some

relationship between the rate for the first leg and the rate for the second, (e.g., the rate uphill is half the rate downhill).

- Given a particular schema, generate all the possible problem structures. A problem structure is defined as a particular configuration of given and goal variables.

- Given a problem structure, generate and/or select a problem context. Thus, the round-trip schema could be presented in a hiking context, a boating context, and so forth.

- Given a context, vary the noun referents for problem variables and generate different sets of values for given variables. For example, "Juanita" becomes "Tom" and the total time changes from 10 to 20 hours.

- Given a context, noun referents and variable values, generate a natural language cover story.

We envision embodying the above functionality in an integrated system that offers more to the test developer than just item-generation capabilities. Ideally, such a system should offer the following types of functionality:

1. *Item Creation, Classification, and Tracking.* These are basic word processing and database functions that form the backbone of functionality for the system. Users should be able to type in items, edit them, import graphics, and so forth. Items that are created with the system should be compatible with test delivery software. Item management features should allow the test developer to track the location and status of an item throughout its life cycle. In addition, items would be arranged in a searchable and browsable library in terms of whatever conceptual frameworks are used in the automatic generation and/or analysis of items. The text/graphics of these library items should be directly accessible by the item creation tools; that is, the user should be able to edit the text of a library item to create a new item.

2. *Item Analysis.* The system should be able to perform analyses of items that attempt to predict level of difficulty in a principled way. The analyses should be based on psychological theory that relates features of the items to item statistics (e.g., Enright, Morley, & Sheehan, 1999; Sebrechts, Enright, Bennett, & Martin, 1996; Sheehan & Mislevy, 1994; Tatsuoka, Birenbaum, Lewis, & Sheehan, 1993). Depending upon the set of features that need to be extracted, the analysis may proceed completely automatically or may require some intervention. To the extent that well-defined cognitive structures can form the basis of item generation, fairly deep automatic analyses should be possible.

We and our colleagues have built such an item creation tool, called the Mathematics Test Creation Assistant (TCA), that is our initial attempt at fleshing out the vision described earlier in a production environment.

The TCA contains an editor and facilities for model browsing, model creation, and variant generation. The editor is Microsoft Word. In the TCA, a model represents a schematized description of a class of questions from which draft test items are automatically generated for the test developer to review and revise. To begin, the developer selects an existing model or creates a new one either from an existing test item or anew. Existing models can be varied by the developer to form a model "family" (i.e., that a collection of models that shares variables, constraints, and invariant text).

Within a family, models can be hierarchically organized by their underlying schematic structures. The hierarchy is defined in terms of shared schema equations, such that a child schema inherits all the equations of its parent schema, and perhaps supplies one or two more. Parent–child relationships between schemas are designated in the interface by indentation in the list of models, as is done in many displays of directory–subdirectory structures for computer file systems.

Figure 14.1 shows the TCA's Model Workshop, where the test developer creates and edits item models. These models are created within Microsoft Word templates designed around particular item types. Currently the TCA supports three such templates: standard multiple choice, quantitative comparison (used on the Graduate Record Examination [GRE] General Test and the SAT I), and data sufficiency (a Graduate Management Admission Test [GMAT] item type). The test developer can very easily use the standard multiple-choice template to create constructed-response item models simply by not filling in the distractor fields. These constructed-response models may be as lengthy as the developer desires because the stem field is of variable length. Figures, charts, tables, pictures, audio, and video—indeed, any Microsoft Word object—can be incorporated.

Creating an item model from an existing item is basically a two-step process: First, the user replaces literal strings of text and/or numbers in the original stem and options with variables. Second, the user defines constraints that tell the system something about how the variables should be instantiated, or given values. A critical feature of the system is that these constraints are defined declaratively: The user simply states the constraints and it is the system's responsibility to figure out how to solve them simultaneously. Alternatively, the user could have been required to write a procedural program that would explicitly derive the values of all variables and would propagate the constraints between variables. In our judgment, this would have rendered the system unusable by nonprogrammers.

The TCA screen in Figure 14.1 shows the results of this process for a word problem. In the top left section of the screen is the variablized item stem, with the variables shown in bold. All remaining elements are literals that remain constant across variants. Those variables with numeric extensions (e.g., $SVar.1$) are elements of $n$tuples; that is, string variables whose values change in synchrony with other members of the $n$tuple,

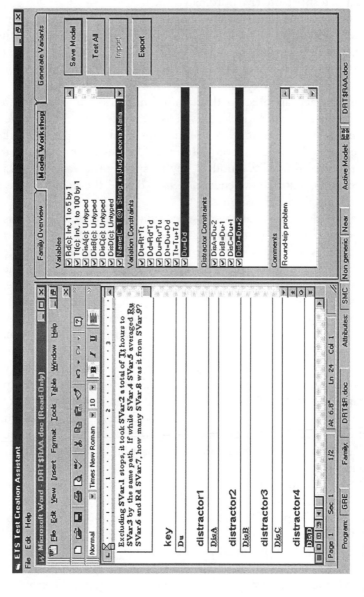

FIG. 14.1. The TCA's Model Workshop.

thereby allowing the situational context to be changed from one variant to the next in a substantively coordinated way.

In the right-hand pane, are the variable definitions, variation constraints, and the distractor constraints. Variables are defined by indicating their type (string, real, integer, untyped) and specifying the values they can take on. For string variables, the test developer may either type in a list of values or import them from library files built specifically to support the instantiation of nonnumeric variables. In the case of numeric variables, the user can define a range for the variable, as well as step size (e.g., the variable may be specified as ranging from 1 to 100 in steps of 5). By specifying the range and step size, the user can control critical features of the variants that may affect problem difficulty. Another way to specify the values for a numeric variable is by writing new equations that derive the value of the current variable from the values of others.

The variation-constraints window contains the schema equations for the round-trip problem. The distractor-constraints window shows how each of the distractors is computed, in this case by adding or subtracting a constant from the key, Du, the distance for the first leg of the trip. Thus, the system automatically defines as constraints the equations that characterize the item's schema. The variables in the schema equations automatically become variables that can be referenced in the model, and any values supplied by the system for these variables will necessarily satisfy the schema equations.

One important feature of the system is that it is quite easy to modify the models themselves and thus greatly increase the range of variation associated with a particular parent item. In our current example, by switching information between the stem and the options, it would be quite easy to create a new model that would ask the examinee to determine the return rate given the distance from the starting point to the midpoint of the trip. This amounts to changing the configuration of givens and goals across problems.

At the bottom of the screen, general information about the model is given. This model is a member of the DRT family, which is headed by the simple (or one-legged) DRT schema. The current round-trip-schema model is a child of the two-legged DRT schema, which in turn is a child of the simple DRT schema. In each case, more equations are added as one moves down the hierarchy. The simple DRT schema has only the first equation shown for the round-trip schema, and the two-legged DRT schema has the first five but not the sixth. The general information also indicates that the model is associated (for purposes of this example) with the GRE Program, is standard multiple choice (SMC), nongeneric (a memorability classification), and of a type that will produce "near" variants, meaning ones that differ only in surface features.

When developers believe the model is ready for generating variants, they can test the model to make sure that it is sufficiently constrained. To aid in model debugging, variables, variation constraints, and distractor constraints can be tested simultaneously, as classes, or individually. When the model tests successfully, the system is prepared to generate variants.

Figure 14.2 gives a variant produced by this item model. As shown, the values of all variables are consistent with the constraints specified in the model. This variant can, of course, be edited. The developer may wish to change the word "canoe" to motor boat so as to make the item more realistic or polish the text in other ways.

In Figure 14.3 is a preliminary TCA tool that allows the test developer to estimate item difficulty. This tool incorporates initial models for both the GRE and the GMAT. All model variables are entered by the test developer. The GRE model includes the domain (arithmetic, algebra, geometry), whether the item is real or pure, the type of computation required, cognitive demand (procedural, conceptual, higher order), and whether certain concepts are involved (e.g., probability, percent of a percent, percent change, linear equality). The variant pictured in Figure 14.3 was coded as an algebra real, requiring integer-level computation and conceptual-level cognitive demand. The model predicts it to be relatively easy, with an IRT b in the neighborhood of -0.2. Work is continuing to refine these models of difficulty for quantitative items (Enright et al., 1999).

As noted earlier, the Test Creation Assistant is a production tool that test developers use to generate operational items for the quantitative sections of the GRE General Test and Graduate Management Admission Test. To make this possible, the TCA has been connected to the ETS Test Creation System, which banks items centrally, routes them among test developers for review, lets production artists refine their layout, and then prepares them for operational delivery.

Prospects for Automatic Item Analysis

As mentioned earlier, currently all item features in the Math TCA are hand-coded by item authors. But if items are classified according to their schema types, we seem to be in quite a good position to do automatic item analysis. Having this kind of handle on the deep structure of a problem may provide us with a host of important features that can be derived automatically and that may help in estimating difficulty. We have just begun to think about the implications of schema-based item authoring for automatic analysis, but here are some preliminary thoughts:

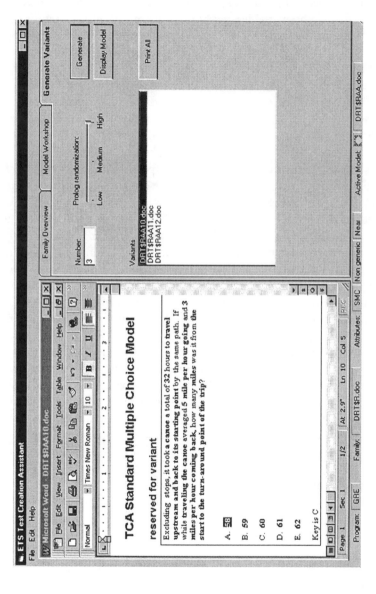

FIG. 14.2. A variant generated from the item model.

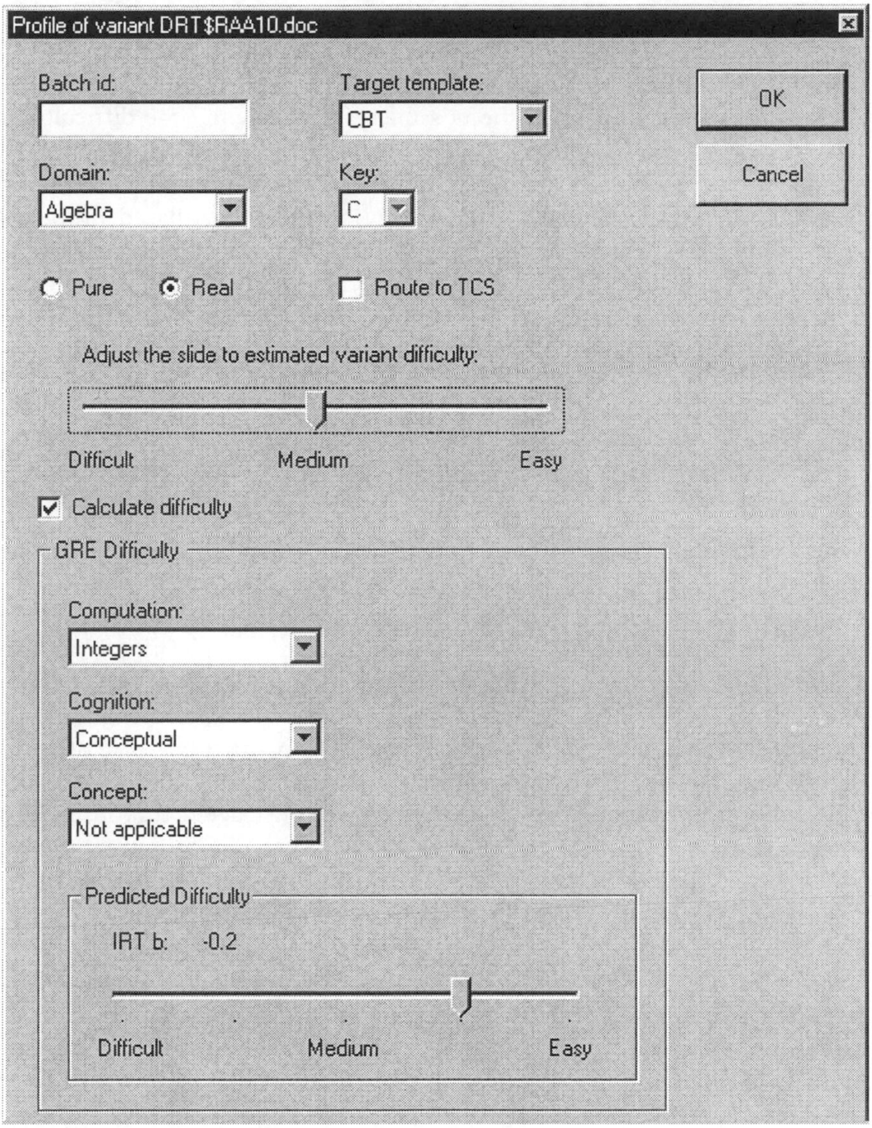

FIG. 14.3. The GRE-quantitative item-difficulty model.

First, the schematic category from which an item is drawn may itself be a predictor of item difficulty (Marshall, 1995). So, for example, round-trip problems may on average be more difficult than two-legged DRT problems. One could imagine studying this at the rather molar level of the schemas themselves, or being more analytical and trying to predict the difficulty of individual schemas from their constituent equations. Using the latter approach, the round-trip and two-legged DRT schemas should operate very similarly because they share so many constituent equations.

Second, we might explore the possibility of predicting the difficulty of items based on the complexity of their search spaces. Indeed, the Schema Compiler described later in the chapter essentially provides us with a fledgling cognitive model that can actually solve schema-based problems and characterize the complexity of the solution process. The search spaces derived by the Schema Compiler are the product of an exquisite interaction between the problem representation (the schema) and the problem-solving strategy (means–ends analysis). This interaction is such that two problems that involve the exact same set of four equations (i.e., have the same structural description) may have dramatically different search spaces.

BEYOND ITEM GENERATION

When attempting to develop automatic item-generation algorithms, one necessarily learns a lot about the underlying structure of the problems. This knowledge of problem structure is indispensable to making progress in generation, but it may also be useful for other applications. In the remainder of this chapter, we report on our attempts to apply the linchpin of our automatic item-generation efforts, schema theory, to the analysis of multiple-line solutions and the delivery of instruction. We try to demonstrate that we have in schema theory a general framework for integrating test creation, automatic analysis of constructed responses, and test preparation.

ANALYSIS OF MULTIPLE-LINE RESPONSES

Being able to track and score multiple-line constructed responses is important from two perspectives. First, it provides a basis on which to assign partial credit. Presumably, if an examinee spends a significant amount of time solving a complex problem, one would like to make finer discriminations than simply whether the answer is completely right or wrong. The test may be throwing away information that took valuable time to collect if a complex response is only summarized as a single "bit." Second, it offers information about the individual steps or the path the examinee took toward solution. Whereas information about precisely how the examinee solves problems may not strictly be needed for admissions testing, it should be valuable for self-assessment, particularly when supplemented with error and other qualitative process information.

We have shown earlier a sample solution for the Juanita problem, an example of what we call the round-trip schema. Unfortunately from the standpoint of analysis, there are many other ways than the one shown for an examinee to arrive at an answer to this problem. Furthermore, there are many ways in which an examinee might evidence some level of partial understanding in an errorful solution. For example, an examinee might show the following work when solving the *Juanita* problem:

$$t_u + t_d = t_t$$
$$t_t = 10$$
$$2d + 3d = 10$$
$$d = 2$$

This solution is incorrect, but much of the work shown is valid and it therefore may be deserving of partial credit. How do we systematically analyze such responses?

Of course, there are problems of mathematical paraphrase ($p = 3.1d$ should be regarded as equivalent to $d = p/3.1$) and numerical imprecision (should 3.1 be regarded as equivalent to 3.14?). But in addition to these problems, there are many others.

- Many different strategies for solving a problem exist; all valid strategies must be accommodated in the analysis.
- Substeps may be combined; the examinee is free to determine the granularity of each step.
- Substeps may be skipped; certain calculations or symbolic transformations might be done in the examinee's head.
- Substeps may be inconsistent; one step may directly contradict another.
- Substeps may be partially correct; a single step may be composed of correct and incorrect elements.
- The solution trace may make use of multiple symbol systems (e.g. figures, tables, mathematical symbols, natural language).

For the purposes of the present work, we have assumed that the examinee's response will be composed entirely of syntactically correct expressions or equations involving numbers and mathematical symbols, and all the variables that appear in the solution must be defined in terms of their problem referents. (Such constraints could conceivably be enforced at the user interface.) We have chosen to defer the analysis of supporting figures and tables for now.

The Schema Prover

Given these assumptions about the kind of input we receive from examinees, we apply techniques from *constraint logic programing* to analyze the examinee's response. Constraint logic programing is an extension to logic programing (e.g., Prolog) that allows for the declarative representation of a quantitative problem as a set of linear constraints. Once represented in this way, the answer to the problem can be easily *proven* by propagating the constraints. If the problem is underdetermined (i.e., there are an insufficient number of constraints to uniquely determine the solution), the system can derive the most constrained functional relationship between the goal variable and other variables in the problem. We are using constraint logic programing, not to solve problems directly, but rather to determine the relationship between a canonical representation of the constraints of the problem (the schematic description) and an examinee's response. For the current project, we built a system called the Schema Prover that attempts to derive the examinee's response from the schematic description as a kind of *proof.*

As outlined earlier, we first develop a structural, schematic description of the problem we are analyzing. This description is composed of a set of primitive equations, a set of given variables, and a goal variable. With this problem description in hand, we do a two-pass analysis of the response.

Correctness. We first determine whether the response is correct, that is, whether what is presented in the response is consistent with the problem description. To do this, we try to determine whether the response can be derived from the problem description. We frame the problem in terms of a logical proof: Given the problem description, is it possible to *prove* the response? If it is, we at least know that the equations and values of variables presented in the response are consistent with the problem description. However, we still do not know whether the examinee has represented *all* of the problem constraints in the response and has derived the final answer.

If we determine that the examinee's response is *not* correct, we then systematically vary the constraints in the problem description and try again to prove the correctness of the response. In other words, we try alternative sets of premises (alternative problem descriptions) and see whether any of these sets can prove the conclusion (the response). For example, we may propose a different problem description that replaces all primitive constraints of the type $d = rt$ (equations 3, 4, and 5) with the errorful variant $t = rd$. If, after degrading the problem description in this way, we are successful in proving the response, we have a very specific account of the error in the response: We know which constraint has been misrepresented and in what way. (It turns out that in the sample response shown above, two errors of this type are present in the third line.)

Completeness. Once the analysis for correctness is finished, we must analyze the response for completeness. To determine whether the response is complete, we simply reverse the premises and conclusions of our earlier proof: Given the examinee's response, is it possible to *prove* the problem description? If it is, then we know that at some level all of the relevant constraints are represented in the response, and the response is complete. If it is not, we attempt to determine what is missing in the response. We do this through a procedure very similar to the one outlined above for correctness: We systematically supplement the response with constraints from the problem description and attempt to determine the minimal set of constraints from the problem description that, when added to the response, make it possible to solve the problem. In this way, we can once again pinpoint precisely which constraints are missing from the examinee's response. For example, consider the following correct yet incomplete response to the Juanita problem:

$$d_u = 2t_u$$
$$d_d = 3t_d$$
$$2t_u = 3t_d$$

All of the work shown is correct, but the examinee has failed to provide all of the constraints necessary to uniquely determine the value of d_u or d_d By systematically supplementing this response with constraints drawn from the problem description, we can determine that, with the addition of the constraints $t_t = t_u + t_d$ (equation 2 above) and $t_t = 10$, the problem is solvable. Thus, once again we have a precise description of what is present and what is missing in the response.

In sum, our approach involves representing a particular problem as a set of schematic constraints, and then determining which (if any) of those constraints is violated and/or absent in the response. By reducing a particular response to the set of quantitative constraints it represents, the analysis bypasses many of the problems outlined earlier concerning variations in the surface forms of responses: multiple strategies, skipped steps, composed steps, and partially correct steps. According to this approach, two responses are equivalent if they can be reduced to the same set of primitive constraints.

Such an approach lends itself well to the implementation of partial-credit scoring rubrics. Subscores can be associated with each constraint in the problem description. The presence or absence of the constraint in the response can either increment a base score or decrement a total score for the problem, respectively. Also, subscores can be associated with common errors (i.e., common degradations of the problem description). In addition, such rubrics need not be created for each individual problem; they can be created once for an entire class of problems if they are done at the level of the problem schema.

INSTRUCTIONAL APPLICATIONS

The constraint logic programing system described earlier for analyzing multiple-line responses is optimized for a certain kind of scoring task: the assignment of a partial-credit score on the basis of an analysis of an entire response. This optimization resulted in an analytical engine that is less than optimal for instructional applications, however, for the following reasons:

1. The constraint-logic analysis is holistic in that responses are characterized rather abstractly in terms of the presence or absence of correct and buggy schema equations in the entire response. Analyses of individual lines of the response are not performed, and the internal structure or logical progression of the response is not appreciated. Thus, the system is not in a very strong position to offer remediation.

2. The analysis is optimized to detect completely correct responses or near-misses: responses that deviate from correct responses by the relaxation or absence of one or two constraints. This was done because presumably any response deserving of partial credit would necessarily be fairly close to the correct response. Thus, the system devotes most of its attention to doing a very thorough exploration of the space of responses very close to the correct response, and relatively little attention to those further away from the correct response. As a result, the system does less well analyzing partial responses (or responses-in-progress), which an instructional system presumably would be called upon to do.

We envision an instructional system based on schema theory that would not simply assign a score to a student's multiple-line response, but would offer immediate feedback and remediation on each line of the response as it is being entered. Its analytical capabilities would strive to approach those of a human tutor: The system would understand exactly where the student was in the solution of the problem, and would be able to offer help to the student based on a dynamic analysis of the best path from the student's current state to the goal state of the problem (Singley, Anderson, & Gevins, 1991). In some cases, it would also be able to detect and remediate errors. In order to build such a system, we have designed and implemented another schema-based analytical engine (a companion to the constraint-logic system described above) that is optimized for instructional applications.

The Schema Compiler

The goal of the Schema Compiler is to take a minimal schematic description of a math problem (a set of schema equations, a set of variable assignments, and a goal variable) and generate from it a solution graph that represents all possible problem states and all valid transitions between states. An instructional system should be able to use such a graph to (a) represent whatever state a particular student is in, and (b) generate the "best" path from the student's current state to the nearest goal state. The Schema Compiler generates a solution graph in two basic steps:

Step 1: Determine means–ends solutions. First, the system must determine whether the problem is solvable, and if so, which subset (or distinct subsets) of schema equations are required. It does this not only for the goal variable of the problem, but for every unknown. (In the instructional system, a student should not be limited to determining just the stated goal of the problem, so paths involving the derivation of other unknowns need to be modeled.)

The system uses a general problem-solving strategy borrowed from artificial intelligence and cognitive psychology known as *means–ends analysis* to determine these sets of equations. Means–ends analysis is a depth-first, recursive, working-backward strategy that has been widely used as a method for solving systems of equations (Newell & Simon, 1972; Larkin, McDermott, Simon, & Simon, 1980). In means–ends analysis, the program first retrieves a schema equation that contains the goal variable. (If more than one schema equation contains the goal variable, there is more than one starting point for this process; this is represented as an "OR" node in the search tree.) This equation would be examined to determine whether or not the goal variable is already constrained sufficiently so that its value is determined. (For example, if all the variables in this first equation other than the goal variable are known, the process terminates: only a single equation is required to solve for the goal.) However, if there are other unknowns in the first equation, subgoals are set recursively to find values for them. In order for this ultimately to become an equation solvable for the goal variable, the values of *all* the other unknowns must be determined, so these subgoals are linked by an "AND" node in the search tree. As the system recurses, additional schema equations are retrieved that contain these other unknowns, and again the system checks to see whether the variables are sufficiently constrained to allow for solution. This process is performed exhaustively to generate a search tree that represents all possible means–ends linkages of equations. A particular branch of the search tree terminates when either (a) the system runs out of schema equations to retrieve and apply (failure condition) or (b) the schema equations retrieved serve to constrain the goal variable sufficiently to allow for solution (success condition).

Figure 14.4 shows the means–ends analysis search tree generated while solving for the goal variable (d_u) of our example *Juanita* problem. (Again, similar search trees are generated for the other unknown variables of the problem.) As shown in the figure, there are six distinct solution branches generated, but only two of these lead to success. This reinforces the claim made earlier that, in addition to activating the appropriate schema, a significant part of problem solving in this domain is determining which subset of schema equations is required to solve the current problem.

Step 2: Derive problem graph. Once all the means–ends solutions have been found (in the *Juanita* problem, there are eight: two each for each of the four unknown variables), the Schema Compiler uses them to generate the problem graph. The problem graph represents all possible problem states that can be derived from the schema and all valid transitions between states.

In our example, the means–ends analysis for the goal variable d_u produced two solutions. In both cases, these solutions amounted to linear

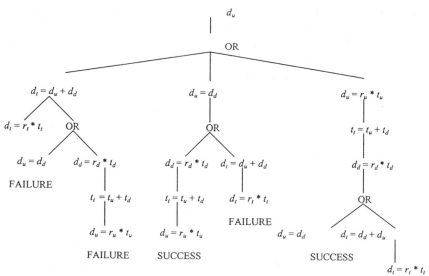

FIG. 14.4. AND-OR search tree generated by means–ends analysis for the goal variable (d_u) of the *Juanita* problem. Any node not marked as an "OR" node is an "AND" node. Terminal nodes of each branch are marked with either "success" or "failure."

chains of equations.[1] The task of the Schema Compiler at this point is to generate all permutations and combinations of the schema equations on these paths, while preserving the linkages in the original search tree.

Figure 14.5 presents the portion of the problem graph generated by the Schema Compiler for the two means–ends solutions for d_u. (This is a small fraction of the entire graph, but perhaps that portion most frequently

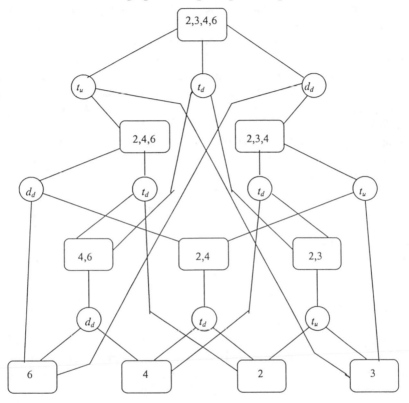

Nodes:

(2) $10 = t_u + t_d$

(3) $d_u = 2 * t_u$

(4) $d_d = 3 * t_d$

(6) $d_u = d_d$

(2,4) $10 = t_u + (d_d/3)$

(2,3) $10 = (d_u/2) + t_d$

(4,6) $d_u = 3 * t_d$

(2,4,6) $10 = t_u + (d_u/3)$

(2,3,4) $10 = (d_u/2) + (d_d/3)$

(2,3,4,6) $10 = (d_u/2) + (d_u/3)$

FIG. 14.5. A small portion of the problem graph for the *Juanita* problem. Shown are the nodes and links for the modal means-ends analysis solutions for the goal variable, d_u.

---

[1] The solutions were linear chains because, in each schema equation retrieved and applied, there was a single unknown. This rendered all of the AND nodes in the successful portions of the graph degenerate. Other topologies (e.g., trees) for solutions are possible, however.

traversed by students who are making progress solving the problem.) The rectangular nodes of the graph represent all the different equations a student might write that are directly on-path to solving for d_u, and the links between the nodes are all the possible ways these nodes might combine to produce more complex equations. The circular nodes that join the links represent the variables that are replaced when one node is composed with another. One rectangular node in the graph (2, 3, 4, 6) is distinguished in that it represents the equation that can be solved for the value of d_u. In this case, it represents the particular composition of four primitive schema equations that eliminates the unknown variables d_d, t_u, and t_d but preserves the goal variable d_u. (In the full graph, there are other distinguished nodes that can be solved for the values of the other unknowns.)

This, then, is how the problem graph is constructed. However, several complications should be mentioned:

Each rectangular node in the graph does not represent a single equation but, in fact, an entire set of equations. This is because students can write the same equation at different levels of instantiation (i.e., they can either use values for known quantities or variables). So, for example, the equation $d_u/2 + d_u/3 = 10$ could alternatively be written by the student as $d_u/r_u + d_u/r_d = t_t$. This equation is perfectly valid; it simply does not make use of all the information given in the problem. In this example, because there are three known quantities in the equation, there are 2^3 different ways the equation might be instantiated.[2] All the different equations that can be written for a single node are called the node's *projections*. The one projection that contains values for all known quantities in the problem is called the node's *modal projection*.

The logic of the problem graph is really based on linkages between the modal projections of the nodes. If the student has not written equations that are modal projections, those equations must be turned into modal projections before the logic of the problem graph applies. This is the problem of *underinstantiation*, and it is fairly trivial to address: Presumably, the instructional system would encourage the student to plug in values for any variables used by the student that are given values in the problem statement. A different, thornier problem arises when, as an intermediate step in solving the problem, the student solves for the value of a variable that is not the goal variable of the problem. This is the problem of *overinstantiation*: a variable other than the goal variable changes its status from unknown to known in the middle of the problem. Because the logic of the means-ends analysis is entirely predicated on the designation of

---

[2] We are currently dealing only with equations that are underinstantiated, that is equations where variables are being used for known values.

certain variables as either known or unknown, this invalidates the logic of the problem graph. To deal with this problem, we in fact generate means–ends solutions not only for the problem as it is originally stated, but also for the problem restated to include values for all the unknown quantities that (a) are replaced in the modal means–ends solutions and (b) whose values can be derived from the original problem. Thus, the means-ends solutions we have described so far are in fact only the *modal* means–ends solutions. We run the analysis a total of 2^5 (32) additional times to determine the best solutions when the values of other unknowns have been derived midstream in solving the problem.[3]

Finally, it should be noted that, in addition to the correct schema equations, we have allowed for "buggy" versions of those equations to be submitted to the Schema Compiler. Thus, the Schema Compiler can generate subgraphs that include equations representing common errors, as well as compositions of errors with correct equations or compound errors. (The inclusion of compound errors in the graph might in many cases result in a combinatorial explosion that would be prohibitive, however.)

To summarize our example, when we submit the *Juanita* problem to the Schema Compiler with one additional buggy equation ($d = r/t$ rather than $d = r * t$), the resulting problem graph consists of 32 nodes having 142 distinct projections and 64 distinct linkages. The total number of distinct problem states that can be represented by the graph is therefore 2^{142} different combinations of projections times 2^5 different levels of overinstantiation for a total of 2^{147} different states. Although the number of possible states for these problems is astronomical, the graph that represents these states is actually fairly compact. The graphs can be precompiled and stored efficiently so that it is practical to use them in real-time instructional applications. The problem graph generated by the Schema Compiler can be used to understand in precise detail exactly where a student is in solving a schema-based problem and to deliver advice about how best to complete the solution given the student's current state. As students write equations, the system matches those equations to individual projections in the problem graph using an evaluation-based matching strategy. The system can detect buggy equations written by the student and offer appropriate remediation. When the student asks for help, the system inspects the student's current state and, using the logic of the problem graph, *dynamically* computes the best path between the student's current state and the nearest goal state.

---

[3] The number of additional means-ends analysis is 2^5 because there are five unknowns in the problem other than the goal variable. Each of these may or may not be determined midstream in the problem.

DISCUSSION

We have tried to demonstrate how schema theory provides a general framework for integrating test creation, automatic analysis, and test preparation. The same deep-level item description (i.e., the item schema) can be used for classifying items, generating question variants, predicting difficulty, assembling tests based on a chosen range of content and item difficulty, delivering feedback as students solve problems, and scoring multiple-line responses. In terms of efficiency, the schema-constraint processing approach explored here is a substantial advance over a more traditional knowledge-based approach and, we believe, has reached the point of practical utility for at least some initial applications. Unlike a more traditional knowledge-based approach, large problem classes can be specified with relatively little work and with essentially no technical skill beyond mathematical content knowledge.

We first showed how schema theory could be applied to the development of item models that could be used to automatically generate item variants. We described a tool, the Math Test Creation Assistant, that provides test developers with an environment in which such models can be specified declaratively and variants are generated with the aid of an automatic constraint solver. Thus, a mathematics content expert can build models and generate variants without the need for procedural programing. The tool has already been used to generate hundreds of items for operational use at ETS. Most of these items are not word problems but rather "pure" items that involve abstract mathematical concepts and no cover story. These items lend themselves especially well to deeper kinds of variation.

We then applied schema theory to the creation of two new analytical engines for multiple-line responses, one for assessment and the other for instruction. The Schema Prover uses constraint logic programing techniques to explore the correctness and completeness of responses by attempting to "prove" the response from the schema specification, and *vice versa*. This scoring engine is optimized for the analysis of full responses involving the assignment of full- and partial-credit scores in assessment situations. The Schema Compiler uses means–ends analysis to generate a problem graph that represents all possible states of a schema-based problem and all paths from these states to goal states. This scoring engine is optimized for the analysis of partial or emerging solutions in instructional situations. The analyses in both cases depend critically on having the right representation of the schema. Although actually entering the schema is trivial, the analyst must strive to cast the schema at the finest level of granularity possible and to include all possible quantities and relationships found in the problem situation. This results in the most extensive coverage of problem states and paths and minimizes the chance for "gaps" in the analysis.

Presently, both the Schema Prover and the Schema Compiler are limited to linear systems of equations, or, at least, systems that are linear once they are instantiated with known quantities. Future work will focus on extending our analytical power to nonlinear equations and other kinds of elementary functions, for example, trigonometric and transcendental functions.

Although the Schema Compiler represents our first attempt at a cognitive model from which one could derive predictions of difficulty automatically, much work remains to be done. First, the schemas themselves need to be validated psychologically, as well as the strategy for searching them. The minimal means–ends analysis engine we are using now is almost certainly inadequate in that it is a purely working-backwards strategy that may be avoided by examinees because it imposes a severe working memory load (Sweller, Mawer, & Ward, 1983). We should explore the incorporation of some working-forward elements as well as elements of generate-and-test to better model the actual behavior of examinees. Protocol analyses of examinees solving problems would appear to be indispensable for informing this effort.

In our research, we have tried to lay the groundwork for a future generation of computer-based tests that broadens how and what we test. Schema theory offers exciting possibilities for doing that, including more cognitively based test designs, better automatic scoring methods, and feedback that can be used for test preparation or for new approaches to assessment (e.g., "dynamic" assessment). Considerable work remains to be done before these improvements are realized. We must still determine how broadly we can apply the schema framework in terms of content coverage, how well it will predict difficulty, how accurate it is in deciphering student responses, and how acceptable it is to mathematics test creation staff members.

ACKNOWLEDGMENTS

This work was funded in part by the Graduate Record Examination Board; we gratefully acknowledge their support. We also thank our many colleagues at Educational Testing Service (ETS) who made large contributions to this work: Mary Morley, Pete Brittingham, Krishna Jha, Rob Rarich, Mark Zelman, Irv Katz, Mary Enright, Kathy Sheehan, and Jim Fife contributed greatly to the development of the Test Creation Assistant. The Schema Prover was implemented in large part by Krishna Jha and Pei Wang; the Schema Compiler was implemented in large part by Eric Gold. We thank them all for their unique contributions.

REFERENCES

Enright, M., Morley, M., & Sheehan, K. (1999). *Items by design:The impact of systematic feature variation on item statistical characteristics* (ETS Research Report 99-20). Princeton, NJ: Educational Testing Service.

Marshall, S. (1995). *Schemas in problem solving*. New York: Cambridge University Press.

Mayer, R. E. (1981). Frequency norms and structural analysis of algebra story problems into families, categories, and templates. *Instructional Science, 10*, 135–175.

Sebrechts, M. M., Enright, M., Bennett, R. E., & Martin, K. (1996). Using algebra word problems to assess quantitative ability: Attributes, strategies, and errors. *Cognition and Instruction, 14*(3), 285–343.

Sheehan, K., & Mislevy, R. (1994). *A tree-based analysis of items from an assessment of basic mathematics skills* (ETS Research Report 94–14). Princeton, NJ: Educational Testing Service.

Singley, M. K. (1995). Promoting transfer through model tracing. In A. McKeough, J. Lupart, & A. Marini (Eds.), *Teaching for transfer: Fostering generalization in learning*. Hillsdale, NJ: Lawrence Erlbaum Associates.

Singley, M. K., Anderson, J. R., & Gevins, J. S. (1991). Promoting abstract strategies in algebra word problem solving. In *Proceedings of the International Conference on the Learning Sciences*. Charlottesville, VA: Association for the Advancement of Computing in Education.

Sweller, J., Mawer, R., & Ward, M. (1983). Development of expertise in mathematical problem solving. *Journal of Experimental Psychology: General, 112*, 639–661.

Tatsuoka, K., Birenbaum, M., Lewis, C., & Sheehan, K. (1993). *Proficiency scaling based on conditional probability functions for attributes* (RR-93-50-ONR). Princeton, NJ: Educational Testing Service.

Discussant Remarks

Rick Morgan
Educational Testing Services

I come to this role as discussant from a different perspective than do my colleagues from the Research Division. Being from the Assessment Division my role is to try to aid in the production of the best and fairest measures within reasonable costs for the testing programs to which I have been assigned. A major part of my job is to explain to both ETS clients and ETS staff the psychometric/statistical reasons why we should made some adjustment in our current testing practices. The psychometric knowledge of some of the clients and staff is somewhat limited. I also have to explain our current testing methods to customers ranging in level of technical expertise from the generally low levels of many parents and students to groups as almost psychometrically wise as those assembled here.

The role I'll try to take here is that of the person who needs to convey to current and future clients and ETS staffers why they should consider the application of item generation to the testing program. For example, I plan on presenting techniques discussed at this conference to save some of the cost of pretesting multiple-choice items. Currently, multiple-choice items for the Advanced Placement Program (AP) are pretested at colleges in order to gauge their approximate level of difficulty. Over time the level of participation of the colleges has diminished to such a level that pretesting is becoming impractical. As result of the conference discussion AP is now investigating ways to estimate item difficulty using the methods outlined by Singley and Bennett. Efforts to utilize item-generation techniques like those outlined by Bartram and others in this conference to create variants of multiple-choice items are also being investigated. I also feel that the application of item-generation techniques can lead to improvements in efficiency in both the production and the scoring of constructed-response questions. Consequently, I will seek answers to questions for my own edification and perhaps the edification of others rather than make sterling points about the papers.

Dr. Bartram's paper provides a very lucid roadmap for the thinking that is necessary for the application of item-generation techniques to developing new batteries of tests. A lengthy array of tests was created. Two issues raised during the first morning's discussion are addressed in this paper; the creation of test items and test forms on the fly and the scoring of constructed response/open-ended tasks. A question I have concerning the creation of tests on the fly is whether the computer stores the items administered to each examinee? The storing of the item record would make it possible to reduce the exposure of the same item in subsequent administrations to the same candidate and future candidates.

The scoring of the exams appears to range from model-based algorithms to the scoring algorithm used for the Landing test. The algorithm devised to score the Landing test was based on first asking expert raters to provide judgements of the landing approaches and then correlating the ratings with five measures (final height, horizontal alignment, proximity to the end of the runway centerline, rate of descent, and speed control). What is the percent of variance in the expert ratings that is explained by this approach?

Those working on the project were faced with the problem of attempting to design tests that had both predictive validity for the later stages of pilot training and face validity for the trainees. Without either a model of the relationship of abilities to performance, or the necessary sample sizes to establish the best links between underlying cognitive components and performance, the test battery evolved into having tasks more in common with work/job samples approaches than assessments of one dimensional underlying abilities. Due to the need to rapidly produce multiple equivalent versions of the tests, the approach soon led to the need for a computer to generate items for the different tasks.

When test takers are presented with different tasks, a key psychometric issue becomes the parallelism of tasks across administrations. In the paper the author lists many of the aspects of each of the task dimensions that are varied systematically because they contributed to item difficulty (radicals) and those aspects of task dimensions that are allowed to vary randomly (incidentals). I'd be interested in knowing how the task dimensions that were item radicals and those that were incidentals were determined? How long did this procedure take? What is being done to control for interactions among task dimensions that would lead to easier or harder tasks than expected given main effects models? How well do these task dimensions generalize across groups of examinees?

The paper indicates that many tests never saw the light of day because of either unreliable scoring protocols or the large number of dimensions that were radicals and the small number of tasks dimensions that were incidentals. Could you please give a couple of examples of tests that never became part of the battery?

A few additional questions follow:

1. The reliabilities of the measures range from .25 to .99, with an average in the low .80s. At what point were tests removed from the battery based on the inability of the tests to produce consistent scores?

2. What are the correlations among tasks and were factor analyses carried out which may help to limit the number of tests required for each pilot candidate?
3. What evidence is there that the second-stage predictive validity was solved by the administration of the current battery of exams?
4. What were the key lessons learned from this approach that would generalize to other attempts at item generation?
5. Besides the development of scoring rubrics, developing measures to capture the necessary complexity of the tasks, and differentiating radicals from incidentals what were other challenges to the construction of the tests?

One comment in the paper that I believe those thinking about embarking on item-generation techniques should particularly remember is that: "It is generally fairly easy to identify the parameters that are likely to make a task easier or harder. It is less easy to find those that have no effect on difficulty."

The paper by Goeters and Lorenz examines the PARAT tests. The tests are versions of paper-and-pencil tests that have been adapted to create multiple parallel test versions. The study determines which properties of test items influence item difficulty, how the impacts are moderated by other properties, and how item difficulty is moderated by individual differences. Two levels each of five item dimensions were completely crossed to create 32 Sternberg memory-search tasks. Reaction time and percent error served as the dependent variables for analyses of variance. Counterbalancing of the tasks was not done so that the observed effects may have been underestimated since more difficult tasks were given later in the sequence.

The analyses indicated that all the cognitive functions except for task load significantly impacted the dependent variables. Additionally, most of the second and third order interactions of the properties were significant. Factor analyses of the reaction time and the false rejection rate yielded separate factors for the visual sub tests demanding visual search and the auditory sub tests with dichotic listening. The clustering of these tasks on separate factors provided evidence of distinct abilities in the visual and auditory domain.

In the section of the paper describing the Rotation of Dice exam there is a discussion of how preconceived ideas about what are item radicals and what are item incidentals can change. Test takers are first shown a six-sided die with a cross on one plane. The examinee is then given information concerning several tilts (right, left, etc.) of the die. The examinee then indicates the final position of the die. Speed of information and number of tilts are obvious radicals. However, testing showed that the number of tilts was incidental to difficulty, while the location of the tilted plane was a radical. This finding speaks to the importance of empirically testing theoretical notions about item radicals and incidentals.

The paper also addressed the coaching issue that was brought up earlier in the conference. Coaching to the test was one of the stated reasons for using item-generation technology. As a result of differential amounts and quality of coaching, information was supplied to all examinees describing the test principles and providing miniature tests. Thus trying to standardize to a certain degree the pretraining. How successful has this approach and the implementation of item generation technology been in moderating the impact of coaching?

Four other questions follow:

1. Have the results of the study influenced the battery of the tests administered to the applicants and if so, how?
2. How were item generation principles applied to the stimuli chosen in the study? There were five radicals (modality, task load, memory load, probe quality, and task variable response), but what were the incidentals?
3. What are the plans for the collection of validity evidence relating criterion performance to the tests?
4. Because these tests can be taken multiple times, is exposure to the same items limited?

The paper by Singley and Bennett presents the application of schema theory to the generation and scoring of items, as well as the production of instructional feedback. The tools for automatic item generation look very practical for item cloning and the estimation of difficulty levels can help test developers more quickly provide needed pretest items to pools. Reading through the first part of the paper lead me to the following questions:

1. What is the correlation of the predicted difficulty estimates with the actual difficulties?
2. Which of the item characteristics are item radicals and which are item incidentals?
3. How were the incidentals and radicals determined?

With the continuous testing feature of computer adaptive tests requiring so many items, I would also like to know the authors' perspective on the research steps needed to estimate item parameters for use in high stakes tests.

I believe that schema theory could also be used to create the distracters for the multiple-choice items. Currently, theory plays less of a role in the creation of distracters than it should. Schema theory suggests that the distracters be based on common errors in the application of the schema.

The use of the Schema Prover for the scoring of mathematical constructed responses seems as practical as the scoring of essays using regression based scoring models. Being theory based instead of being based on a regression model, schema theory is likely to be a more valid solution to essay scoring than some of the current methods utilizing computer scoring.

The instruction and test preparation aspect seem complex with millions of different problem states creating a significant challenge. However, if the marketplace is as willing to invest in learning aides, as it is to invest in assessments, then this aspect may prove to have the most long-term benefit.

In summary, the three papers show that item-generation techniques can be used to create and score both multiple-choice and open-ended items for high stakes tests. The technique requires sophistication of both software and test development specifications. A major task for the future is to determine if the item parameters of cloned items are stable enough to support fungibility in test administration.

DISCUSSION

BRAUN:

Thank you. Well, Rick, I hope you've had as much fun preparing this discussion as we have had listening to you, and I hope that none of your managers are in the audience! But seriously, I think Rick has not only well summarized the papers, but issued some challenges, on the order of a PhD oral, to the speakers. All our speakers are very distinguished, but it seems to me that if they're willing to accept this challenge, then I would invite them to make at least a partial response to some of the issues that Rick raised, and then we can have the general discussion. Dave, would you like to say just a few words?

Bartram's response

BARTRAM:

I think I've noted down all the questions, but I may have missed some. I'll try and give some quick answers to what really deserve much longer answers.

The first question is about creating items on the fly. We did explore the impact of varying tests on the fly in our research. Most of the tests, when used executively, were not free to vary. In the case of most of the item-based tasks, we had set constraints on the generation so that we could sample randomly from a set of known versions (in effect we had a number of parallel forms). In the case of the most of the dynamic tasks, content was generated randomly on the fly within the constraints designed into the task. Item generation on the fly tends to be more of a problem with what I was calling item-based tests than with task-based tests.

The second question referred to the modeling of expert scoring within Landing. I do not remember the percentage of the variance of the expert score related to the actual measures as we derive them. But I do recall that it was fairly high. The group of experts we had agreed very well with each other in terms of performance, because there's a lot of variance in performance on that landing task. It's pretty obvious when people are doing it well and when they're doing it badly. And the extent to which we could capture their judgment was very, very good. So, while I couldn't give you a figure, it was very high. The computer-generated internal scores weren't simply based on regression weights. Regression was used as a measure to get some estimate of the weights, and then they were rationalized into a scoring rule. The outcome was a little more robust than the regression weights would have been. We found very good agreement then, between subsequent expert ratings and the computer generated scores. I cannot recall the exact figure, but correlations were in the region of 0.8.

Your third question was about how we decided what were radicals and what were incidentals. At the time, of course, we didn't call them that as Sid hadn't invented those phrases then. We simply talked about the things that were going to make it more or less difficult, and the things that we didn't worry too much about. But essentially, there were two main techniques. First, we used the cognitive psychology literature, the literature in particular on psychomotor control and tracking. There was a lot of information on what makes psychomotor tasks easy or hard: things like control laws, display-control compatibility, and all those sorts of issues which are fairly well-documented in the literature. One could identify these fairly easily. Second, we explored the impact of the various parameters in relatively small scale studies, usually run by postgraduate students, with fairly small numbers of people, to check out particular combinations of conditions, seeing if they made differences or didn't make differences to the performance. In this way we could start mapping out very crudely the level of difficulty, or the impact of different variables on difficulty. By no means calibrating it precisely, but just giving us a ballpark feel for what things were affecting the task, and what things weren't. Since then, there has been an iterative development process. As the tests go through trials, what tended to happen was that the conditions would become refined with feedback from field trials, certain conditions would be dropped out, because they were redundant, or because they either proved to be too difficult or too easy to discriminate. The final test versions, in a sense, evolved in that fashion.

The sense of direction test is a typical example of the way in which various studies were carried out to look at what made the test difficult. For example, we found that if you used 16 directions and more than 4 legs on a journey, it became impossible, so there wasn't any point putting those sorts of conditions on the test. But having said that, we did know beforehand that these were the variables that affected difficulty. What we didn't know was what levels of each variable were difficult enough.

You asked about the generalization of radicals and incidentals across different groups. I don't know the answer to that, but I suspect you're probably right that there are certain things which may be incidental with one group, but become a radical with another group. In the sense that we've been operating with a fairly well defined population of pilot applicants on these tests, they are generally a homogeneous group, so I don't think we've had that as an issue.

Which of the tests did we try but throw out and why? Well, there were quite a few false starts. There's one I remember that I thought was a wonderful test. This simulated landing a helicopter onto a flight deck. It tried to represent the acceleration of the rate of streaming of visual patterns that occurs as you descend vertically towards a surface. This was to give the visual cues needed to control the rate at which you descended onto the flight deck. We gave that one up because it was impossible to program on the technology then. It would probably be very easy, and would be a nice test to do now. Another one, which I mentioned in the paper, was 4-dimensional tracking. This was an overly complex task, and wasn't possible to get a clear understanding of how people had performed it, in a way of getting a coherent set of measures that had any clear construct validity. It was too complex. People could perform it in all sorts of different ways, and could manage the complexity in different ways, which we couldn't control well enough. Generally, though, the tests that we dropped were just too long, or had to be too long if we wanted to make them reliable enough.

You mentioned some of the unreliable measures that we had, but 2 or 3 measures that are noted in the paper as being unreliable, are not actually used, they're put in there for completeness. The very high reliability (0.99), if I remember rightly, was compensatory tracking. It's the Spearman–Brown corrected average correlation between three trials. Compensatory tracking is a very stable, reliable characteristic. That's one estimate from one study. It varies from about .92 to .99, I think, on that variable.

We did carry out various factory analyses of the tests on different sets of data, but I should add that Cathay Pacific people are only using five of the tests in the executive battery, they're not using all of the tests that are being described in the paper. The choice of which tests to use was partly informed by using factor analysis, and looking at the redundancy of variables, so that they're using a minimally redundant set. One of the analyses we did included some of the BARB tests. This produced four main factors, one looks like a general ability factor, as you might expect, there's a clear psychomotor factor, and one that is probably spatial (it certainly has loadings on the tests which correlate with paper-and-pencil spatial-ability tests). The fourth factor is not easily interpreted, but I suspect it may be some sort of speed factor.

Your final question related to validity. There are a number of papers that actually do give you the answer to that question, but it wasn't a major feature for the paper for this session. The predictive validity estimates are around .4 to .5 for correlations with operational training outcome. Chris Elshaw has more recent MOD data on the Micropat validity studies.

Klaus-Martin & Berndt's response

BRAUN:

Thank you, thank you very much. Klaus-Martin, would you like to take an opportunity?

GOETERS:

Thank you very much. There was a question concerning the PARAT test. Yes, they are paper-and-pencil tests. At the time we constructed these tests we took already known item principles, and we created versions of tests based on these principles. The new thing was that we schematized test construction, we defined clear constraints, and this resulted in a set of rules to reach parallelism on the different versions.

One of the especially interesting PARAT tests is the Dice test. It is interesting because it uses only acoustic information. All information to the candidates is given via earphones, or loudspeaker—the position of the cross on the dice, where they start, and the rotations. The interesting thing is that this acoustically presented test correlates with figural materials, the typical, classical tests of spatial orientation or visualization.

LORENZ:

Another question regarded the interaction patterns, which obviously bothered you a lot. The interaction patterns are very important according to additive-factor logic. I have given at least one example, which was very sound in the conclusion that can be drawn. That is that the visual search component is self-terminating; it shows up in that kind of pattern. Due to the large sample size (396), we did find some other significant interactions on the Sternberg task, but though significant, they were small in R^2.

As to the question, what is an incidental in the Sternberg test: We used single-syllable consonants, randomly chosen from a whole set of consonants. For the auditory, it was clear that we not use things that would be a radical, for the auditory as well as for the dichotic, it was important not to use a double consonant pair "S" and "F"—too hard to differentiate.

One influence this research has on the application of the test battery, was that the application of the standard test was more of a shotgun approach to see task variables that have an obvious relation to the abilities we're tapping, and to see how we can construct componential tests. The next step would be to construct more complex tests involving dichotic listening, monitoring, and visual search, and timesharing ability. A lot of literature shows that you have to prioritize tasks—that was simply lacking in our simple Sternberg tests. And you must have a management of priorities. Lessons learned from our complex test was that you have good predicted validity from a work sample test, and complex task scenarios are more valid than single tasks. And inherent in that is a kind of priority management must be achieved.

With rotation of dices, we have a paper–pencil (PARAT) and a computerized version. We took advantage of the new technology. In the PARAT test, the voice has a given pace—"left, right, forward, forward, left, right"—and you have to imagine where the cross is now on the dice. And that is of course, more difficult if you have a more lengthy series of tilt instructions. One can get lost. The length of tilting instructions is a radical. We changed that type of task to a self-paced task, what we normally can't do with acoustic information. It was a challenge to do that in the transfer to acoustic test, to do self pacing. And the pacing itself is then the reaction time measured. If one can self-pace his instructions, then the length of the instruction he paced himself, is no longer a radical, it's an incidental. What we found is that where the cross is, maybe it is on top, and then, say left, OK, then it turns to left. If it's then left then it turns to the bottom, and if the cross is on the bottom, and there is then left, then it turns to the right. And that is the turning that has the largest impact. That was a radical. So what we found was that in the former paper–pencil version of the test, not enough precautions were made about where the cross is. We had only one study showing that if the cross is unchanged by the distraction, it's left as we see, forward, backward, then it stays on the left side, and this is a very easy one, so the algorithm we used for the paper pencil construction, took precautions of that, but not of the other thing that the number of bottom instructions were parallel.

Singley and Bennett's Response

BRAUN:

Thank you very much Bernd, Kevin or Randy, would you like to respond? It was really a great adulatory review. I'm very surprised!

SINGLEY:

The first question I recall is, "What were the correlations for those difficulty predictions?" As I said, what I showed was last year's version of the difficulty model. It's being replaced with a better version. But I think for that version, I think the variance accounted for was around 30%. When the test developer sorted the item into one of the three categories—higher order, conceptual, or procedural—then it went up to around 50% if we also asked the item writer to do a self-rating of how difficult the item is.

BRAUN:

I think it went up to .55 from Mary's presentation.

SINGLEY:

The next question concerned the practicality of the schema prover. We had a project with the College Board on the math level-2 achievement test, we actually took some handwritten responses that they had, and some of their rubrics. It was an interesting exercise. I think we did pretty well. One thing we discovered was that a lot of the rubrics were spotty. The people who write the rubrics are limited by the kinds of errors they can imagine occurring. And in fact, lots more errors happen than are similar to ones they imagine. As I understand it, in the scoring sessions, the first day or two they spend uncovering more and more cases that hadn't been uncovered by the rubric, so it's very labor intensive to whip these rubrics into shape.

I think the schema approach may be a more systematic way of handling this. And I think we did pretty well with the score. The impracticality was that they had no plans in the near future to go to any kind of computer based administration, so we had all this paper-and-pencil data sitting there with a computer program sitting next to it waiting to analyze it.

MORGAN:

One further question I have is that I have seen applications that generate items. I see a nice big application for scoring the items for test preparation development.

BENNETT:

I guess I'm not really sure in the sense that it's a business question from one point of view. Where does ETS want to go? Given that we have that capability, or could develop it the way that would allow us to take advantage. So at the moment it's hard to see where it is we're going. But we could go in either direction.

Distractors

ALMOND:

I wanted to follow up on that comment about the distractors, because I think it's an interesting one that a lot of people could think about, using the schema and distractors. When I was interviewing here, Howard posed this rhetorical problem to me, and it can be described pretty handily with Kevin's schema. It was key, key times 2, key with the wrong units, key with the digits transposed, key + 1. He generated a number of distractors in that way, and it was pretty easy to key this particular item without a stem. And so I think there's a big issue. A lot of what the question is measuring, depends on how the distractors are coming in the schema. I saw a number of papers here where the distractors were almost an afterthought. They were thinking maybe there's something in the distractors that could predict difficulty, but they weren't thinking very hard about it. I think that's certainly an area that a lot of these projects could go. It's the next step for them—to think about how the distractors fit into the schemas.

MISLEVY:

The way you grade the distractors ought to be part of the rationale of what aspect of this you're getting at.

Precision in modeling

MISLEVY:

The other thing I wanted to mention was this notion of trying to model item parameters, and knowing that we can't do it perfectly, that there's some uncertainty. It goes in a range. Howard showed a 15% needed increase in test length. That's a worst case with existing item types, no data at all, a first shot. A much better case we would aspire to is the one Dave Wright showed, where the uncertainty had no negligible impact. As statisticians, we're happy to say that ok, there is some uncertainty, we'll integrate over that, and we'll count on the law of large numbers, averaging, to make things better. So if there's a certain amount of noise in one item, well, if you've got 40, you're much better off. What Rick Morgan said that got me thinking, though, was when he was talking about explaining this to lawyers. Lawyers don't think like statisticians. So if there's that much noise on one item, and now that you've got 40 with that much noise, we'll you're really in big trouble then! So we're going to have to do some work on explaining that.

Final Thoughts

BRAUN:

Thank you very much. I'd like to just say a few words. When I introduced the conference yesterday morning, I said I hoped it would be a milestone in the area of item generation. I think it has not missed my hopes, and I hope that you all feel as excited and energized, and more intelligent, in whatever metric you happen to use, as a result of participating in the conference. So I want to thank the speakers, the discussants, the audience, for staying with us, and particularly, Kathy Howell isn't here today, but again, thank her for her enormous work in getting the conference off the ground. Pat, for his financial and logistic support, Sid, for his conceptual and organizational support, and please pay attention to Sid because that book is going to come out. So thank you again, and for those of you who are traveling home, have a safe and pleasant journey.

Author Index

A

Abram, M., 62, 71, 331, 337
Ackerman, P. L., 358
Advisory Group for Aerospace Research and Development (AGARD), 341, 343
Akin, O., 208, 210, 214
Albert, J. H., 281, 286
Almond, R. G., 103, 108, 127, 202, 214
Anastasi, A., 225, 248
Anderson, J. D., xviii, xxiv, 116, 127, 277, 286, 323, 331–332, 334, 344, 353–354, 359
Anderson, J. R., 256, 274, 376, 384
Armstrong, R. D., 11, 28
Atherton, R. M., 17, 31

B

Babkoff, H., 251, 274
Baddeley, A. D., xviii, xxiii, 10, 15, 28, 215, 251, 257, 274–275
Banerji, N., 335–336
Bartram, D., xix, xxiii, 3, 28, 317, 319–320, 330–331, 336–337
Battig, W. F., 261, 274
Baxter, P., 319, 336
Bayliss, R., 331, 336-337
Bejar, I. I., xvi, xxiii, 3, 10, 13, 15, 28, 122, 127, 130, 157, 161, 177, 199–203, 205–210, 214–217, 331, 337
Bennett, R. E., 130–131, 157, 202–203, 206–207, 212, 215, 365, 384
Berger, M. P. F., 114, 127
Beringer, J., 345, 358
Bevans, H. G., 18, 28
Bird, A. S., 20, 22, 33
Birenbaum, M., 365, 384
Bittner, A. C., Jr., 254, 274, 352, 356, 358
Blizzard, R. A., 20, 22, 33
Bloom, B. S., 169, 177
Bock, R. D., 135, 158, 230, 248, 281, 287
Boer, L., 357–359
Boies, S. J., 14, 33
Bongers, S. H., 16–17, 28, 30–31
Bormuth, J. R., 159, 177, 199, 215, 323, 337

B (continued)

Bortkewitsch, L. von, 290–291, 305
Bradlow, E. T., 214–215, 217
Braun, H. I., 208, 215
Bredenkamp, J., 173, 178
Brennan, R. L., 214–215
Bridgeman, B., 209, 215
Brieman, L., 136, 157
Bunderson C. V., 6, 28
Burke, E., 317, 319, 331, 337
Byrne, R. M. J., 42, 45, 51

C

CTB/McGraw-Hill, 208, 210, 215
Cape, L. T., 17, 32
Carpenter, P. A., 15, 32, 161, 177, 202, 215, 226–230, 233–234, 243, 247, 249, 257, 274
Carretta, T. R., 319, 337
Carroll, J. B., xviii, xxiii, xxiv, 3–4, 12, 28–29,117, 127, 221, 225–226, 249, 323, 334, 352, 358
Carter, R. C., 254, 274, 352, 356, 358
Cattell, R. B., 225, 249
Chaffin, R., 117, 127, 200, 215
Chaiken, S. R., 257, 259, 274
Chalifour, C., 122, 127
Chase, W. G., 5, 15, 29, 260, 274
Chiu, C. W. T., 212, 214–215
Chomsky, N., 200, 215
Christal, R. E., xviii, xxiv, 3–4, 16, 18, 21, 23, 25, 29, 31–32, 244, 249, 257, 274
Clark, H. H., 5, 15, 29, 43, 51, 260, 274
Clark, L. A., 135, 158
Collins, A. M., 58–59, 62, 71
Collis, J. M., 3–4, 8, 11–12, 16–18, 24, 27, 29–31, 117, 122, 127, 335, 337
Cooper, L. A., 161, 177
Cronbach, L. J., xv, xxiv, 3, 27, 30, 129, 157, 214–215, 221–222, 249

D

Damos, D. L., 356, 358
Daneman, M., 257, 274
Dann, P. L., xviii, xx, xxii, xxiv, 3–4, 8, 10, 12–14 16, 30–31, 33, 58, 71, 116, 122, 127, 277, 286, 323, 331–335, 337, 344, 353–354, 359
Davis, J. H., 5, 18, 33
Dayton, C. M., 121, 127
De Boeck, P., 214, 216
Dempster, A. P., 281, 286

Dennis, I., xx, xxii, xxiv, 3–6, 12–13, 30–
   31, 34, 58, 62, 71, 117, 127, 267, 274,
   278, 281, 286, 335, 337
Diehl, K. A., 242–243, 249
Dresher, A., 214, 216
Dumais, S. T., 270, 275
Dunlap, W., 251, 274

E

Eißfeldt, H., 340, 344, 356, 358–359
Educational Testing Service, 35–36, 39,
   51, 63, 71, 210, 215
Eichelman, W. H., 14, 33
Ekstrom, R. B., 340, 344, 358
Elithorn, A., 331, 337
Elizur, D., 219, 249
Elliot, S. M., 209–210, 215
Elshaw, C. C., 17, 32, 62, 71
Embretson, S. E., xvii–xviii, xx, xxiv, 14,
   16, 30, 116, 122–123, 127–128, 130,
   157, 200, 212–213, 215, 221–222,
   236–237, 243, 249
Engle, R. W., 257, 275
Englund, C. E., 256, 274
Enright, M. L., 118, 124, 127, 130–131,
   157, 365, 369, 384
Ericsson, K. A., 39, 51
Estes, C. A., 210, 216
Estes, W. K., 6, 33
Etzel, S., 165, 172–174, 177
Evans, J. St. B. T., xx, xxii, xxiv, 4–6, 10,
   14–16, 18, 30–31, 42–44, 51, 267,
   274, 335, 337

F

Feynman, R. P., 302, 305
Finell, G., 339, 343, 359
Fischer, G. H., 121, 127, 280, 286
Fitzpatrick, F., 163, 178
Fleck, D., 334, 337
Fleishman, E. A., 344, 358
Flynn, I. N., 327, 337
French, J. W., 340, 354, 358
Friedman, D., 209, 215
Friedman, J. H., 136, 157
Furneaux, W. D., 5, 30
Furnival, G. M., 145, 157

G

Gao, X., 214–215
Gerritz, K., 123, 128
Gevins, J. S., 376, 384
Gitomer, D. G., 105, 128
Gitomer, D. H., 103–104, 128
Glaser, R., 129, 157, 259, 275
Gleser, G. C., 214–215
Goeters, K-M., xix, xxiv, 3, 13, 30, 339–
   340, 342–344, 347, 353–354, 356–
   359
Gopher, D., 356–357, 359–360
Greig, J. E., 16–17, 28, 30–31
Grenzebach, A. P., 22, 31
Groen, G. J., 15, 31
Guttman, L., 219, 249

H

Habon, M. W., xvii, xxiv, 3, 31, 163–166,
   177, 220, 249
Haertel, E. H., 101, 108, 127
Hambleton, R. K., 280, 286
Hamilton, P., 15, 31
Harbeson, M. M., 254, 274, 352, 356,
   358
Harris, R. I., 11, 31
Harsveld, M., 357–358
Hayes, J. R., 210, 216
Hegge, F. W., 256, 274
Heineke, M., 339, 359
Hermans, P. H., 357–358
Herskovits, E., 103, 109, 127
Hetter, R. D., 296, 305
Hitch, G., xviii, xxiii, 15, 28, 354, 359
Hively, W., 116, 127, 199, 216, 219, 249
Hockey, G. R. J., 15, 31
Hoffman, M., 219, 249
Holroyd, S. R., 17, 31
Holzman, G. B., 202, 216
Hombo, C. M., 214, 216
Hone, A., 206, 217
Hörmann, H. J., 339–340, 356, 359–360
Horn, J. L., 225, 249
Hornke, L. F., xvii, xxiv, 3, 31, 161, 163–
   166, 168, 170, 172–173, 177–178,
   220, 249
Hough, P. V. C., xvi, xxiv, 10, 31
Houghton, A., 292, 305
Hunt, E., 14, 31, 356, 359
Huttenlocher, J., 44, 51
Hutwelker, R., 161, 177–178

I

Inouye, D. K., 6, 28
Ippel, M. J., 259–260, 264, 274
Irvine, C. D., 20, 22, 31
Irvine, S. H., xviii, xx, xxii, xxiv, 3–4, 9–
    14, 16–20, 22–24, 27, 29–34, 116,
    122, 127, 277, 286, 323, 331, 335,
    337, 344, 353–354, 359

J

JAA-Joint Aviation Authorities, 340, 359
Jacobs, N. R., 17, 32
Jacobs, P. J., 163, 177
Jacobson, R. L., 288, 305
Janssen, R., 214, 216
Jensen, A. R., 18, 32–33
Jex, H. R., 352, 359
Johnson, E. S., 12, 29
Johnson-Laird, P. N., 45, 51, 260, 274
Jones, A., 331, 337
Jones, D. H., 11, 28, 331, 337
Jones, S. R., 62, 71
Just, M. A., 15, 32, 161, 177, 202, 215,
    226–230, 233–234, 243, 247, 249

K

Kadane, J. B., 169, 178
Kahneman, D., 357, 359
Katz, I. R., 208, 216
Kennedy, R. S., 251–252, 254, 256, 274–
    275, 352, 356, 358
Kenney, J. F., 208, 216
Kerr, M. O., 331, 337
Kirsch, H., 13, 32
Kitson, N., 17, 32
Klamm, A., 346, 361
Kluge-Klaßen, A., 170, 177
Kokorian, A., 317, 331, 337
Kornbrot, D. E., 18, 32
Koslowsky, M., 251, 274
Kotovsky, K., 210, 216
Krause, M., 254, 274, 352, 356, 358
Küpper, A., 165, 177
Kuse, A. R., 161, 178
Kutschke, T., 18, 31
Kyllonen, P. C., xviii, xxiv, 3–4, 16, 21,
    23, 25, 32, 244, 249, 256–257, 259,
    274–275

L

LaDuca, A., 202, 216
Laird, N. M., 281, 286
Lamschus, D., 343, 359
Landauer, T. K., 270, 275
Lanham, D. S., 252, 274
Lansman, M., 356, 359
Larkin, J. H., 169, 178
Laudauer, T. K., 15, 33
Lawton, D. H., 17, 32
Lescreve, F., 317, 331, 337
Lewis, C., 365, 384
Lewis, J., 14, 31
Loevinger, J., 323, 337
Loftus, E. F., 169, 178
Logie, R. H., 251, 275
Lohman, D. F., 5, 15–16, 32, 129, 157,
    260, 275
Lord, F. M., 4, 32, 203, 214, 216
Lorenz, B., 339, 341, 343, 353–354, 356–
    357, 359–360
Lorenz, J., 339, 341, 359
Lunneborg, C., 14, 31

M

Maclean, A., 15, 31
Macready, G. B., 121, 127
Mann, A. H., 20, 22, 33
Manzey, D., 339, 341, 359–360
Marshalek, B., 256, 275
Marshall, S., 362, 371, 384
Martin, C. J., 317, 331, 337
Martin, K., 130–131, 158, 365, 384
Maschke, P., 339–340, 344, 358–360
MathSoft, 281, 286
Mawer, R., 383–384
Mayer, R. E., 131, 157, 169, 178, 362,
    384
McBride, J. R., 242, 247
McDonald, J. E., 22, 31
McDonnell, J. D., 352, 359
McKean, K. E., 5, 33
Meade, A., 12, 29
Meehl, P. E., 221–222, 249
Merwin, J. C., 199, 216
Messick, S. J., 4, 33, 97, 99, 127, 211,
    213, 216
Metzler, J., xvi, xxiv, 12–13, 15, 33, 161,
    178
Meulders, M., 214, 216
Miller, G. A., 5, 33

Mislevy, R. J., xxiv, xxii, xxiv-xxv, 3, 12–14, 18, 33, 103, 104, 108, 121–123, 127–128, 130, 135, 157, 202, 214, 216, 230, 248, 281, 283, 286, 365, 384
Mispelkamp, H. B., 166, 177
Montague, W. E., 261, 274
Morely, M., 124, 127, 365, 369, 384
Moreno, K. E., 242, 247
Mosier, C. I., 331, 337
Moyer, R. S., 15, 33
Munster, E. W., 292, 305
Muraki, E., 212, 215

N

Nährer, W., 161, 178
Nanda, H., 214–215
Neimark, E. D., 6, 33
Nelson, J., 209–210, 215
Newell, A., 116, 128
Newstead, S. E., 42, 51
1994 Profile of SAT and Achievement Test Takers, 295, 307
North, R. A., 356, 360

O

Olsen, J. B., 6, 28
Olshen, R., 136, 157
Oltman, P. K., 214–215
Ortmüller, S., 349, 360
Osburn, H. G., 210, 216, 323, 337

P

Parkman, J. M., 15, 31, 33
Page, J. M., 219, 249
Page, S. H., 116, 127
Paige, J. M., 169, 178
Palmer, S. E., 171, 178
Patterson, H. L., 116, 127, 219, 249
Pecena, Y., 356, 359
Peirce, L., 117, 127
Pellegrino, J. W., 129, 158, 259, 275
Phatak, A. V., 352, 359
Poltrock, S. E., 356, 359
Polyakov, V. V., 339, 341, 360
Ponsoda, V., 200, 216
Posner, M. L., 14, 33
Potts, G. R., 44, 51
Powers, D. E., 122, 127
Pregibon, D., 135, 157

Price, L. A., 340, 344, 358
Prince, M. J., 20, 22, 33
Prinsloo, W., 9, 14, 32

Q

Quillian, M. R., 59, 71

R

Radatz, H., 169, 178
Rajaratnam, N., 214–215
Rathje, H., xix, xxiv, 3, 30, 342–343, 347, 359
Raven, J. C., 225, 249
Raymond, M. R., 209–210, 216
Reeves, A., 357, 360
Reeves, D. L., 256, 274
Restle, F., 5, 18, 33
Rettig, K., 161, 165, 170, 177–178
Reuning, H., 9, 14, 32
Revuelta, J., 200, 205, 216
Rost, J., 245, 249
Royer, F. L., 6, 33
Rubin, D. B., 281, 286
Ruzius, M. H. B., 357–358

S

Scheuneman, J., 123, 128
Schiewe, A., 341, 361
Schmeiser, C. B., 210, 216
Schoeman, A., 9, 14, 32
Schum, D. A., 98, 121, 128
Sebrechts, M. M., 130–131, 157, 365, 384
Segall, D., 121, 128
Sheehan, K. M., xxii, xxv, 18, 33, 118, 121–122, 124, 127, 130, 157, 214, 216, 221, 249, 302, 305, 365, 369, 384
Shell, P., 226–230, 233–234, 243, 247, 249
Shepard, R. N., xvi, xxv, 12–13, 15, 33, 161, 178
Shingledecker, C. A., 256, 274
Shye, S., 219, 249
Silberztein, M., 200, 216
Simon, H. A., 39, 51, 116, 128, 169, 178, 201, 210, 216
Singley, M. K., 363, 376, 384
Snow, R. E., 129, 158, 256, 275
Spearman, C., 225–226, 249
Sperling, G., 357, 360

Staples, W. I., 202, 216
Stecher, B., 210, 216
Steinberg, L. S., 103–104, 108, 127–128,
  202, 214
Sternberg, R. J., 5, 33, 221, 249, 259, 275
Sternberg, S., 14, 33, 341, 344, 352–353,
  356–357, 360
Stevens, G., 62, 71
Stocking, M. L., 120, 128, 205, 216, 296,
  305
Stone, C. J., 136, 157
Storm, E. G., 171, 178
Storm, G., 170, 173, 177
Suppes, P., 169, 178
Swaminanthan, H., 280, 286
Swanson, L., 120, 128, 296, 305
Sweller, J., 383–384
Sympson, J. B., 296, 305

T

Tapsfield, P. G. C., 3, 8, 11, 30–31, 33–
  34, 116, 122, 127
Tatsuoka, K. M., 18, 25, 33, 365, 384
Tatsuoka, M. M., 18, 25, 33
Taylor, R. J., 14, 33
Templeton, B., 202, 216
Thacker, C., 335, 337
Thiele, G., 339, 359
Thorndike, R. L., 289, 305
Thorne, D. R., 256, 274
Thurstone, L. L., 12, 33
Tirre, W., 257, 259, 274
Tryon, R. C., 210, 216, 323, 337
Tuerlinckx, F., 214, 216
Turnage, J., 251–252, 256, 274–275
Turner, M. L., 257, 275

U

Urbina, S.,

V

van der Linden, W. J., 121, 128
Van Raay, P., 317, 331, 337
Vandenberg. S. G., 161, 178
Vandeventer, M., 163, 177
Veerkamp, W. J. J., 114, 127
Vernon, P. A., 18, 33
Viola, M. V., 292, 305

W

Wainer, H., 4, 33, 214–217, 302, 304–
  305
Walker, R. F., 18, 32
Wang, X., 214–215, 217, 302, 305
Wang, Z., 11, 28
Ward, J., 163, 178
Ward, M., 383–384
Weber, W., 317, 331, 337
Weibull, W., 18, 33
Weiss, D. J., 244, 249
Wenzel, J., 339, 359
Wesman, A. G., 160, 178
Wetzel, C. D., 244, 249
White, P. O., 5, 18, 26, 33
Whitely, S. E., 166, 178
Whittaker, J., 103, 128
Wilding, U., 168, 170, 177
Wiley, D. E., 101, 108, 127
Wilkes, R. L., 251, 274
Williamson, D. M., 206, 217
Wilson, J. W., 169, 178
Wilson, K. P., 256, 274
Wilson, R. W., 145, 157
Wingersky, M. S., xxii, xxiv, 3, 12–14, 33,
  121–123, 128, 130, 157, 214, 216
Wippich, W., 173, 178
Woltz, D. J., 12, 15–16, 21, 32, 34, 257,
  275
Wright, D. E., xxii, xxiv-xxv, 3, 5, 11,
  13–14, 17–18, 25, 30–31, 33–34, 116,
  122, 127, 278, 281, 286

Y

Yocom, P., xvii, xxiii, 13, 28, 130, 157,
  200–201, 215

Z

Zipf, G. K., 289, 305

Subject Index

A

ADTRACK—One-dimensional Adaptive Pursuit Tracking Test, 321, 327–328
ARE 97, 208–221
Abstract reasoning items, 219, 225, 236, 240, 243, 246
Adaptive Control of Thought (Act) theory, 256
Adaptive Digit-span Test, 326
Advanced Placement Program (AP), 385
Admiralty Interview Board (A.I.B.), 56
Airplane-Position Test, 347–348
Algebraicness, 131
Analogical reasoning, 200
Analytical Reasoning (AR), 35, 53, 63, 67–68
Approach 1, 57–58, 62–63, 67–69, 200
Approach 2, 63, 67–69, 200
Armed Services Vocational Interest Battery (ASVAB), 23, 89–90, 207
Army Personnel Research Establishment (APRE), 317
Army Regular Commissions Board Battery, 11, 24
Assembly specifications, 114, 120
Assessment design, 98, 122, 207
Assignment rules, 47
Associative memory, 354
Attitude to Risk Test, 325
Automated Item Generation (AIG), 73, 287, 298–301, 303
Automatic item-generation-See Item generation

B

BETTERAVEN, 227–228
BILOG, 135, 230, 237
Back coding, 200
Background complexity, 171
Bandwidth fidelity dilemma, 264
Base form, 202–204
Base pool, 202–204
Basic Models
assembly, 102, 114

delivery, 102, 114
environment, 102
evidence, 101, 105, 118
student, 100–103, 119, 183
task, 101, 112–113, 115, 183
Bayses-net fragments, 109–111, 121, 122, 124
Behaviored anchoring, 124
British Army Recruit Battery (BARB), xix, xx, 11–12, 15–17, 20–21, 79, 81, 91, 192, 277–278, 393

C

COMP2D—Compensatory Two-dimensional Tracking Test, 321
CONQUEST (CONstruction of QUESTionaires), 345
Category order, 261
Chronobiology, 253
Class membership (cla), 166
Clearance (CLE), 347
Coachability, 78–79
Cognitive
approach, 168
complexity, 224, 234
design system approach, 221–223
models, 239
performance, xx
psychology, 260
tests, 20
theory, 201, 219–221, 226
Cognitive Abilities Measurement (CAM), 256–259, 270–271
Cognitive Task Analyses (CTA), 106, 116
Compactness, 172
Compensatory tracking, 393
Completeness, 375
Complexity, 131, 140, 148, 172–173
Computer adaptive (CAT), 113, 146, 150, 296–297, 308
Computer Assisted Testing (CAT), 343–345, 355
Computerized Placement Test (CPT), 301
Conceptual
analysis, 39
theoretical foundation, 117, 119–120
understanding, 146
Conceptual Assessment Framework (CAF), 100–102, 110, 222

405

Concrete odd word out, 58
Conditional
     probability distributions, 108–109,
        122, 124
     rules, 45
Constraint logic programming, 373–374,
     376
Construct
     analysis, 201–202, 209, 213
     centered approach, 116
     representation, 130, 212, 222–223,
        225, 246
Content, 43
Context, 131, 140
Continuous opposites, 257
Control of Velocity Test (CVT), 318
Correctness, 374
Curricular approach, 168

D

D-Models, 5
DLR, 339–340, 343, 345
DRT, 137, 140–144, 368, 371
Decision time, 47–48
Delivery model, 114
Delta, 254
Development/Conversion (dev), 166
Dichotic Listening Task (DLT), 357
Differential Item Function (DIF), 77–78,
     85–86
Difficulty modeling, 130, 145
Dimensional relation (dim), 166
Discrete Bayesian Networks, 103–104
Discrete cognitive components
     approach, 319
Disjunctive rules, 46
Directions and Distances test, 53–55, 57,
     66–67
Double counting, 121
Dualtask Test, 324
Dynamic learning, 74

E

ETS-Kit of Reference Tests for
     Cognitive Factors, 340
Educational Testing Service (ETS), xxi,
     180, 184, 200, 289, 304, 310, 362
Emperical Bayes, 302
Enemies list, 121
Error detection tests, 19
Error rate, 49

Evidence rules, 106–107, 112
Expectation Maximisation (EM)
     algorithm, 277, 281

F

FAIRAVEN, 227–228
Factor
     loadings, 244
     models, 110

Features
     controlling, 55–56
     noncontrolling, 55–56, 59, 69,
Fleishman Job Analysis Survey, 344
Flexilevel exam, 203
Fluid intelligence, 225–226, 244
Focusing evidence, 119
Four-dimensional Compensatory
     Tracking Test, 335
Four-term ordering, 257, 260–261, 263
Function (fun), 166
Fusion, 240

G

g-items, 77, 89
g-loaded figural tests, xvii
Generative
     assessment, 206–207, 213
     framework, 60
     program, 64–65
     testing, 199
Generic item types, 63
God's Eye View (GEV) items, 54–55
Graduate Management Admission Test
     (GMAT), 366, 369
Graduate Record Examination (GRE),
     35, 39, 44, 63, 98, 106, 110, 113,
     117–118, 122–123, 129, 140, 145–
     146, 156, 181, 289–290, 297, 310,
     366, 368
     Big Book, 35–36, 39, 63
     CAT, 104, 109–110, 113–114, 120,
        145, 294–296
     quantitative measure, 157, 182, 184
     P & P, 106, 113
     Psychology Achievement Test, 123

H

HYDRIVE, 98, 105, 107, 109, 111, 115,
     118–119, 124–125

Hierarchical models, 110
Higher order thinking, 146
Homogeneity, 172
Human Assessment Laboratory, 10

I

INTEX, 200
Imagery, 173
Incidental factor, 260–261, 386
Initial scenario, 40
Inspection time, 173
Instrumental comprehension test (INS-B), 318
Integrated representation, 44
Integrativeness, 208
Intelligence, xv
   Factor-g, 225–226
Isomorphs, 201, 205–206, 210–212
Item
   analysis, 365, 369
   biserial correlation, 123
   classification, 130, 146, 365
   construction, xxi
   creation, 365
   generation, xv, xvi, 57, 86, 183, 219–220, 234–235, 247, 251–252, 323, 364, 372, 389
   generation methods, 9
   structure, 235
   tracking, 365
Item Design Rules, 160–161, 165, 169, 171–173, 175–176
Item Response Theory (IRT), xxii, 27, 74, 87, 104, 109–111, 114, 120–124, 135, 138, 147, 149, 155, 265, 279–280
Item Variability Principle, 273
Item-difficulty, 12, 123, 130, 136, 146–147
Item-Generation Design Principle, 273

K

KSA's (knowledge, skills, and abilities), 97, 105, 208–210
Kaplan Educational Center, 288
Knowledge, 99

L

LANDING—Landing Approach Test, 321–322, 329, 335, 386

Latency models, 73, 110
Latent semantic analysis, 270
Learning Abilities Measurement Program, 253
Levels of generativity, 199–200
Line deletion, 171
Linear Logistic Test Model, 280

M

MANIKIN—Test of spatial Orientation, 321
MATHICA, 148
MICROPAT, 317, 319, 321, 333
Management/work behavior, 160
Markedness, 43
Market basket score, 126
Markov chain Monte Carlo (MCMC), 277, 281
Matching, 261
Mathematical modeling, 230
Mathematical-Logical Reasoning (RAG), 353
Mathematics Test Creation Assistant (TCA), 362, 365–367, 369, 382
Matrix completion problems, 220, 225–227
Means-end analysis, 377–378, 381
Mechanical Comprehension Test (TVT), 351
Mechanical/Comprehension/Knowledge (MK), 354
Memory load, 240–241, 352–353
Memory Test (MEK), 346
Mental Arithmetic-Acoustic (KRN), 351
Mental Concentration Test (KBT), 347–348
Mental models, xvi
Mental rotation, 160–161
Model semantic, xx
Modal projections, 380
Multiple Task Coordination Test (MTC), 357
Multiple-line constructed response, 372, 376

N

NAVCALC—Test of Navigational Calculations, 318
NAVOR—Test of Navigational Orientation, 318
NCARAB, 312–313

Natural language processing, 90
Negation, 43, 261
Negation/Opposition (neg), 166
Nodes
    AND, 378–379
    Child, 136
    OR, 378
    Parent, 136
Nomothetic span, 213, 222–225, 243
Nonverbal g, xvii
Not-All-Tests-Are-Alike Principle, 273
Number problems, 160, 168
Numberacy and Literacy tests, 53, 58,
    66–67

O

Observable variable, 105, 107–108, 111,
    122
Odd word out items, 59
Operation span, 257
Order items, 63
Overinstantiation, 380

P

PARAT (PARAllel Testing) program,
    342–345, 349–350, 387
POPLOG, xx
Paper and Pencil (P & P), 113
Parade Ground (PG) items, 54–55
Part/Whole (p/w), 166
Pattern
    complexity, 161
    simplicity, 171
Perceptual Maze Test, 331
Perceptual Modality, 352
Perceptual speed, 354
Performance Evaluation Tests for
    Environmental Research battery
    (PETER), 254
Personality, xv
Physics Knowledge Test (TQ), 351
Portal project, 100, 120, 126, 189, 202
Principled assessment design, 181, 187
Principled Component Analyses (PCA),
    354, 356
Pro Facts, 174, 185
Probability problems, 132, 134, 141
Probe quality, 352–353
Procedural
    framework, 223
    knowledge, 146, 271

Psychometric
    analysis, 231
    approach, 168
    properties, 237

Q

Quantitative
    factor, 244
    reasoning, 129, 354

R

RAF Officer and Aircrew Selection
    Centre (OASC), 317, 319
RT2, 58
RT3, 58
Radicals, 116, 260–261, 264, 386–387
Rapid serial visual presentation task
    (RSVP), 357
Rasch model, 231–232, 237, 239, 245–
    247
Rating
    problems, 131, 133, 137–138
    scale models, 110
Ratio score approach, 267
Raven's Advanced Progressive Matrix
    tests, 220, 225–226, 230–234, 243–
    244, 246, 248, 310
Reaction time, 46
Reading time, 41
Repeated performance testing, 252
Restriction rules, 41
Right/wrong model,
Root mean squared error (RMSE), 341–
    342
Rotation of Dices (ROT), 343, 349–350,
    387
Royal Navy's Recruiting Test (RT), 58

S

S-Plus, 281
SAT I, 366
SP80A, 53–54
SCHEDULE—Test of Scheduling
    Ability, 321, 329
SUBTRACT—Test of Speeded Mental
    Arithmetic, 321
Schema, 361, 364
Schema Compiler, 362, 372, 377–379,
    381–383

Schema Prover, 362, 373–374, 382–383, 389
Schema theory, 361–364, 376, 382, 388
Scripts, 210–211
Scorability, 205–206
Scoreright, 214
Semantic hierarchy, 59, 61
Sensory-Motor Apparatus (SMA), 318
Sentence Transformation, 58, 60
Serial learning, 160
Simulator models, 115
Single model problem, 45
Skill level classification, 146
Space splitting, 125–126
Spacial Orientation Test, 324, 354
Spearman
    cognitive theory, 225
    psychometric theory, 225
Speed Decision Making Test, 325
Speed tests, 265
Standard deviation, 285
Standard multiple choice (SMC), 368
Statistical model, 108–110, 122
Sternberg Memory Search Task, 342, 345, 352, 355–356, 387, 394
Student model variables, 107–108, 112, 114, 120–121, 123–125
Structural analysis, 40

T

Target of inference, 99
Task
    construction, 117, 122
    design, 97
    generation, 326
    load, 353
    model variables, 97, 112, 119, 120, 122, 125
Term, 261, 268
Test design, 201–202, 207, 210
Test items
    impossibility, 42, 50, 63, 66
    necessity, 42, 50, 63, 66
    possibility, 42, 50, 63, 66
    possible model, 42, 63, 66
Test of English as a Foreign Language (TOEFL), 123, 187
Test of Navigational Calculation, 322–326
Test of Navigational Orientation, 322
Test of Speed Mental Arithmetic, 324

Test use, 181, 187, 202, 204, 210, 213–214
Think aloud protocols, 38–39
Three parameter logistic model (3PL), 181, 184, 190, 232
Three-term series problem, 42
Time limit,
Transformation complexity, 162
Transitive inference, 42
Tree-based techniques, 135–136
Two parameter logistics (2PL), 230, 232, 234, 237, 239, 308

U

USAF CAM Experimental Battery, 4
Unbiasedness, 181
Underinstantiation, 380
United Tri-Services Cognitive Performance Assessment Battery (UTC-PAB), 256
Unstable Tracking Test (UTT), 351
Use Variable (UseVar), 137

V

VISAN-test, 170
Validation, 89
Validity, 187
Variant, 201, 205
Verbal
    analogies, 160, 166
    memory, 173
    strategies, 44
Visual
    analysis, 160, 170
    memory, 160, 172
    strategies, 44
Visual Perception Test (OWT), 351

W

Walter Reed Performance Assessment Battery (WRPAB), 254
Work product, 105, 108, 112

X

XYZ Assignment, 257

Z

Zipf's Law, 291–295

About the Editors

SIDNEY H. IRVINE

Formerly Professor of Differential Psychology at the University of Plymouth and now Emeritus₁ Professor Irvine established the Human Assessment Laboratory. With his colleagues in that unit he devised BARB, a computer-based series of tests for recruitment selection in the British Army. This went operational in 1992 and its original features include algorithm generation of items in real time to prescribed levels of difficulty. In 1993 he inaugurated The Spearman Seminar, a symposium on the nature and measurement of human intelligence. This takes place every four years in the University of Plymouth. The 1997 Seminar was a cooperative venture with Educational Testing Service.

Professor Irvine is no stranger to North America, having been the U.S. Public Health Service Visiting Scholar at ETS in 1967, and thereafter spending 11 years in Canadian Universities in teaching, research, and administrative roles. He was United States National Research Council Senior Fellow for 1997–99, in residence at The Air Force Laboratory, Brooks AFB, Texas, having enjoyed close collaboration with its scientists during the previous decade.

His doctoral research was on the structure and nature of abilities in African groups. Continued fieldwork in this area resulted in the publication of several papers on problems of cross-cultural assessment, leading in 1981 to the award of the Simon Biesheuvel Medal for the Study of Man In Africa. He is a Fellow of the British Psychological Society and a Chartered Psychologist. His most comprehensive work, published by Cambridge, is *Human Abilities in Cultural Context*, a collection edited with John Berry.

PATRICK C. KYLLONEN

Patrick Kyllonen is the Director of the Center for New Constructs in Educational Testing Service's Statistics and Research Division, in Princeton, NJ, where he has been since 1999. He received his B.A. from St. John's University and Ph.D. in 1984 from Stanford University. Before joining ETS, Dr. Kyllonen held positions at the University of Georgia (1985-1988) and the Air Force Research Laboratory in San Antonio, Texas (1982-1985; 1988-1999). He is a Fellow of the American Psychological Association, and a recipient of the American Psychological Association Division 15 Outstanding Early Contribution Award, the Air Force Science and

Technology Achievement Award, and the Technical Cooperation Program Achievement Award. He serves on the editorial boards of the journals Intelligence: A Multidisciplinary Journal, and Human Factors. Recent publications include *Learning and Individual Differences: Process, Trait, and Content Determinants*, with Phillip Ackerman and Richard Roberts; "Structure and organization of psychomotor ability," in *Cognitive Psychology*, with Scott Chaiken and William Tirre; and "Options and Alternatives to the Academic Career: Jobs Outside of Academe," in J. M. Darley, M. P. Zanna & H. L. Roediger's *The Compleat Academic: A Career Guide (2nd ed)*.

DATE DUE